COLLEGE ADMISSION

COLLEGE ADMISSION

FROM APPLICATION TO ACCEPTANCE, STEP BY STEP

Robin Mamlet and
Christine VanDeVelde

THREE RIVERS PRESS
NEW YORK

Originally published in the United States in slightly different form by Three Rivers Press, an imprint of the Crown Publishing Group, a division of Random House LLC, New York, in 2011.

Grateful acknowledgment is made to the following for permission to reprint previously published material:

National Association for College Admission Counseling: "Five Secrets to Success for Undocumented Students" from the *Journal of College Admission*, Winter 2010 issue, number 206, copyright © 2010 by National Association for College Admission Counseling. Reprinted by permission of National Association for College Admission Counseling.

George Waters, TheWaBlog.com: excerpt from "Sick of Standardized Testing? Bubble THIS in" by George Waters. Reprinted by permission of George Waters, TheWaBlog.com.

Library of Congress Cataloging-in-Publication Data
Mamlet, Robin.
College admission : from application to acceptance, step by step / Robin Mamlet, Christine VanDeVelde.
p. cm.
Summary: "Anxiety about getting into college has never been greater, and as an admission dean at Stanford, Swarthmore, and Sarah Lawrence, Robin Mamlet has had a front-row seat to all the angst and antics. Now she reveals the truth about admission, and the simple, honest approaches that really do work. Journalist and coauthor Christine VanDeVelde is a parent who has experienced the process firsthand and knows the questions, anxieties, and concerns of students and parents. *College Admission* directly addresses all the questions that plague parents and students along the way to an acceptance letter and will be their definitive resource during the sophomore, junior, and senior years of high school." —Provided by publisher.
1. Universities and colleges—United States—Admission. 2. College choice—United States.
3. Student aid—United States. I. VanDeVelde, Christine. II. Title.
LB2351.2.M24 2011
378.1'980973—dc22   2011007978

ISBN 978-0-307-59032-9
eBook ISBN 978-0-307-59033-6

Printed in the United States of America

Cartoons by Mark Anderson

Cover design by Alison Forner
Cover photography by Image Source

6 8 10 9 7

Updated Edition

To Austin, Chloe, Don, and Roark

Contents

PART III

BECOMING COLLEGE-BOUND

PART IV

WHERE TO APPLY

PART V

APPLYING

PART IX

SPECIAL CIRCUMSTANCES

PART X

APPENDICES

Acknowledgments

A project of this scope and comprehensiveness is not possible without the contributions of many. We would like to acknowledge with a heartfelt thank-you all of the individuals who made this book possible.

FIRST AND FOREMOST

Don Luskin

Alice Kleeman

THE DEANS OF ADMISSION

Amy Abrams, formerly of Sarah Lawrence College

Seth Allen, Pomona College

Ken Anselment, Lawrence University

Philip A. Ballinger, University of Washington

Nancy Benedict, formerly of Beloit College

Michael Beseda, Willamette University

Donald Bishop, Notre Dame University

Tamara Blocker, Wake Forest University

Jim Bock, Swarthmore College

Jon Boeckenstedt, DePaul University

Shawn Brick, University of California

Thyra Briggs, Harvey Mudd College

Nancy Cable, formerly of Bates College

Arlene Cash, University of the Pacific

Mary Chase, Creighton University

Douglas L. Christiansen, Vanderbilt University

Robert S. Clagett, formerly of Middlebury College

Lee Coffin, Tufts University

Dennis Craig, Purchase College

Vince Cuseo, Occidental College

Yvonne Romero Da Silva, University of Pennsylvania

Charles Deacon, Georgetown University

Randall C. Deike, Drexel University

Tom Delahunt, Drake University

Jennifer Delahunty, Kenyon College

Rick Diaz, Southern Methodist University

Stephen M. Farmer, University of North Carolina at Chapel Hill

William Fitzsimmons, Harvard University

Katie Fretwell, Amherst College

Patricia Goldsmith, formerly of Scripps College

Christopher Gruber, Davidson College

Christoph Guttentag, Duke University

Stephen Handel, University of California

Katharine L. Harrington, University of Southern
California
Pamela T. Horne, Purdue University
Monica Inzer, Hamilton College
Jeannine Lalonde, University of Virginia
Maria Laskaris, Dartmouth College
John Latting, Emory University
Jean Lee, Yale University
Jess Lord, Haverford College
Garrett Marino, Purchase College
Quinton McArthur, Massachusetts Institute of
Technology
Kitty McCarthy, West Virginia State University
Nancy Hargrave Meislahn, Wesleyan
University
Richard Nesbitt, Williams College
Alton Newell, formerly of Washington &
Jefferson College
Jim Nondorf, University of Chicago
Tom Parker, formerly of Amherst College
Angel B. Perez, Pitzer College
Delsie Phillips, Newberry College
Bruce Poch, formerly of Pomona College
Jenny Rickard, University of Puget Sound
Lorne T. Robinson, Macalester College
Arnaldo Rodriguez, formerly of Pitzer College
Nancy M. Rothschild, Syracuse University
Daniel J. Saracino, formerly of University of
Notre Dame
Stuart Schmill, Massachusetts Institute of
Technology
Richard H. Shaw, Stanford University
Ted Spencer, formerly of University of Michigan
Fumio Sugihara, Juniata College
Steve Thomas, Colby College
Roger Thompson, University of Oregon
Keith Todd, Reed College

Kelly Walter, Boston University
James Washington, Jr., Dartmouth College
Christopher Watson, Northwestern University
Leigh Weisenburger, Bates College
Rebekah Westphal, Yale University
Jarrid Whitney, California Institute of
Technology
Susan A. Wilbur, formerly of University of
California

FINANCIAL AID OFFICERS

Vincent Amoroso, The Ohio State University
Sally Donahue, Harvard University
Maureen McRae Goldberg, Occidental College
Leslie Limper, Reed College
Mary Morrison, Stanford University
Alison Rabil, Duke University
Diane Stemper, The Ohio State University

HIGH SCHOOL COLLEGE COUNSELORS

Charlene Aguilar, University Preparatory
Academy, Seattle, WA
Ali Bhanji, Collegiate School, New York, NY
Natalie Bitton, Lycée Français La Pérouse, San
Francisco, CA
Melanie Choukrane, Grace Church School, New
York, NY
Robert Clagett, St. Stephen's Episcopal School,
Austin, TX
Mark Clevenger, Menlo School, Atherton, CA
James Conroy, New Trier High School,
Winnetka, IL
Neal Cousins, The Haverford School,
Haverford, PA
Susan Dean, Castilleja School, Palo Alto, CA
Aliza Gilbert, Highland Park High School,
Highland Park, IL

Deb Kelly, Newman Central Catholic High School, Sterling, IL

Alice Kleeman, Menlo-Atherton High School, Atherton, CA

Marybeth Kravets, formerly of Deerfield High School, Deerfield, IL

Brad MacGowan, Newton North High School, Newton, MA

Rod Skinner, Milton Academy, Milton, MA

Laura Stewart, The Ensworth School, Nashville, TN

Patricia Ustick, formerly of Portsmouth School and East Greenwich High School, East Greenwich, RI

Jan Williams, formerly of Dartmouth High School, Dartmouth, MA

EDUCATORS

Jeff Brenzel, Yale University

Carmina Cianciulli, Tyler School of Art, Temple University

Gina Coleman, Hillcrest Educational Centers

Linda DeAngelo, Higher Education Research Institute, University of California, Los Angeles

Emily Froimson, Jack Kent Cooke Foundation

Leslie Hawkins, Higher Education Research Institute, Graduate School of Education and Information Studies, University of California, Los Angeles

Rob Mullens, director of intercollegiate athletics, University of Oregon

Denise Clark Pope, Stanford University School of Education, founder of Challenge Success

Holly Thompson, Castilleja School, Palo Alto, CA

Doug Tiedt, associate athletic director, University of Wisconsin

Bruce VanDeVelde, associate athletic director, University of Wisconsin

Belinda Wilkerson, Steps To The Future

MaryJo Yannacone, principal, Strath Haven High School, Swarthmore, PA

EXPERTS

Scott Anderson, The Common Application, Inc.

Maureen Brown, executive director, Challenge Success

Jon Erickson, senior vice president, ACT, Inc.

Carrie Evans, co-founder, Educators for Fair Consideration

Katharine Gin, co-founder, Educators for Fair Consideration

Scott Gomer, ACT, Inc.

Rob Killion, formerly of The Common Application

Jim Montoya, The College Board

Jodi Palmer, ACT, Inc.

Erica Pierson, Naviance, Inc.

Martha Pitts, The College Board

Rose Rennekamp, ACT, Inc.

Jay Rosner, executive director, The Princeton Review Foundation

Bob Schaeffer, Fair Test

Linda Gray Sexton, author

Joyce Smith, National Association for College Admission Counseling

Kathleen Fineout Steinberg, The College Board

Ellen Sussman, author and writing teacher

Edward Walters III, ACT, Inc.

Kris Zavoli, The College Board

PARENTING EXPERTS

Michael Riera, author of *Uncommon Sense for Parents of Teenagers,* head of school, Brentwood School, Los Angeles, CA

Michael Thompson, Ph.D., author of *The Pressured Child*

Rosalind Wiseman, author of *Queen Bees and Wannabes*

INDEPENDENT COUNSELORS

Jeff Haviland
Jane McClure
John Perlman
Irena Smith

READERS

Amy Abrams, formerly of Sarah Lawrence College
Charlene Aguilar, University Preparatory Academy
Seth Allen, Pomona College
Vincent Amoroso, The Ohio State University
Chloe Atchue-Mamlet, student
Natalie Bitton, Lycée Français La Pérouse
Daniel Cherry, student
Melanie Choukrane, The Grace Church School
James Conroy, New Trier High School
Claire Costantino, student
Jennifer Delahunty, Kenyon College
George Dowdall, St. Joseph's University

Maureen McRae Goldberg, Occidental College
Jeff Haviland, formerly of Strath Haven High School
Roark Luskin, student
Fern Mandelbaum, parent
Ayesha Rasheed, student
Sarah Ringer, parent
Rod Skinner, Milton Academy
Irena Smith, writing teacher and counselor
MaryJo Yannacone, Strath Haven High School

CARTOONISTS

Mark Anderson
Randall Munroe

EDITORIAL ASSISTANTS

Kristin Maynard
Katherine M. Miller

AND LAST BUT NEVER LEAST

Our agent, Jennifer Joel of ICM, an incredible guide from start to finish
Our editors, Heather Lazare and Mary Choteborsky of the Crown Publishing Group, the best counsel step by step

Foreword

Robin Mamlet: It was spring of my senior year of college, Occidental graduation was in a few weeks, and I'd heard there was an opening in the admission office. The job sounded engaging and fun—I'd get to travel around the country and talk with interesting young people about their hopes and dreams, the value of a liberal education, and what Oxy could offer.

And I fell in love with it. I loved spending time with seventeen-year-olds, and loved coming to know them—both in person and through what I came to refer to as my "flat friends," because through the years at Sarah Lawrence and Swarthmore and Stanford, I certainly spent more time each year with all those application files (which for many years were paper rather than electronic) than I did with real people. Like so many college admission officers, I found the work endlessly interesting—whether talking with a roomful of seniors about how to write their college admission essays, learning what made an individual student tick when I interviewed him or her, or working my way through that night's stack of application folders.

When you are an admission dean you know a great deal that could be helpful to students and families. So I have been writing this book for a very long time. For my last few years at Swarthmore and certainly my entire deanship at Stanford, I was dying to speak and write about what I thought the college admission process was doing to our brightest young people. But there was no time.

I was also—and remain—keenly aware that the public's exposure to college admission is both far greater than ever and woefully insufficient. This exposure leaves in its wake a public ravenous for real information, as well as untold numbers of young people unaware of the amazing college options available to them.

If admission deans lack the time to speak and write more about the college admission process, they also are not very trusting. Too often there is not enough column space to handle the nuanced view a question deserves, and the information is therefore treated simplistically; as a result, it is misleading. Too often a reporter is working quickly, under deadline, and can't take the time to check back and ensure he got it right. Too often one is quoted out of context, adding to the misinformation. Too often what admission deans say is used to back a point the reporter had set out to prove before learning fully about the issue. Too often one's quote is edited down in a way that leads the reader to a false conclusion.

I would discuss this periodically with my fellow deans. You want to be helpful to families, but the complexities of so many of the issues do not make for quick sound bites, and besides, there are so many applications still to be read before you can sleep that night. There is also a reluctance to surrender to the quickly reduced tidbit of a story that often inflames fears rather than calming them. The issues that students and parents want to know about are often nuanced and complex, and deans themselves are not professional writers—not everyone has access to a Christine VanDeVelde, who easily untangles the overly labored response and makes complicated subjects understandable.

And so most deans are very selective about whom they will talk with. In the absence of the experts themselves speaking out, many people charge a great deal of money for advice and counsel that may or may not be helpful to students, and often is harmful. And in the absence of calm and sound guidance, fear grows. This book is born of a desire to share information—not to take the quick route and disclose the "secret sauce" to getting in, because there isn't any, but to speak with empathy and expertise to students about how to approach this process, step by step, and end up with a happy result.

Christine and I hope this book will make life easier for college aspirants around the country (and abroad), not to mention their parents, teachers, counselors, and others who care about them. While many students have access to sound school-based college counseling, far too many are not so lucky. Some find strong college counseling outside their schools, while others pay too much for less sound advice, and still others—the vast majority, in fact—get no help at all. Christine and I hope this book will provide expert counsel to students from all backgrounds, everywhere.

Christine VanDeVelde: This is the book I wish I'd had when my daughter was applying to college.

I was surprised by the amount of bad information out there about college admission—from the covertly competitive "advice" of other parents to the come-ons from private counselors and the scare tactics in the media and on the Web. And amid the explosion of information about applying to college, there wasn't one reliable, comprehensive resource available to students and parents for what has become a fairly complex process.

Being a good parent to my daughter was and is the primary objective in my life, and I thought seeing her off to college would be another milestone, another first—like her first word, first day of kindergarten, first best friend. But shortly after the beginning of her sophomore year in high school, I discovered the college admission process might not be just another happy challenge—for her or for her parents. I wish I'd had a book like this one to help me.

My family found ways to ignore the hype and avoid the most painful and expensive pitfalls. My daughter's story did have a happy ending—she was accepted at her first-choice college with early admission.

My story did, too, because my friend Robin Mamlet and I decided to write this book. Robin brought to this project all the knowledge amassed in having made over 100,000 admission decisions. Then we called on almost a hundred other experts for their advice and insight—deans of admission and financial aid, high school counselors, educators, parenting experts, and the professionals at places such as ACT and the College Board and the Common App.

Our goal has been to create the first expert, comprehensive, authoritative, and step by step guide to applying to college.

Robin's experience is the guiding hand that informs this book. She made sure we hit hard all the things that she wished students and families had known all the years she was a dean of admission. I made sure the book included everything that I understood families need to know from their perspective on the other side of the desk—like whether you need a private counselor, whether you have to include community service on an activity list, the etiquette of a college visit, and how to parent well amid so much pressure and misinformation.

Robin and I tried hard to present all this with a sense of humor and a big dose of common sense about handling the hype and the anxiety. Our touchstone throughout was "Is this helpful to the student?" We asked ourselves that question hundreds of times as this book was written. Then we set out to present all of this in the most rational, sympathetic, coherent, and unambiguous way. I think we have. I hope we have.

Part of the difficulty of the college application process is that along with the SATs and the essays, students and parents are always anticipating not just the finish line of the fat envelope but also what that means as a life passage for the family. When I was fretting about how much I would miss my daughter when she headed off to college, a dear friend said to me, "Don't worry about it. It's just another part of the adventure." That helped me—and continues to help me. Because it turned out it was true.

I hope that this book provides you and your family with all the information and advice you'll need to make this time in your lives just another part of the adventure—one with a happy ending.

PART I

THE
BIG PICTURE

CHAPTER 1

Don't Skip This Chapter!

More than three-quarters of students are accepted
by their first-choice college.

—Higher Education Research Institute, University of California at Los Angeles[1]

What that means is that college-bound teens have an excellent chance of getting into a school that is right for them if they prepare properly. And that's what we will be showing students and parents how to do in this book: how to get from application to acceptance, step by step.

We know you're used to hearing scare stories about getting into college. But we're here to tell you the true story. There are more than 2,200 public and private four-year colleges and universities in the United States to choose from. And the vast majority of those colleges—79 percent—admit more than half the students who apply.[2]

There are many colleges, and there are many paths to get to them. In this book, we'll provide you with a comprehensive road map. We'll have the best advice, strategies, and recommendations for you, whether you want to attend your state university, a mid-sized college, or a small liberal arts school. If

you're one of the thousands of students who want to go to one of the schools that top the *U.S. News and World Report*'s "Best Colleges" list, the challenge is greater, but we'll have the best advice for you, too. And if you have special circumstances—if you are attending a high school where there is no counseling, are the first in your family to go to college, or are applying from abroad—we'll address the steps you will need to take as well. If you want to go to college, you can.

And here is why we know this is true. One of the authors of this book has thirty-one years of experience in admission and has made over 100,000 admission decisions as the dean of admission at Swarthmore, Sarah Lawrence, and, most recently, Stanford University. The other author is a journalist and parent who, when her daughter applied to college, felt ambushed by the anxiety and misinformation families faced, was surprised there was no authoritative guide available to lead them through the

Checkpoints ✍

✔ Applying to college is hard work, but you can and will succeed.

✔ Whether you want to go to Princeton, Ohio State, Vanderbilt, Long Beach State, Kenyon, Columbia, Rice, or Colorado College, we will tell you the steps to take—and the truth—at every stage of the admission process.

✔ Don't fall prey to media madness, numbers games, scare stories, or gossip.

✔ Don't try to game the system.

✔ Make sure the student is in the driver's seat.

process, and decided to remedy that. This book also benefits from the participation of more than seventy prominent deans of admission from across the country—from Yale on the right coast to Stanford on the left coast, and everywhere in between—as well as educators, public and private high school counselors, educational psychologists, and parenting experts.

OKAY, LET'S GET STARTED

We're not trying to look at college admission through rose-colored glasses. We know it can feel intimidating. But it's not as bad as you may fear, and it's certainly not as bad as the media—or various interested parties, including some parents—might suggest.

So here's a mantra to use when you get discouraged or confused:

Getting into college is not rocket science. It's a lot of work, but it can be done.

You might be surprised at how often you will need to repeat this to yourself.

DON'T LET MEDIA NEGATIVITY SCARE YOU!

When it comes to college admission, the media work hard to bring home an A+ in sensationalism. A *New York Times* article headlined "Great Year for Ivy League Colleges; Not So Good for Applicants" was illustrated front and center by a photograph of an iron gate, chained and padlocked, while an ivy-covered brick building—Harvard, presumably—loomed out of reach in the background. The story began, "Harvard turned down 1,100 student applicants with perfect 800 scores on the SAT math exam."

The media constantly resort to scare tactics, fear mongering, and sob stories. Some samples:

- "The College Admissions Freak-Out Countdown #3: The Squeeze Play—Early Decision, Budget Cuts, and No Vacancy Signs" —*Huffington Post*
- "University of California Sees Applications Surge: Students are applying to the University of California in record numbers, with increases in freshman applications from other

states and countries far outpacing those from within the state." —*San Francisco Chronicle*

- "Athletes Are the Problem: Like it or not, 40 percent of the class at most top colleges are reserved for 'hooked' kids." —*New York Times*
- "The Swarm of the Super-Applicants: Ivy League mania has created a generation of high-school kids so overqualified it's a wonder they even need college. But will they get in?" —*New York Magazine*
- "Dirty Secrets of College Admission: In a Daily Beast exclusive, college admissions officers reveal just how whimsical the selection process can be." —*Daily Beast*
- "Admit it. All you want is for your kid to go to MIT, Harvard or some other status school.... It's not going to happen." —*Worcester Telegram & Gazette*

Today, the news cycle about getting into college is year-round, as the admission process itself has become. Stories and sound bites about the desperate state of high school applicants and the grim gatekeepers on college campuses are everywhere, all the time.

When you come across harrowing headlines, be aware that the media are usually just trying to sell papers or page views. Even when what you read in the media is factual, often its focus is so narrow it doesn't really apply to you at all. For example, the media almost always cover the same five or six most highly selective colleges, where the chances of getting in are smallest. This feeds the fear that

it's impossible to get into college at all. But that's simply *not* the case.

Unfortunately, the campaign to manufacture admission anxiety is by no means limited to the media. At every school gathering, in the grocery aisles, and over drinks at dinner parties, "well-meaning" parents are there to counsel other parents—letting you know that if your son or daughter wants to go to a "good" school, you need to immediately get her a $40,000-per-client counselor, sign him up for SAT test prep twice a week, send her off to South America on a social service mission, or make a significant donation to your alma mater to enhance your child's "legacy" status. Students have to deal with an onslaught of misinformation, too. In the hallways and cafeteria, they hear that Princeton turned away thousands of high schoolers with a 4.0 grade point average and no one cares about National Merit Scholars anymore because *everyone* is a National Merit Scholar.

So how do you weather the perfect storm whipped up by the media, other parents, peers, some independent college counselors, and, yes, even a lot of admission books? Just remember you can't believe everything you read or hear—even when it's in the *New York Times* or on CNN. And, alas, proud parents will be proud parents. You know what we mean.

Learn how to be a savvy consumer of media. Look at any source of sensationalism—newspapers and magazines, network television, blogs, and secret-sauce admission guidebooks—with the knowledge that these "experts" often have their own motives and may be doing their best to strike fear into the hearts of teenagers and parents everywhere. There's usually another side to the story.

THERE IS A HAPPY ENDING—DON'T WORRY, YOU'LL BE FINE

Because the reality of college admission isn't all that scary.

Yes, there are more applicants than ever before—each year between now and 2020, about 3.2 million students will graduate from high school.[3] Add to the mix online applications, expanded financial aid, and the widespread adoption of the Common Application, and you've got more students applying to more schools.

But what does this actually mean? If you are interested in one of the handful of top-ranked schools, such as Columbia, Yale, or Amherst, where the competition is fiercest, these numbers have an impact. Elite schools that good, solid students used to be able to count on getting into are now more selective,

simply because of the crowding-out effect caused by the avalanche of applications.

But for the typical applicant, the numbers are nowhere near as intimidating as they appear. Remember: more than three-quarters of students *are* accepted by their first-choice college. And 79 percent of the 2,200 four-year colleges in the United States accept more than half the students who apply. The average acceptance rate among all schools is still 64 percent.[4] A study by Stanford economist Caroline Hoxby confirmed that while a few selective colleges have become more difficult to get into over the past fifty years, most colleges are now easier to get into.[5]

College-bound students should not be intimidated. They instead should look realistically at the current picture, and build with care the list of schools they are applying to in order to make a good match, which we'll show you how to do in Chapters 8 and 10.

That way *you* can be part of this happy group:

Nearly eight out of every ten college graduates would attend the same college if they could go back and do it all over again.[6]
—AMERICAN COUNCIL ON EDUCATION

And that happy ending is worth it in more ways than one. Seventy percent of the top earners in this country hold a college degree. Lifetime earnings for a high school graduate total about $250,000, and lifetime earnings for those with a bachelor's degree total

$1,050,000. And college graduates not only earn more, but they're also more likely to be employed, have greater job satisfaction, and be healthier. Finally, investing in a college education has greater returns than investing in gold, housing, the stock market, or government securities.

GETTING INTO PRINCETON ISN'T THE ONLY KEY TO SUCCESS

We know that some of you probably want to attend one of the most selective schools in this country. And throughout this book we will be letting you know what that takes, as well as reporting what the deans of admission at some of these top schools have to say. But we have one request: please don't fall prey to the myth that the prestige of admission to one of these schools is the only way to ensure future happiness and financial security.

When it comes to the most highly selective schools, things are not always what they seem or as the media would like you to believe. In *Looking Beyond the Ivy League*, Loren Pope analyzed eight consecutive sets of scores on the Medical College Admission Test and found that while Caltech produced the highest-scoring students, Carleton College trumped Harvard, Muhlenberg outflanked Dartmouth, and Ohio Wesleyan bested Berkeley.

In fact, a degree from the handful of

We'll continue to address and debunk the myths, scare stories, and numbers games in the college application process on our website at college admissionbook.com.

"Look Who Harvard Blew Off" —Headline in the *New York Post*, May 2007[8]

Among those who went on to "fame, fortune, and charitable giving . . . to other institutions," according to *02138*, the magazine whose title references the zip code of Harvard's campus:

- Über-investor Warren Buffett
- Former *Today* co-anchor Meredith Vieira
- *Simpsons* creator Matt Groening
- *Rolling Stone* founder Jann Wenner
- Turner Broadcasting System founder Ted Turner
- Journalist Tom Brokaw
- Senator John Kerry
- *New Yorker* editor and Pulitzer Prize winner David Remnick
- Memorial Sloan-Kettering Cancer Center president Harold Varmus
- Singer Art Garfunkel
- Columbia University president Lee C. Bollinger

And, of course, this is only a small sample of those who went on to fame and fortune elsewhere.

schools that have become status symbols doesn't always result in the sure outcome students and parents are so desperately seeking. Two studies by Princeton economist Alan Krueger and Stacy Berg Dale of the Andrew Mellon Foundation found that if you were smart enough to get into Harvard, then it didn't matter so much whether you actually went there.[7] Success in life is the result of

CEO Alma Mat(t)ers

If you think going to one of the most highly selective colleges in the country is the only way to ensure wealth and happiness, take a look at where these people went to school.

- Steven Spielberg, principal partner, Dreamworks: Cal State Long Beach
- Richard Rosenfield, co-founder, California Pizza Kitchen: DePaul University
- Oprah Winfrey, chairman, Harpo: Tennessee State
- Les Wexner, chairman and CEO, Limited Brands: Ohio State University
- Anna Deavere Smith, actress and playwright: Arcadia University
- Marc Andreessen, founder, Netscape: University of Illinois
- Dr. Phil McGraw, self-help guru: North Texas State University
- John R. Strangfeld, CEO, Prudential Insurance: Susquehanna University
- Dr. Peter Agre, Nobel Prize winner in chemistry: Augsburg College
- Paul Allen, co-founder, Microsoft: Washington State University
- Indra Nooyi, CEO, PepsiCo: Madras Christian College
- Jimmy Smits, actor: Brooklyn College
- Timothy D. Cook, CEO, Apple: Auburn University
- Ralph Lauren, chairman, Polo Ralph Lauren: Baruch College
- Lyndon B. Johnson, thirty-sixth President of the United States: Southwest Texas State Teachers College
- Roger Goodell, commissioner, National Football League: Washington & Jefferson College
- Ed Catmull, president, Walt Disney and Pixar: University of Utah
- John W. Thompson, CEO, Virtual Instruments: Florida A & M
- Brian Krzanich, CEO, Intel: San Jose State University
- Stephen King, writer: University of Maine
- Mary Barra, CEO, General Motors: Kettering University
- T. Boone Pickens, financier: Oklahoma State
- Craig Jelinek, co-founder and CEO, Costco: San Diego State University
- John Chambers, CEO, Cisco: West Virginia University
- Ronald Reagan, fortieth President of the United States: Eureka College
- Daniel M. Delen, CEO, Reynolds America: Washington State University

the effort and innate capabilities of an individual, not an education at any particular school, however elite it might be.

A survey of Silicon Valley CEOs found that two-thirds of those leading the largest public companies earned their undergraduate degrees not from a highly selective school but from public universities, state colleges, and regional schools.[9] And four of the technology industry's wealthiest and most prominent players were college dropouts—Bill Gates of Microsoft, Larry Ellison of Oracle, Michael Dell of Dell Computer, and Steve Jobs of Apple and Pixar. If you need a little more evidence that it's the person and not the place that makes the difference, take a look at the box on page 8 to see where some of the most prominent people in America attended college.

PARENTS: PUT YOUR KID IN THE DRIVER'S SEAT!

Here we'd like to talk directly to the parents reading this book. We realize many parents don't know what to do to be most helpful to your teenager in the college admission process. Others may be worried that if you don't do what everybody else is doing—no matter how crazy it seems to you—you're disadvantaging your son or daughter. Still others of you are hurting your college-bound students by misguiding them, all with the best of intentions.

Here's the most important thing to remember through every step of the journey to an acceptance letter: the student must be in the driver's seat. The process of applying to college and the decision about where to go should be theirs alone, because when they get there, they will be alone and will have to live with that decision alone. If their decision is based on their true abilities, interests, and temperament, then they will develop the resilience, autonomy, and self-confidence necessary for a happy life—and a happy college experience.

Throughout this book, we will advise you about how much help is too much and how to mix the perfect parental cocktail of high expectations and a lot of support. What students need at this point in their lives is parents who stand with them, by their side, yet far enough away so they have room to behave like the grown-ups they are becoming. So when your high school junior tells you she is dropping AP history to take photography or he wants to leave behind ten years of piano to start a rock band, you may want to remember why everyone hates Miss X. Who? Read on and find out in the sidebar on page 10.

KNOW THE JARGON...

Fat Envelope

A "fat envelope" is an acceptance letter from a college, stuffed with the information a student needs to enroll. A "thin envelope" is a rejection letter. These expressions are mostly outmoded. Today acceptance letters are typically in thin envelopes, and most colleges are forgoing envelopes entirely, instead notifying students of decisions electronically.

> **"Know what you love to do and dedicate yourself to it. It doesn't matter what it is. Authentic, authentic, authentic!"**
> —ALICE KLEEMAN, college advisor

The applicants who get the attention of admission officers are those who know who they

Why Everyone Hates Miss X

In 2003, Miss X—we aren't mentioning her name, in hopes that she can live down her unhappy college admission story—was named co-valedictorian with another student at their high school in a wealthy New Jersey suburb. But Miss X didn't want to share the title. Her parents hired an attorney—a local legal legend whose Atlantic City roster of clients included "Little Nicky" Scarfo and "Skinny Joey" Merlino—and sued the Board of Education, obtaining a temporary restraining order making Miss X the sole valedictorian and asking for $2.7 million in punitive and compensatory damages. The community was outraged—along with plenty of talk show hosts, news anchors, school administrators, college counselors, and admission officers.

Miss X quickly became the poster child for the self-promoting, ultracompetitive high school student, coached and coddled by overinvolved parents. "A Bobo version of the Texas cheerleader case—a combination of obsessive pursuit of academic credentials and parental ambition run amok" is the way one reporter described the situation.

Diagnosed with a type of chronic fatigue illness (the exact nature of which was never disclosed) and therefore classified as being "disabled," Miss X had been allowed to complete most of her high school course work at home. This allowed her to use private tutors, take more AP courses than would normally be available, and skip requirements such as gym class, where even the highest grade of A+ would have lowered her overall GPA (because it's not an honors course). In addition, her home schooling meant that she had about half as much classroom time as her high school peers, which gave her an advantage when it came to extracurricular activities. So despite her chronic fatigue, in 2001 she was awarded a Congressional Gold Medal, which requires that the student perform "400 hours of voluntary public service, 200 hours of personal development activities, 200 hours of physical fitness, and four consecutive days and nights of an exploration or expedition."

Why did the school district decide that Miss X should share the honor of being named valedictorian? Primarily because there was negligible difference in the students' GPAs (4.689 to 4.634), and the other student had played an active part in the high school community. But there was also evidence that Miss X's father, a Superior Court judge, had worked with her in manipulating her GPA, exploiting every subtlety of the grading system. So in addition to helping her out with her volunteer activities, including driving groceries to the local food bank on her behalf, Miss X's father pressed his daughter's case whenever there was a way to polish her transcript, including testifying before a child study team that she was exhausted and needed to be withdrawn from an AP course where her grade was an A-minus, which would have been one of the lowest grades on her transcript.

At the time of the lawsuit, Miss X had been accepted at Harvard, Stanford, Duke, Princeton, and Cornell. But when she notified Harvard she would enroll, she found that her notoriety had preceded her to Harvard Yard. In the wake of the lawsuit and its attendant publicity, 2,700 students signed an online petition asking the admission office to rescind her acceptance. Shortly thereafter, it was found she had plagiarized speeches by President Clinton as well as various Supreme Court decisions, failing to credit her sources in opinion columns she wrote for the local newspaper. In July 2003, citing Miss X's plagiarism, Harvard decided that she would not be a member of the Class of 2007. She eventually enrolled in a university abroad.

are and what they are looking for, and don't try to fake it by "packaging" themselves as something they are not. That means *they*—the students—have to be in charge. But never fear, there is a role for parents in this process.

The best way students can reach their destination in this process and arrive there healthy, whole, and ready to take on new challenges is to *follow their own path* and *be themselves*!

With this book, we'll help both students and parents find the right paths.

CHAPTER 2

Is There a "Secret" to Admission?

"The big secret in college admission is that there is no big secret."

—Fred Hargadon, former dean of admission, Swarthmore, Stanford, and Princeton[10]

We know the college admission process—and its results—can feel confusing, mysterious, and sometimes downright capricious. That's because you know what *you* want—to get into college! But you can't be sure what the college you hope to get into wants. This chapter is about helping you understand the college's point of view. You'll end up seeing that what every college most wants is *authenticity*—for you to be honest and to show them exactly who you are in your application. The rest of this book will explain how you can do that. But before we start, here's why authenticity counts.

IS IT JUST A ROLL OF THE DICE?

Every year in the spring, at high schools across the country, college-bound teens and their parents will at some point hear a story that goes something like this: The class president receives a thin envelope—a rejection—from Harvard, while the teenager who seemed least likely to go Ivy is admitted. Somehow every gossip in the grocery checkout line "knows" the class president's grades and SAT scores, which of course are far higher than those of the lucky teenager now headed to Cambridge. And while the class president was cramming for the exams that produced those A's and dancing in *The Nutcracker* and building houses for Habitat for Humanity, the future Harvard Crimson was playing so-so basketball and partying. "It's just not fair," goes the familiar refrain. Why do some get admitted and others get waitlisted, deferred, or rejected?

Students and parents often feel like the admission process is unfair or a matter of sheer luck. But that's because they are too immersed in their own role in the process, according to Alice Kleeman, who heads the College and Career Center at Menlo-Atherton High School in Northern California, where she counsels about five hundred students a year. "Parents and students have no clue about comprehensive review, institutional priorities, the actual numbers of students admitted and denied," she says. "It's easier to say it's just random. But when they say that it's random, that implies there's not a lot of care given to who is admitted and who is not. And there's an enormous amount of care given to those decisions."

UNDERSTANDING HOW COLLEGES THINK ABOUT ADMISSION POLICY

Admission policy is shaped by two schools of thought. Most public universities take an approach that's more quantitative. It's sometimes referred to as the "panty hose" method, like the chart on the back of the panty hose package, where you can use height and weight to determine size. For these colleges, specific criteria, such as scores and grades, are used to determine admission—at least in the preliminary stages of the process.

Most private universities, on the other hand, are holistic in their review of applica-

tions. In addition to scores and grades, these schools consider an applicant's extracurricular activities, athletic ability, special talents, nonacademic interests, background, legacy status, experiences, and aspirations. In the later stages of admitting a class, even public universities using statistical equations may consider some of these factors as well.

KNOW THE JARGON . . .

Comprehensive (or Holistic) Review

"Comprehensive review" or "holistic review" is an admission process that takes into account criteria beyond grades and scores, including a student's extracurricular activities, teacher and counselor references, essays, and—where available—an interview.

This is where the process gets messy. There are no computers adding up the numbers and making the decision. Human beings are making judgments—about talent, motivation, character, leadership, and ability. As soon as a school starts considering anything other than grades and scores, the process can no longer be reduced to a formula, secret or

Institutional Priorities

"Institutional priorities" are the strategic needs of a school as it considers whom to admit. For example, one year a school may seek tenors, female engineers, fullbacks, or geographic diversity. Institutional priorities can change from year to year, though some may carry over.

otherwise. And that's what many anxious applicants and their parents are really looking for—the secret formula that would ensure admission to Notre Dame or Dartmouth or the University of Michigan.

What Are the College's Priorities?

What happens in a college admission office is not about selecting a group of students with the highest grades or the most awesome talents—it's about putting together a class that meets the school's needs. It is driven by institutional priorities—that is, every college's own self-interest. And every school's self-interest is different and ever-changing, dependent on the college's leadership, its values and aspirations, and its heritage and culture.

So, students, it's not "all about you."

But don't let that intimidate or discourage you. It's an advantage to realize you're dealing with people who have their own goals and needs. And colleges want you to realize that. An understanding of a college's institutional priorities and the policies behind them doesn't guarantee admission to your school of choice. But if you understand how colleges view admission and their applicants, you'll be better able to understand the judgments admission officers have to make and even see

where the opportunity may lie for you and your unique talents.

What do institutional priorities consist of? At public universities, the priority is often a mandate from the legislature to educate the best students in the state, as defined by GPA or class rank. For private colleges, it's also about the institution's mandate, as reflected in its mission statement. They will seek applicants who reflect the characteristics that fulfill that mission statement—which might be leadership, intellectual ability, or dedication to public service.

But it's more complicated than that.

Admission officers must also listen to all of a college's voices. They must listen to the faculty—the engineering school that wants more women, the mathematics professors who want to see conceptual creativity in their students, the social scientists who want students who will push issues and provoke discussion, the physics department that wants Intel Science Talent Search winners, and the biology researchers who want at least *some* students who are genuinely interested in biology rather than studying it as a stepping-stone to medical school. They must listen to those in student life who want leaders who will run the student organizations, writers who will fill the student newspaper, actors to walk the stage, athletes who will fill the stands, and the just plain nice kids who will make the residence hall a fun place. Finally, they must listen to the administration, which hopes for geographic, cultural, and socioeconomic diversity.

And then there is another layer of consiforation and complication. Some colleges have cultures and personalities that can become an important part of their admission criteria—perhaps they are seeking quirky intellectualism, highly social students, or international applicants.

So, then, what are colleges looking for? All of the above.

Transparency—an admission process where everyone can understand the simple rules—is a quality often discussed and yearned for. It's believed that if there were transparency, if students and parents could see exactly how the colleges make their decisions, then the process wouldn't feel unfair or random.

But the rules are not simple, and they are ever-changing. And it is not always in schools' best interests for their priorities to be completely transparent. Here's why: If a school says they're looking for female engineers who tap-dance, classicists who play the oboe, and a new defensive line for the football team, then the following year, every applicant will be just that. But by then the priorities may have changed, with the school now needing male math majors, female premeds, and a center for the basketball team.

Colleges also have to watch how much they divulge about what they are looking for in order to prevent applicants from presenting themselves falsely—and to encourage applicants to show honestly who they really are. Charged with building a class that meets the school's priorities, admission departments need to know what the applicants are really like. That's why there is one word heard over

and over when admission officers are asked what they are looking for in applicants: *authenticity*.

WHAT DOES IT MEAN FOR AN APPLICANT TO BE QUALIFIED?

So is the college admission process meritocratic? Yes . . . and no.

The problem with the subject of merit is that what it means depends upon who is doing the talking. The applicant who has high SAT scores and low grades defines merit as high test scores. The student with high grades but low SAT scores defines merit as high grades. The student who is not strong academically defines merit as "emotional intelligence" or leadership ability, a state championship in soccer, or legacy status.

Actually, all of these types of merit can come into play in the admission process. But the focus in college admission is going to be on an individual's merit in the context of the total applicant pool, and in light of the college's own institutional priorities.

That's a good thing. Yes, the subjectivity of the process creates stress for students and parents. But it means that a school is looking at applicants as individuals, not as numbers. Remember, your particular "merit" may be just what a school is seeking for its next class of freshmen. So once again, students, show colleges who you really are!

Because, in the end, it's all about fit. To understand whether a school is a good fit, students will want to learn as much as they can about a school's institutional priorities and campus culture. But don't use that information to tailor yourself to fit into their priorities. Instead, figure out the schools that will be a good fit for *your* personality, abilities, interests, and aspirations. Read the mission statement on the school's website. Look at recent public statements from the school's leaders. Visit the campus. Ask questions. With some astute observation, it will be apparent if a school's priority is, for example, diversity, public service, or recruiting women engineers. If what that school values will make it a good fit for *you,* then just present yourself authentically so they can see that you're a good fit for them, too.

Believe us when we tell you that schools are not looking only for the student with the highest test scores, the most impressive talents, or the best writing. They are looking at what students have done with what is available to them, in order to identify young people who have committed themselves to one or a few things in which they have achieved some level of success—whether that's graphic novels, high school musicals, mathematics, soccer, a part-time job, American history, research at a local hospital, or playing the oboe.

Using a student's transcript, test scores, application, and essays, looking at what a student does with her time, considering letters of recommendation and, when available, an admission interview—with all of that, schools try to figure out what a student will do with the four years of her college career and in the span of her lifetime. This is no small task, and you will see in this book—and, we trust, be reassured—that it is done with an open mind, great care, generosity, and deep respect for the applicant.

PART II

GETTING ORGANIZED

CHAPTER 3

The 9th and 10th Grades: Before You Begin . . .

> "Learning is supposed to be joyful! Challenge is supposed to be exciting! And mistakes are supposed to be made!"
>
> —Denise Clark Pope, Stanford University School of Education

The hype surrounding college admission has spun so far out of control that headlines hawking tutoring, test prep, and campus visits for students in elementary school are commonplace. When a magazine for Harvard alumni set out to produce a tongue-in-cheek guide to preparing a child in utero for admission, the editor complained it was almost impossible to satirize the subject because every ridiculous recommendation they came up with was actually in use.

So when should the college application process really begin?

Elementary school is way too early. But students and parents can also make the mistake of starting way too late. For most students, the formal application process will begin in the junior year of high school. Before that, most students should simply enjoy being in high school—discovering who they are and exploring what they like to do. Rod Skinner, director of college counseling at Massachusetts' Milton Academy, says, "Build a life and the colleges that work for you will come."

VERY FIRST STEPS: FRESHMAN AND SOPHOMORE YEARS

During the freshman and sophomore years of high school, there are a few things that students can and should do. But these things should be done in the spirit of being aware of college as a goal and making decisions that keep doors open—not with a fat envelope in mind.

Course Work

Selecting the right courses is the earliest step a student will take on the path to college. You should meet with your academic advisor early in your freshman year and become familiar with the requirements for graduation and the

Checkpoints ✍

- ✔ For most students, the college admission process will begin in junior year.
- ✔ During 9th and 10th grade, students should pay attention to course work and grades, find and invest in some extracurricular activities they love, and spend a good dose of time daydreaming.
- ✔ Too much pressure to perform can have serious negative consequences for health and learning.
- ✔ For families who will be applying for financial aid (and this is the majority of families), keep saving and practice good record keeping.

Navigating with Naviance

Many schools subscribe to Naviance—a Web-based service for academic planning and the college admission process, used by guidance counselors, administrators, students, and families. Some schools may introduce Naviance components as early as 9th grade, including tools to manage course selection; resources for tracking extracurricular activities, tasks, and milestones such as awards; and "interest inventory assessments" that identify learning styles and potential careers. Later, Naviance is used to manage aspects of the college search and admission process, including providing academic and admission data about colleges, test prep, financial aid planning, and other resources, which we will discuss further in Chapter 8.

appropriate college-prep curriculum. Courses should be mapped out along the timeline of your four-year high school career in order to create as many options as possible. Decisions made in 9th and 10th grade set the table for junior and senior year, particularly in cumulative subjects such as science, math, and foreign language. Don't close any doors by not taking math, for example, just because it's not a favorite subject. Also look through the course

Student Athletes

Student athletes who are being recruited by Division I schools or who play sports where identification as a college prospect occurs early in high school will likely have to start thinking about college earlier than other students, including mapping out a four-year plan of course work that meets NCAA standards. See Chapter 18 for more guidance.

Underresourced Students

Students whose needs may be underserved by their high school's resources or who are the first in their families to pursue higher education have a different timetable for the college admission process. When a college-going culture is not present in either the home or the school, students need to begin preparation earlier than junior year of high school. They must be extremely purposeful as early as possible, even as early as middle school. Emily Froimson, vice president of higher education programs for the Jack Kent Cooke Foundation, which supports gifted low-income students through its programs and scholarships, warns, "Some of these students will get twenty minutes of guidance counseling during their entire high school career."

Here are some actions to take:

1. **Find a mentor.** Start learning what steps it takes to apply to college. Ask a teacher in your high school or a faculty member at a local college. Anyone you know who has attended college can help answer your questions.

2. **Talk with your high school college or guidance counselor.** Ask about advising opportunities in community-based organizations and support programs such as the Jack Kent Cooke Foundation and the National College Access Network. If it's difficult to get time with an overworked counselor, just keep trying. Persistence could get you what you need.

3. **Sharpen study skills.** Read, read, read! Choose challenging course work. If challenging courses are not available at your high school, look for online opportunities or local community college classes.

4. **Tap resources at community colleges.** Look for mentors among faculty and admission officers and take the opportunity to visit these campuses. Community colleges can often be a good resource for students whose high schools offer little college support.

5. **Get involved in precollege programs.** Organizations such as Upward Bound, Advancement Via Individual Determination (AVID), and federal TRIO programs offer support for students preparing for college.

lists and think ahead to higher-level electives that may interest you; then make sure you include any prerequisites in your course work.

The goal is to enroll in a variety of classes, aiming for a course load that is challenging but not overwhelming.

Additional tools and resources for underresourced students are available in Appendix IV and on our website at collegeadmissionbook.com.

Grades

Academic preparation is important, and so is finding out what you most enjoy studying. Rather than working toward a grade in a class, learn to have fun academically, and let yourself be captivated by a subject. When we tell you not to worry about grades, we are by no means saying don't study. Your grades will count, and they will count more than anything else in the colleges' admission decisions. But students who develop a love of learning early on will usually find that good grades follow.

Activities

Students should use these early high school years to explore activities and identify what they love to do, outside the classroom and beyond the school. Resist resume building—it's not about the number of activities on your list or about how busy you can be. This is a time for discovering passions and developing natural talents. So volunteer, write for the student newspaper, run cross-country, try out for the school play, start a garage band—the goal is to do a lot of different things in order to figure out what motivates and excites you.

Downtime

It's true for all the high school years but especially these first two—this is the time for thinking about "Who am I?" and "What do I like to do?" Make some time for what Castilleja School college counselor Susan Dean calls "navel contemplation" to discover who you are—as well as daydreaming, hanging out with friends and family, and recreational reading, whether it's graphic novels or Gabriel García Márquez. All of this prepares a student to be a great candidate for college.

Parents: Start Your Financial Planning Early

One of the most important things parents can do during a student's first two years of high school is to prepare for the expenses of college.

- **Continue saving.** For the 2013–14 school year, tuition, room and board, and fees at private four-year colleges can run as high as $60,000; at a four-year public college the total can approach $30,000.
- **Keep good financial records.** For families who will apply for financial aid, make sure your record keeping is in good order. The following documentation can be necessary in applying for financial aid:
  - Federal income tax returns
  - Untaxed income records, including veterans' benefits, workers' compensation, and child support

A Practice PSAT?

The PSAT (Preliminary SAT) is a standardized test that provides practice for the SAT. It is typically administered in the fall of 11th grade. However, some public high schools and many private schools offer students the option of taking a "practice" PSAT in 10th grade. If this is offered and a student would enjoy taking it, it can be a good chance to become familiar with standardized testing. But it is not required. The PSAT is used by the National Merit Corporation for its National Merit Scholarship Competition, but a 10th grade "practice" PSAT is not considered. Scores are accepted only from a PSAT administered in the 11th grade. See Chapter 7 for further information. (Keep in mind that the world of college admission is constantly evolving. The College Board has announced changes to the PSAT and SAT for 2015 and 2016. Please see Chapter 7 and the sidebar on page 91 regarding these changes. And to make sure you have the most current information, visit our website at collegeadmissionbook.com or sign up for our free weekly newsletter.)

The Perils of Overscheduling College-Bound High School Students

Denise Clark Pope of Stanford University's School of Education likes to ask parents and teens to perform a thought experiment: "Imagine if Steve Jobs had no time to tinker in his garage because he had to go to piano lessons and SAT prep class and art class and was on a travel baseball team that had practice five times a week and away games on the weekend." What if he hadn't had the downtime to dream up Apple, design the Mac, create Pixar Studios, and put an iPad in every backpack?

Right from the start of high school, parents and students need to recognize that there is an epidemic of overscheduling, says Pope, who is also the founder of Challenge Success, an organization working with schools to reduce excessive stress. When students' schedules are so full that they feel they can't meet expectations to perform—when, for example, there is so much homework that it becomes a choice between sleep and studying—the result is stress, and serious consequences for health and learning.

Depression, anxiety disorders, sleep disturbance, alcohol abuse, self-injury such as cutting, shoplifting, and substance abuse, particularly of prescription drugs such as the stimulants Adderall and Ritalin—educators are seeing a rise in all sorts of negative behaviors. These are the coping strategies of teenagers faced with an unhealthy level of challenge in their lives.

Worse, stress also takes a toll on the desire to learn. Students who are pushed too far too fast will disengage—the exact opposite of the focus and enthusiasm that are optimal for learning. Pressed to perform in myriad ways from the basketball court to the biology lab, teenagers will feel like they can't do it on their own. Just when they should be experiencing some independence, they can be made to feel they need tutors, extra coaching, more help. They learn that who they really are is not enough. One result: cheating is rampant. Ninety percent of 11th and 12th graders confessed to cheating at least once during high school, according to a Challenge Success study.

A little stress can be a good thing—it's normal to feel stress when a final exam is looming in biology or there's a big game against a tough opponent coming up. We know the pressure to indulge in the bounty of activities and athletics available today comes from all sides: teachers, parents, the media, peers, colleges, and the students themselves. But what happens to creativity and engagement when a student is stressed out, exhausted, and afraid to make a mistake? As Pope says, "Learning is supposed to be joyful! Challenge is supposed to be exciting! And mistakes are supposed to be made! That's how you learn."

Pope's best advice? Make a priority of reserving some downtime. And parents—*listen* to your teenagers when they say it's all too much, and support their efforts to achieve balance.

- Bank statements—checking, savings, and mortgage information
- Business and farm records
- Investment records—stocks, bonds, retirement accounts
- Custodial documents in the case of divorce
- Alien registration or permanent resident card
- **Watch out for big purchases, especially if you have to borrow to make them.** Paying

interest and principal on debt—whether it's a mortgage, consumer loan, or credit card—cuts into your spendable income. But when you apply for financial aid, colleges won't take your debt costs into account. Your aid will be based on total income, and that can be a problem, because the reality of what you can afford is based on your income after you've dealt with your debt every month. So if you think it will be a stretch to pay for college, don't get any deeper in debt.

Parents: Follow the Student Leader

Early in a student's high school career, parents need to set the stage for an ongoing discussion about grades, activities, family time, and college applications. Dr. Michael Riera, author of *Uncommon Sense for Parents of Teenagers* and head of school at Brentwood School, says the biggest mistake parents make in these discussions is trying to control the agenda. When students are allowed to lead—encouraged to make decisions about activities, course work, and how they spend downtime, as well as to deal with the consequences of those decisions—they acquire good decision-making skills and learn who they are. This is a critical step in making the long-term college admission process a success. We spoke with Riera to get his advice:

- **Don't ask about grades.** Ever spent time with a cultural anthropologist? Probably not, but if you had, you'd know that their interview technique is to ask you about your life and your assumptions, beliefs, and interests—they get you talking by making you feel like you're the most fascinating person in the world. The same technique works to get high school students talking. Anything you do that makes teens feel more interesting will make them want to keep you close at hand and talking to you.

  So avoid outcome-based questions such as "What grade did you get?" or "Did you score a goal?" Instead, ask questions that are really about them, not about your goals for them. Questions such as these have staying power: "When you made that painting, how did you know you were done?" or "You're studying the American Revolution. Is there anything applicable to today's politics?" Ask questions that encourage students to look at pieces of their experience they might have missed. "You seemed to study differently for that test; what did you do with those note cards?" Teens won't push you away when you're really interested in them and not interested in judging them.

- **Encourage students to embrace confusion.** Successful people have a relationship with confusion—it doesn't frighten them. It's uncomfortable, but they know it's a sign: if they can get through it, there will be an insight on the other side. So let your teenager be confused! Encourage her to appreciate it. Don't jump in with solutions. Experiencing confusion will teach strategies for dealing with it. Perhaps your son needs to take a run. Or your daughter needs to study differently—looking for themes instead of memorizing. Sometimes calling a friend or talking to a teacher is the solution. A healthy relationship with confusion can show a student how to work hard, problem-solve, and take an idea and follow through on it.

- **Talk when they're ready to hear you.** There are two times when teenagers will talk and listen more than any other—in the car and late at night. In the car, they're a captive audience. But don't take advantage. If you talk to a high school student for more than five minutes about an idea *you* think is important, he may check out. Discipline yourself and stop at four minutes. Conversations can also go well late at night when both teens and parents are tired and relaxed. It's a natural time for teenagers to reflect on things, and parents tend not to jump in with questions and mini-lectures, so they can hear what their son or daughter is thinking about. As one high school student said, "We all know that tired parents make better listeners!"
- **There are more than twelve colleges in America.** If the subject of college comes up during the first two years of high school, parents need to follow the student's lead. Make it clear your expectation is that they will go to college, but show them right from the start that it's all about fit—not name brands or bragging rights. By spending these years helping your teen see which decisions and experiences are a fit and which are not, you're preparing her for a successful college admission experience.

FROM THE DESK OF THE DEAN

An Extended Generational Apology to High School Sophomores and Freshmen, 8th Graders, and Others

JON BOECKENSTEDT, ASSOCIATE VICE PRESIDENT, ENROLLMENT MANAGEMENT, DEPAUL UNIVERSITY

First and foremost, we're sorry. We didn't think your parents were listening, and maybe we stretched the truth to make a point. Let me explain.

Fifty or so years ago, college was little more than a dream for most Americans. Only a quarter of high school graduates attended. Many went for only two years, and that was fine, because just going to college said something about you in those days.

But then Americans started to believe higher education was part and parcel of a better life. When our parents looked around, one thing was unmistakable: the wealthy and

The 9th and 10th Grades: Before You Begin . . . 25

successful were college graduates and those on the middle and bottom economic rungs of society were not. If cause and effect may have been reversed in a classic case of *post hoc ergo propter hoc,* who cared? Aspire, regardless. Go to college.

So college became a part of parents' dreams for their children. The enthusiasm was contagious. Even the government got involved, creating special grants and loans to make college possible for those who couldn't have imagined it. (Hard to believe, but for most of history, if you wanted to go to college, you had to pay for it yourself.)

I was a part of this education boom. And as I started my work in college admission thirty years ago, my colleagues and I also started beating some things into your parents' heads.

Most notably: "Choosing a college will be one of the most important choices you will ever make." Dramatic? Sure. We probably should have said, "Hey, you have a few more choices than you might think. Exercise them," and been done with it.

The truth is, you do want to do a good job choosing a college that fits your talent, ability, temperament, and worldview. But I've learned that your choice of a specific college is far less important than your investment in learning once you arrive there.

We also told you, "It is *never* too early to start preparing." What we really meant was that March of senior year was a bit too late. Subtle hyperbole wasn't our strong suit.

So the generation that benefited most from just "going to college" started wondering, "What would happen if my kid got into the *best* college? I must start grooming her *now*!"

Your parents had not only heard our message but embraced it, squeezed out any nuance, exaggerated it, and passed it on to you. Who knew they'd be so . . . so . . . so literal?

Really, we had no idea.

Several years ago, the *Chicago Tribune* ran a story about kids who played unorganized baseball. No uniforms, no parents, no umpires. Just fun. That this is newsworthy was disheartening. But it made me realize you can take back your adolescence. You have my permission to skip your choice of debate, violin, tennis, Model UN, or your job in the nuclear physics lab.

And, again, please accept our apology.

College Counselors and Advisors

"Get to know your high school college counselor.
They are your greatest advocate."

—James Conroy, department chair, Post-High-School Counseling,
New Trier High School

As students make their way through the college application process, a counselor may act as a coach, consultant, expert, psychologist, drill sergeant, mentor, or hand-holder. A college counselor can be a powerful advocate for a high school student during this time and can have a significant impact on a student's aspirations, achievements, and admission results.

Families may encounter two types of counselors during the application process:

- **High school college counselors** are employed by schools to provide information, advice, and guidance to students.
- **Independent counselors** are fee-based consultants employed directly by students and their families.

HIGH SCHOOL COLLEGE COUNSELORS

A high school college counselor's primary objective is to help students and families manage the application process. Counselors can be a significant resource on everything from navigating the Common Application to filing for financial aid and where to find a Starbucks during a college visit. Here is what you can expect a college counselor to do:

- **Provide guidance on creating a list of schools.** One of the counselor's most important duties is to help students put together the list of schools to which they will apply. Most counselors expect students to come up with an initial list. Then they will use their knowledge of the student, the colleges, and the admission history of the high school to help edit and refine the list. "Students and their families feel most powerful and in charge when they're putting together their list," says Melanie Choukrane, director of college counseling at New York City's Grace Church School. "That is the point at which the counselor can be most helpful by balancing

Checkpoints ✍

✔ High school college counselors provide influential parts of the application such as a recommendation letter.

✔ Students should get to know their high school college counselor!

✔ Hiring an independent counselor may benefit some students, particularly those who need help with organization, who have special circumstances, or who do not have access to high school counseling.

✔ Independent counselors must be carefully vetted.

✔ When admission offices have questions or concerns, they will call the high school college counselor, *not* an independent counselor.

✔ There are serious pitfalls in trying to "package" an applicant.

the list and making sure students are not too vulnerable, suggesting schools they may have been unaware of, pushing them to look widely, and getting them to expand their thinking about this next step." For example, using college profiles and student test scores and grades, a counselor can help students understand their realistic chances of being admitted.

- **Provide letters of recommendation.** Applications usually require a letter of recommendation from a secondary school official. In most high schools, this letter will be written by the college counselor. (An academic advisor or guidance counselor may sometimes write the recommendation as well.) When these letters provide a thorough, personal, holistic view of a student, they can have a significant impact on an admission decision.

- **Provide counseling.** If the student requests it, college counselors will offer advice and

help with decisions about college essays, application forms, courses, and activities. They can dispel myths and rumors that create unnecessary anxiety, manage crises (such as accidentally pushing the "Send" button before the application is complete), provide constructive and candid perspective, and be a sounding board for students as they manage their emotions throughout this process.

- **Help students stay on track.** The admission process is full of deadlines—testing, financial aid, filing of the application, and requesting recommendations. While counselors won't ride herd on a student, many will help organize the process by providing timely information for important steps.

- **Be a strategic voice.** Family dynamics are a part of the college admission process, too, and when the goals of a student and her parents differ, the counselor can help them figure things out as a family.

- **Provide a safe haven.** Counselors can help students manage external factors such as peer buzz, athletic recruitment, and campus gossip. They view their job as providing a safe haven for students to make good decisions. Be open and honest about the influences you may be juggling—whether it's the expectations of your family, a boyfriend, or a coach.

When Will a Student Get Started with a High School Counselor?

The first one-on-one meeting between the student and a high school college counselor will typically occur during junior year at most schools. Prior to that time, students and their families may attend one or more group meetings with the counseling staff, and the student will receive information from the counselors on course work, testing, and preparation for the admission process.

In order for a counselor to successfully advise a student about her college list and write a compelling recommendation, it is essential the student get to know the counselor. Counselors can do a lot for a student during the application process, but they can't do it well unless they know the student.

Whenever possible, students should be proactive. Make an appointment with your counselor, introduce yourself, find out when would be a good time to meet, and ask how he would like you to stay in touch. A student who takes the initiative will make a very strong, positive impression.

Then stay in touch. Drop in periodically to talk, perhaps during a free period. Keep the counselor informed of what is going on in your life, what you're excited about, and what challenges you. You might say, "I know you're busy, but I just wanted to tell you how things are going. I've got the lead in the musical." It's your responsibility to cultivate this relationship so that when the time comes, the counselor can be your advocate.

We realize a personal relationship with a college counselor is not possible at all schools. If your counselors are overburdened, you will need to be aware of their constraints and plan accordingly. We'll have more advice for you later in this chapter.

KNOW THE JARGON . . .

School Report (SR)

The School Report (SR) is completed by the high school counselor and provides colleges with a profile of the school and the student. It includes information about class rank, GPA, curriculum, and the percentage of the student body attending four-year colleges. It usually requires the counselor to evaluate the difficulty of a student's course load, to report any disciplinary violations or suspensions, and to explain any special circumstances the student might have experienced. In other words, it provides a context for the student within the school—a holistic, personal overview.

◉ Best Advice

- Get to know the college counselor. Drop by to chat and provide regular updates about your life. Start early—even before junior year, if appropriate at your school.

- Be honest and open. The counselor is your ally.
- Meet deadlines. This is your process; own it! Don't expect the counselor to do your work for you.
- Respect boundaries. Counselors won't take phone calls at home on the weekend, or fulfill requests the moment they are made.
- A good relationship with your counselor will help her guide you appropriately throughout the process and is crucial to obtaining a recommendation letter that is detailed, is reflective, and portrays the person behind the data for admission officers.

Get to Know Your High School Counselor

High school counselors can be great resources for students and stand ready to answer specific questions about individual colleges, test prep, recommendation letters, extracurricular activities, course selection, scholarships, and much more. Get to know them and take advantage of their expertise!

That said, colleges understand that students often do not have close relationships with their college or guidance counselors. The opportunity to get to know a counselor will depend on the individual high school and counseling program. It is certainly more difficult in large high schools. But even students from large or underresourced schools can potentially find a way to stand out in the crowd.

Here are some ideas:

- Don't wait until senior year to speak with your counselor—go early in junior year or even earlier if your school assigns academic advisors throughout all high school grades.
- Drop in during your free period.

Here are some of the things high school counselors will not do:

- Counselors will not do any writing for a student, whether it's filling out the application or composing the essays.
- Counselors do not set up college visits.
- Counselors do not make decisions for students. They will not tell a student, for example, where he can or cannot apply. They will advise students, provide information, and serve as their editor and advocate, but a counselor's goal is for the student to practice thoughtful decision making.
- Counselors do not share information about other students.
- Counselors will not meet with parents before they have met with the student.
- Counselors do not have a vote in the process. They cannot make promises about admission.

College counseling is structured differently from school to school. At some schools, college counselors and academic advisors work together to guide students. At others, college counselors and academic advisors work with students separately. At still others, there may be no college counselors, but academic advisors or guidance counselors who provide college counseling. For students whose schools do not provide college counseling, see our advice on page 34.

- Drop in just the way you would drop in on a teacher.
- Make an appointment, if available.
- Find out the counselor's open-office hours, if available, and attend once in a while.
- Pay attention to announcements and bulletin boards so you know when opportunities to meet with the counselor are available; mark the dates and times in your calendar, and then follow through by attending.
- Have your list of questions ready for when you do speak with your counselor. Ask how she would like to interact with you, what information you can provide that would be most helpful in writing your recommendation, and her best advice for you.

Here are some of the questions you may want to ask:

- What kind of colleges do you think I'd do well at and why?
- I don't know where to begin. Can you help me take the right steps toward coming up with a college list?
- What courses should I be taking if I'm interested in attending College X?
- Can you put me in touch with graduates from our high school attending College Y?
- Can you go over my transcript with me so I can see where I stand?
- What can I tell you about myself that will help you give me input and feedback on my college list?
- Can you help me design a list of criteria to help me research schools?
- What is the best way for me to communicate with you in the future? An appointment, email, drop in, phone?

Lessons from Orange County

Don't feel like making the effort to get to know your high school counselor? Well, watch the movie *Orange County*, starring Colin Hanks as a high school senior and Lily Tomlin as his clueless college counselor. You don't want to end up like Hanks' character, Shaun Brumder, a serious surfer, academic overachiever, class president, and aspiring writer who dreams of going to Stanford. When his application is rejected, he pays a visit to his counselor, Charlotte Cobb, only to find that she doesn't recognize him and, worse, sent the wrong transcripts to Stanford.

COBB: And you didn't get into Stanford? Too bad. Tough break. Where else did you apply?

SHAUN: Nowhere. You said I was a shoo-in.

COBB: Not even a safety school?

SHAUN: You said "shoo-in."

COBB: Calm down. Let's see. I'm just going to pull up your file. Well, looks here like your GPA is 2.5 and your SATs combined are 940. That's low.

SHAUN: No, I had a 1520.

COBB: No, it says 940.

SHAUN: That's not my transcript. That's Shane Brainard's transcript.

COBB: And *you* are . . . ?

Disclaimer: We would like to note that we do not know any counselors like Charlotte Cobb. But don't let what happened to Shaun happen to you! Get to know your high school college counselor.

Former Castilleja School college counselor and Stanford admission officer Susan Dean has some good advice: "Developing self-confidence and being the initiator of opportunities for your counselor to know you can be hard. But this skill will serve you well in becoming a leader, when interviewing for a job or with a college, and ultimately in being seen by admission officers as ready to take on the challenges of college. You are a work in progress, so no one expects you to be an expert yet—jump in and take a chance!"

As you begin to apply to colleges, you should feel free to consult with your high school counselor about everything from interpreting test scores to starting your college essays. They are there to support you, guide you, and provide constructive and candid perspective.

How Parents Work with High School Counselors

Most high school counselors see parents as allies who can help them arrive at a fuller understanding of the student. That said, while it is understood that parents will be part of the process, they play a secondary role.

If there is an opportunity for parents to meet with the high school counselor during a student's junior year or sooner, they should certainly make the effort in order to find out what services will be provided and to reassure themselves that they can have confidence in the person who will be advising their college-bound teen.

At large schools where counselors are serving many students, it may be difficult to bring parents into the process. In those cases, there will probably not be one-on-one meetings, but there may be group information sessions or websites that keep parents up to date on testing, financial aid, and important deadlines.

Questions for Parents to Ask the High School Counselor

Counselors understand parents are not experts in applying to college, so it's entirely appropriate in an initial meeting to request a calendar of events and ask the counselor to help you understand the basic vocabulary of applying—terms such as "FAFSA," "selectivity," "NMSQT," and "Naviance." Here are some other questions you may want to ask:

- What resources are available through your office to research colleges?
- What classes should my teenager be taking?
- Which tests should my teenager be taking?
- Has my teenager developed an appropriate college list?
- Are there schools on the list that my teenager can get admitted to?
- When should we start visiting schools?
- Where can I find out about financial aid?
- How do I keep my teenager motivated?
- Which colleges would be a good fit for my teenager?
- What trends are you seeing in admission at public universities? At small liberal arts colleges? At the most selective schools?
- Where do students from this school attend college?
- What has been this school's track record for acceptance during the last few years at College X?
- What can we tell you about our teenager that will help you to know him better?

As the college application process unfolds, it is also appropriate for a parent to check in periodically with a counselor by email or phone to inquire about where the student is in the process and what the parent can do to help. Parents should keep in mind, however, that while all counselors want to engage with them, in the final analysis it is the student's process. In general, parents should respect the wishes of the student when it comes to parent-counselor interactions.

How High School Counselors Interact with Colleges

College admission officers and high school counselors from both public and private high schools routinely interact. Admission officers frequently visit high schools, and, when possible, high school counselors travel to college campuses to get an in-depth view of the classes, student life, and admission review. An admission officer may call a high school college counselor with questions about a student's file, to request a misplaced recommendation, or, in the case of a spring waitlist, to inquire whether the student is staying engaged academically. Likewise, high school college counselors talk regularly with college admission officers to do follow-up on an issue reported by a student, provide perspective on the rigor of a student's curriculum, or elaborate on a special circumstance, such as a student undergoing treatment for cancer.

Many college admission offices also extend the courtesy of speaking with high school counselors about specific applicants. In these calls, a student's chances for admission may be discussed once she has applied. And, yes,

> ## Starting the Parent-Counselor Relationship Off on the Right Foot
>
> - **Back off.** Put the student in charge. After an initial meeting with the counselor, the student needs to run with the ball.
> - **Get everything out on the table early.** Talk to the counselor about the family's finances, your student's struggles and successes, alma mater issues, priorities in the college search such as religious affiliation or diversity, and, of course, your hopes and dreams.
> - **Remember how vulnerable your student is in this process.** Even the most well-meaning parents can expect too much in a process where, once the application is in, the final decision is out of the student's and counselor's hands.
> - **Don't ask who else is applying to a school.** Counselors do not share any information about other students.
> - **Don't bet the counselor is wrong.** Disregarding counselors' advice can be foolhardy. Counselors are professionals who have relationships with admission departments and access to the past history of their high schools with the colleges.

counselors do sometimes advocate on behalf of applicants when appropriate—primarily because they care about their students. In these conversations, college admission officers listen intently to what counselors have to say, and information the counselor provides may inform an admission decision. But a counselor's advocacy, a push for a certain student, will not dictate a decision.

No high school college counselor is in

a position to "get his favorite students in," either because of the school where he works or because of relationships he may have built. Admission officers operate from the presumption that counselors support all of the students they recommend.

Families who may consider pressuring a counselor to call an admission office should think twice. Counselors know when these phone calls are appropriate and are reluctant to second-guess admission offices. They know that when they do decide it's right to call, the fewer calls that have been made, the greater the impact. In nineteen years, Alice Kleeman, advisor at Silicon Valley's Menlo-Atherton High School, says she has called an admission office just four times to inquire about an applicant outcome.

Schools with No College Counselors (or with College Counselors Who Don't Have Enough Time!)

College admission officers do not expect every student in a large public high school to have a deep relationship with a counselor—or even have a counselor at all. They know that at many schools there is no counseling department, or counselors have large student caseloads. Under these circumstances, students will have to rely more on their academic advisor, teachers, and other available mentors, and will need to be more proactive at each stage of the process.

It will take time and effort. But it can be done. Colleges are not asking high school students to do anything they are not completely capable of doing on their own—or at least with some support from teachers and parents

or other mentors. Scores of students every year get into colleges that are right for them without the attention of a guidance counselor at every turn. The most important parts of the application will be from the student and his teachers.

INDEPENDENT COUNSELORS

Independent counselors—also sometimes called "consultants"—work outside of public or private high schools, providing private fee-based services directly to students and their families. The number of independent counselors is on the rise, and they get a lot of publicity in the media, generating sensational headlines about sky-high fees and promises of fat envelopes.

The issue of whether to hire an independent counselor is complex, and the decision to use outside help can have numerous ramifications for a student and the eventual outcome of the application process. Parents should consider carefully the costs and benefits to their family and the student's future.

In reality, most students will navigate the college application process perfectly well on their own or with their high school counselor. Independent counselors are not necessary to a successful college application process.

But there are situations where independent counselors can be helpful. Those who might consider hiring an independent counselor include:

• Students who attend high schools where there is no counseling available or where the counselors don't have enough time to spend with each student.

- Students who have chronic problems staying organized or who will require constant guidance to complete the process, especially when it is not healthy for the parent to perform the role of "reminder in chief."
- Students with special circumstances such as a learning difference or talent in the arts and athletics, where the process can start much earlier and be more complex. For example, arts students are usually required to submit extensive portfolios, often on a deadline earlier than that of a regular application.
- Students who are the first in their families to attend college and whose high schools lack counseling resources. Many independent counselors offer their services pro bono to families who lack economic resources and whose students attend high schools that are underresourced.

As a rule, the impetus for hiring an independent counselor should come from the student, who should feel it adds value to the process. A word to the wise: It is never a good idea to hire an independent counselor simply to obtain a competitive advantage. That strategy can just as easily backfire, and we'll talk about that risk throughout this chapter. For now, students and parents should keep in mind that no matter how good a counselor is, the real work still belongs to the student. And parents, who often drive this decision: Be careful about the message being sent when hiring an independent counselor. Make sure it isn't seen as a vote of no confidence in the student's ability to handle applying to college.

Services and approaches vary widely among independent counselors. Some may meet with students a few times at a reasonable hourly rate to provide input on a list of colleges that are a good match. Others perform comprehensive consulting on everything from activities to essay writing beginning early in high school, with a final price tag that can exceed the cost of a couple of years of tuition at Yale.

Generally independent counselor services include:

- Assisting students in developing a balanced list of schools that fit their strengths, goals, credentials, needs, and interests
- Consulting with students on extracurricular activities, summer programs, and internships—but with the goal of helping students further pursue their interests, not pretend to be someone they're not
- Test preparation
- Review of students' transcripts, test scores, and any other evaluations
- Essay preparation (but advice and editing only—no actual writing)
- Application review
- Mock interviewing in preparation for college visits
- Logistical planning to keep a student on track and meeting deadlines
- Collaboration and coordination with other individuals involved in the student's application process, including coaches, music teachers, social workers, tutors, and the high school counselor

Here are the things that independent counselors cannot and will not—or at least should not—do.

- Write recommendation letters. These letters must come from the student's high school counselors and/or teachers.
- Contact college admission offices to advocate for students. For more on this, see below.
- Urge the student to take on unwanted extracurricular activities in order to "package" him for admission.
- Ghost-write essays or any part of the application.
- Handle the logistics of college visits.
- Tamper with the student's authentic self in any way. Anything that makes it harder for admission offices to see who a student really is makes it harder for the student to gain admission.

How Independent Counselors Interact with the High School Counselor

Every high school has a different policy about independent counselors. At one end of the spectrum are schools that will not work with independent counselors and will not share any information about a student. At the other end are schools that have built strong relationships with local private counselors and will provide a list of those they recommend.

Some high school counselors are skeptical because they have had experiences with independent counselors who got in their way or provided information to a student that was detrimental. In most cases, high school counselors are willing to cooperate with independent counselors if their caseload permits. In those cases, it is critical that a student inform the high school counselor that he is working

with an independent counselor from the beginning of the relationship.

Parents may worry that the high school counselor, who communicates directly with the colleges, might be offended or hurt if he thinks parents don't have confidence in his ability to help the student. But our best advice is to be open about it. That's because the larger worry is what happens if the student gets caught in the middle—when she gets conflicting messages from the independent counselor and her high school counselor and then is told to keep the relationship with the independent counselor a secret! Then the parents' best intentions to help their student become a point of frustration and confusion.

If you need another reason to be open about hiring an independent counselor, remember that if there is any question about a student's application, the admission office will call the high school, *not* the independent counselor. Also, independent counselors do not have access to the high school's past history with colleges, relationships with the student's teachers, or an understanding of the context of a student's class as a whole in terms of applications to particular colleges or the competitiveness of the admission pool in any given year.

So if you do employ an independent counselor, don't put the student in the middle. Let your high school counselor know about the relationship—while telling him how much you value his participation—and grant permission for both counselors to communicate and work cooperatively.

How Colleges Interact with Independent Counselors

At the most selective colleges, admission offices will generally not communicate directly with independent counselors about individual applicants. On occasion, the admission offices of less selective colleges may interact with an independent counselor, but most are, in general, reluctant to discuss specific students with them.

In fact, admission officers treat calls from independent counselors very differently than those from high school counselors, making an important distinction between them. The colleges' allegiance is always to the high school counselor. Colleges do not accept letters of recommendation from independent counselors, and if any questions arise about a student's application, the admission office will call the high school counselor, not the independent counselor, no matter how long that counselor may have worked with a student.

The reason? An independent counselor is not impartial but is being paid by a family to represent a student. High school counselors are presumed to be objective because they represent and work on behalf of all their students who are applying to a college.

"It's important that parents recognize there is a kind of firewall between the independent counselor and the college, just as there is with a high school counselor. Only with the independent counselor, it's a little bit higher," says Jennifer Delahunty, dean of admissions at Kenyon College. "For example, we will review a transcript with a high school counselor, or talk about a student's chances for admission after they have applied, but we won't do that with an independent counselor."

How to Find an Independent Counselor

Most families find independent counselors by word of mouth—talking to other parents about their experiences. When doing so, parents should specifically question fellow parents about why they liked their counselor, what their child reported back to them, and why they thought the counselor was helpful.

Independent counselors may also be located through the websites of several professional organizations that serve the industry, including the National Association for College Admission Counseling (NACAC) at nacacnet.org, the Independent Educational Consultants Association (IECA) at educationalconsulting.org, and the Higher Education Consultants Association (HECA) at hecaonline.org.

Questions—and Advice— for Parents Evaluating an Independent Counselor

Our best advice? Buyer beware! These are shark-infested waters. There are counselors who truly understand what is required to apply to college and whose services provide real value to students and families. But there are also counselors out there who prey on families' anxieties or, worse, don't know what the process actually requires and are handing out bad advice. Take the time and effort to interview counselors you're thinking about hiring.

Here are some questions to ask:

- **Are you a member of any professional organizations?** Expect affiliations with NACAC, IECA, or HECA.
- **What is your philosophy?** A counselor's philosophy, mission, and ethics should reflect the standards and principles outlined by the National Association for College Admission Counseling, which can be found on their website at nacacnet.org.
- **What are your fees and how is payment structured?** Fees can range from an hourly rate of $150 to a multiyear "package" costing more than a year of tuition, room, and board at Columbia. Make sure all fees are spelled out contractually.
- **Do you have certification or an academic degree in counseling?** Credentials should go beyond having had their own child go through the application process or attending a workshop.
- **What is your experience?** Look for a counselor who has years of experience—the more the better—on both the high school and college sides of the desk. But get the specifics—for example, a part-time reader at a college admission office has never actually made an admission decision, nor will an assistant or volunteer in a high school typically know about important trends or campus cultures.
- **What is your track record?** The best track record is happy families. Get references and follow up on them. Run for the hills from a counselor who boasts about personal connections or says, "*I* got these students

into these colleges." You want a counselor who says, "Students who have worked with me have been admitted to these colleges." Remember that no one outside of a college admission office can faithfully predict or guarantee admission.
- **How often do you visit college campuses and meet with admission officers?** If a counselor is to advise a student about his list, she must be up to date with the campus culture and admission practices of a school.
- **What kind of students have you worked with in the past?** There should be a good fit between the counselor and the student. This is especially true for students with a special circumstance, such as athletes, students in the arts, international students, or those with learning differences.
- **What services will be provided to the student and to the family?** Is the counselor offering short-term counseling, individual "à la carte" services such as test prep or essay editing, or comprehensive, multiyear consulting services? Once that is established, make sure the counselor isn't promising something she can't deliver. Hightail it out of there if the counselor says she knows how to get a student into a particular school, or uses the pronoun "we"—as in "So when we look at the essays we are going to turn in . . ." And steer clear of the counselor who tells you it's too bad you didn't hire him when the student was in 7th grade.
- **What is your working style?** Make sure the counselor believes applying to college is the student's job and isn't planning on doing anything the student ought to be doing. No counselor should ever put pen to paper on the essay or application. Also, blackball any

counselor who dictates activities, classes, or a college list.

- **What services are you providing that our child's school counselor isn't?** There should be some value added by hiring an outside counselor. But avoid a counselor who touts her value with talk about "angles" and "hooks" or "packaging" a student for his "dream" school.
- **What would you do if . . . ?** Ask specific scenario questions, just as you would with any interview for an important service: "What would you advise if our son was waitlisted at his first-choice school?" "What would you say if our daughter wanted to take a gap year?" "What would you advise if our son got a C in a core course?" "If our daughter wanted to take a higher-level math course where she might struggle or receive a lower grade, what would your advice be?"
- **How will you assess the student?** Counselors will typically want parents and students to complete extensive questionnaires and participate in personal interviews in order to assess a student's academics, activities, and preferences about colleges.
- **How often will the student or family interact with you?** Counselors should be accessible, though not constantly available. The schedule should also be reasonable for the student, who will be taking time spent with the counselor away from family, friends, activities, and regular schoolwork.
- **Do you help students with financial aid or scholarships?** Be wary of scams when it comes to fee-based services here. See Chapter 16.

There is a crucial difference between a student's relationship with an independent counselor and the relationship with a high school college counselor. With the high school college counselor, it is necessary for the student to be the driver of the relationship from the very beginning. But with independent counselors, of necessity the parent will take the lead in initiating the search, conducting it, negotiating the fees, and so on—elements that don't exist in the high school counselor world.

This makes it essential for students to meet the independent counselor prior to a final selection. Students should not be put in the position of evaluating a counselor, but a high level of trust and some chemistry have to exist for a successful collaboration. The student should feel the counselor is genuinely interested in her and should emerge from an initial meeting feeling that she had a good conversation with an adult who was able to draw her out and who "gets" her. If the counselor talks nonstop and the student can't get a word in edgewise, that's a red flag.

If the student is worried that such a meeting might feel awkward, he might want to have some questions in mind, such as:

- What kind of colleges do you usually recommend to students?
- How does this process work?
- What do you expect of me?
- How often will we meet?
- Are you familiar with my high school?

Finally, all of the particulars that are discussed with a counselor should be spelled out in a contract, including a provision that allows cancellation without penalty if things don't work out.

"Packaging"

There is a widespread perception that college admission has become intensely competitive. In reaction, some families believe a student can be "packaged" into an applicant who is more appealing to colleges and therefore has a better chance at admission. But what often happens is overpackaging. When a marketing campaign is waged on every page of an application to make the student seem "perfect," it hurts at least as often as it helps. In fact, a school may prefer an "imperfect" applicant who is real and sincere.

The overpackaging of applicants is often associated with independent counselors. But any overinvolved adult can compel a too-slick sales pitch—including parents. Neither an experienced, professional independent counselor nor a thoughtful parent should attempt a makeover—or takeover—of a teenager. And if you're tempted, keep in mind that admission officers have read literally thousands of essays and applications. There are admission deans who can perform the parlor trick of guessing an applicant's SAT scores within thirty points upon reading an essay. They're old pros at detecting the supposedly invisible hand of coaches.

Here a group of admission deans weigh in on overpackaged applicants.

KNOW THE JARGON...

Overpackaging

The term "overpackaging" refers to students whose applications have been manipulated to present a picture that is believed to be more appealing to colleges. To produce a teenager who will look "good" on a college application, there may be an attempt to game the system—for example, by having her take the ACT multiple times until a certain score is achieved, or engage in activities that are not aligned with her true interests.

WILLIAM FITZSIMMONS

Dean of admission and financial aid, Harvard University

➡ There are lots of dangers with overpackaging. In a sense, you can lose your soul in this process. And in the case of one who is developing a worldview and a value structure, it can hinder the development of the core of the individual. And that's rather frightening.

What you do not want is admission to a college that's not appropriate or may even do permanent damage to a student, because of some package that was put together by a third party or the parents or both. It is terribly important that the student end up at a college that's the right match. So you can outsmart yourself in a variety of ways. You can really damage your son's or daughter's life.

There is this "Do you have a hook?" obsession. The truth of the matter is that we're going to admit 2,100 or 2,200 people, and the vast majority of them are going to be what many will say are people who don't get into places like Harvard. In other words, they're good all-arounders. Now, they're good at a very high level—academically, extracurricularly, personally. We always say character and personal qualities should be the foundation for each case. But there will only be a certain number of people in the world every year who apply to Harvard who will be so unusual that that will provide, in a sense, the hook for the case.

What we are trying to do is look for people who have been presented with the following opportunities in their families, in their neighborhoods, and in their schools. What have they made of those opportunities? What do their accomplishments at this point project for their next four years at Harvard, and beyond, the next fifty or one hundred years?

It's unwise to have a highly professional, slick, embossed-stationery, high-quality package—I mean literally a package. Because we get packages. But we also read guidebooks and we realize what people think is required. And there is no set of requirements. Less is more. Colleges right now are very wary of the overpackaged candidate—candidates who appear to be too slick, candidates whose essays are written in iambic pentameter despite the fact that they have B's in English. Colleges are really trying to hear a genuine voice emerge from an application.

I don't have a one-size-fits-all answer here. In many high schools there are no counselors left because of budget cuts, and in many high schools the ratio of counselees to counselors is 500 to 1 or more. So especially in those situations, it would seem, if parents can afford it—and a lot of independent counselors take on a considerable number of pro bono clients—using an independent counselor might be a rational thing to do. But it's not an easy call. There are many highly effective independent counselors who do not go over the line and overpackage candidates. Many of them are just there to give advice about college and talk about visiting colleges and the application procedure. They're not writing essays for people. They're not essentially creating a different candidate from the real candidate as they help people think about how to put their applications together.

There's no right way to apply to college. The vast majority of people apply to Harvard without an independent counselor. But there's a whole industry out there that has decided that packaging is *the* way to get into college. It's very unfortunate.

JENNIFER DELAHUNTY
Vice president and dean of admissions and financial aid, Kenyon College

➡ Kenyon is not a highly competitive college. It is a selective college. So I don't see a tremendous number of really overpackaged applicants like Brown or Stanford might. But I can sniff out when there has been some adult involved in the process. You can smell it in the essays and the way everything is presented—especially if you've met the student and what you see on the page doesn't square up with what you saw when he interviewed.

Does it work against the student? It depends on whether the kid has tried to make sense of the resources and opportunities he's had. He's been led to water and he either drank or sat. Parents clearly engineer a lot of these things—the tremendous summer and after-school opportunities. Do you punish the kid for ambitious parents? I think you do try to see if the student has internalized any of these experiences, rather than just going through the motions.

I also have to say that those students who really manage the show on their own, fill out their application on their own, make their own appointments for interviews, correspond with you on their own email account—those students get extra points because they're managing their lives. They're managing this complicated process and they're showing that they can manage their life, and sometimes those are little signals that parents forget about but colleges are paying attention to.

It's a tough dance. The best thing for parents to do is just let their kid follow her heart, her gut, be herself. Let her make mistakes. Let her follow her passions. Colleges will appreciate that more than somebody who appears to be perfect.

JIM NONDORF
Vice president and dean of admissions and financial aid, University of Chicago

➡ Everything in an application file should hang together. When some pieces of a file are more polished than others or the person coming across in the essays is not reflected in the teacher or counselor recommendations or extracurricular activities, then it's clear that somebody else has been involved.

There are a lot of ways packaging can go awry. Sometimes the quality of the packaging can torpedo the student. You lose his voice. Frankly, seventeen-year-olds don't sound like forty-five-year-old independent counselors. As much as independent counselors might have good information to offer a student or understand how we make decisions, they are not experts on the tone or the vibe of a kid. They'll package the kid up so tightly that the student's uniqueness can't come through. The way students write our essays, for example, is going to be different from the way they write them for Yale or Harvard or another of our peer institutions. And sometimes the packaging is structured so that it's one package for everybody, and that kills our ability to see the unique fit.

At other times, we'll look at an extracurricular list and there's no community service until senior year and then there's loads of it and the essays are all about it. You think, "Okay, they've hired an independent counselor who told him we want community service, so they had him join all these clubs and then they wrote the infamous 'building a hospital in Ecuador' essay." There's nothing wrong with a student who likes music and didn't do a lot of community service.

Our best advice is to be yourself. Don't stress about what we want. Tell us who you are.

SETH ALLEN
Vice president and dean of admissions and financial aid, Pomona College

➡ When students get "packaged," it's sometimes the case that they are offered the advice "Go with your strengths and ignore your weaknesses." This can leave the admission committee in a very uncomfortable situation. For example, the very solid math student who takes calculus and the grade goes from an A- to a C+. The admission committee has to assume the worst if the student doesn't address the situation or take responsibility for it. But if the student addresses the situation proactively and tells us what he's going to do differently in the future, turning a seeming weakness into an educational moment, it allows us to make an informed judgment and it demonstrates the student is mature and self-aware. He's not perfect. But that's okay. That's not going to derail you. Help us make sense of the application.

The other thing that can happen when parents inappropriately take over their child's role in this process by hiring an independent counselor, or muscling in and rewriting the essays and reordering activities themselves, is that the seventeen-year-old gets taken out of the application. But the seventeen-year-old is the expert in this process and can be highly creative and original. There needs to be a part of the application where the student makes a telling case about why we should admit him to our institution and the seventeen-year-old needs to tell us that in his own voice. That's what we find interesting, not the adult voice. I have gotten to know parents so well in this process and thought so highly of them. But the fact of the matter is that they are not applying and they won't be admitted.

There is an appropriate role for parents or counselors—as editors, making sure there are no spelling or grammatical mistakes, that the application to Grinnell doesn't say Amherst College. But they shouldn't try to take the seventeen-year-old out of the application. We are looking for authentic. We know they have imperfections. They're going to college to work on those things. If, at their tender age, they are already a superstar, why go to college at all?

KATIE FRETWELL
Dean of admission and financial aid, Amherst College

→ Admission officers are professionals who read hundreds, even thousands, of applications each admission cycle. In their quest to find a student's true voice, they are sensitive to polish that suspiciously exceeds even an exceptional adolescent's capabilities. In certain geographic corridors of angst, many families embarking on the college process are convinced by other "successful" families who utilized the support of independent packaging services that the only way to gain the needed edge in the application process is through hired support. Too often, however, a student's true direction and voice are lost in the process of over-handling and excessive packaging. Fabulous candidates can and often do come in compact, uncomplicated packages! Parents need to focus on allowing students to claim ownership of the application process. They can do this by supporting their children's voices, encouraging their passions and ambitions, and, of course, by keeping an open line of communication about finding the right college fit.

Questions You May Have

My high school doesn't have a college counselor, so who will write my recommendation letter?

Your guidance counselor or academic advisor may write your recommendation and complete the School Report (SR). Teachers—or even an administrator—may also do double duty and write your recommendations. When admission offices read applications, they usually read "in context"—in other words, taking into account the school from which the student is applying. They will know if your school doesn't have a college counselor, and they do not weigh one student against another in such a way that the one with a guidance counselor comes out ahead. They are just trying to build a picture of the applicant.

Also, for students with a disability or learning difference, letters of recommendation may be written by their case manager.

Is it true that certain prep school counselors go over their "slate" of students with college admission officers and discuss which applicants should be taken and which should not?

That is not what happens. If a high school counselor from any school requests it, admission officers will often speak to them about their candidates. The information counselors provide in such a conversation enriches the applicant's file and allows colleges to make better-informed decisions.

Can college admission officers tell if a private counselor is used, and how will they react?

Many colleges read applications by school group—admission officers are seeing the application, essay, and teacher and counselor recommendations of every student applying from a particular high school. So patterns emerge that inform the reader, and inconsistencies stand out. A brilliant essay that's not supported by the Critical Reading or Writing SAT score or the teacher recommendations, for example, is a dead giveaway. At one highly selective college, the admission dean was tipped off when she received a crop of applications from the same school during an admission season—all boasting essays with the same theme of "cultural awareness."

When admission officers see the heavy hand of an independent counselor—or any adult—in an application, they are still going to give the application a full read. But the officer may begin to wonder what other parts of the application aren't authentic. If there is anything else that rings false, it will make them wary. If the college that suspects adult involvement is one that values independence or those who are self-starters, it may be a negative and students viewed as co-applicants may go to the back of the line. Individuality is one of the things schools seek in applicants.

What about online counseling services?

As college advising in high schools has become limited by burdensome caseloads, Web-based counseling services have sprung up to meet the demand for information. But the sheer volume of information on the Internet can be overwhelming, and it is critical to carefully evaluate the services offered.

When considering signing up for online services, ask these questions:

- How well will they get to know me and what is right for me?
- Is it possible for them to get to know me within the context of my high school?
- Are there other ways I can get answers to my questions?
- I'm paying for this advice. Is it really better than what I could get from a teacher or guidance counselor?
- If they have experience in college admission,

where did they work and how recently? One website, for example, prominently lists its advisors as veterans from the admission staffs of top-name colleges. True, but what they don't tell you is that they worked at those colleges twenty years ago, and not in decision-making positions. If that is the reason you're thinking of purchasing their services, find out how current and relevant their experience is.

There may be specific pieces of any one website—such as a section on essay writing—that can be useful if you don't feel you are getting this help elsewhere. But if you're at a school where the curriculum includes instruction in writing essays, then you're probably set. Also, before signing up for anything that requires a fee, check out free resources available, such as those at collegeboard.org and nacacnet.org.

What if we feel we've made the wrong choice after our child starts working with an independent counselor?

If you are hiring someone to help you with this process and you're paying a significant amount of money for those services, your expectations should be very high. If you feel you've made a mistake after your child has worked with a counselor for a month or two, if there is a lack of trust or chemistry, or if the counselor is giving you bad advice, cut your losses, move on, and find someone else. Make sure any contract that you enter into allows you to terminate without significant penalty.

What should I do if I feel like my high school counselor doesn't like me?

Speak directly to the counselor. Applying to college is a long process, with many significant decisions to be made along the way, and emotions can become involved. At most schools, it isn't possible to switch from one counselor to another. So it's important to address any conflicts that may arise.

You might start the conversation by saying, "I feel as if you and I haven't gotten off on the right foot. Can we talk about it? Because it's important to me." If, despite these actions, things aren't going well, you should discuss the situation with your parents, a teacher, or another guidance counselor. It is possible for a student to obtain the letter of recommendation or School Report from another administrator.

The independent counselor wants me to start working with her in 9th grade. Is that necessary?

Most students begin work with an independent counselor at the end of sophomore year or the beginning of junior year. If a counselor is suggesting starting earlier, find out exactly what she is proposing—in terms of the topics she wants to cover, the frequency of meetings, and the expense involved. Meeting a few times to get to know each another and talk about what the student cares about is not problematic. But a counselor who proposes more than that raises concerns about whether a student will be overpackaged and not given room to explore what excites and motivates her academically and outside the classroom.

If a student at a school with good counseling hires an independent counselor, is that a red flag to colleges?

It can be. Admission officers are well aware of which schools offer top-flight counseling and spend plenty of time getting to know the students. If an independent counselor's presence is detected, an admission officer may wonder why the student felt extra coaching was needed.

If a student has a special circumstance such as a learning difference or is an athlete, is it worthwhile to work with an independent counselor?

Students with special circumstances, such as athletes, musicians, international students, or those with a learning difference or disability, do not always need to work with an independent counselor; in fact, most do not. If families feel they need extra counseling to make the best match between a student and school, such as in the case of a school with support for disabilities, or to navigate unfamiliar terrain, such as NCAA requirements, they should make sure whoever is hired has considerable experience in the relevant specialty. Also, see Chapters 18, 19, and 20, where we discuss these special circumstances.

PART III

BECOMING COLLEGE-BOUND

CHAPTER 5

The Academic Record

"Students who pursue a tough curriculum are more willing to take academic and intellectual risks. They want the challenge. They see something bigger for themselves."

—Leigh A. Weisenburger, dean of admission and financial aid, Bates College

The academic record—the classes students take and grades they earn—is the cornerstone of every college application. Grades in college preparatory courses and the difficulty of the curriculum are top factors in the college admission decision.

IT ALL STARTS WITH YOUR ACADEMIC RECORD

When admission offices examine a student's academic record—classes and grades—they look for:

- The level of difficulty in the student's classes and a pattern of increasing difficulty through senior year
- Grades that are consistently high or grades that trend upward in the midst of increasingly challenging classes

The academic record reveals a student's academic ability. This signals to colleges whether a student is likely to succeed if admitted. So in virtually all universities, academic ability is one of the primary criteria for admission. For the highly selective and most selective schools, it is *the* most important variable in the application.

"Intellectual horsepower" is the way Katharine Harrington, vice president of admissions and planning at the University of Southern California, describes it. "Academic ability is the ante to get into the game," she says. "We start by ensuring, to the best of our ability, that the students we're looking at have the academic ability to be successful. It doesn't guarantee anything. But it needs to be there. It is the first necessary condition."

Checkpoints ✍

✔ Grades and classes are fundamental criteria in a college's admission decisions—often the first two variables examined in review of an applicant's file.

✔ Colleges desire students whose course of study is characterized by appropriate challenge and rigor.

✔ Admission offices go to great lengths to understand the high schools from which students are applying—from the demographic composition and size of the student body to the course offerings and grading standards.

✔ Do colleges want to see high grades or tough courses on a student's transcript? Most say they want students to opt for more demanding classes.

CLASSES

Much of the work you need to do for admission to college begins with choosing the classes you will take in high school. (See a recommended course of study in Appendix II.)

Core Courses

The best preparation is a challenging curriculum in the five core areas: math, science, English, social studies, and foreign language.

The basic requirements for a college preparatory track are:

- **Math**—three to four years
- **Science**—three to four years
- **English**—four years
- **Social studies**—three to four years
- **Foreign language**—three to four years

However, selective and highly selective schools, including many public universities, will want to see four years of study in all five of these core areas. And don't make the mistake of assuming that if you complete your high school's course requirements for graduation, you will necessarily meet the admission standards of selective colleges. Be sure to find out what's required by the colleges to which you may apply.

Electives

After fulfilling core course requirements, students can round out their course work schedule with electives. Electives provide students the opportunity to explore new topics, pursue more in-depth learning experiences, and further develop intellectual passions. These courses might include philosophy, music theory, computer science, journalism, or even yoga. Just remember that if you are interested in the most selective colleges, these classes should continue to showcase academic achievement. Before signing up for multiple electives, confirm that core course work requirements for college admission have been met.

"Challenge" and "Rigor"

When the subject of a college prep curriculum arises, you will frequently hear high school counselors and admission officers talk about "challenge" and "rigor." But what do they mean?

They want to see evidence in the course transcript that students are willing to stretch intellectually and academically in the core areas of the curriculum, and that their choice of classes demonstrates a pattern of increasing difficulty. For example, if a student wants to study science, she would take progressively more demanding courses in that core area. This is an important signal for college admission officers. In fact, one report found that taking progressively more difficult and higher-level courses increased an applicant's chance of being accepted at a competitive college—more so than a higher grade point average.[11]

We asked three college admission deans to share their thoughts on challenge and rigor in a curriculum.

STEPHEN HANDEL
Associate vice president, undergraduate admissions, University of California

➡ We are interested in how students maximize their academic opportunities within any given educational context. The curriculum at high schools across the country may vary enormously and we try to take account of this by recommending that students complete the most challenging courses available to them at their particular school.

When we talk about challenge and rigor, the signal we're sending is that while college is a transformative, often life-changing experience, it requires serious preparation. We believe that students are in the best position to maximize their experience at our institution when they complete challenging and rigorous classes that are offered at their high school.

Students don't do themselves any favors by trying to pump up their GPA by completing a non-college-prep curriculum. Avoiding courses that prepare one for college is not an effective strategy—and it is at odds with the very purpose of higher education. Students who complete a rigorous, college preparatory curriculum demonstrate that they not only have the skills to compete academically, but also possess the habit of mind—call it tenacity, commitment, resolve, or grit—that will prove valuable and essential in helping them earn a college degree.

DOUGLAS CHRISTIANSEN
Vice provost for enrollment and dean of admissions, Vanderbilt University

➡ On the Common Application, in the section the college counselor fills out, they are asked to rank the applicant's course selection. Did the student take the most demanding, very demanding,

demanding, average, or below average curriculum offered? Did they take what is perceived in the school to be the most elevated classes?

We want the student who has pursued the greatest rigor in her course work, the most demanding curriculum. But that has to be put in context so as not to penalize a student who does not have the opportunity. Here's an example: A suburban high school offers twenty-eight AP courses and a student takes three. An inner-city high school offers two AP courses and a student takes two. All else being equal, the inner-city student taking two may look more favorable, because we are looking for students who took advantage of the opportunities available to them in the context of their environment.

Our philosophy is that we're not recruiting students to fill a class. We're recruiting students to build a community. We want them to come here and push and take the very best classes—not come and take the easy way out. So the challenge and rigor in their course work is a good indication of their ability to do the work, but also of their motivation.

Course selection and rigor also go much deeper than just being about how to get into college. If a student prepares well and takes the most rigorous courses, that student will have a much higher likelihood of a successful college career. You should be taking these courses so that you will be better suited for college, and also to be successful once you're there.

FUMIO SUGIHARA
Vice president for enrollment, Juniata College

➡ A student's high school provides the context for determining the level of challenge in the curriculum. Admission officers look for advanced-level courses (relative to the high school) and academic work that identifies the student's program as challenging. We look for students who seek challenge by taking full advantage of the opportunities presented to them, in the hope that these students will take full advantage of the academic resources presented by the college. When students challenge themselves with their courses, it indicates they're engaged rather than simply going through the motions.

Advanced Courses

Advanced courses present students with greater academic challenge and rigor, and are designed to reflect introductory college-level work. Two of the most common advanced course programs in high school are the College Board's Advanced Placement (AP) classes and the International Baccalaureate (IB) diploma. Some high schools have opted out of programs such as AP or IB and offer their own challenging curriculum.

The course designations you are most likely to encounter include:

- **Honors.** At some schools, honors classes are the top-level class available. At other schools, these classes may be more rigorous than the regular academic offerings in a subject, but a step below courses with the AP designation.

- **Advanced Placement (AP).** The most widely available program, Advanced Placement offers more than thirty college-level courses, from art history and calculus to Japanese and U.S. history, each of which culminates in a rigorous subject exam.

- **International Baccalaureate (IB).** The International Baccalaureate diploma program is a two-year course of study focusing on international perspectives, with examinations in six core subject areas. It requires completion of an extended research essay, a course titled Theory of Knowledge, and participation in the arts, sports, and community service. Students may take IB courses without enrolling for an IB diploma.

- **Dual enrollment.** Dual enrollment programs allow qualified high school students to enroll in classes at local community colleges or universities, usually for a reduced fee and with credit toward high school graduation requirements. Dual enrollment is useful for students whose schools don't offer AP or other advanced courses, or for students seeking further academic challenge. Credits earned may be transferable to the college where a student eventually enrolls full-time.

- **Cambridge (AICE).** The Cambridge Advanced International Certificate of Education program is a comprehensive diploma program in math, science, languages, and the arts and humanities. The AICE diploma requires passage of exams in six core subject areas, and may be used for college credit at many colleges and universities.

Colleges realize that advanced programs differ from high school to high school. So no matter what your advanced classes are called—one of the designations above, or another such as "accelerated"—don't worry. Colleges will use their knowledge of your school and the school profile submitted with your transcript to understand your course work.

Advanced courses taken in high school can also influence a student's course work in college. Many four-year colleges and universities in the United States and in Canada grant incoming students credit, advanced placement, or both for qualifying grades on AP or IB exams or in dual enrollment classes. Students who do not take an AP class in a subject can take the AP exam and potentially earn credit as well. But every college and university handles AP and IB credit differently, so students must check the individual policy of each school. For example, at some colleges, course credit is not awarded, but students can

> Remember—enrollment in your high school's advanced courses may require a teacher recommendation, completion of introductory classes, or a satisfactory baseline grade in prior classes. So plan ahead!

be placed in higher-level classes. Or in dual enrollment, some colleges do not provide course credit if the student has received credit for the class in high school. Information on a school's credit policy can be found on the colleges' websites and the websites of the College Board at collegeboard.org and the International Baccalaureate program at ibo.org.

How Many APs?

Admission officers are used to hearing this question: "How many APs—or other advanced courses—do you want?" Unfortunately, there is no clear answer. Suggestions like this are a continuing dilemma for admission officers: how can they be straightforward about the importance of academic preparation but prevent students and families from going crazy and taking every AP course in sight?

When it comes to APs, don't get fixated on a number; instead, focus on a concept. Colleges want students to take as many APs as they can *reasonably* handle. They will look to see that you are challenging yourself within the available classes at your high school. If there are AP courses (or IB or other advanced classes) available, colleges don't necessarily expect you to take every single one of them. But if you're not taking any of them, they will consider that a negative.

Challenge yourself in the areas of your interests and strength. Don't just sign up for the most difficult classes available in every discipline, especially if that leaves you struggling. Find a balance among regular course work and advanced classes that reflects your sincere interests and takes into account the colleges you will apply to, personal obligations, extracurricular activities, desire for time with friends and family—and your capacity for stress.

Think carefully about your aspirations, and then match your efforts to those aspirations. If you want to go to one of the most highly selective colleges, you will have to take a rigorous course load with more AP than regular classes. If you want to spend more time with friends or take that photography class instead of another AP, there are still hundreds of schools out there for you.

The Best Course of Study

Students should work with their academic advisor and/or high school college counselor to figure out the best course of study based on their abilities, their goals, and the colleges they would like to attend. Information on the course work guidelines and requirements for individual colleges can usually be found on the colleges' websites. And once again—because it's so important—students should be aware that the graduation requirements of their high school may differ from the academic course requirements of the colleges where they are applying. For example, a high school may require only two years of a foreign language, but some colleges will want to see four years. Conversely, high schools have requirements for graduation, such as physical education or arts classes, that colleges may not consider as part of the academic record.

Students from high schools that lack a rigorous curriculum can build up their academic profiles by taking evening and/or summer courses at a community college. These courses can be affordable and may even be free if the high school has a dual enrollment agreement with the institution. There are also enrichment programs available for first-generation and underresourced students. For example, the Center for Student Opportunity promotes these programs across the country; information can be found at ImFirst.org.

GRADES

Grades are the second half of the academic record equation. Like the rigor of a student's curriculum, grades in core courses tell colleges about a student's probability of academic success in college—as well as his study habits, perseverance, motivation, time management skills, and resilience. In fact, studies have shown that high school grades, used alone, are the single best predictor of success at most colleges.[12]

Remember, one of the most relevant decision-making factors for college admission offices, particularly at the more competitive, selective schools, is an upward trend in grades in the face of increasing rigor—in other words, as classes get more difficult, a student becomes stronger academically. So a student's grades and grade point average (GPA) are never viewed in isolation from course work. An A in physical education is not the same as an A in AP calculus. One of the ways some high schools demonstrate the rigor of a student's course work is with a weighted GPA, which takes into account the difficulty of course work by assigning more points to advanced courses. For example, an A in a regular-level physics class is worth 4.0 points; an A in AP physics is worth 5.0 points.

You are probably used to thinking of a student's GPA as an objective piece of hard

It's Fine to Study French but It's Better to Study Chinese—*Not!*

It used to be Russian, then Japanese. If everyone could just get together and decide which country was going to be the next superpower, we would all know what language to study. Seriously, when it comes to course selection, Chinese—the language of the emerging superpower du jour—is *not* better than French. Colleges want to see a student who studies French because he adores French, *not* a student who studies Chinese because she's been told it looks better to an admission office. High school—and the college application process—is about finding out who you are and what you love, not simply trying to create the image that you've heard is going to impress a college *this* year. Here's the truth: there is no one decision that a student is going to make in high school that will determine the college she's going to get into or preclude her from getting into a particular college.

data. But high schools have dozens of ways of calculating and reporting grades. Some schools include every class in calculating the GPA, even physical education and band. Some schools don't calculate pluses and minuses in grades. Some schools use a 100-point scale instead of a 4.0 system. Some schools don't convert letter grades to numbers at all. A high school might actually report multiple GPAs using various formulas on a student's transcript.

But don't worry—college admission offices have ways of dealing with these

An A Student with a C?

If a student receives a grade in the sophomore, junior, or senior year that is inconsistent with her overall record—for example, an A student who received a C, or a high-achieving student with a semester of low grades—she should explain the circumstances to the admission offices of each college to which she has applied. The high school guidance counselor may address such circumstances with the admission office. But it is best if the student proactively explains the circumstances of atypical grades. This may be done within the application, but if the form doesn't provide space, the student should attach an extra paragraph or send a separate letter. It is a positive sign to an admission office when a student steps forward in this situation. But the admission officer will also look for the student to take responsibility—so don't blame the teacher or complain that everyone received a low grade. Even in the case of extenuating circumstances such as illness, a college will want you to explain what you have learned from such an experience. Resilience is a critical quality in college—it's a positive sign to an admission office when a student stumbles but gets up and keeps going.

differences so that they are comparing apples to apples when evaluating applicants. Many colleges recalculate a student's GPA based on their own guidelines—for example, they might omit freshman-year grades or include only grades from core courses.

Even if schools don't recalculate, they are looking at the GPA in context. Admission officers realize that differences in curriculum and grading standards from one school to another mean that an A at School X may not be the same as an A at School Y. A student's grades may be viewed in concert with the range and median of student GPAs from his high school, the grade distribution of his graduating class (for example, the percentage receiving A's, etc.), and even the grade distribution in a particular course.

Rank

The other piece of hard data often mentioned in any discussion on grades is rank. Rank uses the GPA to rate a student's academic performance in comparison with other students in the class. As with grades, high schools calculate and report rank in multiple ways. A weighted rank takes into account the difficulty of a student's course work. Nonweighted rank simply lists a class of 400, for example, from 1 through 400. Percentile ranks assign students by groups such as deciles (10 percent slices of the student body, where "top decile" means the highest rank), quintiles (20 percent), quartiles (25 percent), and so on.

Colleges use rank to obtain a quick read on where a student stands. They know, however, that differences in grading standards are so widespread that rank is not as accurate or reliable a measure as it once was. And rank can be skewed by the size of a high school, the rigor of the curriculum, and grade inflation (see the box on page 59).

Many high schools have eliminated rank. Some believe unweighted rank punishes students who take more difficult courses. Other schools have determined that rank magnifies irrelevant differences among students—for example, there was often negligible difference between the student ranked number two and the student ranked number fourteen.

Public universities sometimes use rank as part of a formula to determine eligibility. But the rank used is most often based on a formula specific to each state system, not the rank reported by a high school.

Even high schools that continue to rank students sometimes don't provide this information to colleges, leaving disclosure up to

Grade Inflation

Between 1980 and 2012, according to a Higher Education Research Institute study, students reporting an average grade of A to A+ in high school increased from 7.5 percent to 24.3 percent. Today's parents who attended school when a GPA of 4.0 put a student at the top of the heap may be surprised to learn that their son's or daughter's 4.0 GPA may not even place them in the top 10 percent of the class. Does that mean that everyone has gotten smarter? No—it's grade inflation, students receiving higher and higher grades for the same quantity and quality of work. It has become an increasing concern for college admission officers.

Extra-credit calculations for advanced courses, turbocharged students who take on heavy advanced course loads, and gerrymandered formulas for calculating grades can add up to GPAs that in some schools climb as high as 7.0. Parents and school boards are blamed as well for lobbying teachers to raise the "gentleman's C" to a B in the belief that too-tough grading standards harm students competing for college admission and scholarship funds. The result: grade inflation makes it harder to use a student's GPA as a reliable measure of academic achievement.

The rising tide of grades is one of the reasons colleges continue to use standardized test scores—such as the SAT, ACT, and Advanced Placement exams—in order to place grades in context. Because there is some correlation between high school grades and test scores, comparing the two helps college admission offices balance out grade inflation. When grades are high but test scores are low in a school district, grade inflation is often—though not always—the culprit.

But high grades and low test scores are not necessarily a problem for a student. In the case of a student whose scores are low but higher than the average test scores in that school, it may suggest the student has really challenged himself in that environment. In addition, admission officers know there are issues of gender and ethnic bias in testing, as well as students who simply don't test well.

And don't worry if your school *doesn't* suffer from grade inflation. You can rest assured that you will not be harmed in the admission process. Colleges are not simply looking to admit students with the highest GPA. They examine a student's academic record employing many different variables, from the school district's test scores to a graph of exactly which grades were awarded in AP English during your junior year. And, again, they always read in context—with an awareness and understanding of the school a student attends and how that influences the transcript.

the student. If your school doesn't provide rank, private colleges that conduct holistic reviews may use GPA, test scores, and their knowledge of a school to compute an estimated rank. But even colleges that note rank don't just take it at face value and will delve deeper into the transcript to really figure out what kind of student an applicant is.

The Academic Record in Context

Throughout this chapter, we have referred again and again to admission officers evaluating course work and grades "in context." In other words, applicants' academic records will be looked at within the context of their high school and what it offers. High school education is vastly uneven across the country, and therefore colleges must take into account disparities in course offerings, grade calculation, academic rigor, and competitiveness of the student body.

When we say admission officers go into considerable detail in evaluating the schools from which students are applying, we are not exaggerating. It means college admission officers know that at a particular school, for example, Latin was cut in the student's junior year, and that is why she takes no foreign language as a senior. It means knowing which high schools require four years of physical education, resulting in a lower GPA since it's not an honors course. It means knowing which social studies teacher gives only one or two A's every year. It means that this student's grades dipped in the first semester of senior year because he lost a parent to cancer, and that while this high school may be racially

mixed, this student is the school's first-ever Latina to take calculus.

How do admission officers know these things? They read applications from the same school year after year, and often visit those schools and talk with the faculty and students there. But there are thirty-six thousand high schools in America. So in order to give an application a highly informed reading, they also use the information from the School Report (SR) and the high school profile. The SR includes information about curriculum, the number of students attending four-year colleges, and GPA, as well as a counselor evaluation that rates the rigor of a student's course work and academic achievement. Some schools also provide the college with a profile that describes the curriculum, faculty, student body characteristics such as size and ethnicity, class rank, GPA ranges, awards, and even grade distributions for the class in every offered subject. Ultimately, if the admission officer still feels she doesn't have enough information, she may call the high school for further details.

Students and parents should be reassured that colleges go to great lengths to understand the educational backgrounds of their applicants and endeavor to never lose sight of the complex details of the very real young people whose lives are being assessed.

Parents, What Grade Are *You* Looking For?

Grades are an all-too-familiar source of anxiety for many students. The pressure to perform—and perform well!—can be a maddeningly mixed message when it comes at

FROM THE DESK OF THE DEAN

What's More Important: High Grades or Tough Courses?

Once upon a time there was a high school student who liked math. For the first three semesters of high school, she took advanced courses. She struggled a little but enjoyed the challenge. She didn't earn A's in the courses. So her high school academic advisor suggested she not pursue an advanced math course in the final semester of her sophomore year. She followed that advice, but found herself bored and easily earning an A. She wanted to get back into an advanced class for junior year. She knew an A was probably out of reach—but she didn't mind. She preferred to feel engaged in the classroom. To get into the course, her parents would have to intervene with the school's guidance counselor. But they were uncertain about what was best. They didn't want to discourage their daughter's academic initiative. But would her future—that is, her college search—be better served by a transcript with an A in the regular math class, or one with a B in the tougher course?

Students frequently wrestle with questions such as these as they choose their classes, especially during the last two years of high school. And parents wrestle with how best to advise them.

What do colleges want? Most, hands down, want students to opt for the challenge of tougher courses. Here a group of admission deans answer the question: What is more important—the high grade or the tough course?

RANDALL DEIKE

Senior vice president for enrollment management and student success, Drexel University

➡ We would prefer to see you take the more rigorous course—an AP course, for example, or an honors course—rather than a course where you're not going to be challenged but you might be able to get a better grade. The highest GPA isn't always the best. What's important is the degree to which we believe the student has really been engaged in a rigorous curriculum. So do your best work! Work hard! Challenge yourself! Now, none of us can actually do that every day all the time. But when you deviate from that, there can be consequences in terms of the college decision.

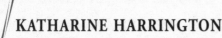

KATHARINE HARRINGTON
Vice president of admissions and planning, University of Southern California

➡ I want to see high grades *and* tough courses: high grades *in* tough courses. Honestly, families to a great extent (and to a lesser extent, students) are hoping for formulas where they can just plug it all in, because it gives them what feels like a sense of certainty. Thus the worry about "Should I encourage my child to challenge herself intellectually and be more engaged in a classroom or do we have to make sure she gets A's?" Challenge yourself, for heaven's sake! And for those institutions where we can't admit all the people who can do the work, a formula doesn't help. There are already way too many people who can be successful here. So I'm sticking with high grades *and* tough courses.

LEIGH A. WEISENBURGER
Dean of admission and financial aid, Bates College

➡ Evidence of a rigorous curriculum, especially in the final two years of high school, is a key indicator of a student's readiness for college. Since the late 1970s, our nation has catapulted into grade inflation, so grades themselves don't mean as much as they did (even ten years ago). The rigor of the curriculum is more revealing of a student's aspirations and level of preparation and should be in line with the level of the selectivity of the college to which he or she is seeking admission. As an admission dean, I admire records with a B in senior AP and/or IB courses from kids who got A's in everything else. The curriculum suggested that the student was willing to try, and had aspirations for her own level of college preparedness. Students who pursue a tough curriculum are more willing to take academic and intellectual risks. They want the challenge. They see something bigger for themselves, and that's an important predictor of success in college.

the same time as the directive to find balance between the hard work it takes to achieve that and the rest of a student's life: downtime, extracurricular activities, friends, family, and, of course, college applications.

Students get these contradictory messages from many sources, but the sources they are most exquisitely attuned to are their parents—whether it feels like that to parents or not. "Parents want it all," says educational psychologist Michael Thompson, author of *The Pressured Child*. "They want their child not to be frantic and anxious and overworked and stressed, and at the same time, they'd like them to take a lot of APs and do well in them." When parents give their children what Thompson calls this "double-bind strategic advice"—"Take these APs and you'd better get A's in them"—it sets some students up for failure and almost all for anxiety.

Because students are constantly reading their parents in order to resolve for themselves the right thing to do, parents need to be clear about what *they* want. Do you want your child to take a lot of APs and shoot for top grades? Or do you want her to take fewer APs and be less stressed? Then meet one of the tests of parenting a teenager: be straightforward and clear with your child about what you want, but be prepared to support what he or she chooses to do. And mean it! "Because what parents should really want is a successful young adult, and that means being independent, loving, moral, and productive. It doesn't mean a great college or a great first job offer," says Thompson. "People who define things that narrowly are putting their kids at risk."

Questions You May Have

Do the most highly selective schools evaluate a student's academic record differently?

The same basic principles hold for any college evaluating a student's academic record. But the more selective the college is, the less room there is for students who are anything but the strongest academically.

I attend a school where most of the students don't go on to four-year colleges and the curriculum is not challenging. How should I explain that to an admission office?

Colleges always take into account the context of a high school's curriculum, and many have a core mission of growing and maintaining socioeconomic diversity. Such schools will consider any student who has fully taken advantage of all of the academic opportunities afforded in his or her setting, such as summer enrichment, dual enrollment, or "bridge" programs for underresourced students. No need to particularly highlight the lack of academic challenge in your high school—just explain it and highlight your own commitment to a good education.

I transferred high schools. Will that affect my college admission?

Admission offices are accustomed to reviewing transcripts from multiple high schools when students transfer, and this situation will not ordinarily put you at a disadvantage. Double-check to make sure records from all schools attended are provided to the admission office. If you are applying to a more selective school, you might write a letter to the admission office explaining the reason a change was made and how you adjusted—especially if the change was made in senior year.

Do pluses and minuses in grades show up on a transcript?

Every school has different reporting standards and customs. Most schools report pluses and minuses on the transcript because they are different grades and represent different levels of performance. Other schools do not include them on the transcript. Sometimes pluses and minuses are shown on the transcript but not factored into the reported GPA. This is one reason colleges read "in context" (see page 60).

? I am in my senior year and thinking of dropping a class. Do admission offices care if I change my schedule midsemester?

First of all, make sure that dropping a class doesn't affect your eligibility for high school graduation or admission at the colleges to which you are applying. Then, in addition to consulting with your parents and high school counselor, you should also call the admission offices at the colleges to which you have applied. Colleges expect you to complete the academic year the way you told them you would. If you make changes without notifying them—before or after an acceptance—your admission may be rescinded.

? If I passed up the opportunity to take a particular AP class my senior year, will that affect my application?

High school isn't just a trajectory toward maxing out on advanced courses. Choose your course work and aim for grades relative to your abilities and aspirations. If you feel further explanation of your course work is needed, inform the schools to which you are applying of your reasons for the choices you have made. One caveat: if this situation

represents a change in your schedule after the start of the senior year, inform the schools where you have applied.

? If I finish an AP language class in my sophomore year, do I have to take another two years of another language to satisfy a requirement of four years of a foreign language?

When it comes to language—and math as well—colleges look at the level completed by a student, not the cumulative number of semesters spent at it. In other words, a student who completes the highest level in a class, such as Latin IV, in the freshman year is generally considered to have completed four years of language, even though she only took the class one year. However, your high school may have different requirements for graduation, so be sure to follow its rules as well.

? Will an abbreviated schedule with a shortened day during senior year affect an application?

It depends on what you do with your time and the colleges to which you are applying. If you just want some playtime, that usually won't be viewed favorably. But if you have satisfied your graduation requirements and taken on a job to help pay for college or supplement your family's income, those are circumstances that are understandable and laudable. Or if you're a ballet dancer spending the afternoons dancing with a professional company or a student with an interest in medicine who has an internship at the local hospital, those are experiences that underscore for a college admission office your passion and commitment.

? Are my junior-year grades the most important part of the transcript?

Colleges want to see strong course work with good grades all the way through. But beyond that, the most important grades on a transcript are always your most recent grades. For example, if a student is applying under an early decision program in November of senior year, the most important grades are second-semester junior-year grades (and many times the college will also call your school for a progress report on how your senior year is going). For students applying under the regular admission schedule, the most important grades are those from the first semester of senior year. "What have you done for me lately?" is the relevant question for admission officers.

? If I take a course at a local community college and earn a grade of C, do I have to report that on my college applications?

Most colleges request that the student provide official transcripts from all educational institutions the student has attended since 9th grade. In the Education section of the Common Application, applicants are asked to list where and when they have taken college/university courses for credit or enrichment and whether an official transcript is available from the college. The student signature on an application affirms that the information on the application is accurate and complete, so failure to disclose *any* course taken jeopardizes your admission if that omission is discovered by the college.

CHAPTER 6

Extracurricular Activities

MYTH #1: A student must be well rounded to get into college—you have to do everything, and do it well.

MYTH #2: A student must be exceptionally good at one thing to get into college.

MYTH #3: A student must build a school in a developing country, attend a summer program at Oxford University, and perform hundreds of hours of community service.

MYTH #4: A student must do all of the above.

When it comes to the role of extracurricular activities in college admission, myths such as these abound, causing unnecessary anxiety. In the worst cases, misunderstandings about what colleges are looking for cause students to ignore their true interests in order to devote time to something they mistakenly believe will be valued more highly.

The reality is there is no ideal mix of extracurricular activities that guarantees getting into college. Students should pursue activities that truly interest them. That's

what admission officers really want to see—students being their authentic selves.

WHAT ARE COLLEGES LOOKING FOR?

Colleges expect students to have spent middle school and the first years of high school exploring enough activities to begin to discover what they are really interested in. Then, as students progress through high school, it's expected they will commit time and effort to those that most capture their interest. That might mean a combination of a sport, theater, debate club, and student government. It might be an after-school job that contributes income to the family or the student's college fund. Or for the student who finds a single driving passion, it might mean robotics, robotics, and more robotics.

Colleges see extracurricular activities as strong predictors of how applicants will contribute to the academic and social environment of the community—in the computer labs, the theater, the newspaper office, the history department, or on the basketball team. While there is no one thing a student must be doing during his high school years, it will be regarded negatively if he has done absolutely nothing with his time outside of the classroom.

A student's extracurricular activities help build a picture of the applicant for a college admission officer, providing a sense of what the student cares about and values. The choices a student makes about clubs and jobs and sports can demonstrate the qualities that student may possess—kindness, leadership, musical talent, creativity, entrepreneurial instinct, humanity, athletic skill, international perspective, intellectual prowess.

 Best Advice

Figure out what you care about and then do those things with gusto, integrity, and commitment. As with much of the admission process, there is no formula.

While a list of activities will be different for every individual applicant, there are some criteria colleges may seek.

Depth Versus Breadth

Colleges aren't looking for the busiest students. Overscheduling a student with loads of activities rarely helps her get into college. An applicant with twenty clubs and sports on his list will not automatically be admitted over the student with a more reasonable schedule of three or four activities. When it comes to extracurriculars, the level of commitment is more important than the length of the list. Depth is more important than breadth.

By junior year in high school, most students will have identified their talents, strengths, and interests and devoted time and energy to them. So admission officers will try to understand your level of commitment. They will look at the time you have committed, your level of accomplishment, and whether you have taken on additional responsibilities or exhibited initiative and leadership.

Colleges want to see progression when you have had years of involvement. For example, a student who has played the violin in the orchestra for four years may progress to first or second chair, or a student who starts out as a reporter for the student newspaper may progress to the position of columnist or editor by senior year.

They will also look for evidence of the impact you have made, that your participation has enriched the activity for all involved; for example, the director of the school musical who has the ability to bring together the group, not just boss around the cast, or the member of the softball team whose enthusiasm makes everyone else play better.

More than minimal participation is critical, but students do not need to excel at everything. Admission officers recognize that students are young people, still trying to find themselves. Some of you do have a significant talent or strength in an area and will have devoted considerable time to it. But others will exhibit curiosity, engagement, and self-motivation in multiple activities. The important thing is the substance and length of involvement. Admission officers are not fooled by students who suddenly join five clubs in junior year.

Extracurricular Activities and the Most Highly Selective Colleges

A student's level of achievement outside of the classroom is a larger consideration at many of the most highly selective schools. They are creating their classes from a pool of the most gifted applicants. Almost everyone who applies is accomplished and academically gifted. Not always, but often, those who are admitted are pursuing extracurricular activities at a level beyond the context of their high school.

Whether it is music, drama, art, service, athletics, leadership, writing, or science, these applicants have often received national recognition for what they do. They are students who aren't just on the debate team but have won state or national competitions; athletes who aren't just the captain of their high school teams but have led those teams to regional or national championships; writers whose work has been published somewhere beyond the school literary magazine.

For most colleges, a student's activities add depth to the application but are secondary to the academic record. Activities become most influential when a college is comparing students with similar academic achievements; at the most selective schools, where many applicants have perfect academic records, activities can sometimes make the difference.

And remember, there is no formula. If you are a student who delights in being involved in many different activities, there is no need to suddenly develop an "expertise" in photography or squash. Rest assured that admission officers appreciate students who are involved in a number of different activities because it's a positive experience for them. They can tell the difference between these students and those who are tackling every activity in sight because they think it will look good to the admission office.

Why Do You Do What You Do?

Model UN, filmmaking, lacrosse, choir, quilting, math club—it doesn't actually matter what activities you choose to pursue. What colleges care about is the why and how of what you do.

Colleges want students who have demonstrated through their actions an ability to see and connect with a world that is larger than they are. A college will want to understand how you have internalized and learned from your experiences—why writing makes you happy, how a position in student government helped you develop as a person, whether a work experience or volunteering provided an opportunity for you to reflect on a larger context for your life. You could work for Domino's Pizza or Dell Computer—colleges don't care as long as you are able to tell them why you work, why it's important to you, what you are getting out of the experience, and why you continue with it.

It's your job to tell this to the colleges. Do things that you have a genuine interest in—and then do enough self-analysis to be

Getting into College: This Is Not Hard

"One art you should learn to master is properly listing your extracurricular activities. Sure, plenty of people have played for their junior varsity tennis team, but how many high schoolers have spent fifteen hours a week doing 'physics research: effects of various levers on trajectories of spheres.' Advantage: you, am I right! Tennis! The point is that you need to phrase things the right way."
—Advice from *The Harvard Lampoon's Guide to College Admissions*[13]

Consumer alert: Do *not* take this advice. Please note the source!

prepared to communicate why you do what you do. Most applications will require you to rank-order your list of activities and to elaborate on extracurriculars in the essays. Recommendations may provide further support for your involvement. Finally, if an interview is offered, an admission officer will probably talk with you about why you do what you do. It's much easier to convey the meaning of an activity if you are doing things that you believe in and value.

Passion

"Passion" is one of those words that gets invoked a lot when admission officers talk about extracurricular activities. It does not mean a student has to have found the meaning of life through chess club or baseball or working the counter at McDonald's. There needn't be a sense of urgency or cosmic fulfillment about every activity a student pursues. Neither does the activity have to be unique, or even something at which a student excels.

What admission officers seek is involvement that shows you are not just going through the motions but truly care about and are committed to what you are doing outside the classroom—a joyful participation. So when admission officers talk about passion, they mean a student should have a strong and genuine interest in an activity evidenced by sustained commitment, whether it's to horseback riding, a church group, English literature, theater, a job, graphic fiction, or golf.

Passion can make a student interesting to an admission officer. It is often the most reliable indicator of an applicant's authentic self. It's a sign of dedication, motivation, and follow-through—qualities admission officers value because they enrich college life for all.

Leadership

Some schools seek leadership in an applicant as part of fulfilling their mission statement, and may actively seek students who exhibit that quality. This is especially true at the most highly selective schools. But colleges know a leader is not always the person holding the highest title in a club or on a team. A leader may be the hardest-hitting tackle who inspired the team or the secretary of an organization whose passion and commitment got results.

Colleges know that not every student can be the president of the student body or the captain of the football team or the founder of the film club. Admission officers actually

shudder to think about a freshman class made up of nothing but leaders. Leadership is not something every applicant has, nor does every applicant need to demonstrate leadership in his activities. Colleges admit many students who show a genuine interest in an activity and pursue that interest in a way that's fulfilling to them without having to run the show.

And, by the way, it's a bad idea to take on a leadership position simply to pad a college application, and then fail to follow through on the commitment. This tactic will become obvious to an admission officer in the essay, recommendations, and interview.

Hooks

A "hook" is some special talent, quality, interest, achievement, or background characteristic that is so distinctive it sets a student apart and makes him more desirable to a particular college. It's something the admission department can "hook on to" as it evaluates the student. It might be athletic ability, culture or ethnicity, exceptional academic credentials, alumni connections, where in the country or the world the student comes from, or an outstanding personal accomplishment such as scientific research that resulted in a breakthrough or the publication of a book of poetry.

The most important thing for students and parents to realize is that for nearly every college in the country, students with hooks represent a minority of any incoming freshman class. In many cases, hooks are intangible qualities over which students have no control, such as ethnicity or where they come from. Being the captain of your high school basketball team, having a 5.0 GPA, or playing

Well Rounded or Specialist?

There was a time when it was believed applicants needed to play a sport *and* run for office *and* sing in the choir *and* join the debate team. That's because colleges used to prefer students who could be characterized as "well rounded." Today, though, admission officers talk a lot about creating a "well-rounded *class*," in which some students may have only narrow interests. Parents worry that's admission-speak for a game plan that seeks only "specialists"—the virtuoso violinist, the science nerd, the academic superstar—leaving no room for well-rounded kids.

"I want to show my colleges I'm well-rounded, so I wrote a poem in Spanish about how chess club has made me a better quarterback."

The real change in policy is that in creating today's well-rounded classes, there is room for both kinds of students—some well rounded and some specialists. It's not that there's no room for the well-rounded kid, but that at many colleges being well rounded is no longer the only ticket to admission. Think about it for a minute—you can't have a class made up of half tuba players and half Intel Science Talent Search winners . . . and especially not all class presidents. Some colleges may lean more toward specialists, some toward the well-rounded student. But most colleges want some of both.

in a community orchestra does not constitute a hook.

In the case of activities, students should never cultivate an interest simply to develop a hook they think will impress an admission committee. Forcing a student to invent a hook shortchanges the multiple dimensions of a young person and makes it more difficult for an admission officer to see who a student truly is. That can be detrimental to a student's chances of admission.

Also, it can be very difficult for a student and her family to identify what would be an appealing hook for any given college. One college might find a fanatical roller-coaster rider to be an exciting explorer of popular culture, while another college might find him to be only a lightweight hobbyist. This may be the year that Princeton needs a shortstop—or not. Trying to micromanage a hook can be chancy as well as insincere.

WHAT DO YOU DO WHEN YOU'RE NOT IN THE CLASSROOM?

For most colleges, that question is how extracurricular activities are defined. It encompasses students who play football or flute; whose intellectual gifts lead them to the library or lab; who serve in church youth groups; who hold a job; who pursue hobbies like carpentry, auto mechanics, or quilting; and who spend twenty hours a week caring for younger siblings because both parents work. Here are some of the many ways high school students spend their time outside of the classroom.

School Clubs and Organizations

Student council, band, computer, French club, peer tutoring, prom committee, anime appreciation, improv, Young Republicans—most schools provide many opportunities for students. Colleges don't have a checklist of activities that applicants need to complete, but they do desire students who have taken advantage of available opportunities.

Keep in mind that intellectual pursuits can be as important as organized activities such as sports or clubs. For example, an applicant whose class in Russian literature has prompted her to independently read Chekhov, Dostoevsky, and Tolstoy while studying the Russian language is involved in a scholarly pursuit that would make her very attractive to an admission office.

Sports

Participation in organized or individual athletics can demonstrate valuable qualities for a college applicant—drive, determination, dedication, teamwork, and motivation. Exceptional athletes may be recruited by

colleges, and in Chapter 18 we discuss how the admission process can be different for such students. But some schools, such as smaller liberal arts colleges, may value students who will participate on club teams as well. Whether or not you plan to continue your sports participation in college, your experience can provide meaningful information to an admission officer.

The Arts

Theater, visual arts, new media, orchestra, jazz band, opera, ceramics—the practice and appreciation of a fine or performing art is valued by many colleges. Involvement can illustrate creativity, commitment, and a willingness to experiment. Some arts, such as orchestra or theater, are also about teamwork. They may provide opportunities for leadership, such as acting as concertmaster or being the arts editor of the school paper. Students with significant accomplishments in this area that they want considered as part of their application will find guidelines in Chapter 18.

Community Service

Tutoring, conservation work, volunteering in a nursing home, temple or church activities, fund-raising, and even political work are all examples of community service.

While all schools desire students who have shown they have devoted time and effort to volunteering or service, admission officers want these activities to be of genuine, heartfelt interest. Colleges can tell when community service is more than fulfillment of a school requirement or an attempt to look good on the application. A student's level of involvement, evidence of leadership, and recommendations will paint a picture of an applicant's true motivation.

Some colleges actively seek students who have been involved in community service as part of fulfilling their mission statement. But it is simply a myth that applicants must show some community service work on their activities list.

 # Best Advice

Extracurricular activities should never compromise a student's academic work. The academic record—classes and grades—is still the most important part of a student's application.

Summer Activities

Summer is a time when many students participate in enrichment programs, leadership training, or academic programs. It is a myth that some of these programs can especially enhance your chances of getting into college. Leadership training programs—for example, the Congressional Youth Leadership Council or the National Youth Leadership Conference—position themselves so that when the "invitation" arrives in the mail, students might think they have been specially selected to participate.

But even if there are baseline GPA requirements and teachers are required to nominate students, these programs are not selective and have a hefty price tag of thousands of dollars. Undertake such an activity only if it aligns with your interests and is something you'd do even if colleges were never to learn

about it. Participation will usually not be a plus factor in an admission decision.

On-campus academic programs and camps can also be excellent experiences for students if they align with the students' interests, affording them an experience of independence and a taste of college life. But use caution! Attending a precollege on-campus program doesn't necessarily mean a student will be experiencing college-level work or earning college credit. Many of these programs simply use a campus as their site. Students are not in classes normally offered by that college and are not being taught by the school's teachers.

If you are considering such a program, here are some questions to ask to determine what you're getting:

- Is this a standard class at this college or is it being taught only for the summer?
- Is this a college-level course or a high school course?
- Will there be students in the class who are enrolled full-time at the college or just students who are attending the summer program?
- Who is teaching the class? Is it being taught by a college faculty member or by someone from outside the university?

Like leadership programs, most of these on-campus academic programs are not selective. They do not usually have an affiliation with the admission office on the campus where they are being hosted and won't give you an advantage when applying. Even when a representative from the college's admission office may make a presentation as part of the program, there is still no formal tie to or leg up in that college's admission process. The absence of any of these programs from a list of activities in an application is not at all detrimental.

While most of these programs are not considered distinctive by college admission officers, there are a handful that are highly selective and may figure in an admission decision, such as the Telluride Association Summer Program (TASP) and the Massachusetts Institute of Technology MITES program for minority students.

Finally, don't worry that you have to cram every minute of your summer full of "worthwhile" activities. College admission officers appreciate students who know how to use their downtime to take a break from academics and other activities and come back stronger than ever.

Hobbies

A student may also devote considerable time to a hobby, such as magic, gardening, cooking, scuba diving, or mountain climbing. Sometimes these pursuits are ignored by students when they consider how they spend their time. If you have developed considerable expertise or skill in a hobby, pursuing it over years, then that is an activity that tells an admission officer a lot about you. An example? A student who is an accomplished seamstress and spends hours in thrift stores buying dresses and remaking them. Her passion may not fit the conventional idea of an extracurricular activity, but it illustrates her authentic self, initiative, and creativity—qualities valued by colleges.

Jobs and Work Experience

Jobs and work experience, in particular, can illustrate how students interact with people outside their immediate circle of home and high school. Whether it's scooping ice cream, camp counseling, or assisting in a hospital lab, a job can be an important experience that teaches time management, responsibility, and people skills.

Internships have become a popular way for students to learn more about a field in which they may have an interest, such as retail, law, medicine, journalism, or technology. These experiences are often not paying jobs, but they can be valuable for a student.

Colleges do not expect every student to have job experience. They know you are busy with classes, sports, and other activities. They are certainly not looking for students to work forty hours a week. But even a part-time job that takes up four hours a week can demonstrate for an admission office who you are—and, in some cases, what you need to do. After all, many students must work to supplement their family income or to pay for their own education.

International Experience

Foreign travel can be an educational experience, whether a family vacation, an overseas class or job, or community service work. If a student has such an experience on his activity list, some colleges may find it of value. But admission officers will want to see that the experience arose from a student's authentic interest and will look for a thoughtful response in the essays or interview about what was learned.

Sometimes an activity such as an "adventure vacation" or international volunteer work can become faddish among the college-bound, and families feel obliged to provide an experience for their teenager they think will be impressive to an admission officer. There is greater focus on globalization in almost every aspect of American life now. But there is no preference in college admission for exotic experiences or international volunteer work. Such experiences are not more valued than any other activity a high school student might pursue. Again—find something that interests you sincerely, and do it with passion and commitment.

TELLING COLLEGES ABOUT YOUR EXTRACURRICULARS

The challenge for all students, whether they travel to Costa Rica to work in an orphanage or shovel snow for pocket money, is not just

Real-Life Experience

What do you do when you're not in the classroom? Answer this question in the most inclusive manner. Colleges are interested in all the ways students spend their time—even in activities that are not organized or formal in any way.

If you think you don't have anything to enter in an activity list, think again. Step back, look at yourself from the vantage point of someone who knows nothing about you, and consider from that perspective what is interesting or unusual about your life. Many students have family obligations that prevent them from participating in organized activities but which are nevertheless valuable ways to spend their time. For some students, your day-to-day life may be so unusual that what you simply do every day qualifies as an extracurricular activity.

- A student may have responsibility for helping a grandmother living at home.
- A student may attend private school and work fifteen hours a week to supplement her scholarship.
- A student may have younger siblings to take care of after school because both his parents work.
- Students whose families are first-generation American or embody two cultures can have unique experiences that tell a college a lot about them. Are the rules in your household the same as they are for your classmates? Do you have the same holidays? Eat the same foods?
- Underresourced students also have experiences that many other students do not. They may not have joined band or played soccer because they were commuting to community college three days a week in order to push themselves academically. What classes did you take and why? How were you able to afford the extra classes? Are you the first in your family to attend college?

Real-life experience is respected by admission officers and has often provided the material for a memorable application. So remember to think about *all* that you do when asked how you spend your time.

to list their activities but to find the meaning in them and then communicate that meaning in the college application, essays, and, if available, an interview. This is key. Don't assume the admission officer knows what leadership means at your school or how long it takes to learn an aria.

Remember you are painting a picture of yourself. One applicant described her competitive horseback riding experience as "pairs figure skating with a 1,200-pound partner." Another applicant wrote an essay describing how Dungeons and Dragons taught him about diplomacy, tact, and cooperation. "Do you hide in the shadows until the fight is over and then pounce on the treasure or leap into the fray with a Flaming Battle Ax of Dismemberment? Plus, all you needed to play was dice, paper, some Cheetos, and Mountain Dew." We'll discuss further how to memorably communicate in the essay and on the application form in Chapters 13 and 14.

The Truth . . . and Nothing but the Truth

Admission officers can add. They know there are only twenty-four hours in a day and seven days in a week, but sometimes a student's activity list aims to convince them otherwise. So if you only volunteer at the soup kitchen for two hours a week, don't inflate that number by claiming you're there for twelve. Do not pad your resume with made-up clubs or leadership positions. And finally, don't aggrandize what you do—one admission dean lamented that students were substituting "independent child care provider" for babysitter.

Exaggerating, embellishing, or outright lying about extracurricular activities can have serious consequences, including having an offer of admission rescinded. Most colleges verify grades and test scores but do not substantiate a student's activity list. Nevertheless, inconsistencies in the rest of the application can catch a fibber out. For example, recommendation letters may not support your claims of involvement in the senior musical or a local church group. Such discrepancies can prompt a quick call to an applicant's high school, and there may be consequences. A student's values and integrity are a fundamental consideration at every step of the admission process.

Since 2003, the University of California has had a formal program for spot-checking students' claims. Each year an investigative team randomly selects applications for review. If there are questions about claims made in a student's essays or activity lists, the university follows up with a letter requesting evidence to support the claims. In a typical year, about 1,000 students may be asked for proof of anything from working for J. C. Penney to discovering a planet. Most are able to provide it. In 2010, Stanford and Harvard also instituted random audits of prospective students' applications to ensure accuracy and honesty.

PARENTS, YOU'RE NOT CRUISE SHIP DIRECTORS

In a survey of almost nine thousand students from high-achieving schools, the majority said they participated in extracurricular activities because they enjoyed them. At the same time, 27 percent also reported they were often or always stressed by their participation.[14]

FROM THE DESK OF THE DEAN

On Extracurriculars

We asked several deans of admission for their perspective on how applicants spend their time outside of the classroom.

DANIEL J. SARACINO

Former assistant provost for enrollment, University of Notre Dame

➡ Parents, don't ask us what looks good on a resume! Don't ask us what looks good on an application! Don't ask us what students should get involved in! We should be encouraging our children to follow their own interests and passions. I get very disappointed when parents ask me, "What will help my child stand out in terms of extracurriculars?"

I encourage parents to help their children identify those things they do that they're really passionate about, and then maybe just let go of those things that their children do out of obligation, without any sense of excitement. By the end of middle school, children probably know what they really enjoy. They will realize that playing soccer doesn't engage them as much as debate or forensics, for example.

We should encourage them to follow their passions. The advantage of encouraging our children to go with what they really enjoy and not what they think will look good on an application is that they will be happier and will develop a confidence in themselves that carries over into many other aspects of life.

We, as parents, have a responsibility to help our children be the best they can be, to not have a definition of what that is, and to let our children create that definition with their involvement. And if we encourage them in that way, they're going to be fantastic! They're going to be passionate about those activities that they're involved in, that make them who they are.

KATHARINE HARRINGTON

Vice president of admissions and planning, University of Southern California

➡ My job is to bring in a well-rounded class. That does not mean that every student has done everything. I routinely advise students to be themselves. Yes, push themselves, but be themselves. We admit people who haven't done anything since third grade but go to school, come home and do their homework, and practice the oboe. We also have plenty of kids who have worked on the school newspaper, been student body president, and gone to New Orleans to help clean up after Hurricane Katrina.

We are looking for students who are authentically themselves and who are distinctive not because we can go through a checklist of things they've accomplished, but rather because of who they are. And that takes all different forms. With some students it includes a variety of different activities, and with other students it just doesn't. We have room for all of these kinds of students.

CHRISTOPHER GRUBER
Vice president and dean of admission and financial aid, Davidson College

➡ A couple years ago, one of my fraternity brothers called and mentioned that his daughter was about to enter high school. He then proceeded to ask, "What should she get involved in during her high school years so you college folks will find her attractive?" What a horrible question! I am looking for commitment over quantity, and true impact rather than resume building. I also appreciate how interests both evolve and dissolve over time, am intrigued, and want to hear the "why" behind these changes.

KATIE FRETWELL
Dean of admission and financial aid, Amherst College

➡ Some institutions have highly visible admission priorities that are consistent from year to year. Others, however, have shifting institutional ambitions across admission cycles that are not always visible to the untrained eye. This can make for some mystifying admission decisions. It is never inappropriate for a candidate to inquire about a college's current enrollment goals to best understand how a candidate's profile might be perceived—but it is never appropriate to force a student to conform to an institution's priorities. Parents should support their children's passions, which will ultimately and naturally reveal themselves in college applications in the form of follow-through, leadership, commitment—yes, and sometimes even talent! These are all sought-after attributes by college admission offices. It is also safe to say students who commit themselves to just a few nonacademic commitments quite seriously over time will have greater appeal in the evaluation process than those who juggle dozens of activities with minimal degrees of commitment.

JIM BOCK
Vice president and dean of admission, Swarthmore College

➡ Pursue what you enjoy and then find the college that fits with those interests. A lot of the anxiety in the admission process exists because students do things because they think we want them to, rather than doing what they want and then finding the school that fits with those interests.

Also many students are just trying to do it all and haven't stopped to think about why they're doing any of it. They're in the mind-set of "More is better" and "Let me show you this incredible list of activities." But we care more about why you do anything than what you do. Few students have truly given thought to why they pursue any of these activities. They're often descriptive in their presentation of the activities with very little analysis as to why any of it is important to them.

Having said that, though, we also want to know what they would do if their true interests were taken away—if they were in an accident and split their lip and couldn't play trumpet anymore, for example. How would you benefit from being on our campus? Because we very much expect students to grow and change and try new things. So we're also looking for openness, risk-taking ability, and a willingness to be exposed to things they've not tried before.

That's the catch-22 that can occur with students and their extracurricular activities. It can make it difficult for parents to know how to advise their teenagers.

Many very capable teens can handle what may seem like a prodigious number of activities. For them, the relevant question is whether there is pleasure in the pursuit or it is just clocking in and out of obligations. For students who are less motivated or less capable of handling stress, overinvolvement can result in a subtle grinding down, according to educational psychologist Michael Thompson. Sleep deprivation is often both a symptom and a part of the problem. At the far end of the spectrum, students can develop eating disorders or experience depression.

Studies have shown that the most negative effects occur primarily when students are doing things for the wrong reasons. The biggest mistake admission deans see is students who pursue activities because they think it will look good to a college—a strategy that can backfire when it comes to college admission.

Stanford University's Denise Clark Pope says parents should be "consultants, not cruise ship directors." Talk to your teenager; discover what activities she is excited about every time she does them. Reflect back to her in conversation those times when she seems most happy and engaged in an activity—this strategy helps her discover what she most enjoys. Then support her in pursuing those activities.

Pope has an acronym for what every student of every age needs every day: PDF— playtime, downtime, family time. Even if your child enjoys having a lot on his plate, be on the lookout for signs of stress and exhaustion. And help him do some advance planning by looking at the ebb and flow of the academic year: if she has a featured role in the spring musical, look at what else she's doing, such as taking the SAT or planning the prom.

Questions You May Have

What if I have spent a lot of time pursuing an interest that I can't adequately explain by simply including it in an activity list—for example, gourmet cooking or beekeeping?

The essay provides you with a great opportunity to tell the story of an interest that may be slightly out of the ordinary. If you feel you don't want to write about the activity in an essay, you can always send in an additional letter explaining the interest or even some supplemental materials. (Check with the admission office first!) For example, one applicant who was a pastry chef sent in photos of her best efforts. But don't send in a portfolio of your best plated entrees if the interest is only casual. It's okay to showcase an interest that is unconventional, but you then must clearly illustrate to the admission office that your involvement is thoughtful and has grown over time.

I'm not that involved in activities. How should I fill out the activities section of the application?

A student who truly does nothing but goes home after school and watches television is not going to be an appealing candidate to a college. But before you decide that you really don't do anything, perform an exercise by asking yourself these questions.

- What did you do last Saturday? Last Sunday?
- If you didn't have school this week, what would you do?
- If you didn't have to work, what would you do?
- If you had to list three things that you care about, what would they be?
- You get home and do your homework. Then what do you do?
- What is your favorite way to spend time?
- What chores do you have to do every day?

Remember, family obligations or jobs are experiences colleges value. Also, informal hobbies or household duties count—babysitting, tinkering with computers, repairing cars, skateboarding, reading a lot, teaching yourself guitar. These activities are of interest to colleges! Take this exercise seriously—or do it with your parents or guidance counselor—and at the end of it, you will probably have an activity list. Also, colleges don't expect you to fill out every line on an application. They understand that if a student takes advantage of the academic offerings in his school and assumes some responsibility in the home, there isn't an abundance of time left over.

What if I haven't found a sport or activity that really interests me? Is it okay to still be experimenting with activities in junior and senior year?

It's not fatal to an application, but ideally by that time you are finding things that capture your sincere interest. It can be a valuable experience to experiment and find out what you don't like. But by the last two years in high school, it's important to have found something that you do want to hold on to. Many of the most highly selective schools in particular will want you to show interest and increasing involvement in specific activities beginning in the 10th grade.

What if I quit an activity in my senior year after participating in it for a long time?

If you're going to quit an activity you've been doing, what are you going to do instead? Why are you quitting? Are you just tired of it, or do you have other things competing for your time that you want to pursue? If you have good reasons for quitting, explain them to the admission office. For example, if you gave up a chair in the orchestra in order to pursue baseball and that change ended up making you a more competitive player, that's quite a different situation from one where you just got bored with playing the cello. There is also a difference between quitting and taking a break. Often, taking a break can be valuable, allowing a student to return to an activity more committed than ever.

It's also quite different to quit one activity one time as opposed to exhibiting a pattern of quitting. Admission officers often look for patterns in students' activities, and a student who quits activities as soon as a significant commitment is required is a red flag. The bottom line is that colleges know students are finding themselves, and when they look at how you spend your time, they are looking

for who you are, not for a resume from the perfect college candidate.

How large a role should my extracurricular activities play in picking which schools I apply to?

A college is a learning environment, so your first priority should be finding a school that is a good fit academically. But the happiest students are those who participate both in the classroom and in the college community beyond it. Look for a balance that offers the kind of classes and teaching style you prefer, as well as opportunities to participate in the life of the college—whether that's volunteering or pledging a fraternity or sorority. And be creative when you think about your extracurricular possibilities. An Olympic kayaker chose a school that didn't have kayaking as a sport, but it did have an engineering program he was interested in. He brought his rowing machine and enrolled in classes where he could learn how to design and build a better kayak.

Is it ever a good idea to submit supporting materials, such as a portfolio elaborating on my extracurricular activities and academic work?

Forty-page art portfolios from students who want to go into undergraduate business programs aren't unheard of, but they are often frowned upon. While most colleges probably wouldn't hold submission of these kinds of materials against a student, at best they will probably be ignored at selective colleges. See Chapters 14 and 18 for guidelines about when submission of supplemental materials is appropriate.

CHAPTER 7

Taking the Tests

"Bubble *This* In . . .

$(x - y) = 4x - 4y$ is a good example of:

a. Things I used to know

b. What am I, Stephen Hawking?

c. I was never very good at geometry

d. I missed that lesson because my piercing totally got infected"[15]

—George Waters

Students will invest a lot of time, money, and mental energy on the battery of standardized tests that begin as early as sophomore year. So it's important to start out with a sense of humor—or at least perspective—on the subject.

All kidding aside, here's the truth: testing counts far less than most students and parents think it does, but more than most colleges are willing to admit. Testing provides one piece of information among many, all of which are used to help an admission office understand the whole student. It's an important piece of information, but in most cases a test score alone will neither get a student in nor keep a student out.

Every year, standardized tests—the PSAT, ACT Aspire, ACT, SAT, and SAT Subject Tests—are administered to millions of students. For most colleges they remain an important factor in admission decisions. They're also the catalyst for a lot of headlines and classroom conversations, which give rise to a lot of questions. What do the tests really measure? How do colleges use them? Will a good score guarantee admission? Will a bad score obliterate your chances? Can coaching produce a higher score? How many times should you test?

The results of standardized tests are most often part of a complex weighing by colleges of grades, classes, extracurricular activities,

Checkpoints ✎

✔ Testing matters less than students and parents think, but more than most colleges are willing to admit.

✔ Students need a plan for the series of tests they will take beginning in sophomore year.

✔ Students should become familiar with the testing format of the ACT or SAT with practice tests—including the PSAT and ACT Aspire if available through your school.

✔ Expect to take the SAT or ACT twice unless you are satisfied with your scores on the first try.

✔ Colleges are always examining the criteria used to make admission decisions. As a result, there are now some schools with alternative requirements. But they may still require some testing.

✔ To do well, become familiar with the test, get a good night's sleep, and eat a healthy breakfast before heading to the test center. And read, read, read!

recommendations, and a student's essays. But not always. There are some universities and colleges where tests are optional, and some that don't use test results at all. Testing is in a period of evolution—what should be tested, how long the test should be, which colleges will require testing and which will not—all is shifting. (For more information, see the sidebar on changes to come on page 91.) So there are alternatives for students today. There is a college out there for everyone.

Nevertheless, for now, beginning in sophomore year, you will have to pick up your No. 2 pencils—or more likely these days put hands to keyboard—and guess. Just kidding—we mean *test*. We'll walk you through the tests most students choose from and talk about timing, preparation, scoring, and strategy. And we'll also discuss test-optional schools and what a college's testing policy tells prospective students.

It may seem that the length of this chapter belies the fact that testing is not as important as parents and students believe it to be. But please don't be misled by this chapter's reach. Testing really is less important than you probably think it is. But it has a lot of moving parts. We believe that when students and parents are armed with the relevant information about a step in the admission process such as testing, it allows them to feel more confident and reassured. So we hope this extended discussion has the intended effect—and students and parents recognize that testing is simply another step in the admission process, and not even the most important one.

PSAT/NMSQT AND ACT ASPIRE

The two standardized tests you are probably most familiar with are the ACT and the SAT, and these are the ones used by most colleges in admission decisions. One of the most effective—and easiest—strategies for doing well on the ACT and SAT is to be familiar with the tests.

For the SAT, there is a preliminary version that you can take as practice—the PSAT/NMSQT (Preliminary Scholastic Aptitude Test/National Merit Scholarship Qualifying Test). Slightly shorter and slightly easier than the SAT, it tests the same content in the same format. The PSAT/NMSQT will be revised in 2015 in preparation for a revamped SAT in 2016. Please see the sidebar on page 91 for information on those changes.

In 2014, ACT discontinued its PLAN test, which was a preliminary version of the ACT. The ACT Aspire, which replaced the PLAN, essentially tests the same content as the ACT. However, schools have the option of testing only one of the five subject areas. If your school does not offer the ACT Aspire in its entirety, the best preparation is to take a practice test, which we address later in this chapter.

Your performance on the PSAT/NMSQT and ACT Aspire (if offered in its entirety by your school district) can provide important feedback about where you need improvement. Since all colleges accept both the ACT and SAT, if students have the opportunity to take both preliminary tests—the PSAT/NMSQT and ACT Aspire (in its entirety)—the results may give them an idea of which one they are better suited for in the long run. The PSAT/NMSQT also includes a component that assesses a student's academic and career interests and a component that enables colleges to send students information, called the Student Search Service.

Also, when the PSAT/NMSQT is administered in the junior year, a student's score acts as a qualifier for the National Merit Scholarship Program, a large, prestigious recognition and academic scholarship program. Hence the acronym PSAT/NMSQT. From now on, we'll just call it "the PSAT."

Colleges do not see PSAT or ACT Aspire scores, and they are not used for admission. Both tests are meant to be risk-free tools to help students learn their testing strengths and weaknesses. But students can opt to share some of their results with colleges, scholarship organizations, and others, in order to receive material from those institutions. Under this scenario, colleges never see an individual student score, but they may see the range of scores into which the student falls.

Test fees for the PSAT are considerably less than those for the SAT, so it's relatively inexpensive to take advantage of this practice test. Usually students pay the fee in advance, but some high schools, school districts, and states don't pass the cost on to the student. For low-income students, fee waivers are

Testing, Testing . . .

Both ACT, Inc., and the College Board offer extensive information about their tests and provide free practice materials on their websites: actstudent.org and sat.collegeboard.org.

THE PSAT

Subject	Number of Questions	How Long It Takes
Critical Reading	48	50 minutes: two 25-minute sections
Math	38	50 minutes: two 25-minute sections
Writing Skills	39	30 minutes: one section

available for the PSAT when the test is taken junior year. Students apply for fee waivers through their school, not through the testing services. The ACT Aspire is paid for by the school district or state.

Here are more specifics for each test:

The PSAT/NMSQT

The PSAT is offered every October by the College Board. Most students take it in the fall of junior year. But some schools offer students a "practice" PSAT—that's right, it's a practice before a practice—in the fall of sophomore year. The PSAT currently includes multiple-choice and fill-in response (or, as the College Board calls them, "grid-in") questions in five sections: two in critical reading, two in math, and one in writing skills.

The test lasts 2 hours and 10 minutes. The format and content of the PSAT are the same as the SAT. It measures reasoning skills as opposed to specific classroom knowledge. However, the PSAT writing section is multiple-choice only and does not require an essay, as the SAT does.

Students register for the PSAT through their high school, not through the College Board.

Scoring is reported on a scale of 20 to 80. Juniors taking the test can simply tack a zero onto their score to estimate how they may perform on the SAT, where the range is from 200 to 800. But keep in mind that because you have gained greater familiarity with the test and have another year of study under your belt, most of you will score higher on the SAT after taking the PSAT.

National Merit Scholarships

While PSAT scores are not used as a criterion for college admission, they are used to qualify students for the National Merit Scholarship competition, the best-known scholarship program in the country. The PSAT is also used to identify students for the National Achievement Scholarship Program, which is open to African American students, as well as the National Hispanic Recognition Program, the Telluride Association, and some other programs.

Only scores from the PSAT taken in the junior year can be used to qualify a student as a National Merit Scholar. No matter how high a student scores as a sophomore, only scores from the junior-year PSAT will be considered.

Students are informed if they have qualified for National Merit Scholar recognition in April following the fall administration of the PSAT. The approximately fifty thousand highest-scoring students are then offered the opportunity to name two colleges or universities to be notified of the honor. For schools that look for you to actively demonstrate interest as part of their admission decision, this notification can be important—it tells them you have identified them as one of your first choices. (You will see more about demonstrated interest in Chapters 8 and 9.)

Status in the National Merit Scholar competition is initially based on the "selection index," a total of a student's critical reading, math, and writing skills scores, which are reported on a scale ranging from 60 to 240. For example, a critical reading score of 76, a math score of 69, and a writing skills score of 73 would sum up to a selection index of 218. There are four levels of recognition: Commended Student, Semifinalist, Finalist, and Merit Scholar Designee.

- **Commended Student.** About 34,000 of the highest-scoring students receive letters of commendation but do not continue in the competition for National Merit Scholarships.
- **Semifinalist.** Approximately 16,000 students qualify as Semifinalists. Qualifying scores vary from state to state and year to year. To move on in the competition and be considered for a scholarship, they must submit an essay, their school's recommendation, and their SAT scores and academic transcript.

- **Finalist.** In February of the senior year, approximately 15,000 Semifinalists advance to Finalist by meeting high academic standards and other requirements.
- **Merit Scholar Designee.** Most but not all Finalists become Merit Scholar Designees and may receive a Merit Scholarship award or a corporate- or college-sponsored award.

Many of the most highly selective colleges and universities do not participate in the National Merit program because their financial aid is limited exclusively to need-based awards or because National Merit Scholar status, though meaningful and prestigious, may be the norm in their applicant pool rather than a distinction. Some colleges have chosen not to participate because they object to a competition that bases awards on the results of a single test. Additional information on this process can be found at nationalmerit.org.

ACT ASPIRE

ACT Aspire is a comprehensive assessment system students may begin testing with as early as third grade. In high school, the test may be offered in a student's freshman or sophomore year, anytime between late August and late May. The test is computer-based,

THE ACT ASPIRE

Subject	Number of Questions	How Long It Takes
English	48–52	30 minutes
Math	27–35	40 minutes
Reading	18–20	20 minutes
Science	23–28	25 minutes
Writing	1	30 minutes

though there is a paper-and-pencil option—the testing format will likely be determined by your high school. It includes five sections: English, writing, math, reading, and science. Questions include multiple choice, essay or short answer, and technology-enhanced options.

Total testing time when all five sections are administered is 4 hours and 10 minutes. Like the ACT, ACT Aspire tests academic skills and knowledge.

ACT Aspire is administered at the discretion of the high school or school district, so students should check with their guidance counselor to see if it will be offered. The Early High School portion of the ACT Aspire provides a "predicted" ACT score.

THE BIG TWO: THE SAT AND THE ACT

The SAT (which used to be called the Scholastic Aptitude Test) and the ACT (formerly the American College Testing Assessment) are the most important standardized tests in the admission process. We'll refer to them here as "the SAT" and "the ACT."

A student's results on these tests are an important factor in the admission decision at many colleges. Today, almost every four-year college and university in the country that requires standardized test scores in admission accepts the ACT or the SAT.

But that doesn't mean students have to take both tests. We'll give you a snapshot of each before we move on to a discussion of which test to take, how many times to test, and how best to prepare.

In the meantime, when you think about ACT or SAT test dates and No. 2 pencils, don't freak out. These are hard tests, but they are grounded in what you have been studying since you started high school, so most of the questions are similar to those you've already encountered in the classroom.

The SAT

The first SAT was administered in 1926 and based on questions that had been developed by the U.S. Army for selecting and assigning World War I military recruits, thus the idea of testing aptitude—originally the "A" in "SAT." Though the test has evolved, it essentially still tests the ability to reason, problem-solve, and think critically. The way the College Board explains it is that it is grounded in student learning, covering subjects that are part of the high school curriculum—testing both what you know and how well you apply that knowledge. (Please see the sidebar on page 91 regarding changes to the content of the SAT as of 2016.)

The SAT is administered seven times a year: October, November, December, January, March, May, and June. (It is offered six times

Filed Under: The Now-Extinct College Major in Household Management

This math question appeared on an SAT test from the 1950s:

A woman allows 15 minutes per dress in her ironing schedule. At what time in the afternoon must she start ironing if she has 10 dresses to iron and wants to finish ironing at 4 p.m.?

a year at international sites.) Specific test dates, as well as test center locations, which are usually high schools, can be found online at collegeboard.org or in the SAT Registration Bulletin, available from high school guidance counselors.

The basic fee for the test includes four score reports for colleges. (Up-to-date fee information can be found at sat.collegeboard.org.) Unlike the PSAT, the student is responsible for submitting payment for the SAT—but fee waivers are available. Students should apply for fee waivers through their high school. (Beginning In 2016, the College Board will provide fee waivers directly to financially eligible students who will no longer have to go through high school counselors.) Also, unlike the PSAT, students register for the SAT directly with the College Board, either by signing up online at sat.collegeboard.org or by returning the form in the registration booklet available from a high school counselor.

The SAT lasts 3 hours and 45 minutes and tests three areas:

- **Critical reading**—how well a student comprehends and analyzes text passages
- **Math**—skills in arithmetic, Algebra I and II, geometry, and statistical probability
- **Writing**—grammar and vocabulary skills, as well as the ability to develop and support a point of view on an issue, and including an essay.

The SAT scores each of the three areas (excluding the experimental section) from 200 to 800, with a maximum total score of 2400. The essay is scored from 2 to 12 and scaled into the overall writing score that includes the multiple-choice sections. It accounts for about one-third of the overall writing score of 200 to 800. But because testing is in a period of evolution, there will be less and less emphasis on the essay. While officially a 2400 scale will be in place until 2016, it is common to hear scores discussed with a 1600 scale. (To understand scoring scale changes, please see the sidebar on page 91.)

Most students take the SAT for the first time in March or May of junior year. Some take the SAT for the first time in January of the junior year—that way they can retest in the spring of junior year if they are dissatisfied with their scores. It can be helpful to take the test for the first time on one of the four dates when the College Board's Question-and-Answer Service is available for a fee. This service provides students with the test booklet and a report that includes a breakdown of their answers, the correct responses, and a guide to where they need improvement. (Students using fee waivers receive this service free.) More information on test dates when this service is available can be found at sat.collegeboard.org.

Word to the wise: test centers fill up quickly—especially on these dates—so register early. It's no fun to get up an hour early and head off to a testing center fifteen miles away because the one two blocks from your house is full.

The ACT

The ACT was first used as a college admission exam in 1959. Developed by a statistician who partnered with a former

The Essay

In 2005, both the SAT and ACT added a written essay as part of their tests. The essays on both tests ask students to address a prompt—a question or statement designed to incite students to respond to a topic. Students are asked to use examples and supporting arguments from their own experience or studies to develop a point of view in response.

The written essay is scored by two individuals, often high school or college teachers, who have been trained and tested by the College Board or ACT, Inc. The essays are evaluated on the basis of organization, clarity, development of ideas, and basics such as grammar and use of descriptive language.

On the SAT, you have 25 minutes to complete the essay, which is a required element of the writing section. (As of 2016, the essay is optional on the SAT; please see the sidebar on page 91.) This part of the test also includes two multiple-choice sections that cover skills such as sentence structure and language usage.

On the ACT, the writing test is optional and consists only of the written essay. Students are given 30 minutes to complete it. Students must sign up for the ACT writing test when they register for the ACT and pay an additional fee. Many colleges require the ACT essay if a student is submitting only test scores from the ACT. Check the policies of the colleges to which you are applying.

Also, students, take note: colleges may use the SAT or ACT essay as a point of comparison for students' application essays to confirm that the student, not a parent or outside counselor, is the author.

For more information about the essay section, including an explanation of how it is scored, practice prompts, and test tips, go to sat.collegeboard.org and actstudent.org.

University of Iowa dean of admission to found the American College Testing Program, the ACT Assessment was based on a student's achievement—what he had learned in the classroom.

The ACT and SAT test many of the same skills, such as reading and writing. But the questions on the ACT are closely tied to classroom content and based on the material taught in grades 7 through 12.

The ACT is administered six times a year, in September, October, December, February, April, and June. Beginning in 2015, students have the option of taking a computerized version of the ACT. Specific test dates and center locations can be found online at actstudent .org or in the ACT Registration Packet, which can be ordered online or obtained from your high school guidance counselor. (Check the ACT website for test dates and registration information for international centers.) Students can register online or with the form in the Registration Packet. The basic fee includes reports for four colleges designated at the time of registration. An additional fee is charged for the optional writing test. Up-to-date fee information can be found at the ACT website at actstudent.org. Fee waivers are available—check with your high school for eligibility requirements and how to apply.

The ACT test lasts 2 hours and 55 minutes plus scheduled breaks; add another 30 minutes if you have opted to take the writing test that is the essay. So the total test time is just over 3 hours and 25 minutes. The test consists of four sections, plus the optional essay, covering:

- **English**—grammar and sentence structure, as well as rhetorical skills such as organization and style
- **Math**—arithmetic, algebra, geometry, and trigonometry
- **Reading**—comprehension and analysis
- **Science**—inductive reasoning in the natural sciences, including biology, earth science, chemistry, and physics
- **Writing test**—an optional essay test of composition skills

The ACT scores each section from 1 to 36, with a maximum composite score of 36. The optional essay is reported separately, scored from 2 to 12, and the student receives a combined English/writing score where the essay accounts for approximately one-third.

Students often take the ACT for the first time in the spring of junior year. On test dates in December, April, and June, the ACT offers Test Information Release (TIR): for a fee, students receive a copy of their test with their score and an answer key. If you take the writing test, you will receive a copy of the essay and scores assigned by the readers. This information can be helpful in determining where you might need improvement if you are dissatisfied with your scores and plan to retest. More information on test dates and TIR can be found at actstudent.org.

Colleges' Test Requirements

Testing requirements vary from college to college, so students must check the requirements for each school where they are planning to apply.

At colleges that require standardized testing for admission, test requirements are usually fulfilled by one of the following:

- ACT (many schools require the writing section; check the colleges' requirements)
- SAT
- SAT and two SAT Subject Tests (see page 94 for information on Subject Tests)

Which Test Should You Take?

There is no need for students to take both the SAT and the ACT. Virtually all four-year colleges and universities that require standardized tests for admission accept either test.

So which test should you take? There is

Ch-ch-ch-ch-Changes . . .

Standardized testing for college admission is in a period of evolution. In 2014, the ACT's PLAN was discontinued and replaced with ACT ASPIRE, explained in full earlier in this chapter. In 2015, the ACT will be administered by computer, though also available to be taken with pencil and paper for some time. Also in 2015, the College Board introduces an updated version of the PSAT/NMSQT. And in 2016, a redesigned SAT will be administered.

The principal changes to the redesigned SAT are as follows:

- The essay will be optional and scored separately. Students will be asked to read a passage and analyze how its author used evidence, reasoning, and stylistic elements to build an argument. The essay will be scored on the strength of that analysis, as well as writing ability.
- There will still be three sections: "evidence-based" reading and writing, mathematics, and the essay. "Evidence based" simply means students will be asked to back up answers with specific passages from the readings and to analyze both text and data.
- Math questions will focus on data analysis, problem solving, algebra, and topics leading into advanced math with emphasis on linear equations; complex equations or functions; and ratios, percentage, and proportional reasoning. Calculators will be barred on some parts of the test to help gauge proficiency.
- Overall scoring will return to the iconic 1600 scale, based on a top score of 800 in both reading and math. Scores for the essay will be reported separately.
- "SAT words" are out. Vocabulary words more widely used in classroom and work settings will replace more obscure words. That means you won't see "depreciatory" on the test but you may see "synthesis."
- The test will be available on computer and paper.
- The "guessing penalty" will be eliminated. Students will no longer have a quarter point deducted for each incorrect answer.
- The exam will be three hours, with the optional essay requiring 50 additional minutes. The earlier version was three hours and 45 minutes, including the required essay.

a lot of subjective information—and downright misinformation—about that. Several examples: *Fast readers do better on the ACT and strong readers do better on the SAT. The SAT favors good test-takers and the ACT favors academic overachievers. The ACT is easier and the SAT is trickier.* Don't pay too much attention to such characterizations—they can be misleading. Most students perform equally well on the two tests.

 Best Advice

Familiarize yourself with both the ACT and SAT and take the one with which you feel most comfortable. You can try your hand at the SAT by taking the PSAT and at the ACT by taking a practice test. Practice tests are available for both the ACT and SAT in the registration booklets or online at their websites.

Again, there is no hard evidence that students consistently score higher on one test or the other.

Concordance tables that estimate how students of comparable ability would score on the ACT and SAT can be seen in Appendix V.

PREPARATION

There is no easy path to a high score on the SAT or ACT. The best preparation is to take rigorous courses in high school, work hard, and read, read, read. But there are two steps you can and should take to prepare.

Get Up Close and Familiar with the Test

For many students, familiarity with the test can improve scores. In fact, no student should ever go into a test cold. Spend time familiarizing yourself with the following:

- **Instructions.** Get familiar with directions on the test so you're not wasting time the day of the test figuring out how the SAT math section "grid-ins" work or what the "No Change" response means on the ACT English section. You'll find the directions on the SAT and ACT websites.
- **Content.** Refresh your knowledge and skills on any subjects where it's been a while since you've studied them in school—for example, in algebra or geometry.
- **Strategy.** Test-taking skills matter. Understanding how to approach the tests

strategically can help you do well. For example, because there is no penalty for wrong answers on the ACT, there is an advantage in completely finishing each section. So go ahead and guess—the right guesses will help, but the wrong guesses won't hurt. For students taking the SAT prior to 2016, there is a penalty for wrong answers on the SAT, so don't guess randomly. Narrow your alternatives and guess strategically—the rule of thumb is to guess only if you can eliminate two of the five choices on a question.

- **What to expect on test day.** Alleviate test day anxiety by scoping out where you'll be going so you're not late. Also, know what you need to bring as well as what isn't allowed at the test center. There are specific guidelines for calculators (no QWERTY keyboards), snacks (yes, you'll need them during breaks), cell phones (forget about it), and other paraphernalia you may consider essential to your survival (like an iPod—which is not allowed). Don't forget identification! Most students use their driver's license, but if you test before you've earned your license, you will have to bring another form of photo identification that bears the exact same name as your admission ticket, such as a school ID or passport. (Familiarize yourself with the identification requirements at sat .collegeboard.org and actstudent.org.)

Practice, Practice, Practice!

Practice, like familiarity with the tests, will increase scores up to a point. But it's like sports—you can run and run and run, but if you're doing the same thing wrong every day, you're not going to improve. So when it comes to practicing for the SAT and ACT, if you're listening to your iPod and not timing the sections, then you're probably not going to improve your score. Here's how to practice so it means something:

- **Take the PSAT or ACT Aspire if offered by your school.** These are practice tests meant to prepare you. For the PSAT, your answers and the correct answers are available with the score report—great feedback that shows where you need to improve.
- **Make sure you practice with real tests.** There are a lot of test books out there, but the ones you practice with should contain actual test material from the ACT or SAT. The test services call these materials "disclosed" tests—in other words, they are actual ACT or SAT tests from prior dates. Practice tests are available at no charge directly from the College Board and ACT, Inc., on their websites. You can also find guides in the library or bookstore, but make sure they contain disclosed tests. In addition, both the ACT and SAT offer a "question of the day"— the ACT's is available on its website (act.org), and you can sign up for the SAT's on Twitter.
- **Practice under actual test conditions.** Both tests require you to perform in a fixed amount of time. Sit down in your kitchen with a test book and have a family member time you. Or better yet, have a testing party. See the box on this page.
- **Use feedback.** Take advantage of the SAT's Question-and-Answer Service and the ACT's Test Information Release (TIR) service to understand where you need further preparation.

- **Timing matters.** Preparation, particularly for test-taking skills, is more effective close to the test date. On the other hand, we do not advise you to save it all for the last minute. The best approach is to begin preparing in the summer between sophomore and junior year. Then refresh your knowledge and test-taking skills as test dates draw near.
- **Work diligently.** Enough said.

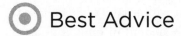 ## Best Advice

KRIS ZAVOLI
Former senior director, The College Board

➡ Challenge yourself. And read—it's a very strong and important skill that you need for success in college.

You're Invited to Test . . .

Alice Kleeman, the college advisor at Silicon Valley's Menlo-Atherton High School, suggests students throw testing parties. Get a group together on a Saturday and take a timed SAT or ACT together. (Quality control tip: let the parents do the timing.) Then provide some further motivation by planning to do something fun together afterward—go out to lunch, attend a concert, go bowling, shop till you drop.

Let's face it, there is no really fun way to prepare for these tests, but a test party is better than studying on your own. An added bonus: it simulates real conditions—you're surrounded by other sighing, fidgeting teenagers, just as you will be at a test center.

JONATHAN PERLMAN
Testing coach

➡ Prep with real past tests and take the test for the first time when you can get your test booklet back along with the answers.

JON ERICKSON
President, Education and Career Solutions, ACT, Inc.

➡ Become familiar with what it's like to have to perform in a fixed amount of time. And disregard the age-old myth I've heard from several sources that "When in doubt, check C." I'll tell you for a fact, that doesn't work.

NATALIE BITTON
College counselor, Lycée Français La Pérouse, San Francisco

➡ Have a plan and never go into a test cold; always know the basics.

BRAD MACGOWAN
Director of college and career counseling, Newton North High School, Newton, Massachusetts

➡ There are options out there—what tests to take, when to take them, how many times, how to prep. Look at the options and make a plan. There are ways to avoid overtesting and overprepping while still being able to send good scores to colleges. Also, many colleges are test-optional for all or some applicants, and many colleges offer other options for their requirements. Check out the fairtest.org website.

CHARLENE AGUILAR
College counseling, University Preparatory Academy, Seattle, Washington

➡ Be wary of spending significant amounts of time studying for standardized tests to the neglect of academic course work. The single most important element in any college application is your transcript. So balance is your goal.

SAT SUBJECT TESTS

SAT Subject Tests are standardized tests administered by the College Board that measure a student's knowledge in particular subject areas. Twenty Subject Tests are offered in the areas of English, history, math, science, and language. You can see a complete list at the College Board website, sat.collegeboard.org.

While most colleges do not require Subject Tests, most selective schools require or recommend them in the admission process. The general rule is that the importance of Subject Tests increases with the selectivity of the school. Our advice is to take the Subject Tests if they are recommended by a school to which you're applying, even if they are not required.

Most colleges that consider Subject Tests ask for scores from two of them. However, since the College Board allows you to take three Subject Tests on the same test date, consider testing in three subjects. That way colleges can choose to use your best two scores. Colleges also may have preferences or requirements about exactly which tests are submitted. For example, engineering schools may want physics and/or Math II. Other schools will want a student to show scores from two

Do I Need a Coach or a Class to Prepare?

The billion-dollar business of test preparation would like you to think that everybody is taking a class or hiring a coach in order to prepare. But that's just not true. The vast majority of students test with no formal organized preparation—they download some practice tests and take some timed sessions on their own.

The sole major study on the effectiveness of commercial test prep found that prep courses resulted in only modest benefits—an average score gain of 30 points on the SAT and less than 1 point on the ACT.[16] That's less of a gain than many students experience simply by retaking the test.

If you have the means to pay for prep and either a class or coach will make you more comfortable about the test or more disciplined in your preparation, then go ahead. But don't overdo it! Test prep is expensive and time-consuming. Courses from for-profit prep companies can cost thousands of dollars, and a private test tutor may charge $100 an hour or more. Students also need to consider the amount of time classes or coaching sessions require. It's a mistake to let prep cut into your academic work. Don't spend too much time studying for these tests. We've said it before and we'll say it here again: the most important part of the college application is your transcript—grades and course work.

While no one absolutely needs test prep, there are some students who may benefit from it:

- Underresourced students with preparation gaps in the subjects covered by the test. (Check with your high school to see if discounted test prep classes can be arranged.)
- Students with learning differences.
- Students who experience test anxiety that affects performance.
- Students who aren't motivated to prepare on their own.

Manuals, guides, online resources, software programs, commercial courses, school-based coaching, and private tutoring—test prep comes in many shapes and sizes. But whatever the form, buyer beware! The source, quality, and content of practice materials are important. Test prep company pitches can be misleading—"guaranteeing" score increases of 100 points or more. So read the fine print. Ultimately, no class or coach can produce a great result—you have to practice.

SAT Subject Tests are not considered "coachable"—so we don't recommend investing in prep services for them. Because they are based on high school curricula, the best preparation is completing the highest-level course in the relevant subject. However, refreshing by reviewing the material in the subject can be helpful, particularly if you completed the class months earlier. The College Board offers practice Subject Tests online at sat.collegeboard.org.

different areas of study—for example, in history and science.

Subject Tests are each one hour in length and consist entirely of multiple-choice questions. They are scored, like the SAT, from 200 to 800. Colleges will see all of your scores unless you opt not to send the score reports by using Score Choice (see page 99). You can also cancel scores—see the College Board website at sat.collegeboard.org for details.

Students can take Subject Tests at any time during high school. But there is optimal timing: test as close as possible to when you complete the relevant class so that the subject matter is fresh in your mind. For example, if you complete the highest level of Japanese in your sophomore year, take the Subject Test in Japanese at the end of sophomore year. Or if you're in AP Chemistry, take the subject test in May or June while you're prepping for the AP test. (See our discussion of AP classes in Chapter 5.)

Subject Tests are offered six times a year, usually on the same dates as the SAT. Students can take up to three Subject Tests on a single date but cannot take the SAT and Subject Tests on the same date. Scores must be submitted to most of the selective colleges no later than December of your senior year—earlier if you are applying under an early decision program (see Chapter 15). Plan accordingly. (See our sample test plan on page 97.)

When you register for Subject Tests, you will indicate which subjects you plan to test in, but you can change and select any subject on the day of the test except in the case of the foreign language with listening exams. There is a basic fee for each sitting, plus fees for each exam (up to three exams) and additional fees for foreign languages with listening. Up-to-date fee information can be found at sat.collegeboard.org. Also, check the schedule online for additional charges for phone registration and other circumstances. (Fee waivers for Subject Tests are available for those who qualify.)

PLANNING

Students usually take the SAT or ACT for the first time in the winter or spring of junior year in order to capitalize on having just completed Algebra II, as well as further course work in English. Most students will want to take either test once by the end of junior year so they can retest if they are not satisfied with their scores. There is no single timetable for testing that suits all students, but all students need a good plan.

The Last Word on Preparation

Follow the advice your parents have been giving you since your first standardized test in elementary school:

• Get a good night's sleep.

• Eat a good breakfast.

What's a Good Breakfast?

Your morning meal should have three components: protein, a complex carbohydrate, and fat. Some good choices? Bacon, eggs, and whole-grain toast; peanut butter and jelly or tuna on whole-grain bread; even beef barley soup. No doughnuts, Pop-Tarts, or coffee—you might crash from a sugar or caffeine high in the middle of reading comprehension.

Have a Plan

With multiple standardized tests and multiple testing dates, it's important to map out a testing plan. Here are two examples to use as templates, depending on your course work and college plans.

Are you enrolled in multiple advanced courses? Here's a sample plan.

10th Grade	SAT	ACT
September to May		ACT Aspire*
October	"Practice" PSAT/NMSQT[†]	
May	AP exams (if enrolled)[‡]	AP exams (if enrolled)[‡]
June	SAT Subject Test in modern or classical language[§]	
11th Grade	**SAT**	**ACT**
October	PSAT/NMSQT	
January	SAT	
February		ACT
May	AP exams[‡]	AP exams[‡]
June	SAT Subject Tests (2 or 3)	
12th Grade	**SAT**	**ACT**
October	SAT	ACT
May	AP exams	AP exams

Not enrolled in as many advanced classes? Here's a sample plan.

10th Grade	SAT	ACT
September to May		ACT Aspire*
October	"Practice" PSAT[†]	
11th Grade	**SAT**	**ACT**
October	PSAT/NMSQT	
May	SAT, AP exams (if enrolled)	AP exams (if enrolled)
June	SAT Subject Tests (2 or 3)	
12th Grade	**SAT**	**ACT**
September	SAT	ACT
October	SAT	
May	AP exams (if enrolled)	AP exams (if enrolled)

* ACT Aspire is given at the discretion of the high school anytime between August and May.

[†] Some of you may have the option to take a "practice" PSAT in 10th grade. (See page 84.)

[‡] We advise students taking more than two Advanced Placement tests *not* to take the SAT in May. Students *cannot* take SAT Subject Tests and the SAT on the same day. (Advanced Placement courses are discussed in Chapter 5. Subject Tests are discussed on page 84.)

[§] The Subject Test in language should be taken only if the third year of study has been completed.

Please note that while we have included opportunities to test twice on the ACT or SAT, there is no need to retest if you are satisfied with your scores. Also note that while we have used the example of AP tests in these charts, you will have to take into account the advanced courses offered by your school—such as the International Baccalaureate exams—when determining the testing plan that works best for you. (See Chapter 5.)

And one more thing—we can't say this enough—read a lot!

Underresourced Students and Standardized Testing

Underresourced students may benefit by preparing more intensively for standardized tests. Such students include those who are the first in their family to attend college, those from households where English is a second language, or those with preparation gaps because their high schools lack academic rigor. Completing a few practice tests alone may be insufficient preparation for these students. Here are some steps they should take:

- Take the PSAT and ACT Aspire if offered by your school district. Fee waivers are available for the PSAT. Check with your high school.
- Spend time exploring the SAT and ACT websites to take advantage of free test prep. Both sites also offer customized preparation in specific areas such as algebra or geometry. The College Board and ACT websites offer some of the same tips, hints, and info that students would receive in an expensive tutorial.
- Check area high schools to see if they offer or have access to low-cost or no-cost test prep classes.
- Explore taking classes at a local community college.
- Talk to your high school guidance counselor about organizations that offer reduced-fee or free test preparation and tutoring. Most test prep companies and private tutors offer some pro bono services. See Appendix IV

for organizations that provide resources for underresourced students.
- Read, read, read, read, read.

How Many Times Should You Test?

Our best advice is to expect to take the SAT or ACT twice.

You certainly do not need to take *both* tests multiple times. Decide which test best suits you by taking the PSAT or ACT Aspire (if offered by your school) or by doing some practice tests. Then plan to take either the ACT or SAT during the winter or spring of your junior year. If you are satisfied with your score, you're done. If you feel there is room for improvement, you will have time to test again in the fall of senior year.

If you feel there is further room for improvement or there were extenuating circumstances such as illness on your test day, you could consider testing for a third time. But taking either test more than three times is stretching it—a lot! The likelihood of improvement is small at that point. And it's bad strategy to neglect your studies in pursuit of the perfect score.

Beware of becoming a professional test-taker. Don't box yourself into doing so much testing that you neglect your course work or extracurricular activities. And don't be in such a rush preparing for the next step—college—that you forget to do things that make you happy right now.

Special Accommodations

Both the SAT and ACT provide special accommodations for students with disabilities or learning differences, in accordance with the Americans with Disabilities Act. Such accommodations may include wheelchair-accessible rooms at test sites, large-type test booklets, permission for diabetics to eat snacks, a sign language interpreter, Braille versions of tests, and extended time for testing. The requirements of the SAT and ACT for special accommodations differ. Check each website as early as possible.

Accommodations for students with disabilities or learning differences must be applied for and approved in advance of test dates. Eligibility is determined by the testing services and requires sometimes extensive documentation; for example, simply having an Individualized Education Program (IEP) will not automatically qualify a student for special accommodations. The majority of requests for special accommodations in recent years have come from students with learning differences—a sometimes difficult-to-define category—who are requesting extended time. Parents should work with high school counselors and diagnosticians to carefully document learning disabilities as early as possible in a student's academic career.

Scores

Scores for both the ACT and SAT are usually available online to students, high schools, and colleges within two to three weeks after the test date. (Once both tests offer computerized versions, results may be available even sooner.)

There is a lot of valuable information in your score report, and it is a good idea to sit down with your guidance counselor or high school college counselor to understand your results. For example, in books such as the *Fiske Guide, Peterson's,* or the College Board's *Handbook,* colleges typically report the middle 50 percent range of scores from their enrolling students, so your scores may provide an initial idea of where you fit into a college's statistical profile. We'll discuss this further in Chapters 8 and 10. Also, in Appendix V, you can see concordance tables that show approximately how ACT scores translate into equivalent SAT scores.

Whether you have taken the ACT, the SAT, or both, you need to understand the score reporting policies for each testing service and for each college to which you are applying.

The ACT provides reports for the student, the high school, and each college or scholarship agency the student lists when registering. The ACT automatically sends tests results to the student's high school, but the student must specifically select and list each college or scholarship agency he wishes to receive scores.

For the SAT, students can select Score Choice, which allows them to determine which scores a college receives by designating SAT scores by test date and SAT Subject Test scores by individual test. Under Score Choice, for example, a student would not have to report a low score from a particular test date, or the fact that he tested multiple times. Full reports are still sent to the student and the high school. Students can select the option of Score Choice when registering for the SAT or after scores are received. If students don't select the Score Choice option, all scores from all test dates are sent to colleges.

Note that every college has its own score reporting policy. Some schools require students to submit their entire testing record—all scores from all test dates, regardless of Score Choice. Other schools "superscore," using the highest scores on every subsection from various test dates—in other words, a school would evaluate a student's application using the best score in math from one test date and the best score from critical reading from another test date. Superscoring is possible only if you submit all scores. It is your responsibility to understand the requirements of every school where you are applying and to comply with them.

Our best advice? Provide your entire testing record to the schools where you are applying and then let the colleges do their work in evaluating it. If one score is lower than another, it is not going to be held against you in the admission process. Most colleges prefer to review your testing profile as a whole. Test a reasonable number of times and then share all your scores.

No school has a definition of a "good score"—they know that no test score is a precise measure of a student's ability. Scores can be helpful to admission officers, but they don't tell a college about day-to-day performance, intellectual curiosity, or what one admission officer calls "the fire in the belly" that a student will bring to his or her academic work. Test scores are simply one component of an admission review that also takes into account a student's grades, courses, recommendations, essays, and special talents and abilities.

HOW COLLEGES VIEW STANDARDIZED TESTING

Like many steps in the admission process, when it comes to testing, there is no single simple formula employed by colleges that students and families can look to for guidance. For those colleges that consider standardized testing in their admission decisions, a student's scores are an additional piece of information, along with grades, courses, essays, recommendations, and interviews when available.

Yvonne M. Romero Da Silva, University of Pennsylvania's vice dean and director of admissions, notes:

➡ **Testing is certainly one of the indicators that institutions look to, in order to get a sense of a student's academic readiness. Institutions evaluate testing relative to a student's context, recognizing that there are differences based on geography, family income, gender, and ethnic background, as well as different strengths in different academic areas. At the University of Pennsylvania, we definitely want to see students who are academically prepared. But testing isn't the only measure that we look to to make sure we have confidence in that. Testing is just another element in the file. And we're looking at many different elements when evaluating students. For example, institutions will look closely at the rigor of the course work that students have taken in school and then the** performance in those courses. It is the combination of multiple measures that tip a student in or keep them just shy of being admitted.

When looking at a standardized testing record, admission officers search for overall patterns. Where did the student score high? Or low? How many times did she take the test? Did scores go up? Or down? Does a student have very good grades and very low scores? Or very high test scores and very low grades? If a student has high grades and low test scores, does that mean he doesn't test well or has not been challenged in his course work? If a student retakes a test and the scores go from very low to very high, was that because there was an extenuating circumstance, such as illness, on the day of the initial test? Testing tells an admission officer a story.

Testing is often spoken of as a benchmark or yardstick that is used by schools to compare students from Manhattan to those from Cleveland or Dubai. But colleges do not hold an SAT or ACT score as a hard constant against students from all backgrounds. Admission officers are aware that socioeconomic, gender, and racial biases are reflected in all tests and that there is tremendous variability in the quality of high school education in the United States.

As with many other such variables, test scores are considered in the context of the overall review of the student's application. Admission officers know, for example, that if a student has grown up hearing-impaired or speaking more than one language in the home, she is statistically likely to score lower on the reading or English portion of a standardized test.

In most cases, there is no formula for how a specific college will weigh your test scores. But what you can know, as we said at the beginning of this chapter, is that testing matters less than you think. That's because, as you can see, colleges consider your test scores as one piece of information among many. Even when scores are important information, colleges don't want you to be apprehensive or distressed about this step in the process. It's counterproductive and can lead to behavior such as overpreparation to the detriment of your class work and grades, which are—we know we keep repeating ourselves on this key point—the most important part of your application.

Test-Optional

For a number of years now, many colleges have been looking closely at the use of standardized test scores. Some have adopted a "test-optional" policy, which means they are flexible about submission of standardized test scores. As testing undergoes even further scrutiny and evolution, the number of test-optional colleges will increase.

For some test-optional schools that means students are not required to submit any standardized test results, including SAT or ACT scores. At others, students may be asked to submit the results of AP, IB, or SAT Subject Tests in lieu of SAT or ACT results. Eligibility to not submit test scores may be contingent on other factors, as well—for example, applicants might need to rank in the top

10 percent of their class or have a GPA of 3.5 or above. Furthermore, applicants can sometimes be required to meet alternative admission requirements such as submission of graded writing samples, additional teacher recommendations, or in-person interviews. Make sure you check the testing policy of each school to which you are applying.

Schools choose to go test-optional for many reasons. The *Chronicle of Higher Education* described the decision as "the place where marketing and mission overlap." In other words, some schools want to increase their pool of applicants by encouraging students with lower scores to apply, while other schools have found that data such as GPA or writing samples are more valid predictors of a student's success at their school.

Regardless of their reasons, today there are hundreds of schools with test-optional policies. A list of schools that have de-emphasized SAT and ACT scores can be found at fairtest.org. This list includes a range of colleges and universities, from Wake Forest, Bowdoin, and Bryn Mawr to Arizona State and the University of Texas at Austin. Pay close attention to each school's policy and practices. For example, while test scores may not be used for an admission decision, they may be required for placement or scholarships. Sometimes test scores must be submitted after admission, even if they are not considered in the admission process.

Harvey Mudd College vice president for admission and financial aid Thyra Briggs has an advantageous perspective on this subject. In 2003, Briggs was dean of admission at Sarah Lawrence College when it decided to no longer require test scores for admission. In 2007, Briggs became dean of admission at Harvey Mudd College, where testing remains an essential variable in the admission decision.

➡ **The most important thing for students to know about testing is to put it in the context of the individual schools to which they are applying. Students—and families—need to use every place a school talks about itself as a message about whether or not a school will be a good match for them. Testing plays into this, because one of the ways that a college can tell you an incredible amount about who they are and what they value is through their own admission requirements.**

At Harvey Mudd, for example, we use standardized tests as part of our application review. This makes sense for us since we are a math/science/engineering school and testing is a standard way in which we evaluate our students. So we require all students to submit the ACT or the SAT (the ACT has to have the writing option). We also require every student to submit the results of two Subject Tests and one of them must be Math II. If you don't want to take Math II, then Harvey Mudd is probably not the right place for you.

At Sarah Lawrence, however, while I was there, there were fewer exams. Writing was at the heart of the Sarah Lawrence education, as were the relationships students formed with faculty members. While some courses used testing as a method of evaluation, most relied more heavily on writing. For that reason, we felt comfortable making the decision to no longer use standardized tests in our admission

decisions and placed greater emphasis on additional writing samples such as a graded analytical paper or lab report. This made sense for Sarah Lawrence as the college was at the time. This decision also provided us with additional opportunities at college fairs or in conversation with students to answer the question "If you don't look at standardized test scores, what *do* you care about?" We could then talk about the rigor of a student's curriculum and the value Sarah Lawrence placed on writing.

The myth about testing in college admission is that it's all about numbers. Students seem to think there's a cutoff point for test scores at every school—"If I'm above this, I'm going to get in; if I'm below this, I'm not going to get in." And it just never works that way. The thing for students to know is that it's a range. That means it's probably not going to be as much of a factor in our decision-making process as they think it is. We're going to move on and look at other things.

The danger is that students see themselves in the top end and think, "Well, this is a safety school"—not realizing all the aspects of fit and match that are so crucial. It's why students hear stories all the time about kids with perfect scores who don't get in. These students simply may not be portraying themselves as great fits for the institution.

The flip side is also the case. Students whose test scores are at the lower end shouldn't rule themselves out. That simply means they have more of an uphill battle in terms of admissibility at a school like Harvey Mudd, and the other parts of the application will need to be that much stronger to balance out lower scores.

There is a place for colleges that demand

Questions to Ask About Testing

Students must know the testing policy of each school to which they are applying. Check the school website to determine the following:

- What tests are required?
- Is the optional writing section required if I am submitting the ACT?
- If I submit the ACT with the writing test, are Subject Tests required?
- Are Subject Tests required in addition to the SAT? If so, how many and in what areas?
- Is the writing score used in the decision?
- Does the school use Score Choice, allowing me to decide which scores it sees?
- Does the school "superscore," using only the top scores from different test dates?
- Is it required that students submit their entire testing record? For example, both the ACT and SAT results and all results from retesting?

testing, for colleges that make it optional, and for colleges that don't use it at all. That's the huge advantage of the American educational system. You can find any number of colleges that agree with your philosophy. Students who feel their test scores are not a reflection of who they are now have an incredible range of colleges they can apply to where test scores are not a requirement. This process is not about students making themselves into something that's attractive to a college. It's about figuring out what they value and finding a college that values that as well.

The Testing Controversy

There is a lot of controversy in the educational community about testing. Here are some of the highlights: Testing stresses out students. The billion-dollar prep industry and rankings further fuel unnecessary anxiety. Testing is socioeconomically biased—favoring students who attend strong schools and have the resources for private tutoring and test prep. Tests instigate gamesmanship because they're coachable. There is gender and racial bias in the tests. Tests are too high-stakes— as the deciding factors in admission and scholarships, they perpetuate inequities and inequalities in access. Tests are not the best predictors of success in college. They're not fair. They're not fun. (Okay, that last one was a joke, but barely.)

Colleges, educators, and journalists worry about this. But you shouldn't—it's simply not helpful. Just get familiar with the tests, practice, get a good night's sleep, and eat a good breakfast before you head to the testing center. Worried anyway? Then know this: professional admission officers have been thoroughly trained in all the foibles and drawbacks of the test and know how to interpret individual scores within those concerns. Enough said.

Questions You May Have

Are non-Saturday test dates offered for students who cannot test on Saturday due to religious considerations?

Both the ACT and SAT offer non-Saturday testing for students with conflicting religious convictions. Check their websites for specific requirements. For example, students requesting non-Saturday testing will not be admitted to an ACT test center without a letter from their clergy member or a notarized statement to verify religious beliefs.

Are testing policies different for home-schooled students?

Home-schooled students will have to make arrangements to take the PSAT/NMSQT or ACT Aspire by contacting a local high school. This needs to be done well in advance. You can register online for the ACT and SAT, including Subject Tests. See their websites for more information, including the proper codes to denote home schooling and how to choose test centers.

Note: You will need to check the testing requirements for home-schooled students at each institution to which you are applying. Home-schooled students will usually have the same test requirements as other applicants but may be required to submit additional testing, such as results from as many as four SAT Subject Tests. See Chapter 19.

What influence do test scores have on financial aid?

Test scores are one of many elements that may influence the amount of scholarship and grant monies you receive. See Chapter 16 on financial aid.

What do colleges think about high test scores and low grades?

High scores will not usually balance out a weak transcript. Colleges prefer students who are talented *and* do the work in class.

? I took a practice PSAT as a sophomore. How do I interpret my scores?

Sophomores should look at the percentiles for each subtest, which compare them within the group of sophomores who took the test in the previous year. On average, sophomores can usually expect scores to rise 3 to 4 points in each subtest when they test again as juniors.

? How can I evaluate a test tutor?

Talk with at least two families with whom the tutor has previously worked. Ask for a resume—you want a tutor who has years of experience and an educational background that will allow him to assess a student. For example, a student who has high grades but low test scores may suffer from a learning difference or test anxiety, and a test tutor will not be able to help if he can't make that diagnosis. Question the tutor about the methods used in his tutoring, as well as how he manages special circumstances such as heavy sports schedules.

Request test scores of previous students, both before and after tutoring; while an individual tutor may not have these, companies such as Kaplan and Princeton Review do. Discuss scheduling and cancellation policies—students should not be prepping for standardized tests to an extent that interferes with their regular academic work. Also request the tutor's payment schedule and fees. Average fees can range from $70 to $130 per hour. Premium tutors may charge up to $300 per hour or more.

But remember, ultimately preparation is still up to the student. If she doesn't do the work the tutor assigns, she won't see a good result.

? If my test scores are higher than the average for a test-optional school, should I submit them anyway?

It may be in your interest to send your scores if they are at the top of the range for accepted students at a school that is test-optional.

? Can test scores be appealed?

Neither the ACT nor SAT has an appeals process per se. However, if you believe there has been an error in scoring your test, both services offer a hand-scoring service to verify that a test was machine-scored correctly.

? What if I have proctor or test center problems?

Problems that students may experience on a test date might include a poorly trained proctor who mistimes a test, noise problems in a testing room, or weather that prevents a test from being administered or completed. Both the ACT and SAT have procedures for the reporting and resolution of problems. Students who experience difficulties at a test center should contact the testing service, either by calling the customer service number or by using the email feedback form on the websites.

? How do the testing services handle cheating?

Both the ACT and SAT have strict guidelines governing testing conditions, including the use of electronics such as cell phones, misconduct on the part of test-takers, failure to turn in a test booklet, and other irregularities. Both testing companies have procedures for reporting concerns. If you notice any irregularities, report them to the test center supervisor or the online or help line customer service departments of the testing service as soon as possible. Further information about irregularities in testing can be found on the websites.

PART IV

WHERE TO APPLY

CHAPTER 8

Creating an Initial List of Colleges

"The best estimates suggest that there are at least 70 thousand million million million (70 sextillion or 7×10^{22}) stars in the Universe."[17]

—Royal Observatory, Greenwich

"There's only one Maltese Falcon."

—Caspar Gutman, in *The Maltese Falcon*

"There are 2,242 four-year non-profit colleges and universities in the United States."[18]

—U.S. Department of Education, National Center for Education Statistics

Your task in the next step of applying to college is to turn a four-digit universe—2,242 colleges—into a two-digit list of possibilities: the dozen or more schools you think you might like to attend. If winnowing down thousands of schools to double digits sounds intimidating, don't let it. Most of the time the problem students have is starting with too few prospective colleges on their list. Unlike the Maltese Falcon, there is more than one college.

Remember, the goal here is to create a list

of schools that will provide you with good choices in your senior year. But to get there, you are going to have to be very thoughtful about who you are and what you want—and then figure out where you can find it.

We recommend students use a four-step strategy:

1. **Research yourself.** What do you want? Before you start asking how schools are going to see you, think first about how you see yourself.

Checkpoints ✍

✔ Research yourself and the schools on the front end of creating your preliminary list. We'll show you how. You will regret it if you are casual about this step.

✔ Don't make a list that includes only highly selective colleges.

✔ Applying to ten of the most highly selective schools does not multiply your chances of being admitted by ten.

✔ Each college on your list should be a "first choice"—campuses with compelling reasons for you to attend.

✔ Balance your list among schools according to their difficulty of admission and cost.

✔ The goal is to have options and a happy outcome in the spring of senior year.

2. **Research the schools.** Find out what they offer.

3. **Make some matches.** Pick between fifteen and thirty colleges that look like they can meet your preferences, interests, and abilities. Have fun with it. This is the part where *you* get to make the choices.

4. **Balance the list.** Analyze your list of matches to make sure it includes schools with a range of selectivity and cost. We'll say more about both of these later in this chapter.

Do these four things, and there you go. You have an initial list.

STEP 1: RESEARCHING YOURSELF

Here's where you start—by examining your preferences, priorities, interests, and hopes. You have to look inside yourself before you start looking outside. Before you ask which college is right for you, ask yourself who you are and who you want to become.

For some students, the starting point will be obvious. An interest may have already emerged as a potential life passion. Playing a college sport may be a possibility. Or living in a big city has always been a dream. Many high school students will begin thinking about their list of colleges as early as sopho-more year. However or whenever you start, you will need to do this homework in order to get the best result in your senior year—a choice among a group of schools where you would be delighted to spend four years.

There are many ways to approach this first step. You can find personality tests and "interest inventories" in some reference guide-books such as the *Fiske Guide to Colleges,* or online with a Web-based service such as Naviance. Some of you may seek out friends, family, and guidance counselors to help you

Do You Have to Know What You Want to Do for the Rest of Your Life?

We asked Haverford College's dean of admission and financial aid, Jess Lord, what students need to know about themselves before they start thinking about college. Here is what he had to say.

➡ This is a key question, but students often misunderstand what it really means to "know themselves." I encounter so frequently students who feel they are lost at sea if they don't know a lot about themselves. But they don't need to know what they're going to do for the rest of their lives. They don't need to know necessarily everything they're going to do in college and who they are going to be as an adult.

Students do need to be engaged and active in the process of getting to know themselves. Students don't need to have the final answer, because we adults know you never get to that point. Life is a process of exploration and discovery. But you need to be engaged in that process, because the student who is self-reflective knows what kinds of things to ask about and look for and can test out assumptions and ideas about college and the college process.

There are some practical things students need to know as they go into this process about themselves and the kind of education they want. For example, those who have an interest in engineering need to make sure a school can accommodate that interest. But what students need to know as well is: What kind of experience does any particular college offer? What are the educational values of that college? What is the mission of the college? How does a college describe the education it provides and the experience it wants its students to have? And then does that resonate with the individual student and the kind of experience she envisions for herself?

with this. At many high schools, counselors might ask students to complete a detailed survey of their likes, dislikes, dreams, abilities, and plans for the future. Some schools request that parents respond at length to a questionnaire as well.

We'll add to those approaches with some questions to help you get started. You can contemplate the answers on your own or discuss them with friends, counselors, coaches, clergy, or family. Students often get the best results by writing out their answers—it will be easier to see what really matters to you.

Don't be intimidated by the self-examination required here. These are simply ideas to get you thinking. It's not a test. You don't have to answer every question. Do what you can—but do at least some. For the last few years, you have been stretched and tested and asked to think about life and what's important to you. Now you're just going to think about it a little more.

Who Are You? Part I

Don't forget to think about the "why" of each answer as you proceed through these questions.

Interests and Activities

1. What is your favorite thing to do?
2. What inspires you?
3. Which activity have you pursued outside of school that has been most meaningful to you?
4. What do you hate to do?
5. What are your favorite . . .
   a. Books
   b. Movies
   c. Websites
   d. News sources
   e. Food
   f. Type of music
   g. TV shows
   h. Sports
6. How much do you genuinely like to read, discuss issues, and exchange ideas?
7. What did you do last summer? What do you plan to do this summer?
8. Is there a career you've always dreamed of?
9. Do you see yourself as politically liberal or conservative?
10. Is there an issue of local, national, or international concern that you find compelling?

Personality

11. What are the first words that come to mind when you're asked to describe yourself?
12. How do you go about making significant decisions?
13. How have you changed since 9th grade?
14. Complete this sentence: "People think that I am . . ."
15. What are you most proud of?
16. What are you afraid of being or becoming?
17. Name the three values that are most important to you.
18. What makes you happy?
19. Do you like hustle and bustle or peace and quiet?
20. How are you unique? What can you say about yourself that is only true for you?
21. What do you consider your coolest trait?
22. What do you consider your worst habit?
23. Are you a morning person or a night owl?

Friends and Family

24. What do you most appreciate about your family life?
25. How would your parents describe you? What three words would they use?
26. If you have siblings, how do you get along with them?
27. How would your siblings describe you? What three words would they use?
28. What are you known for in your family?
29. Who are your closest friends?
30. How would your friends describe you? What three words would they use?
31. Describe a fun experience you had with a friend.
32. Describe a difficult experience you had with a friend and how you handled it.
33. What person in your life has been most influential and why?

School

34. If you could start over at high school, what would you change? ("Nothing" is not an acceptable answer!)

35. What are you known for at school?

36. How would teachers describe you? What three words would they use?

37. What teacher do you have an important relationship with and why?

38. What do your friends and teachers not know about you?

39. What has been your greatest challenge in high school?

40. Which activity have you pursued in school that has been most meaningful to you?

As you contemplate these questions, certain priorities and patterns will emerge that will translate into preferences when you start looking at individual colleges. Don't worry about getting anything "right" at this point—your criteria for what you want may very well change. You're just mining for information.

Who Are You? Part II

College is a learning environment. What you want to study and how you learn best should be among your primary considerations even as you begin to think about an initial list. You will also be called on to honestly evaluate yourself as a student in order to figure out what schools are best for you.

Academics

41. What is your GPA? What is the highest GPA reported by your school?

42. Are the majority of your classes advanced, such as APs?

43. What is the most intellectually engaging class you have taken in high school? Why? How did it influence you?

44. What do you choose to learn when you learn on your own? Consider what topics you choose for research papers, lab reports, or independent reading.

45. What subjects have you excelled in?

46. What has been your greatest academic success?

47. What are your weaknesses academically?

48. When you have struggled in your class work, what did you do about it?

49. How do you respond to academic pressure?

Learning Style

50. Are you happiest when you are (a) significantly challenged and must be ever energetic in your efforts to keep up; (b) growing along with the rest of your classmates; or (c) learning while comfortably at the top of your class?

51. Are there any circumstances, such as a learning disability, that have impacted your academic performance?

52. What has been the best learning environment for you—a large lecture class or a small discussion group?

53. Is it important to you to have close relationships with your teachers?

54. What kind of schedule is best for you?

The Next Step

55. Why are you going to college?

56. Do you already have an idea about what you want to study?

57. Is there a career you are intent on pursuing?

58. If not, are there professions you are considering?

59. Which activities have you participated in so far that you are interested in pursuing in college, and what haven't you been able to pursue that you would like to try in college?

60. Is there an activity that you insist on continuing in college?

61. If you took a year off before college, what would you do?

62. What balance of study, activities, and social life are you looking for?

63. Do you like to socialize with a group or one-on-one?

64. Is being in a leadership position important to you?

65. Are there colleges that your family has significant ties to or is interested in having you look at?

66. Are you ready to live far from home?

67. What kinds of surroundings are essential to your well-being?

68. Do you want to live in a community where everybody knows your name, or one in which you can be anonymous?

69. Are you used to advocating for yourself?

70. Do you like being around people like yourself, or do you prefer a lot of diversity in your friends or community?

As you have considered the questions of who you are and what you want, certain priorities will have emerged. For example, you may feel strongly that you want to experience living in a new part of the country or stay close to home, learn everything there is to know about biomechanical engineering or play water polo for a top team, pursue an interest in opera or do improv.

Here's a key step: write down an actual list of these personal priorities. Be sure you have at least five on your list. If you have more than a dozen, then see if you can let a couple go. Be careful to distinguish between needs and wants. Needs will represent your highest priorities, and as you move on to the next step of researching the schools, you must satisfy those criteria first in developing your initial list. Now you're ready to move on to the next step in developing your initial list of prospective colleges.

STEP 2: RESEARCHING THE SCHOOLS

Now you are going to take your list of personal priorities and dive into researching schools. As you figure out what the schools have to offer, you will be looking for those that meet the needs and wants you have begun to establish. Your goal will be to find

Parental Preferences

Parents, if you have strong preferences or requirements with regard to considerations such as cost, religious affiliation, alma mater, geography, diversity, or any other factor, now is the time to have a frank discussion with your teenager and the high school counselor. If you are going to impose any limits or restrictions on the list of prospective schools, do it before an initial list is developed. Don't wait, for example, until your student from New Jersey has his heart set on California schools to disclose that you can't bear the thought or expense of him being so far away.

at least three to five colleges for each priority you have listed. Some schools will show up more than once, if they meet more than one of your priorities. Remember, as you learn about schools, you may also find yourself discovering personal priorities that you hadn't already considered, such as an academic major or political diversity. Just add them to your personal priorities list.

Here are some of the big factors that you will want to consider as you begin your research. These are the elements that are usually most relevant in linking up to students' personal priorities.

- **Location.** Location encompasses considerations of geography, climate, and distance from home. Are you ready to be far from home? Do you want to live in a part of the country or world you've never experienced? If you've spent your life in the South, are you ready for the cold winter of a campus in the Midwest or Northeast?

- **Setting.** Do you want a school with an urban, suburban, or rural setting? Do you want the peace and quiet of a college located in a quiet suburb, the isolation of a school in the Rockies, or the hustle and bustle of a big-city campus with access to museums, shopping, and entertainment? What is the character of the surrounding community? Are there services available—medical, dry cleaning, restaurants?

- **Size.** School enrollments can range from a few hundred students to tens of thousands. Size can impact the range of majors offered, a school's athletics, extracurricular activities, opportunities for involvement, the sense of

community, and the amount of attention a student will receive from faculty and staff.

- **Academic programs.** What courses of study does a school offer? Does it offer a major in the specific subject you're interested in? If you're undecided, does the school offer a range of courses and majors that may ultimately satisfy what you want to do? Can you change from one college to another within the university—for example, from engineering to liberal arts? Does the school have a core or open curriculum? Are classes large lectures or small seminars? Are introductory courses taught by faculty or graduate students?

- **Cost.** If cost is a concern for your family, keep it in mind as you look at schools. But if you're a student with good grades and test scores, don't rule out any school at this point on the basis of cost alone; just be sure your list includes colleges with a range of price points and financial aid. We'll talk more about balancing your list with regard to cost later in this chapter, and you can find more about financial aid and scholarships in Chapter 16.

- **Athletics.** Do you want to be at a school with NCAA Division I athletics? Is a "big-game" atmosphere important to you? Is it important to you to be able to participate in intramural or club sports?

- **Extracurricular activities.** What kind of entertainment is available—music, art, theater, improvisational comedy? Is there a lecture series, and if so, whom do they bring to campus? What kind of public service and volunteer opportunities are there? Is there a strong internship program? Is there an active religious community, such as a Hillel House? Are there ethnic organizations?

"College" Versus "University"

What's in a name? In this case, lots. Whether a school is a "college" or a "university" can make a difference. Understanding how schools characterize themselves may provide important information in creating an initial list.

Most—but not all—colleges and universities offer a liberal education. That doesn't refer to politics! "Liberal" in this case goes back to the original meaning of the word: "unrestricted." It's an educational approach where a student is called on to examine problems and issues from multiple vantage points and learns how to think, communicate, question, and probe. The rationale behind a liberal education is that the world is changing rapidly and training for a specific discipline or job is ultimately less practical than learning how to be ready for a world unknown.

Undergraduate education in the United States is dominated by institutions that hold to the notion that a liberal education is the best way to prepare for a life of significance, meaning, and means. There are, however, also terrific options that do not insist students be liberally educated.

Here are the definitions of the four general categories of selective four-year higher education institutions:

- **Liberal arts colleges** offer a liberal education to students across the arts, humanities, social sciences, and sciences. Primarily awarding undergraduate degrees, their faculties are focused on teaching, although many offer strong opportunities for students to be involved in and conduct research. Usually small to medium-sized schools, they typically enroll fewer than 5,000 students, with most living on campus. Examples include Grinnell, University of Mary Washington, Oberlin, Sarah Lawrence, College of Charleston, Berea, St. Olaf, Bowdoin, Amherst, Haverford, Claremont McKenna, University of North Carolina at Asheville, and Kenyon.

- **Research universities** offer a full range of academic programs in undergraduate, master's, and doctoral programs. They may be either public or private and can have an enrollment as small as 5,000 or as large as 50,000. Research is part of the mission of these schools, and so faculty members are expected to place a priority on research as well as teaching. Research universities are composed of several colleges, including a college of liberal arts, all of which usually share a single campus. They also offer programs in professional fields such as nursing, architecture, communications, the arts, and engineering. Examples include Northwestern, Vanderbilt, UCLA, Yale, University of Michigan, Tufts, Drexel, Rensselaer, Iowa State, University of Massachusetts, George Washington, and MIT.

- **Specialty schools** primarily offer undergraduate and graduate degrees in the fine and performing arts, business, and engineering. Students entering these programs should be confident of and committed to their particular course of study. Examples include California's Menlo College or Massachusetts' Babson College for business, Massachusetts' Olin College of Engineering and the Rose-Hulman Institute of Technology in Indiana for engineering, Parsons School in New York for design and fashion merchandising, New York's Juilliard or the San Francisco Conservatory for music, and art institutes such as Cleveland Institute of Art and Rhode Island School of Design.

- **Comprehensive colleges** are master's universities and baccalaureate colleges. Baccalaureate colleges offer programs in the liberal arts, but also preprofessional programs. Master's universities provide a full range of undergraduate studies, some master's programs, and sometimes a small number of doctoral programs. Examples of comprehensive colleges include Cooper Union, Valparaiso University, United States Air Force Academy, Simmons College, Santa Clara University, University of the Pacific, and University of Portland.

There are also schools that have other attributes you might consider as categories in and of themselves, such as women's colleges, including Agnes Scott, Mt. Holyoke, and Scripps; schools with religious affiliations, such as DePaul and Boston College (Roman Catholic), Yeshiva University (Jewish), and Belmont University (Christian); and historically black colleges and universities such as Spelman, Morehouse, and Lincoln.

While the way a college names itself can provide you with important information, it's smart to dig a little further to specifically understand what a school offers. There can be considerable overlap among the different categories. And, alas, the designations "college" and "university" are not always enlightening. Denison University, Bucknell University, and Ohio Wesleyan University are all liberal arts colleges. Dartmouth College, College of William and Mary, and Boston College are all research universities.

- **Public or private.** At this point your list should probably have a mix of public and private schools. Tuition costs for in-state students at public universities are usually lower, although sticker price can be deceiving—private schools can often offer generous financial aid packages. (See more on this in Chapter 16.) Public universities often have larger enrollments than private schools and can offer a broader range of academic programs.

- **Diversity.** Gender, ethnicity, socioeconomic background, age, politics, and international population can each have an effect on campus culture. Do you like being in a setting where you encounter diversity daily or one in which you will find that most people are like you? Do you want a school that has a good balance of men and women? Does the school have a reputation as being liberal or conservative? Do you want a school with a large international population?

- **Campus culture.** What is the social climate? Is it dominated by a Greek system? Populated by artsy students? Is it known as a party school? Is the library busy on Friday night? What type of people do you encounter on the quad? Is reputation or prestige a factor for you? Do most students live on or off campus?

- **Other factors.** You may have requirements unique to your own situation, such as a school with support for disabilities or learning differences, a study-abroad program, religious affiliation, or specialized academic programs such as architecture or film.

Everything You Will Ever Need to Know

Here are the resources where you will find the information about colleges needed to create your initial list. There's no shortage of information—guidebooks, brochures, view books, email, college fairs, blogs, YouTube videos, websites, and road shows. In fact, one of the challenges is to sort through the abundance and extract meaningful data from the come-ons, hype, and plain old misinformation. The upside is that you have a wealth of resources for finding out everything you will want or need to know.

You're not expected to use every single one of these resources to research a school. This guide to information sources is descriptive, not prescriptive. Find the ones that work best for you and go with them.

Guidebooks

Guidebooks are comprehensive references for basic information about colleges and often have the size and heft of the Gutenberg Bible. These are a great starting point for your college search. Published annually, they are available in most bookstores, libraries, and the office of your high school college or guidance counselor. We'll recommend several, and we guarantee the ones you choose will be well worn by the time you make your college decision.

Guidebooks fall into two categories:

1. **Objective guidebooks** are comprehensive catalogs—providing an at-a-glance overview for each school, with facts and figures on variables such as location, cost, test scores, academics, athletics, and financial aid. These can be excellent

Students of color, women considering historically male colleges or male students considering historically women's colleges, and LGBTQQI (lesbian, gay, bisexual, transgender, queer, questioning, and intersex) applicants will have unique considerations in researching prospective colleges that others will not.

These students may want to ask additional questions about integration and the surrounding community. For example, LGBTQQI students may want to ask if there are counseling and support services for students coming to terms with their sexuality or if there are active LGBTQQI organizations on campus. Students of color should look not just at the percentage of minority-group members or specific ethnicities on campus but what the surrounding community is like. Ask if residence staff and campus police and security have been trained in issues that affect minority or ethnic students, and if the campus social life and surrounding community include restaurants, houses of worship, clubs, or other services that support diversity.

Much of this information can be found online, but we also recommend going straight to the source and asking the admission office to put you in touch with student organizations that are active in your area of interest, whether it is the Korean Students Club, the LGBTQQI Pride Network, the Women's Resource Center, or the Muslim Students Organization. Current students are usually happy to share their views and perspectives.

resources. An example would be the College Board's *College Handbook.*

2. **Subjective guidebooks** provide basic facts about the schools, including info on acceptance rates, cost, and enrollment. But they also "review" the schools the way critics review movies—weaving together fact and opinion about the physical setting, student body, academics, athletics, and other aspects of campus life. They may use feedback and narrative from students, faculty, or alumni and attempt to convey the personality of a school, the vibe of the student body, and a sense of the institution's values. The anecdotal nature of these books makes them accessible, entertaining, and very appealing to students. An example would be the *Fiske Guide to Colleges.*

If you stick to the latest editions from the list in the sidebar here, you won't go too far wrong. But if you look elsewhere, consumer alert! Pay attention to how guidebooks gather their information and from whom—the methodology is usually explained in the opening pages. Confirm that the guides have done their research directly with the institutions they are covering and that the survey process has integrity. Don't put your faith in a book that uses information from sources that don't have direct knowledge of the institution. Stay away from guides that call themselves "objective" but resort to simplistic numerical rankings. Avoid books that feel too gimmicky. And beware of outdated information—statistical data can lag and the admission profile of any one school can change rapidly from year to year.

Unsolicited Mailings

When students take the ACT Aspire test or the College Board's PSAT/NMSQT, they can opt on the registration form to provide information about themselves to colleges. The ACT and the College Board provide that information to colleges based on criteria such as score ranges, geographic location, possible majors, or sports and extracurricular interests of those who opt in on the form.

Students will soon find themselves swamped with brochures, postcards, view books, catalogs, and email. Some of these materials will be helpful and instructive. Catalogs or bulletins, for example, provide in-depth information on course offerings

Browse This Bookshelf

Here's a partial list of the books we think have something to offer.

- **Objective reference guidebooks**
  - *College Handbook*, published by the College Board
  - *Four-Year Colleges*, published by Peterson's
- **Subjective reference guidebooks**
  - *Fiske Guide to Colleges,* by Edward B. Fiske
  - *Student's Guide to Colleges*, edited by Jordan Goldman and Colleen Buyers
  - *Big Book of Colleges*, by College Prowler
  - *The Best 378 Colleges*, by Princeton Review
  - *Colleges That Change Lives: 40 Schools That Will Change the Way You Think About Colleges*, by Loren Pope

and major requirements, and brochures may describe features of college life such as intramural sports or study-abroad programs. Marketing materials such as these can also provide clues about a college's character and environment.

How to Handle Emails from Colleges

If you get an email from a college that you think you might be interested in, be sure to actually open it. Don't simply move it into a folder, read it in a preview pane, or delete it. Colleges can tell whether you actually open their emails. At schools that consider "demonstrated interest," they will take your opening the email as a sign of interest, and failing to open it as a sign of no interest. (Read more about demonstrated interest on page 121.)

Some communications from colleges might seem like a waste of your time; email, often contracted out to third-party direct-marketing firms, may be the biggest offender. Emailed solicitations try to get you excited with urgent instructions to "follow this link" to "10 steps to college success" or "respond immediately" to receive a "college prospectus" because "there are only a few left." If you find these come-ons condescending, don't necessarily let them turn you off to a school that otherwise seems like it could be a good match.

And appreciate the schools that make an effort. Harvey Mudd College used to send a mailing that was marked honestly—but cleverly—on the envelope as "Junk Mail." More recently, they got students' attention

with a flip card that held one way shows an iPhone and held another way becomes a graphing calculator.

In the mass marketing of college admission, schools pitch themselves to students the way credit card companies pitch themselves to consumers—the come-on is just to apply, not to really buy anything. Personally addressed mailings may flatter you with invitations to visit a school's campus or even to apply. But you are not being "recruited" when you receive these sales pitches. These mailers are sent to tens of thousands of students and are nothing more than advertisements. It is not an honor to receive them, nor is it an indication you will be admitted.

These mailings compound the hype, can be misinterpreted by a student or family ("Wow! Wash U really wants me!" Or "Wow, I really can get into Harvard!"), and elevate the anxiety about the admission process in general. On the other hand, for some students, their first exposure to the college they eventually chose was an unsolicited piece of mail that intrigued them.

You may in fact be an exciting prospective student for a particular college, but at this stage in the process it is too soon to tell. Here are several things to remember when you are encouraged to apply to a school, whether that encouragement comes in an email, in a captivating brochure, via Facebook, from your neighbor who went there, or from a representative of a college admission office.

• Encouragement is not a promise of admission. Sometimes it is not even encouragement, but merely a courtesy. Note carefully the words

Demonstrated Interest

Students show demonstrated interest when they take various actions that signal to a school that they are seriously considering it. Some schools don't consider demonstrated interest in the admission decision. Others do, and among them they use different methods to determine a student's level of interest. For example, some schools may note the number of times you have visited or attended an event or whether you have contacted the college directly for information. That information may be included as part of a formula that determines admission. Other schools may look more subjectively for evidence of your interest in your essays. Colleges may or may not disclose whether they use demonstrated interest as a factor in their admission decisions.

Stanford University states clearly that it does not show preference in the admission process for students who demonstrate interest. According to its website:

➡ Contacting the Admission Office is neither a requirement nor an advantage in our admission process. We offer campus tours and information sessions to provide you with the information you need to make an informed college choice, not to evaluate you. We welcome calls and emails for the same reason. Please do not feel compelled to contact us to demonstrate your interest in Stanford; we know by the very fact of your applying that you are seriously interested in Stanford. We do not keep records of prospective student contacts with our office.

On the other side, Christopher Gruber, dean of admission and financial aid at Davidson College, explains why and how his college uses demonstrated interest as a factor in admission decisions.

➡ We look at demonstrated interest in a variety of ways, although I wouldn't go so far as to say there's a calculation that exists. One place where we think about a student's likelihood to enroll is when they're answering the essay question "Why Davidson?" and we can see that they've done their homework. Or if I happen to be hosting a reception in the Los Angeles area and know that an applicant lives three miles away, we certainly expect that they are going to be there. If students live near our campus, we'd love for them to visit. We love to see them corresponding with their admission officers. These are all ways that help us understand our chances of getting that student to ultimately enroll on this campus.

Check the websites of the colleges to which you are applying for their policy or ask the admission office.

used, so you can discern what is really being said.

- Unless the college or university uses a strictly numbers-based formula, no one—not even the admission dean—can predict that you will be admitted based on preliminary contact alone.

- If in correspondence with a college or a conversation with a college representative you are told your chances of admission are "great" but your college counselor is more tempered, then listen to your college counselor. That doesn't mean you shouldn't dream, just that you have to dream realistically so you apply to an ample number of colleges that are likely to accept you. No counselor should ever tell you not to apply to a school.

> A school with a cool website may not be the best one for you. And some great colleges have pretty bad websites, which you shouldn't hold against them. The website, like a college's mailer, is just one piece of information.

Online Resources

The abundance of information and admission tools available online is a boon to students and parents. But it comes with booby traps. Students, you may know how to use the Web best—in fact, better than parents, college counselors, or college admission offices—but don't forget to be appropriately skeptical as you explore it. Here are some resources and guidance about separating fact from fiction as you look for answers online.

COLLEGE WEBSITES

The most reliable source for information about a college is its own website. Almost anything a student wants to know—from the choice of dormitories to available majors—can be found here via virtual tours of the campus, links to academic departments, live chats with current students, podcasts from the admission department, and videos of everything from faculty presentations to football games.

Not only is the information available here

generally illustrative of a school, its students, and its mission, but it is also practical: a definitive source for admission requirements and application deadlines, dates and times for tours and info sessions, and contact information for getting straight to the source on your questions. On the undergraduate admission home page, also click on the link to sections "College Counselors" or "Guidance Counselors"—these often have additional helpful information, including applicant profiles that show test score and GPA ranges.

Our best advice? Start your online search with what a college says about itself—before visiting other sites. By starting with facts, you will be much less swayed by the innuendo and opinion that can be prevalent elsewhere on the Web.

Don't forget to sign up as a prospective student while you're online so you'll receive email notices, view books, and other information from the schools that interest you. And when you make a virtual visit to a school, make sure you get off the admission section of the site and poke around elsewhere. Check out the student newspaper—it's usually online—as well as the Web pages of individual academic departments, on-campus events, and student groups of interest.

SEARCH TOOLS

College search tools on the Web are an easy and fun way to do research. These sites offer large databases of comprehensive information on thousands of colleges and universities. Some sites act as portals with direct links to the home pages of schools. Other sites allow

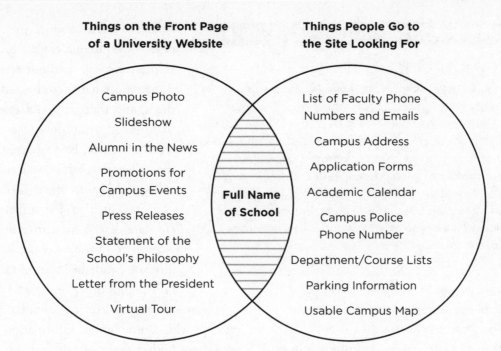

Things on the Front Page of a University Website

Campus Photo

Slideshow

Alumni in the News

Promotions for Campus Events

Press Releases

Statement of the School's Philosophy

Letter from the President

Virtual Tour

Full Name of School

Things People Go to the Site Looking For

List of Faculty Phone Numbers and Emails

Campus Address

Application Forms

Academic Calendar

Campus Police Phone Number

Department/Course Lists

Parking Information

Usable Campus Map

Reprinted with permission of Randall Munroe, xkcd.com

students to help identify schools by inputting criteria such as location, academic interest, religious affiliation, GPA, and sports interests. As part of their counseling or guidance programs, some high schools also provide Web-based college planning portals, such as Naviance, that include databases and search tools.

The lists that result from criteria searches on these sites are great for finding information. But the results can sometimes be all over the map and for a variety of reasons may actually miss colleges that meet your criteria. Look at them as starting points from which to explore further.

Here are some of the most widely used and comprehensive sites:

• The College Board provides data and search capabilities at collegeboard.org. This site also has extensive academic profile information from schools' Common Data Set and other sources.

• The U.S. Department of Education provides data on thousands of public and private institutions with College Navigator at nces.ed.gov/collegenavigator, including information on such topics as campus security and federal loans.

• Portals such as College InSight from the Institute for College Access and Success at college-insight.org and the University and College Accountability Network's U-CAN at ucan-network.org provide detailed data and links to thousands of colleges and universities.

• *U.S. News and World Report* and *The Princeton Review* make some rankings and select information available free of charge at

Common Data Set

The Common Data Set is a collaborative initiative among colleges and universities, high schools, the National Center for Education Statistics, and publishers such as the College Board, *U.S. News and World Report, Peterson's Guides,* the *Fiske Guide,* and others. Its purpose is to improve the comparability of data by providing a standard definition and framework for reporting of information on GPA, class rank, and test scores for the incoming freshman class, as well as acceptance and retention, enrollment, academic offerings, admission requirements, financial aid, and more.

colleges.usnews.rankingsandreviews.com/best-colleges and princetonreview.com/college. Princeton Review also allows students to search by certain criteria with its School Finder. Such rankings can be a good source of initial information about schools but should be handled with care—see the rankings sidebar on page 127.

MATCHMAKING SITES

Social networking meets up with college recruitment in online matchmaking sites like Zinch at zinch.com and Cappex at cappex .com. Students, at no charge, can create profiles, similar to Facebook pages, where they upload video and audio as well as creatively showcase extracurricular activities and talents. Colleges that have contracted with these sites can then search the databases to find and recruit students with specific interests or abilities. Both these sites also include matching programs for financial aid and scholarships.

These may be good sites to browse, but students should demonstrate interest in and learn about colleges—as well as have

colleges learn about them—in other ways. Requests via sites such as these may go without response if the school hasn't contracted with them, and there is no reliable way to know if your query has been received or not. Best advice? Go to the college's website or contact the college admission office directly.

Sites such as Parchment.com are data-driven matchmaking services that purport to predict admission. Students input test scores, GPA, and other info, and these sites generate target lists of schools. These may provide some good information, but take them with a grain of salt and use other sources as well. You might have some schools you wouldn't otherwise consider brought to your attention. But the matching that is done cannot possibly be reliable since it doesn't take into account such variables as letters of recommendation or a college's institutional priorities. The danger is such a site may discourage you from applying to a school where you might be admitted or encourage you falsely to see yourself as more highly admissible than you actually are.

REVIEW-AND-DISCUSS SITES

These websites are basically social networks that offer a little bit of everything— college databases, search tools, admission advice, and financial aid resources. They are best known as stops on the information superhighway where colleges are rated, reviewed, issued "report cards," and endlessly discussed. There's some good insider information at these sites in the form of student reviews that give you the scoop on aspects of campus life you might not learn about from the admission office. But some sites' discussion boards traffic heavily in hearsay and ill-informed opinion masquerading as fact. You need to monitor your intake with an eye to discerning the facts from the gossip.

These sites include:

- Unigo, at unigo.com, is a social network that allows college students to post reviews, photos, videos, and other candid commentary about their schools for prospective applicants. This site's strength is its student-generated reviews—it's the Yelp of college guides.
- College Prowler, at colleges.niche.com, is a student-generated guidebook that issues a report card for colleges. Like "unofficial guides" in general, this site paints a sometimes helpful—and sometimes unusual—broader picture for applicants: grading a campus' girls and guys, as well as its academics. It also has some tools students find beneficial, such as online index cards that allow them to track schools in which they're interested. But, overall, ratings can be misleading—one student's C school may be your A campus.
- College Confidential, at collegeconfidential.com, is best known for its discussion forums, used by students and parents. Personal opinion is often represented as fact or the inside track on this site. For example, on the heavily viewed "What Are My Chances?" thread, students post their grades, scores, and other stats and ask participants to weigh

in on the likelihood of their admission to a particular school. Looking for reassurance is understandable, but this thread is not useful—other students and parents have *no* way of determining whether you are a good candidate for admission. The only way to find out if you're going to get in is to apply and see if you are admitted. If you have a question about a college or a step in the admission process, go straight to the source and email or call the admission office.

ADDITIONAL ONLINE RESOURCES

You may also find valuable information on the following websites:

- The National Survey of Student Engagement, or NSSE (pronounced "Nessie"), at nsse.iub.edu, collects student feedback in five benchmark areas, including academic challenge, student-faculty interaction, and cultural and social environment. NSSE releases only national averages, but many participating schools have chosen to make public their individual results. This site is not an appropriate starting point for information about a college but can add useful information and enrich your picture of an institution.
- The National Association for College Admission Counseling (NACAC) is primarily for professionals in the college admission community—in other words, those on the other side of the desk. But it does feature resources for students, including fee waiver applications, advice for international students, a timeline for college applicants, and their annual College Openings Update of four-year

colleges and universities that have slots available for freshmen after May 1. Go to nacacnet.org (note: *not* nacac.net) and click on the Students & Parents tab.

WEB-BASED PORTAL PROGRAMS

Many high schools offer online portals that allow students to research, track, and plan their college admission. Schools usually provide these free of charge to students and families. The most widespread program is Naviance, but states or school districts may have similar platforms; for example, the Rhode Island Higher Education Assistance Authority sponsors WayToGoRI.org at waytogori.org for its students. Check with your school about online resources.

This list is not exhaustive, and it is in the nature of the Web for new sites to pop up at any time—sites that may or may not offer reliable information. Remember to consider the source and be mindful of the drawbacks of surfing for information on the Web. For example, some search engines provide information only from schools that pay them for the privilege, so they are not comprehensive. Others provide information from schools whether those schools have consented to co-operate with them or not. Also, most of the information and services offered on the Web are free—so while "buyer beware" is not ex-

Check our website at collegeadmissionbook.com for recommendations of new resources on the Web and elsewhere.

actly the proper admonition, do pay attention to the fine print. These sites sometimes offer additional services such as essay preparation or scholarship finders, for which they charge fees. Finally, again, the most up-to-date and accurate information is always available from a college's admission office.

SOCIAL MEDIA

Fan pages on Facebook, Twitter feeds, blogs, Tumblrs, Pinterest pages, and viral videos on YouTube—colleges and universities are now creating content for the social platforms where prospective students play. These can be entertaining ways for you to be exposed to a campus culture. You can follow a school's Twitter feed or Tumblr, ask questions at an admission office blog, and add colleges to your Facebook News Feed.

YouTube offers what may be the widest exposure to the culture of a campus. Here you can find both the portrait of a college uploaded by the school's administration and the panorama of campus life as captured by

Rankings Run Amok

"The richest schools are the most prestigious." That's the conclusion at the satirical website College Ranking Service, rankyourcollege.com, where the ratings are arrived at through the use of "complicated algorithms," the expertise of cabalists, and a phenomenon known as the *kanaydel* effect, so dubbed in honor of the webmaster's mother's Passover matzoh balls. Interestingly, this methodology, according to the webmaster, has produced results strikingly similar to their chief competitor, *U.S. News and World Report*.

The Rankings

College rankings are everywhere. Distracting and sometimes deceptive, they can nevertheless be useful for students and parents.

The number one rank in the ranking pack belongs to *U.S. News and World Report*'s "America's Best Colleges" issue. It's their best-selling issue every year, called by some "the *Sports Illustrated* swimsuit edition." Kaplan/*Newsweek* has "The 25 Hottest Schools in America." *The Princeton Review* lists sixty-two rankings across eight categories, including politics and parties (as in Zeta Beta Tau, not Democratic or Republican). The *Washington Monthly* looks at Pell Grants, ROTC standings, and research dollars to rank schools by how much they contribute to the "common good"—though their definition of that may be different from yours. There are rankings from *Forbes, Kiplinger,* and even *Playboy,* which features a "bikini index."

The rankings are often blamed for contributing to the "frenzy" of the application process. Educators and admission professionals worry that the excessive media attention rained on the top ten or fifteen schools ranked "best" artificially stimulates students' interest, resulting in an avalanche of applications, a run-up in anxiety—and the mass hysteria that just a handful of colleges are the only ticket to success in life. Yet many colleges have a love-hate relationship with rankings, blaming them for injecting hype into the admission process but issuing press releases to announce where they landed on the list every year.

Critics also regard rankings as a beauty contest that creates incentives for colleges to set admission policies and goals aimed at artificially improving their rankings. Overemphasizing data related to selectivity, such as high SAT scores and low enrollment rates, results in strategies such as "ranksteering" where—because schools get judged on criteria such as how many applicants they reject—admission practices that maximize rejections are encouraged in order to steer the rankings in colleges' favor. In the last few years, Emory University, George Washington University, Claremont McKenna College, and Bucknell University admitted to inflating students' ACT and SAT scores and class rank.

Further, *U.S. News and World Report* positions its rankings as a numbers-based "scientific" approach, but they are to a large extent subjective. For example, more than 20 percent of a school's overall ranking comes from a peer assessment survey where presidents, provosts, and admission deans rate one another's institutions. Officials at both Clemson University and University of Florida admitted in the recent past to manipulating their responses to the peer assessment survey.

Even if the rankings were just based on objective numbers, they would still be of limited use. That's because admission is not just a quantitative formula, even at large public colleges. The lack of a formula, though, makes it hard for parents and students. In making the complex and costly decision about college, families want standardized, accessible information that allows them to make easy comparisons among schools. So the rankings have an eager audience. But do they help?

The Rankings (continued)

Despite the controversy among professionals, rankings—used responsibly—can be a good starting point for students and parents. For example, some of the individual data points displayed within the rankings can tell you a lot about a school: faculty-student ratio, class size, and spending per student. That said, the pitfall is that ranking data are just data—and often highly manipulated data at that. They tell you very little about the character, programs, people, or heart of a school.

Rankings are a beginning, not an end in themselves. They can be helpful at the start of a search by bringing to a student's attention the hundreds of colleges beyond the list of fifteen or so always touted in the press. For example, admission deans at some smaller schools such as Swarthmore find it hard to hate the rankings with the vengeance of so many of their detractors in higher education. Because fewer young people have heard about their schools, being ranked as a top liberal arts school in *U.S. News and World Report* can be helpful—particularly for students and families who might otherwise overlook a strong match.

Rankings can also show how colleges change over time. Schools that parents may not have considered when they were applying now offer great educations because of careful investment and strong leadership. Those changes can be reflected in the rankings.

The key to using the rankings correctly is to look beyond the top ten or fifteen schools. It's not always easy. "Best-ism" is part of the larger cultural phenomenon of status competition and celebrity. But don't fall prey to it. Stop and consider—is there really a difference between the number one school and the number seven school? Between number ninety-nine on the "Top 100" list versus the ten colleges that follow? Think of someone you admire and find out where that person's alma mater ranked. Maybe it didn't even make the list. Or try this thought experiment: Perhaps there indeed is a "Best Brunch" in town, according to Zagat. Yet some people like flapjacks, others want omelets, and still others are looking for beignets. Stay focused on what is important to you.

students—a student doing a back flip off the roof of a Middlebury dining hall, a tour of Virginia Tech's Hahn Horticulture Garden, UPenn engineering students playing robot soccer, and a pastiche of beer pong and nodding off in class at Cornell. Just remember that videos such as those posted on YouTube offer very personal points of view—they rarely represent the whole reality.

Admission office blogs can be informative and reassuring to students, on any given day addressing the Common Application, essays, or the status of the waitlist. Many of these blogs have great information, and we encourage you to refer to them. Check your college website's admission page for links to their blogs. Student blogs or blogs without direct links to an institution should be read with care—they will traffic more in opinion than fact.

As with all sources of information, don't rely on communicating with a school solely via social media such as Facebook, a blog, or Twitter. While those can be great for gathering info, phone calls or email often will be more effective in producing answers. Don't hold a college's iPhone app—or lack of one—against it, either. Social media are only color commentary. The college website or the admission office is the best place to find out the score.

College Fairs

At college fairs, admission officers or alumni are present to answer questions and pass out brochures and other information to students and their families. Fairs may be held in a gym where a couple of dozen colleges have set up tables with information or at a convention center where hundreds of colleges host booths. Usually occurring in the spring and fall, college fairs are free and often open to the public. They are a good way to get an introduction to a wide range of schools at once.

These events can be crowded and chaotic, so you need an action plan to ensure that you get the most out of the experience.

- Obtain a list of the participating colleges online or from your college counselor in advance of the fair and determine which schools' booths you will want to visit.
- Do some homework. Check out the websites of the schools you want to visit and prepare a list of questions after you've done some research.
- Do not bring a resume. Schools are not interested in a resume from you at this point.
- College fairs sometimes include information sessions on subjects such as financial aid or the search process, so plan accordingly if you want to attend.
- Leave some time to wander around. A school that you hadn't considered may catch your eye. Take the time to interact with its admission representative and learn more.
- Helpful hint: You can often obtain a bar code with your personal information—name, address, email, phone number—by preregistering for the fair or upon arrival at the event. That way you can quickly provide your information to the schools in which you're interested.

Check with your college or guidance counselor to find out about upcoming fairs in your area, or go to NACAC's website at nacacnet.org to see a posting of national fairs. Also, ask your counselor about fairs that cater to specialized groups, such as students interested in performing and visual arts programs, Hispanic and Latino applicants, scholarship students, and others.

If a college fair isn't coming to a town near you, you can attend a virtual fair online. CollegeWeekLive offers events year-round, free of charge. Students and parents can visit the virtual booths of hundreds of participating colleges and universities to pick up information via electronic brochures, webinars, or podcasts. Special events showcase specific categories of schools such as the service academies, engineering schools, the University of California system, or religious institutions. There are live chat, IM in real time, and interactive Q&A sessions with admission officials. Participants can also catch keynote speakers via live streaming video addressing college admission trends, aid, and tips on applying. Visit collegeweeklive.com for times and dates.

College fairs—whether virtual or real—are a good starting point for your research into schools, but, as with other resources, don't rely on them exclusively. To create the best initial list, you will need to look a little wider and dig a little deeper.

Road Shows

Yet another way to gather information about schools is to attend what admission officers call a "road show." These are regional events where an individual college or a small group of schools makes a presentation to students and parents at the local high school or in a public venue. Road shows are usually held during the evening or on a weekend and last about two hours.

A road show sponsored by an individual school usually begins with a presentation by admission officers and finishes with an open question-and-answer session. College representatives typically address academic programs, campus life, and sports, as well as how admission decisions are made by the school. Students and parents get an in-depth look at a school and may have the opportunity to speak with not only the admission officers but also current students, parents, and alumni.

In what admission officials call "group travel," a number of colleges or universities band together to make a joint presentation. For example, the program known as Exploring College Options includes Duke, Georgetown, Harvard, Penn, and Stanford. Carleton,

Bowdoin, Swarthmore, and Pomona Colleges travel together, and the Colleges That Change Lives program includes representatives from schools such as Agnes Scott, Ohio Wesleyan, and St. John's of Maryland. These road shows usually feature short presentations on each school, followed by a Q&A. Students and parents get an overview of a number of institutions instead of in-depth information.

Both types of road shows provide students with an introduction to a school or schools, which they can then follow up on with more research or a visit. And, parents, if you have a student who isn't doing any research, these events are a good place to help him or her get started. You will receive notice of road shows if you are on a college's mailing list, or your high school counselor may inform you in advance.

College Representative Visits

Admission staff from colleges visit high schools throughout the country each year in the fall. Regional representatives meet with interested students in small groups for thirty to forty-five minutes, to answer questions and provide the latest information about their colleges and admission policies.

Check your high school's policy about attendance at these sessions. Most schools allow their seniors and juniors time off to attend. But there may be different requirements. For example, seniors may be required to notify teachers but will be allowed to miss class to attend; juniors may be allowed to attend only if the session occurs during a free period. Your first responsibility is to your academic work.

Check with your counseling department for the college visit schedule.

It's a good idea to do what you can to attend any session for a college in which you have a serious interest. The regional representative may be one of the admission officers who will review your file if you end up applying. In addition, you will have a contact at the college to whom you can address questions in the future. If the college or university is one that considers a student's demonstrated interest, it is important to attend, since your participation may be noted by the representative. Likewise, your absence may be noticed. If you are very interested in a school but cannot attend, leave a note for the representative with your contact information.

STEP 3: MAKE THE MATCH

Step three is easy. In fact, you have already mostly done it. You have started to figure out what you want and need and made a list of those personal priorities. Next, you started to identify some colleges that meet those wants and needs and have matched those schools to your list of priorities. That's the beginning of your initial list!

So how many colleges did you come up with? Fifty? That's too many. Perhaps you could narrow your list by eliminating the colleges that were strong on only one of your priorities but missed on the others. Keep the colleges that connected to several of your priorities.

Are there only five or six on your list? That's not enough at this point.

Remember, there are more than 2,200 colleges and universities. Go back to the reference guides and pick some more that meet at least one or two of your priorities. See if you can get yourself to at least fifteen choices.

It's not just a question of numbers. Make sure your list has lots of variety, particularly with regard to size, location, and private versus public schools. Don't forget that you're still early in the process and don't necessarily know what you will ultimately want. Many students find they don't really understand the ideal match with a college until they set foot on the campus on an actual visit—something we'll discuss in the next chapter.

STEP 4: BALANCE THE LIST

Wait! You're not quite done with your initial list. You must now begin to objectively evaluate your academic record, because it's crucial that the list you develop includes schools you are genuinely interested in but is also realistic about where you can be admitted. What this means is that the schools on your list must span a range of selectivity and cost—how hard it is to be admitted and where you will

Here's a sample note a student might leave for a visiting college representative if unable to attend a session:

Dear [Mr. / Ms.] [dean name],
I am sorry to have to miss your presentation today, because I am very interested in College X. We have a test today in AP Calculus that I cannot miss.
[Your name, email address, phone number, school, and year of graduation]

be able to afford to attend. You now need to examine your list with these characteristics in mind.

Achieving Balance: For Selectivity

While you must consider the selectivity of a school in gauging your admissibility, your *preferences* for schools should never be based on selectivity. "Highly selective" is

If you are a student who has a learning difference or physical or emotional challenge, you will need to make sure your list includes colleges that provide the support and accommodations you require. See Chapter 19 for further information.

not synonymous with "best." Choose your schools based on whether they are right for you. Then factor in your chances of getting

Parents, Don't Drink the Kool-Aid

Parents, this is where we call you in, sit you down, tell it like it is, and hope you find enlightenment. If you have been drinking the Kool-Aid of "My child has to go to Princeton," or if you are using the royal "we" because you really believe "We are applying to . . ."—well, then you are in need of an intervention.

Here is your role in this step of the process: encourage your child to explore broadly and be supportive of your teenager's choices.

The question your son or daughter should be asking is "What kind of a school should I go to?" The answer is his or her choice to make. Your job is to resist the pressure to play the "name game" or chase prestige. The objective at this stage is to have a list with plenty of different schools on it. Don't be afraid if there are choices on that list you think are off-base. It's important your teenager have a list that includes schools he can react to negatively, as well as schools he can react to positively. Those reactions are where the learning happens. So be supportive of all choices at this point. Let him react to these choices and learn. Don't do the reacting for him.

You should feel welcome to participate in the discussion of what kind of school your teenager should consider, especially with regard to affordability, but pause, take a breath, and gauge how much interaction is needed. Some students are going to see any kind of interaction as pressure or intrusion. So tread carefully. Let your teenager take the lead. Other students welcome quite a bit of interaction. Ask questions to draw your student out, and then reflect back what you have observed over the years. For example, on the question of how she learns best, remind her of how much she enjoyed the philosophy seminar where there was a lot of opportunity for discussion among just ten students.

If you're worried about your teenager's motivation, you should make sure she is seeing her high school's guidance counselor, because this is an important step in the process. Email or call the counselor at the high school and say, "I'd like to see Susie have an initial list of colleges. Could you meet with her?" Your teenager may be more motivated than she appears. Honestly, we see far more cases where students need the pressure taken off them.

in to make sure you have a list that will provide you with those choices. We have to say it again: believe us when we tell you that applying to ten of the most selective schools doesn't multiply your chances of getting in by ten.

Your balanced list should be divided into four designations:

1. **Statistical reach.** A school you would like to attend but where your chances of acceptance seem slim. Nevertheless, because each student is a unique individual with assets and abilities that might interest a college, you may want to have some schools that fit into this category. Remember, even students with perfect grades and test scores should consider the most highly selective schools to be statistical reaches. No one's chances of admission at these schools are high.

Understanding Selectivity

"Selectivity" is the term used to describe the level of difficulty of admission. Schools have to be selective when there are too many qualified applicants given the spaces available, so the school selects who will be admitted. You will often hear schools characterized as "most selective," "highly selective," and "selective." The difference is simple: it's just the degree to which there are more applications than there are seats—and that determines how hard it is to get into a school.

These differences in the three types of selectivity are subtle but are nevertheless important to grasp. For example, for the class of 2017, Yale's selectivity was 6.7 percent. That means for every 1,000 applications, there was room for only 67 students—which is 67 out of 1,000. This would place it among the most selective schools. These are the schools where no one can assume he or she will be admitted, no matter how qualified—such as Columbia, Swarthmore, Stanford, and MIT. These are statistical reaches for everyone—no exceptions.

By contrast, Colby College's selectivity was 22 percent for its incoming freshman class of 2017. There was room for 220 out of 1,000 applicants. Tufts University's selectivity was 18.7 percent—under a fifth of those who applied. The selectivity of these schools would place them among the highly selective. Others in this category would include Emory, Notre Dame, UCLA, and Boston College.

Next consider Lewis and Clark College, where the selectivity was 62 percent—there was room for 620 out of 1,000 applicants, or more than half. Lewis and Clark would be considered a selective school. Others might include Baylor, Northeastern, and Syracuse. Does this mean it's easy to get in? Not necessarily. At Northeastern, for example, 75 percent of the entering freshmen for 2013 scored 640 or above on the math SAT; at Lewis and Clark, 75 percent earned a 3.7 high school GPA or above.

With more and more students submitting more and more applications, almost all schools have had to become more selective. In addition, many schools conduct an holistic or comprehensive review, taking into account factors beyond test scores and grades, such as recommendations, extracurricular activities, particular talents, essays, and interviews. (See Chapter 2 for a definition

Understanding Selectivity (continued)

of "comprehensive" or "holistic" review.) The result is that it can be difficult to predict who will be admitted, no matter how great a student's academic record is.

The good news is that many schools accept the majority of their applicants. As we noted in Chapter 1, the vast majority of four-year colleges and universities in the United States—79 percent—accept more than half the students who apply. The average acceptance rate among all schools is still almost 64 percent.[19] In addition, some public universities have very transparent admission standards where if you meet their guidelines for GPA, test scores, or class rank, you will be admitted.

Selectivity information can be found in most reference guidebooks, including the College Board's *College Handbook, Peterson's,* and the *Fiske Guide.* If only raw numbers are given, you may have to calculate the selectivity. It's a simple formula: number of students admitted divided by the number of students who applied.

2. **Possible.** A school where your chances of being rejected are higher than your chances of being accepted. However, some students with credentials like yours have been admitted.
3. **Probable.** A school where your chances of being accepted are better than your chances of being rejected, though there is no guarantee of admission.
4. **Solid.** A school that seldom rejects candidates with your credentials.

Your objective is to have several schools from your list of matches that correspond with each of these categories of selectivity. Don't worry—you don't have to have perfect knowledge of your chances at each school. You're just going to make some informed guesses about where you fit by comparing your GPA and test scores with the most recently available quantitative profile of the college's enrolled freshman class, while taking into account the school's selectivity.

This information can sometimes be found on colleges' websites (look for the freshman class profile or Common Data Set) and in the College Board's *College Handbook* (available at your counselor's office or the library), or with Web tools such as Naviance. (On the college websites, make sure to check the link to the College Counselors or Guidance Counselors section on the admission home page. But you may have to go to multiple sources to obtain GPA and test score information.) Also, keep in mind that this information can lag up to a year and, particularly at the most selective schools, admission statistics can experience a rapid change in just one admission cycle. So note the date of the data you are looking at.

GPAs are most helpful when reported as the percentage of admitted students who fall within given ranges. For example, the freshman profile at highly selective College A (remember this is the category right below "most selective") might look like this:

- GPA 3.75 or higher: 79 percent
- GPA 3.50 to 3.74: 18 percent
- GPA 3.0 to 3.49: 3 percent
- GPA 2.0 to 2.99: 0 percent

SAT and ACT test scores are shown as a range for the middle 50 percent of enrolled freshmen. Here's what that means. The high-end score means 25 percent of accepted freshmen scored higher. The low-end score means 25 percent scored lower. So the middle 50 percent remaining were somewhere in between.

So let's say College A is a selective school where the middle 50 percent range for Critical Reading on the SAT is 660 to 740. If your scores are well above 740 and your GPA is in the top reported range for that class, College A would be a probable or a solid school on your list.

Note that this is true for a selective college, but not necessarily for a highly selective college, and certainly not for the most selective. Here's why. In an incoming freshman class of 1,000, the profile shows 67 percent of the class—670 students—had a 4.0 GPA (this is hypothetical). Students looking at that statistic may conclude that if they have a 4.0 they are in good shape. But what that statistic doesn't tell you is that thousands upon thousands of students with a 4.0 GPA applied, and the vast majority of them were not accepted. The small minority who were accepted, and the fraction of that minority who

then opted to attend, are the 670 students they're talking about. Such a college would be a statistical reach for all applicants.

The analysis you are going to do at this point is crude, not least because in addition to the above considerations, your evaluation does not take into account the rigor of a high school's academic program, the impact of special circumstances such as a particular talent or geographical desirability, or any of the additional factors considered in a comprehensive review. Nevertheless, this is a good starting point for balancing your initial list with regard to selectivity.

If you find that you don't have a well-balanced list after completing this analysis, then you will have to circle back and do some more research. If you feel you need some guidance at this point, your high school college counselor or guidance counselor can be very helpful in assembling a balanced list. They understand colleges' selectivity and the combination of factors schools are considering; most important, they know the history of students from your high school who have applied to various schools.

Figuring out where you fit into a college's profile is more complicated for students who do not have a high school college counselor or who attend schools where most students do not go on to college. You will have to make your own estimates by doing more research, studying the data closely, and seeking guidance about where former students from your high school have been admitted from sources such as your principal or guidance department.

Achieving Balance: For Cost

If you are lucky enough not to have to worry about paying for college, you can skip this section. But if you are like the majority of families, cost can be a significant factor in your decision about where to attend college. Paying for a college education is a complex subject, which we will cover at length in Chapter 16. Right now, we are simply addressing how to balance a preliminary list of schools with cost in mind.

At this point in the process, do not rule out any college on the basis of cost. Financial aid exists to remove cost as a factor in your decision—leave room for that to happen. Many of the most expensive schools can potentially be less costly to attend than the public university in your state because of strong financial aid programs. Nevertheless, if potential expense is an issue, it's a good idea to make sure the colleges on your list span the cost spectrum.

Including your in-state college or university is the key step to a balanced list. But there are other steps you can take, too—and when it comes to financial aid, it's never too early to start learning about what is a very complex and very important topic. A good next step is to use the financial aid calculator—also called net price calculator—for each school on your list. This online tool will give you a preliminary understanding of the amount you may be expected to pay out of pocket, as well as any aid you may be eligible to receive from the federal government and the colleges themselves.

Financial aid calculators can be found at the colleges' websites and the College Board at collegeboard.org. The Federal Student Aid website at fafsa4caster.ed.gov provides information about eligibility for federal aid, such as Stafford loans and work-study, as well as a family's expected contribution. The results—the cost to you and the aid you may receive—may differ fairly significantly from calculator to calculator and from college to college. See Chapter 16 for a full explanation of financial aid calculators.

Finally, look into schools with strong merit-based financial aid programs. For some, you may not know in advance whether you qualify. Others have clearly defined awards; for example, $10,000 per year if your GPA is 3.5. Look for information on merit aid on the school's website.

> Any students for whom cost is a concern should include their in-state college or university on their preliminary list of schools. These schools will cost less simply because your family's tax dollars are already helping to pay for them. You should still apply for financial aid at these schools if the cost seems higher than you believe you can afford.

Your List Is Done!

And now that you've got a list, you're ready to move on to the next step in figuring out where you will apply for admission—the college visit.

CHAPTER 9

College Visits

"Colleges and universities are a lot like students in that they can be, in some sense, defined by numbers. But there are characteristics of spirit and personality and texture that you can't judge by sterile measures. You've got to visit. Figure out a way to do it."

—Jon Boeckenstedt, associate vice president for enrollment management, DePaul University

The college road trip is a time-honored ritual—it has even been the inspiration for a Disney movie. This annual tradition offers students the chance to try on a college and see if it fits. For parents, it can be an important step in the letting-go process. It is also one of the most important influences in determining where students will eventually apply.

By walking through the classrooms, libraries, and dining halls of a campus and meeting the people there, students get a feel for the personality and "vibe" of a college—and learn more about what they want and don't want in a school. Virtual tours, blogs, and view books are great resources, but they are no substitute for firsthand observation in

helping students fine-tune a list of prospective schools. Parents get to come along for the ride and get a closer look at the particulars of the considerable investment they are about to make in their son's or daughter's education.

Time, distance, and cost are all considerations for families making college visits. Students and parents should sit down in advance and decide together how much time and money can be devoted to visits. In general, try to see all of the colleges on your list where you think you will eventually apply—to make sure you in fact would want to attend, but also because a visit will help you write a better application. Not all students will have the resources to visit—we have some guidance for you, too, if you can't walk the quad of every school on your list.

PREPARING YOUR TRIP

When Do You Start?

Most students will begin making official visits to the colleges on their preliminary lists in the spring of junior year or the summer before senior year of high school. Stepping onto the campuses of a variety of schools will help you get an idea of what is important to you. Sitting in an information session, talking with students, or browsing in the campus bookstore provides students with a hands-on experience that will do more than anything else to help them eventually narrow down their list of prospective schools.

But your first visits don't have to be "official." If your family is taking a vacation, add a college to the itinerary. Or tag along on a business trip with your mother or father and visit a campus together when the meetings are over. Even if you're just driving through campus or attending a football game, try to stop by the admission office to pick up information and let them know you're visiting.

Also, you don't have to venture far. Visits to *any* campus can help you zero in on what's important to you. So take the tour at one or two colleges within driving distance of home, even if you aren't considering applying there. Experience a group information session and a tour so that you get a sense of what a visit is like and what you most enjoyed—or disliked—about your time on campus. These "practice" visits will help you make good firsthand evaluations later, when you visit the colleges you are most interested in attending.

You don't need to visit every college on your preliminary list. Visits to a few well-chosen campuses will provide enough information to help shape your list. But do visit enough schools to get a sense of college life at each of the different types of campuses on your list—the large research university and small liberal arts college, urban and rural campuses, and public or private schools.

Before You Hit the Road

First, do some preplanning:

- Check your high school's policy about time off to visit colleges.
- Review your preliminary list of colleges. Browse their websites to refamiliarize yourself with the schools and take the virtual tour.
- Find out if there are alumni from your high school who are attending the colleges where you will visit, and get their contact information. Consider an overnight stay with one of them.
- Check the college website or call the admission office to find out what opportunities they offer prospective students on campus and whether you have to sign up in advance. Do this as early as possible. Most colleges offer some combination of the following opportunities:
  - **Group information sessions.** In these sessions, an admission officer will provide an overview of the college, including the school's history, academic programs, undergraduate life, athletics, the application process, and financial aid. Offered by most schools throughout the year, info sessions last at least an hour and include a Q&A session for students and parents.
  - **Campus tours.** Walking tours of the college usually follow the information session. Led by students, they typically last up to an hour and a half and take place rain or shine . . . or blizzard. Make sure you wear comfortable clothing and

Advice for Underresourced or First-Generation Applicants

Setting foot on college campuses is especially critical for underresourced students or those who are the first in their family to attend college—the same students who might have the most difficult time managing to visit. Such students may start visiting colleges as early as freshman year through tours arranged by their high school or as part of an enrichment program. If you are unable to visit the schools on your list before applying, you will have to use every other resource available to research them—virtual tours, the college website, local alumni, current students, and faculty (admission offices can often set up these contacts for you). Then make every effort to visit once you have been admitted. Let the admission office know if a school is high on your list but you are unable to make a trip there. More and more colleges are offering to subsidize transportation costs for admitted students or sponsor fly-in programs to bring low-income or underrepresented students onto campus.

shoes—*appropriate* comfortable clothing and shoes. These tours provide a general overview of the campus. If you are interested in touring colleges' art studios, science labs, or other specialized facilities, you will likely have to arrange a special tour or walk over to that department and look around on your own.
  - **Overnight stays.** Some schools provide prospective applicants with the opportunity to make an overnight visit, staying with current students in the dorm, eating in the

dining hall, and attending some classes. There are usually a limited number of these opportunities, and they may be confined to seniors or admitted students.

- **Interviews.** If the school offers interviews, find out if appointments are available during your visit. See Chapter 11 for more information about interviews.

- **Class visits.** Many admission offices will arrange for a prospective student to sit in on a class and/or meet with faculty members. Lists of available classes to visit can usually be found online.

- **Shadow programs.** Being a "college student for a day" by shadowing a current student—attending class, meeting with professors, and hanging out at the student union—provides prospective applicants with an inside look at campus life at some schools. Shadow days are usually limited to high school juniors and seniors.

- **Specialized tours and visits.** In addition to general campus tours, some schools offer introductory visits for first-generation college students, in-depth tours for students studying specific subjects such as the sciences or engineering, informal student forums, and daylong host programs for families of prospective students. Check the colleges' websites to learn about special programs. And get yourself on the colleges' mailing lists so that you are sent invitations to programs appropriate for you.

Now, look at scheduling:

- Take out your preliminary list of colleges and begin to create itineraries by grouping the schools by geographic region. To the extent possible, schedule your solid and probable schools first. Don't miss visiting the schools in which you are most interested and those where you are most likely to be accepted.

- In scheduling, minimize missed class time by visiting when your high school is not in session—during spring break or summer vacation. Remember, your academic record is the most important part of your application.

- Don't schedule more than two college visits on any one day. If a long drive is involved, you will be able to see only one campus. Providing for some downtime to wander the campus or the surrounding area after the info session and tour is a good idea as well. These trips—the travel itself, the long walks, sitting through info sessions—can be exhausting.

- Spring break of junior year in high school and the summer between junior and senior year are the most popular times to schedule visits. If possible, try to visit when the college is in session. We understand this may be difficult as you juggle classes, sports, and the spring prom. Just be aware that a campus may feel different when the majority of students aren't present. Once you've been admitted, you can revisit when the college is in session.

- With some dates in mind for visits, check the website of each of the colleges you plan to visit to obtain dates and times for tours, information sessions, interview availability, and so on. Make a reservation if required. Do this as far in advance as possible so you can get a spot on a date that works for your family. Some schools may not require you to reserve a space for info sessions or tours but ask you to let them know in advance that you're attending. Do this.

- If the college requires or strongly suggests an applicant interview, arrange an appointment for when you are on campus. There are usually a limited number of time slots for interviews, available on a first-come, first-served basis. Most colleges will not interview students prior to their junior year in high school. See more about interviews in Chapter 11.

Keep track of interviews using the worksheets in Appendix III, which are also available as download-able Excel and Word documents on our website at collegeadmissionbook.com.

- Consider seeing if you can make an appointment with the financial aid department if cost is a concern.
- Sign up for any special opportunities that are of interest, such as in-depth tours for engineering or arts students.
- If you would like to talk with someone directly involved with an area in which you have a strong interest, such as a faculty member in mathematics or a coach for a sport, arrange a meeting through the admission office. Make these special requests well in advance of your visit date.
- Schedule *all* appointments with the schools before finalizing your travel plans.
- Once the logistics are worked out, print out directions for each destination, and download campus maps from the colleges' websites. Believe us when we tell you that, even armed with maps, it will take longer to find the admission office—and a parking spot—than you think it will.
- Confirm your visit with the college one week

before arrival—by email or with a quick phone call to the admission office.

Parents, we know that you often act as travel agent for these trips. It's fine for you to make the hotel reservations and purchase the plane tickets—although this might be a great time for students to learn how to plan and manage travel. But make sure your son or daughter decides where you are going and what you will see. Creating your college visit itinerary can be a family conversation, but the student, as with so many steps in this process, should take the lead.

What to Do If Time and Money Are Considerations

While extremely important, visits are not a possibility for every applicant. Consider the following strategies if scheduling and cost prevent you from visiting or if you must be selective about the schools you will visit:

- Visit online. Many schools offer online tours via their websites. In addition, Campus Tours at campustours.com has virtual tours, interactive maps, webcams, and video of college campuses. Their database includes thousands of colleges and universities.
- If you have to pick and choose which campuses to visit, make seeing the solid schools where you are most likely to be admitted a priority.
- If you can visit only once, visit after you've been admitted—but before you enroll. A visit after you have been accepted can be the most productive way to see a campus. The question you're asking yourself isn't prefaced by "If I

The "Aha!" Moment and Following Your "Gut Instinct"

"Can I see myself here?" That is the question students should be asking throughout their college visits. Some of you, after several stops on your college trip, may have an "aha!" moment—where you step onto a campus and say, "Yes! This feels just right." Others may get to the end of their college visits and worry about why they haven't found one that feels like the place they *have* to be.

Don't worry if you don't have that "aha!" moment. For some kids, lightning doesn't strike when they walk across a campus quad. They just have a different temperament, and they will find their niche. If, on the other hand, you're a student who feels things passionately and none of the colleges you've visited really grabs you, wait a few months and try another group of schools. Then try to figure out if it's the time that you visited or the kinds of schools you were seeing. Try to see some patterns and make sense of your reactions.

But while you're making your college visits, be sure to give yourself permission to feel a "gut instinct" about a school. It might surface as an impression, an insight, or an emotion. It might be positive—one student described it as a general feeling of excitement about going to college as she explored the campus. Or it could be negative—that "icky" feeling you got because there were so many cigarette butts on the ground. You're intuitively evaluating a college, taking in the positive and negative messages it sends: how well the admission officer listens, what the students are wearing, the organic munchie mart in the humanities building, the posters in the student union.

Parents will sometimes see your gut instinct as irrational, as in "What do you mean, you can't go to this school because the buildings are too far apart?" In retrospect, parents—including deans of admission who have been through the application process with their own children—look back on those gut reactions their children had and realize how important it is to honor them. While they might have wished for a process that was entirely rational—"I want to go to a liberal arts school with a good classics department"—what was most important was that their son or daughter could see themselves sitting in a classroom, having dinner with friends in the dining hall, and playing Frisbee on the lawn.

So trust your instincts. But also keep an open mind. Get beyond the name, reputation, or idea in your head about a school. Let yourself experience the place and the people on a campus and you might come away surprised—both positively and negatively. With no expectations, you might find a place where you feel most at home. Or, arriving with lots of expectations, you might find that a school just doesn't feel right.

Try not to let one bad experience, such as a blizzard or a pretentious tour guide, turn you off entirely. That one experience on one day may not be an accurate reflection of what it's like to live and learn there for four years. And if you feel excited about a school despite a poorly trained guide or subzero temperatures, then pay attention. You might want to move that school to the top of your list.

get in . . ." Instead, it's "I can go here if I want. Is this the right place for me?" The pressure is off—you're in!—and the college is wooing you.

- Schools understand that not all students may be able to visit, and it should not have a negative impact on your application. However, if you live within a reasonable driving distance, the college may expect you to visit. A campus visit is often considered an indication of demonstrated interest—a quality considered in the admission decisions of some schools. If you don't show up on a nearby campus, they may think you're not seriously interested.

ON CAMPUS

Once you're on campus, pay attention to your surroundings. Are the residence halls pleasant? Clean? You may be living in them for the next four years. What about the library? Again, you could be spending a lot of time there. Is it easy to get online? Do the science labs look like they're up to date and in good condition? Is there a fitness center? What's the surrounding community like? Does it feel safe? How do the students look? Are they dressed up or wearing sweats and flip-flops?

While you're collecting impressions, don't forget to listen for the story the school is telling about itself. Is the admission officer talking about values, programs, and priorities that resonate with who you are and who you want to be? Listen critically. As you sit in the info session and tour campus, test your assumptions and make your own assessments. Is this a place where you can see yourself, but also where you will be challenged by your peers and the faculty to stretch and grow?

Your job on a college visit is to speak to as many people as possible. That way you will get your questions answered from a range of perspectives, learn the school's story, and be able to determine whether that story is consistent. Do the admission officer in the info session and the student in the bookstore *both* tell you that there is a lot of interaction between faculty and students? If you're getting contradictory messages, you'll want to collect more opinions.

Questions for Admission Officers

Admission officers are the best resources for answers to specific questions about the application process, as well as information about a college's mission and future plans. They will also be able to provide you with answers about most aspects of daily life on campus—academics, housing, special programs such as study-abroad opportunities, and athletics. Don't be afraid to have them address broader queries about the who, what, and why of the campus. Here are some questions you may want to ask:

- What impresses you the most in a student's application?
- What are you looking for when you read students' essays?

What *Not* to Bring on a College Visit

Email from a father on the college road trip: "I am writing this during the info session at Cornell. A new low has been achieved. A kid with a dirty T-shirt, baggy shorts, and sandals has brought his dog. A giant, panting, slobbering black Lab."

- What are some of the things you hate to see in an application?
- Is demonstrated interest a factor in your admission decision?
- Are admission decisions need-blind?
- What kind of student does well here? What kind of student doesn't do well here?
- Did you attend this college? What has changed since you've been here?
- What changes do you see taking place on campus in the next five years?
- What are recent alumni doing?
- What do you think your school is best known for?
- How would you describe the typical student here?
- How does the school help freshmen adjust to college?
- How is academic advising handled?
- Are there on-campus jobs available for students?
- How are roommates assigned?
- What is the Internet situation? Is the entire campus wireless? Do you support Macs or PCs?
- How do meal plans work?

- How much of a role does the surrounding community play in students' daily life?
- What kind of opportunities are there for students to participate in research or internships?

Questions for Tour Guides

Tour guides are almost always current students and, though usually well trained, will have a different perspective than the admission office. Tour guides are usually happy to talk about their personal experiences. In fact, they are trained to answer your questions honestly—for example, if you ask them what they did last night, they won't tell you they were at the library if they were at a frat party.

It's in a college's best interest to be honest about who their students are because they want you to make the best match with a school. However, remember that the tour guide may not be like you, or in some cases may be poorly trained and not have adequate information about specifics such as computer support. With those caveats in mind, though, ask away as you walk the campus.

- Why did you decide to go to school here?
- What was your biggest surprise about the school?
- What would you change about the school?
- What do students do on the weekend here?
- What do people do outside the classroom?
- Are there opportunities to participate in community service?
- What's the teacher-student ratio? Are faculty members interested in students outside of class?
- How do you spend time with faculty outside the classroom?

Making Your College Trip a Great Experience for Your Family

The ritual of the college road trip can be a crucial part of the letting-go process for students and parents. Make the most of this time. Many parents say that these trips are highlights of their relationship with their sons or daughters. How can you make that happen for you?

First and foremost, read our lips—it's the student! There is a role for parents as observers and sounding boards. You're there to support your teen and help her interpret her reactions. But the student should be the decision maker on all things, from which colleges to visit to when to stop at Starbucks. Part of the magic here is in recognizing that one of these colleges is going to be your teenager's world, not yours. So act like a helpful houseguest the whole time. It will be enjoyable because it's appropriate. Your son or daughter will be grateful and may respond by rising to the occasion. Here's some more advice for surviving—and thriving—on the road.

- Do support your teen's choices about where and when to visit colleges.
- Don't get territorial. Traveling in close quarters can cause friction. Apply our first rule here, too, by letting the student pick the music in the car, the TV shows in the hotel room, and the restaurants where you eat.
- Do leave the siblings at home if possible. The trip is about your college-bound teen, and she is anxious. Leaving siblings at home will enable a student to explore a campus in depth to determine if she will thrive there.
- Don't go to war with a student over attending an info session or tour if his gut instinct tells him this college isn't going to stay on the list—even if it's just ten minutes after you've driven onto campus.
- Do make your student keep any interview appointments that have been set up even if she's vetoed the tour. It's common courtesy.
- Do encourage your teenager to give a school another chance if he otherwise really likes a college but has found the personality of a single human being—such as a surly receptionist—to be off-putting.
- Do let the student do the talking at the info session, on the tour, and during any downtime on campus.
- Don't use the question-and-answer session to brag about your teenager's accomplishments. The admission officer is not taking notes.
- Do let students—*all* students, not just your son or daughter—go first with their questions. Feel free to make your own inquiries about campus safety, Internet access, or season football tickets, but only *after* it is clear that no student is going to ask these questions.
- Do consider taking a separate tour from the one your teenager is on, if possible. Or let him wander campus alone after the official tour. It may provide a comfort zone for her to ask questions or strike up conversations she otherwise wouldn't.

Making Your College Trip a Great Experience for Your Family

(continued)

- Don't monopolize the tour guide's time. Stay to the back of the group and let the students speak to the tour guide between stops. That's a time when they can ask more personal questions about campus social life or the economics department.

- Do treat *all* the students in the tour group as the tour's "priority." Let all the students walk first into that cramped dorm room to take a look around.

- Don't ask the tour guide what he scored on the SAT. He will not tell you.

- Don't tell the tour guide the number of APs your son takes, his test scores, and his grades, and then ask her to weigh in on his chances of admission. She does not know!

- Do turn your cell phone off.

- Do think about a budget for the big impulse buys of the college road trip—T-shirts and hoodies. Really, what are you going to do with all of them?

- Do remind your son or daughter that the right school is out there and they will discover each other.

"Yes, we have another question. We really like it here, but we're concerned about how many APs we need. Also, when can we expect to hear about our scholarships? And where are good places for us to hang out on weekends?"

And, students, here's some advice for you: lighten up! Every gesture or comment that your parent makes isn't nearly as awful to everybody else as it is embarrassing to you. Do not scold, roll your eyes at, or pick a fight with your parents at any time during or after the information session or tour. Cut your parents a break. It's only fair.

- How big are classes? Do students participate a lot in the classroom?

- What are the athletic facilities like and are they available to all students?

- Are the residence halls places where people study . . . or party? Are they coed? Are there single-sex options? Are there laundry and kitchen facilities available?

- How is the food?

- Do students stay on campus or get involved in activities in the surrounding area?

- Do most students stay on campus on the weekends?

- What type of student is most comfortable here?

- What's a typical student like?

- Is the campus considered safe at night? Is transportation available if you are studying late at the library?
- What is the school's alcohol and drug policy?
- Are introductory classes taught by faculty or grad students?

Getting Off the Beaten Track

Whenever you are serious about a school, make sure you spend some unscheduled time on campus. Walk around, look at the buildings, check out the bulletin boards to see what's happening on campus, pick up the student newspaper—and the alternative newspaper—and visit the study spaces in the library. As you wander the pathways, notice: Do students and faculty look up and say hello? Do the students look happy? Have you seen any faculty out and about with students? Even half an hour spent familiarizing yourself with the campus can be very helpful.

Questions for Current Students

You got the admission office perspective at the info session and on the tour, but don't forget to get the unofficial perspective during

Visiting the Financial Aid Office

If cost is a concern for your family, consider stopping by the financial aid office on your visit. Having a contact in the financial aid office can be a good idea as you move forward. But first check the college's website or email the financial aid office to see if they are able to accommodate visiting students and their families. While some colleges encourage families to stop by and may even have open hours for visiting students and parents, other colleges may not be as well staffed and won't be able to sit down one-on-one. If you aren't able to see someone in financial aid, feel welcome to ask the admission officer in your info session to answer any questions you may have.

But before you even arrive on campus, go to the financial aid section of the college's website and do some basic research. Look for the following:

- The total cost of attendance for one year and what it includes
- Types of financial assistance available
- When and how to apply
- The availability of need-based and merit aid

Once you're on campus, here are some of the questions you might want to ask:

- What percentage of students receive grant aid?
- What is the average indebtedness of a graduating senior?
- What percent of admitted students have their financial need met fully?
- Will a student receiving aid be asked to have employment over the summer?

See Chapter 16 for more information on financial aid.

Making the Most of Your Visit

"What's your best advice about where to get off the beaten path while on a college visit?" We asked a group of admission deans this question. Here are the answers.

JESS LORD

Dean of admission and financial aid, Haverford College

➡ The traditional tour and spiel being packaged and presented by a college has its value. But to really test that and push it, it is absolutely key for students to seek out what the consistent message is from an institution by asking the same question over and over again of different people.

That's essentially what we're doing in the college application process. We don't base our admission decision on one piece of information. We look for the consistent message of the whole application. So students should be looking for the consistent message of the whole institution. Whatever it is that a college asserts about itself—for example, that the school is a warm and friendly place or that academics are rigorous but noncompetitive—you should be asking both admission people and people outside the admission office the same questions about that message.

See how people answer and note the similarities. Then you will get a sense of what is true about a place and what the common experience is for a variety of people. And it also gives you the broader perspective when you hear the different ways that people experience those same qualities or attributes. You might even get some negative responses that will be helpful.

So go have lunch in the dining hall, get in touch with faculty and arrange a short fifteen-minute conversation, go to the library. It takes being a little bit extroverted, but you could also do this via email if you're too shy to approach people on campus or are unable to visit. Nowadays it's easy for students to do this kind of outreach and connect.

PHILIP A. BALLINGER

Assistant vice president for enrollment and undergraduate admissions, University of Washington, Seattle

➡ Get off the beaten track before you even get to campus by seeing what students and faculty are saying about the school on the Web. This may help you determine things you want to focus on or be concerned about during your actual visit. There are all sorts of websites and blogs that aren't connected to the admission office. See what faculty members and current students are saying—or not saying. When you're on campus, go on the official tour, but also consider some of the resources institutions provide that enable you to do your own thing. Sit in on classes, attend a cultural or sporting event, eat the food. If permitted, visiting current students that you know, as well as their friends and dorm mates, is a good idea, too. If an institution is extremely restrictive about allowing you to "do your own thing," find out why. If it's a matter of safety or student privacy, okay. But if it's a matter of controlling visitors' perceptions, wonder why.

ARLENE CASH

Vice provost for enrollment management, University of the Pacific

➡ The official and traditional student-led tour will always give you the basic lay of the land at any college, and I strongly suggest your taking advantage of this resource. Ask your tour guide about his or her favorite professor, favorite study spot, the best-kept secret about the campus and campus life. Schedule time to walk around campus unescorted as well. Visit the campus center, where you can get a real sense of the community. Do you see the kind of diversity among the students you'd expect? Is there interaction or are people just walking through? Look at the bulletin boards to get a sense of on-campus activities, service initiatives, internships, and job offerings. Also visit academic buildings to get an idea of student-faculty interaction. It's one thing to have a low student-faculty ratio, quite another for faculty to actually show up for office hours and have students stop by. See if you are allowed to sit in on a class, and if so, definitely do that. Most students I work with say that they know if a campus is for them within the first five minutes after getting out of the car. Honor that gut feeling and take a moment to stop and reflect on how the campus feels to you before getting back into the car and heading off to the next school. Keep a journal and record your impressions. They tend to meld after a few visits.

KEITH TODD

Dean of admission, Reed College

➡ When a student visits campus, from our point of view, we want to present both an attractive and honest view of what we have to offer. Obviously, our admission office is promoting our college, but we try to do it in a way that reflects reality as well, because we don't want to attract students who aren't going to stay. But if you just come to the show, so to speak, you are missing out. It may not tell you the whole story if you're really concerned about fit or if you really want to get to know the place beyond that. Those students who are willing to explore places and talk to people beyond the admission office may get more out of their campus visit.

So get beyond the physical look of a place. Think about what's happening inside the buildings. Ask questions about the course work and the accessibility of professors. Go hang out in the student center. You'll be surprised how many students will be willing to talk to you. That's a good start. But I wish visiting prospective students would also ask more about the nature of campus life. What is it like to be in this residential community? Are students really active? How do they participate? How do they have a voice within the college? By doing so, visitors get a chance to see more of what our students are like, and that's often a key factor in the final decision about where to go.

JON BOECKENSTEDT

Associate vice president for enrollment management, DePaul University

➡ There are always embedded clues to be found on a college visit. Here's an example: If you take a tour on a Friday afternoon, is the library crowded or empty? Now, there's no right or wrong way for a library to be on a Friday afternoon. But if you're the kind of student who is always studying and is really driven by grades and you see no one in the library on Friday afternoon because they're all at a cookout, that says something. If you're the kind of kid who's going to say college is as much a social experience as an academic experience and the library is jam-packed on a Friday afternoon or Saturday night, then that college might not be the kind of place you want to go.

Look at things like posters in the student center. Is Glenn Beck on campus? Or Maya Angelou? What about politics? Social action? Athletics? Can you pick up on things that aren't part of the official spiel and tour? Look at the students. If a college or university says it's really diverse but all you see are white faces around campus, that may say something to you. If a college says it's well known for science but you don't see much activity in the science labs and science is important to you, factor that into the equation. Have a healthy skepticism about what you see, as opposed to immediately buying into it.

your downtime on campus. The best way to do that is to talk to current students who aren't on the admission office "payroll." Conquer any shyness and strike up a conversation with the girl studying on the quad or the guy in line at the bookstore. Your opening line can be as simple as "I'm visiting because I might apply to come here. Mind if I ask you something?" Get some candid responses to questions such as these:

- Why did you decide to go to school here?
- When students stay up late talking in the dorm, what do they talk about? What classes have interested you the most?
- How much time do you spend studying? Where do you study?
- How hard is it to get the classes you need?
- Do students get along well with each other?
- Why do students like the school?
- What are the drawbacks to going to school here?
- Who fits in here and who doesn't?
- If you could change anything about this school, what would it be?
- How much time do students spend studying?
- How do you meet people on campus?
- What is the social life like on campus?
- What do you like most about the school?
- What was freshman year like? How difficult was the transition?

PROCESSING WHAT YOU LEARNED FROM YOUR VISIT

Evaluating and Documenting the Visit

By now it's probably clear why we recommend you don't schedule more than two college visits a day. There is a lot of information to take in—as well as a lot of hiking across campuses. You may think you will remember which school had the great language labs, vegan cafeteria, or varsity badminton. But trust us, after a while it can all become a blur—especially a few weeks after you return home.

Start to evaluate your visit while the school is still fresh in your mind. Immediately after a visit, try to articulate exactly why you liked a school—or didn't. Pinpoint the factors that provoked a positive—or negative—reaction. Explore any doubts you experienced. If you felt excited about the prospect of attending the school, try to figure out exactly where and when that happened on campus.

Parents, keep in mind that it may take your child some time to process all that he's seen. Just ask your son or daughter some simple questions: "What did you like and why? What didn't you like and why?" Remember to keep it a conversation. It shouldn't be an interrogation.

Listen to your teenager and then mirror back to her what you are hearing. If your daughter found the campus impersonal, suggest that it sounds like she might prefer smaller liberal arts schools. Not only will this help the student remember what's important about a college, but it can also help begin narrowing down the list of prospective schools.

In addition to spending some time evaluating your visit, fix it in your mind by documenting it! If you're the kind of person who enjoys recording your experiences, then have at it with notebooks, pictures, video, Twitter, and expanding files for all the handouts in the admission office. But it doesn't have to be a major project. Here are some suggestions for remembering that on Tuesday it was Haverford and on Thursday it was Hamilton:

- Bring along a digital camera and take pictures. Make the first picture a shot of a building or sign with the college name. Create captions for more detail.
- Take pictures, video, or notes with your phone when there is something you feel you want to remember.
- Bring along a notebook and jot down your impressions. Include any photos you take.
- If you're a list maker, create a list of the characteristics (dorms, athletics, labs) or preferences (Mideast studies major, study abroad program, Greek system) that are priorities for you. Use it as a checklist for each school. One student simply listed her preferences and then put a smiley face next to each of the aspects of the college that met her criteria. Checklists are often available through your high school's online portal program or at websites such as College Prowler at colleges.niche.com.
- Put a stack of index cards in your luggage for taking notes at the end of the day. Or use the "notes" option on your phone or in one of the online programs or websites.
- Collect business cards and email addresses from the admission office, financial aid, students, and any faculty or coaches with whom you meet. Staple them to your note cards or in your notebook.

- But don't be such an obsessive documenter that you don't really experience the college!

Whatever method you choose to document your visit, do it the same day you were on campus! Don't wait or you won't remember. Then look your notes over every time you visit a campus to help you see more clearly what characteristics are shaping up to connote the best match for you in a school.

Should You Visit More than Once?

Ideally, you will be able to visit your top choices a second time after you are admitted—if you can afford both the cost and the time away from your studies. A second visit will afford a much more in-depth view. You can change a lot in the months between your first visit and an acceptance letter, and we'll talk about this more in Chapter 17. Visiting again may prevent you from second-guessing your decision about attending a school.

If you are considering applying to a college under a binding early decision program, we recommend you visit a second time in the fall of senior year before sending in your application. Spend the night on campus if possible and sit in on some classes. It's important to be as certain as possible because if you are admitted, you must attend. (We'll talk more about the timing of your application in Chapter 15.) Once you are accepted under an early decision program, we recommend you also attend any on-campus programs for admitted students in the spring of senior year so you arrive on campus the following fall feeling as comfortable as possible.

Questions You May Have

What if I can't get a reservation for a tour but am going to be on campus?

Most college websites have self-guided tours available—just download and explore the campus on your own. There are also iPhone apps with self-guided tours for many colleges. Even if you were unable to get a reservation for an official tour, make sure that you visit the admission office while you're on campus and ask again if there is room on the tour. They may be able to squeeze you in. If not, fill out a visitor card with your contact information. That way they will know you made the effort to visit.

Will visiting a school increase a student's chances of admission?

It could—at colleges that consider demonstrated interest in making their admission decision. At such schools, your visit may be noted and possibly included in a formula used in determining admission. However, schools may not be candid about calculating demonstrated interest into their decision. Also, at some colleges, it may be that when they're reading the application file, they notice that a candidate who lives locally didn't bother to come in for an interview. They may assume you aren't seriously interested in their school. The best policy is to visit any school that is high on your list if it is within driving distance. Colleges recognize, however, that not all families have the resources to visit far-away colleges. If that's the case for your family, don't worry that it will hurt your prospects.

Are organized tour groups a good idea for students?

Commercially organized tours of college campuses may be worthwhile if that is the easiest way for you to visit schools. But buyer beware! These tours can cost thousands of dollars, and the problems with them are the same as those you would encounter when going on a group tour for a vacation. You will have a group experience that is less tailored to your needs, and you will be reliant on the guide, who will decide, for example, when you will leave a campus—even if you are in the middle of a conversation with a current student. In addition, some of these guides may know something about college admission—but not all of them will. Check out your guide and the tour company before leaning on them for expertise that goes beyond scheduling the trip itself. It's not a reason to forgo a commercially organized tour. It's simply a situation to be aware of if you do sign up.

CHAPTER 10

Turning Your Initial List into Your Application List: The Eight to Ten Colleges Where You Will Apply

"If you've done your homework, you should have several first choices—places where you can thrive academically and socially."

—Jim Bock, dean of admissions, Swarthmore College

Now it's time to make some hard decisions and fine-tune your initial list of prospective colleges, turning it into the list of schools where you will actually apply.

Is there a magic number of schools for an application list? No. What you should aim for is a list that allows you to do a good job in applying to a group of schools that will provide you with options—not unpleasant surprises—in the spring of your senior year.

THIS LIST IS TOO SMALL.
THIS LIST IS TOO BIG.
WHAT LIST IS JUST RIGHT?

One of the perennial scare stories in college admission is that students are commonly applying to fifteen, twenty, or even thirty

schools. In fact, less than 5 percent of students apply to more than ten schools.[20] The right number of schools will actually be different for every one of you. Our best advice? An optimal application list for most students will have eight to ten colleges.

We know some students may apply to fewer than eight schools or more than ten—sometimes for good reasons and other times out of bad judgment. But straying from the optimal guidelines can be problematic. If you're going to do that, know that there are some hard outer limits that you ignore at your own risk.

If you just can't come up with the optimal minimum of eight schools on your application list, please come up with at least six.

Below that, either you don't have your bases covered or you are not stretching to give yourself the possibilities all students deserve. In order to have options at the end of the application process, your list of schools must cover a range of selectivity and—if finances are a consideration—cost. A list with fewer than six schools can't adequately accomplish this. We'll talk about how to cover your bases in the next section of this chapter.

On the other hand, if you just can't help yourself and feel compelled to go beyond the optimal upper limit of ten schools, you will hurt yourself if your application list becomes larger than twelve. You won't be able to get to know each school well enough to know whether you'll like it or—just as important—to communicate to an admission office why you're a good fit. Remember, many schools require individual supplements to the Common Application that can consist of additional lengthy essays or a number of short-response questions. These demand time, care, and energy if they are going to be thoughtful and persuasive. And if you need yet another reason to stay within the guidelines, consider that there's one more application fee every time you hit the "Submit" button.

What if you don't invest time and effort on the front end of this process—that is, you don't create a list with a reasonable number of schools that you've researched well and would like to attend? Then you're running two risks—the risk of not being admitted and the risk of being admitted to schools you may not even like.

 Best Advice

High School Counselors Weigh In on Lists That Are Just Right

Too few? Too many? How do you build your best application list? Some high school counselors offer their thoughts.

ALICE KLEEMAN

College advisor, Menlo-Atherton High School, Atherton, California

➡ I'm more concerned about which schools are on the list than I am about how many. Applying to twelve colleges, for example, none of which is realistic, hoping that the sheer number will give the student a higher chance of being admitted, is folly.

Choosing to do the work on the far end—waiting to tackle the thoughtful winnowing until after being admitted, rather than crafting an appropriate list on the front end—strikes me as somewhat lazy. Are there colleges on the list that are there for the wrong reasons? Trophy hunting? Someone else's agenda? A sense of "I might as well?" A student's college list—of any size—should foremost be thoughtful and appropriate to the individual student.

MELANIE CHOUKRANE

Director of college counseling, Grace Church School, New York, New York

➡ You get too many schools on a final list because there are too many fingers in the pot, families aren't being honest about their intentions, and parents underestimate the amount of work needed to prepare a great application. You get to more than eight or nine schools because people aren't realistic and those lists are top-heavy with the most selective schools. A final list with too many schools risks unnecessary disappointment that can overshadow the good news and skew how the month of April will feel.

ALIZA GILBERT

College counselor, Highland Park High School, Highland Park, Illinois

➡ The question I ask most of students as they build their final list is "Why is this college on your list?" Asking why ensures the student has done due diligence in regard to college research and is not just applying to a college because it was suggested by a counselor or parent, a sibling is attending, or a friend is also applying. Too often, students, parents, and even counselors express concerns that a varied list is a sign that the student has not engaged thoroughly in self-assessment and therefore is unsure about what factors are really important to them. I disagree. Many students do not know exactly what they want in a college at the time of application, but they do know some of the things that they like. I fully support students applying to large research universities and small liberal arts colleges as long as they can articulate what it is about each college that they find appealing. In some cases this is a specific major/program, scholarship, or even simply location.

CHARLENE AGUILAR

College counseling, University Preparatory Academy, Seattle, Washington

➡ There is a wealth of information available to students as they explore colleges. They might visit campuses directly, talk with alumni, or meet with admission representatives at a local college fair or on the high school campus as early as junior year. The goal for each student is to have a list that reflects breadth and depth. If you've done your homework of deep self-reflection and possess a sense of confidence and reality about the person you are and want to develop, you'll have a rich list that anticipates change without going beyond eight to ten colleges.

And while there is no set or right number of colleges to which a student should apply, the list that reaches into the teens suggests a student has not carefully reflected on college match and fit and simply deferred careful thought and analysis to senior spring. At that point, he or she will have only a couple of weeks to make a decision. College counseling experience has shown that this delay often results in an even greater anxiety and is not a formula for solid decision making in April. Keep in mind, too, that applications are complicated, that the paperwork alone requires a major organizational effort, and that each college or university charges a nonrefundable fee (averaging about $70) to process the application.

So how do you arrive at an application list that's right for you? By going through the same process you did in Chapter 8 when you made your initial list—but this time it's going to be more rigorous.

Step 1: Review Your List of Prospective Schools

Over the past months, you've probably picked up new insights and ideas about the schools on your initial list as you have visited and conducted further research. You have more information and have gained confidence in yourself and your knowledge of what you want. Maybe you hated one school on sight when you visited, and maybe there was another you loved. Maybe you changed your mind about majoring in biochemistry and now want to study American literature, or deepened your interest in an extracurricular activity that isn't available at every college on your list.

Take a look at that initial list. What schools have come to really stand out in your mind as winners? Mark them as keepers. Some of the other schools are ones you've lost interest in, so cross them off. If you still have more than twelve on the list, you will have to make more cuts. And if your initial list was too short to begin with, or if you've crossed off too many and now you have fewer than six, then you'll have to add some back that you've cut or go back to the drawing board and add more.

Now you are going to go back one more time and look at every college that remains on the list. Apply this simple acid test: make sure

Application Fee Waivers

Students who qualify can obtain waivers for application fees—either from the College Board, from NACAC, through the Common Application, or by directly petitioning the colleges to which they are applying. To qualify, a student must apply for financial aid and meet guidelines established by the College Board and by the U.S. Department of Health and Human Services. Check collegeboard .org, nacacnet.org, commonapp.org, and the websites of the colleges to which you are applying.

you really know enough about each school to be genuinely interested in attending, that you have good and well-researched reasons for wanting to attend each school, and that each school is a good fit in terms of your intellectual, academic, and personal interests.

Keep asking yourself the tough questions, remembering the "aha!" moments from your visits, and following your gut instinct until you arrive at an application list of eight to ten.

Step 2: Now Factor in Selectivity

Now you are going to perform a reality check by evaluating your list to make sure it includes enough schools where you are likely to be admitted. Revisit Chapter 8 if you need more details about the four categories you should have in a balanced list:

- **Solid.** A school that seldom rejects candidates with your credentials.
- **Probable.** A school where your chances of being accepted are better than your

chances of being rejected, though there is no guarantee of admission.

- **Possible.** A school where your chances of being rejected are higher than your chances of being accepted. But some students with credentials like yours have been admitted.
- **Statistical reach.** A school you would like to attend but where your chances of acceptance seem slim. No one's chances of admission at these schools are high.

Be honest with yourself about where you are. Don't waste time applying to a college that is not really in play for you. If your statistical reaches are downright impossible, take them off the list! If you fail to do this work now and do not ensure that your application list reflects this recommended range of selectivity, you risk having few or no options in April of senior year.

Use Your High School Counselor

Your high school counselor may be helpful here. Because he knows you and your academic history, and has information about how students have fared historically in the admission process at various colleges and universities, a counselor can help you "get real" about your chances of acceptance. Just remember that a counselor should never prescribe which colleges you apply to. He may have recommendations, and you should consider what he says—but he should only advise you. Where you apply is your decision—as long as you are prepared for the consequences.

A counselor can build on and interpret the information you find in the guides, on the

Trophy Hunting Prohibited

If you are applying to one or more of the most highly selective schools—such as Brown, Yale, or MIT—but have no intention of going there, you need to rethink. If you know you won't attend, then this is nothing but trophy hunting and it is unethical even if you are completely qualified to be admitted. Remember, if you are admitted, you're taking away a seat from a student who really wants to attend that school. Skip the bragging rights and stick to applying to schools you would attend.

college websites, and in Naviance. She may know, for example, which colleges admitted only 10 percent of students with a 2400 on the SATs. So stop by or make an appointment with your counselor to discuss your application list. Here are some questions to start the conversation.

- What has been the history of our school's students with this particular college?
- What's the profile of admitted students from our high school at this university?
- How does my academic profile compare to the most recent profiles for the colleges on my list?

Scattergrams

Some schools have organized comprehensive historical data into a "scattergram"—a great tool to help you evaluate your chances

How should the schools on your application list be distributed among these categories? Here's the paradigm:

- Minimum = three solids and three probables
- Maximum = an additional two to four distributed across the four categories

Under no circumstances should the most selective schools—the statistical reaches and possibles—constitute more than half your list!

of admission. A scattergram is a graph that shows the GPAs and ACT and SAT scores of your high school's students along with their outcomes at specific colleges and universities. Using a scattergram, a student applying to any university can see how his statistics match

The Groucho Marx Syndrome

"I don't want to belong to any club that will accept me as a member." —Groucho Marx

Don't confuse selectivity with quality or fit. The place that is best for you may not be the place that is the hardest to get into. The best educational and social experience awaits you at the school that is the best fit for you—not the school where it's hardest to get in.

(FYI, Groucho had only an elementary school education, so he never had to come up with an application list.)

up to previous applicants from his high school over a period of years—whether students were accepted, waitlisted, or denied.[21]

Some high schools create their own scattergrams, others use Naviance, and others do not track information in this way. Keep in mind that tools such as scattergrams provide information, not predictions. Many colleges take into account factors such as extracurricular activities, recommendations, geographic desirability, or an interview, which are not reflected in a scattergram.

Once you have grouped the schools on your list according to selectivity, you will need to make one further evaluation.

Step 3: Now Go Back and Factor in Cost

If paying for college is a factor—as it is for most families—you will need to evaluate your application list once again to make sure at least some of the schools where you have a good chance of being admitted are also affordable. In compiling your initial list, we encouraged you not to rule out any college on the basis of cost. But cost now becomes a factor in shaping your application list. While cost alone should not keep a school off the list, you may be required to add some colleges or do some careful pruning to ensure you have the right affordable options.

It is imperative that students include affordable options in the probable and solid categories of their application list. For most students, that means including your in-state public college or university on the list. While the most selective colleges often offer the

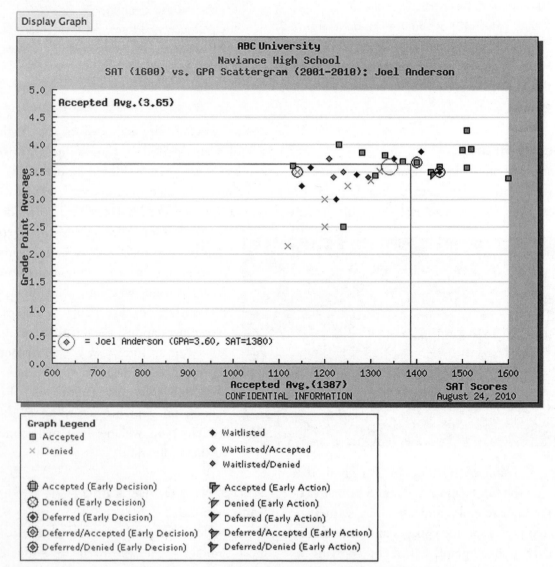

Underresourced Schools

If there is no counseling staff at your high school or your counselor has a heavy caseload, you will need to make your own evaluation about admissibility. Here are some actions you can take.

- Ask a mentor to help you understand and interpret the academic profile information and your academic record. This could be a favorite teacher, a parent, someone at your church, or anyone in an advisory role such as a coach, club advisor, or employer.
- Make an appointment with the principal of your school to talk about where past students are attending college.
- Call or email the admission counselors at the colleges where you are planning to apply, present your credentials, and ask if you are a candidate who would be in the running at their school. Admission staff may be pretty forthcoming. While they don't like to give hypothetical decisions—or to discourage applicants from applying—some valuable information may be gained from a conversation.

strongest financial aid programs, they are, by definition, the hardest to get into.

If your application list doesn't include some affordable solids and probables, you could find yourself in a very bad position— you might get accepted by schools you can't afford, and rejected by the ones you can afford.

So if cost is a factor for your family, make another pass through your list at this

An Exercise in Fine-Tuning Your Application List

Feeling frustrated, uninspired, overwhelmed, or otherwise stymied in the quest to fine-tune your application list? Try this thought experiment for a jump start.

Identify one college on your list—let's call it College A—where you are fairly sure you can be admitted and would be excited to go. Then compare that school to every other college on your list, one at a time, and ask yourself, "Would I rather go to this college or College A?"

If your list is too large, in any case where the answer to that question is "College A," then the other school can come off your list. After all, why would you have any colleges on your list where you like College A better?

If your list is too small, you can use this method to expand your list. If you need more choices, use College A as a benchmark and find more colleges with the same characteristics.

Just be careful to use the most specific, objective, measurable criteria available to determine that you are admissible at the school that fulfills the role of College A. A public university with more transparent admission criteria may be a safer choice for your College A, but some private colleges can fit this role as well, as long as you have up-to-date information and it is a solid on your list.

Go Ahead and Reach If You've Got Solid Options Nailed Down

The best advice is to apply to colleges where you are pretty sure to be admitted and you'll be happy to attend. But once you've done that, then taking a risk—with a possible or even a statistical reach—can be a good thing. So we also encourage you to stretch and strive a little if one or more of the schools you truly want to attend are possibles or reaches for you. We're not saying a more selective college is necessarily better—just that you shouldn't be afraid to set your sights higher in one or two cases. If you can afford the application fee (or will qualify for a fee waiver), are willing to put time and effort into the application, and have some tolerance for rejection, go ahead and include one or two of those schools on your application list. Just don't replace any of your three probable and three solid schools with a statistical reach or possible school.

Sometimes those students who have the most difficulty seeing themselves at selective schools are those who have had less guidance, are the first generation in their family to attend college, or are underresourced. Recent studies have shown that such students often "undermatch"—they fail to apply to the most competitive colleges that would admit them.[22] Yet statistics show attending a college where a student is challenged increases the likelihood that they will graduate. So we particularly encourage such students to stretch and strive a bit—while ensuring that they have fallback options.

point and ensure that it includes your in-state public school and additional colleges in the probable and solid categories that you like and know you can afford, in case financial aid doesn't come through at the hoped-for level.

Now you're almost there. . . .

Step 4: Finally, Ask Yourself One Last Question

Can you picture yourself attending and being happy at each of the colleges on your application list?

If not, go back to Step 1 and repeat this process. Sorry—there's no other way.

Going through this assessment to arrive at your application list—performing the self-evaluation, conducting your research on the front end of the process, and taking care to choose schools that guarantee options and are affordable—is worth the time and effort.

Questions You May Have

Is it important to demonstrate interest at this point in the process?
Yes. Some institutions that take into account how likely a student is to enroll if admitted figure that out in part by looking at how many points of contact you've had with them. See the explanation of demonstrated interest in Chapter 8.

Is it true that if you significantly exceed a college's academic profile, you run the risk of being rejected because the college will believe you won't enroll?

Students sometimes hear this. Whether or not it is true, it is wise for all students to be clear with all colleges on their list about their reasons for wanting to attend and why those colleges are good fits. This is one important reason why you need to confine your list to a manageable number of schools.

As we noted earlier when discussing

Parents, If You Get Too Far Out in Front of Your Own Troops, They'll Mistake You for the Enemy

Parents, you may be disappointed with some of the names showing up on the list of schools where your son or daughter will apply. Perhaps your alma mater didn't make the cut or there are schools you've never heard of. But you need to remember what this is about: you want your children to have choices among schools that are good fits. Don't put your children in the position of feeling they've disappointed you, or of having too few options. Worse, don't go down the road one father did when he told psychologist Michael Thompson that his daughter, who was developing anorexia, would be fine if she got into Princeton. Here Thompson, the author of *The Pressured Child: Freeing Our Kids from Performance Overdrive,* shares some advice about refusing to play the "name game," and how to send the message to your sons and daughters that they are free to make their own decisions about where they will apply to college.

➡ Parents need to keep perspective and remain emotionally steady throughout the college application process. It is the parents who, in their adult wisdom, must remember that this is not a life-or-death process. One senior told me, "This is the biggest decision of my life." But of course it isn't. The college decision gets dwarfed by other life decisions quickly enough. Parents need to remember that and to offer their child help but not insist on it—or force it.

How can parents be supportive?

- Listen, listen, and listen—without getting panicked.
- Ask thoughtful questions.
- Offer guidance in a tentative manner: "Would this really be a help?"
- Don't bring up the subject every day. It's boring, annoying, and anxiety-producing, and it's not motivating for kids. Put yourself on what the Bates College dean of admission once called a "college diet"—mention it only twice a week.
- Don't forget that this is your child's decision, and don't get too far out in front of him. For example, don't become an expert on a school before your child does. One school principal said, "If you get too far out in front of your own troops, they'll mistake you for the enemy."

Parents, If You Get Too Far Out in Front of Your Own Troops, They'll Mistake You for the Enemy (continued)

If you tell your sons and daughters they are free to make the decision about college but you really have an outcome, a name, or a type of school in mind, they will sense it. You can fool younger children, but you cannot fool adolescents. Your own children know you too well by that time. So parents have to really believe that message themselves. A parent has to do the psychological work to come to terms with a child making her own decisions. If a parent has done that work, then he will be able to—as the Buddhists say—manifest inner clarity and conviction.

It's a mistake to become emotionally overinvolved in your child's choice or think you can predict your child's future. I defy anyone to really know for sure what school is the right fit for their child. You cannot predict the really important factors that influence our lives: meeting a great, lifelong friend, or making a relationship with a mentor-professor who inspires you, or simply getting a good freshman roommate. Is there any parent out there who can confidently predict those things from a college view book?

It's tough to get parents to stop talking about the top ten or twenty or thirty colleges. Everyone loves to bandy about the fancy names in idle or covertly competitive cocktail conversation. But there are more than 2,200 colleges and universities in the United States. People come from all over the world to go to our universities—we have an abundance unequaled in the world. If parents only talk about ten or twenty schools, their children are going to feel like failures if they don't go to one of them. You have to be on your child's side and see this through his or her eyes.

Having been a therapist for thirty-plus years, I believe that the internal bottom line for children is love for their parents. It's not an uncomplicated love or an easy love. But it is the bottom line. So parents should be aware that asking a child to look at a college is rarely a casual thing. It goes right to the kid's bottom line.

demonstrated interest, make sure you take advantage of any opportunities to have contact with the school—attend the college representative session at your high school, interview if one is offered, visit the campus, establish a dialogue with your regional admission officer. In addition, if the school has a "Why us?" essay, a student can show through her

response that she "gets it" about the college's mission, purpose, and resources.

Is this sucking up? Done poorly or insincerely, yes. And we want to be clear that this is not what we are suggesting. Your list should have eight to ten schools on it that you honestly want to attend. When you put time and effort into learning about each of those

FROM THE DESK OF THE DEAN

Why We Talk About Fit

"Fit" is a popular bit of jargon used by admission deans to explain the whole complex of factors—academic, social, extracurricular, ethnic, geographic—that indicates you'll be right for their college and their college will be right for you. Here some deans of admission speak about the right fit and what that means for applicants.

CHRISTOPH GUTTENTAG

Dean of undergraduate admissions, Duke University

➡ It's really important for us to acknowledge and be respectful of how uncertain the future is for a high school student. As adults, we really do our children a disservice in the way we talk about and reflect on our lives, because it's very easy and tempting and simple to describe our past as leading to where we are now. It's very easy to make it all appear as if it makes sense—not necessarily that it was preordained, but that everything sort of came together to lead us to where we are now.

But what that leads students to think is that they should be able to look forward in their lives the same way we look back on our lives. In other words, they think that they should be able to prospectively visualize the end point the same way we look back from where we are and go, "Oh yeah, of course. Of course I would end up here! Naturally, this is where I would end up!" We're tempted to do that when, in fact, for a lot of us, there is so much happenstance, so much randomness in how our lives unfold.

So we would be well served by reminding young women and men that, for many of us, life unfolded through a series of steps that we couldn't predict, and that's okay. And that's why fit is so important. Because if you go to a school that's the right place, that enhances your strengths, that helps you shore up your weaknesses, that lets you be challenged but allows you to be comfortable, that's the best preparation for the funny way that life takes us along.

CHARLES DEACON

Dean of admissions, Georgetown University

➡ We hope that students have a chance to get to know the schools to which they're applying. But it's very difficult today. More information has actually made it more difficult

Turning Your Initial List into Your Application List: The Eight to Ten Colleges Where You Will Apply   165 because it has put so many more options in the way of students that it's hard to sort through it all and get to the right place. And then the application process has made it easy to put off that decision by applying to twenty or thirty schools and waiting to see where you get in. That has obscured the idea of fit—that there are one or two or three ideal places where you walk onto campus and say, "This is where I belong."

But the idea of fit is slightly hyped up from where the reality is. There are some misfits, obviously. But most likely students can adapt to the environment of the college where they ultimately are admitted. The bigger problem with fit is that students coming in are going to have certain challenges based on their own circumstances. For example, the student from rural Nebraska may be challenged to fit into the more fast-paced environment of an inner-city campus. "Diversity" is a hackneyed term, but it's important when it comes to fit. The more diverse a college is, the more likely it is that students will fit in, whereas the more homogeneous a college is, the more difficult it's going to be to fit in if you're not from that segment of the population that predominates at the college. So we think that anybody could fit in here at Georgetown as long as they're talented and motivated to do well academically. We aren't looking for a specific kind of person or specific fit. We're really looking for the most interesting people we can find.

JENNIFER RICKARD
Vice president for enrollment, University of Puget Sound

➡ Unfortunately, students often aren't looking at fit up front. They often will look at colleges based on their admission criteria, the perceived prestige of an institution, or what their parents or others think and wait until they are admitted to really get that "gut feeling" about a place. I like to draw the analogy of how we choose our friends to explain why fit is so important in considering a college. We like our good friends for a lot of reasons—usually not for factual or objective reasons. But rather because we have some sense of compatibility, a kind of intuition, a common sense of values, similar interests, an appreciation for each other's way of thinking or sense of humor—those are the things that really bind people together—and create a fit. It's similar with college. You don't want to spend four years with a college that really isn't your "friend." When you're thinking about four years of your life, fit is a really important thing to feel in order to be happy and to thrive.

From our side of the desk, we look at fit through all sorts of intangibles. The University of Puget Sound is one of only five national liberal arts colleges in the Pacific Northwest—a region known for its large flagship public universities. With a student population of just 2,600 from all over the nation and world, the vast majority of whom live on campus, every student here makes a difference in our community. As a result, part of our determination of fit is trying to assess how a student will "fit" in our rigorous academic environment that also values balance and the pursuit of personal interests. We look at a student's interests, what they choose to write about in their essays, the kinds of questions they've asked in an interview, the things they're interested in exploring. Certainly academic criteria are part of fit because students need to be able to succeed here academically. But particularly at a relatively small place like Puget Sound, students need to be active participants in and outside of the classroom, so being able to identify that in a student's application is important. In the end, it's when we can say, "Wow, I could really see that student here." What's great about the process is that a lot of different people "fit" at Puget Sound. There is not a mold we expect students to fit into here—in fact, just the opposite. We want them to be their best selves, not their best attempt at what they think we want them to be. Similarly, there is not just one mold for what the ideal college might be for you. When you do your research, you find that there are a lot of great colleges where you can "fit" and will be happy and thrive.

schools and put time and effort into writing your applications and essays, the fit will show in a way that colleges can recognize.

? Help! I have too many colleges on my list. Any further ideas on how I can pare it down?

Some students have a hard time ruling out prospective colleges. You may have fallen in love with multiple campuses or be afraid you will miss something by taking a school off your list. Try this: Take out a piece of paper. List all your colleges in one column. List your criteria—what you most want in a school—in another column. Any college that doesn't fulfill those criteria can safely be taken off the list and you shouldn't feel you're missing anything. You may also benefit from talking with a teacher,

employer, parent, or friend. Finally, try the fine-tuning exercise we discuss on page 161.

? Will applying to multiple highly selective schools with strong financial aid programs increase my ability to negotiate a financial aid award?

It will depend on the schools. The most highly selective schools often will not negotiate a financial aid award. We'll discuss this further in Chapter 16.

? How should a student who is applying to highly competitive dual degree programs evaluate their selectivity in balancing an application list?

A variety of programs combine admission to an undergraduate program with admission to a professional degree program—for example, joint BS/MD programs or BA/MBA programs. Students applying under these programs—as well as other small, highly competitive specialized programs such as computer science—should treat them as statistical reach options on their application list. Because there are so few spots available, no one can be confident of admission. Such students should balance their list by applying to schools under nondual programs that round out the range of selectivity on their list.

PART V

APPLYING

CHAPTER 11

College Interviews

"If you're late, don't say you're late because you had to stop and get a latte and the lines at Starbucks were too long—especially if you haven't brought a *grande* for the interviewer."

—Rick Diaz, regional director of admission, Southern Methodist University

The college interview is not a test. There are no right and wrong answers. A student is not going to be asked to solve a difficult math problem, or open a window that has been nailed shut so he can be observed under pressure. First and foremost, the college interview is a conversation. It is a chance for an admission officer to get to know the student better and a chance for the student to get to know the college better.

INTERVIEWING 101: THE BASICS

Not every college offers interviews. Many colleges and universities simply don't have the staff. Other schools believe the opinions of teachers and others who have worked day in and day out with a student are more valuable than any insight they might get in a forty-five-minute conversation.

But if an interview is offered, how important is it? While an interview rarely, if ever, outweighs an academic record, it can be a factor in the admission decision at some colleges. The general rule is that the smaller the college, the more important the interview is going to be. Why is that? Just one of the reasons: at a small college with eight students in a classroom, much of a student's intellectual interaction will take place with faculty members, so that school needs to know if a student can carry on a sustained conversation about a substantive matter with an adult. At a larger school, with potentially hundreds of students in a large lecture, a greater percentage of a student's conversations will take place with their classmates.

◎ Best Advice

- Take the time to reflect on who you truly are before you show up at the admission office.

171

Checkpoints ✍

✔ The college interview is a conversation, not a test. Best advice for a student: be yourself and be forthcoming.

✔ Informational, evaluative, alumni, admission office—there are several different types of interviews.

✔ Every college has its own approach. Check the college's website early to find out its interview policy and scheduling requirements.

✔ There is an etiquette to the interview for both students and parents. Follow it.

✔ Students should prepare for interviews by thinking about who they are and what they want. We have lots of questions to help you get started.

The students who emerge most vividly in an interview are those who know themselves best.

- Be on time.
- Be polite—to everyone.
- Be yourself—unless you're chronically late or usually impolite. Colleges want to see who you really are ... within limits. Most important, don't try to be the person you think the college wants you to be. Students and parents are usually off-target when they try to guess what a college wants—and being phony is *always* off-target.
- Be genuine and forthcoming. Your openness and receptivity to connecting with another person are as important as the subject matter discussed. But don't get *too* familiar and let the etiquette of the situation deteriorate.

If an interview is offered and the student lives within reasonable driving distance, she should do the interview. Otherwise, a college may look at the applicant and say, "She's in Maine and she couldn't come to Boston to talk with us? How interested could she be?"

Students who have a sense of who they are and where they are going and who feel they can hold up their end of a conversation are almost always better off having an interview. It will often be to their advantage and will rarely handicap them.

Students who are not comfortable sitting down and talking about themselves with a stranger for forty-five minutes may want to forgo an interview if the college is not within a reasonable distance and an interview is not highly recommended. But if an interview is required, under those circumstances such a student could say, "Interviews are not my strength, but I really wanted to show my interest and be clear about my desire to attend school here. I really have strengths that lie elsewhere." Again, it's all about students knowing themselves—and being true to themselves.

 # Best Advice

Doing a practice interview is good preparation for the real thing. If your high school offers the opportunity for a mock interview, take advantage of it. If not, ask a counselor, parent, teacher, or friend to conduct a mock interview with you. It can help you sharpen your communication skills and prepare you for what to expect.

Informational or Evaluative?

There are two basic types of interviews: informational and evaluative.

- **An informational interview** is an opportunity for the school to tell its story to the prospective student. Subjects might range from housing to the latest superstar professor to join the philosophy department. If an interview is billed as strictly informational, it's primarily a chance for the student to ask questions and find out more about the school.
- **An evaluative interview**, on the other hand, is an opportunity for the school to hear a student's story. The interview might cover anything from world affairs to a student's favorite football team, and affords an admission officer a glimpse of the student as a real person. In most evaluative interviews, while the student will have a chance to ask questions, the interviewer will be doing most of the asking and the interviewer's

impressions will become part of the student's application file.

These represent the two extremes when it comes to interviews. Most interviews consist of both some information and some evaluation, so it's best to prepare and behave appropriately.

An interview is a conversation, not a test. It's merely one part of the admission process.

When Should You Interview?

We recommend you do at least one interview, if possible, in the spring of junior year in high school. You should not interview at your first-choice college at that time. Save the most important interviews—those at schools high on your list—for over the summer or early in senior year. But you can get a sense of what an interview is like only by doing one, and it's better to feel more comfortable with the process before senior year.

Check the website of every school on your list to see when the admission office begins interviewing prospective students. Each college has its own policy. Some colleges do not interview students before the senior year of high school. Other schools will talk with juniors beginning in spring of junior year.

Scheduling an Interview

First, find out if an interview is offered by the schools in which you're interested and whether it's required or optional. Every school's interview procedure and requirements are unique. At Harvard, for example, while there are limited opportunities for on-campus interviews, the university also schedules alumni interviews with applicants, and these interviews are not arranged until an application has been received.

Check the colleges' websites and note the following:

- Whether the interview is required or strongly encouraged
- Whether interviews take place by invitation or at the student's request
- When the college offers interviews
- Where interviews are conducted—on campus, in the student's hometown, or online
- Deadlines for requesting an interview

Don't make the mistake of waiting for the college to contact you to schedule an interview. In the majority of cases, interviews are scheduled at the student's request. Such requests can often be made online. Also, pay attention to deadlines! And don't expect to schedule an interview on short notice. Appointments book up, and if a student calls only two weeks ahead, much less one day, he may not be able to talk with someone one-on-one. For most schools, the more lead time, the better. Use the worksheet in Appendix III to keep track of which colleges offer interviews and when yours are scheduled.

Sometime in the junior year, your family should sit down to plan when and where college trips are going to occur. Then you'll have an idea about when interviews might take place and you can make appointments accordingly. This is just another element of approaching the application process wisely by being organized enough so that students and

parents are not constantly nagged by doubts and concerns.

If you miss the deadline or wait too long to schedule an interview, you should still visit the admission office when on campus. There is often an admission officer on duty, so you may have the opportunity to talk one-on-one, or perhaps to participate in a small group interview. It will not usually be a formal interview that is written up and placed in the file, but it's still an opportunity to show interest and learn something about the school.

Who should schedule the interview? Admission officers will say they prefer that the student handle this, but the truth is they won't know. Parents often set up the logistics of appointments for their teenagers—a trip to the orthodontist, an MRI for a sports injury, a haircut before the prom. College interview appointments are not that different, and many times the phone calls setting up those appointments need to be made during school hours, while the student is in class. That said, if the student takes responsibility for making interview appointments, it demonstrates she is in charge. If a student needs to own this process and is not taking the lead, having her make the appointments can reinforce that she needs to step up.

Who Will Conduct the Interview?

Admission office interviews are usually conducted by the more junior members of the admission department staff. The dean of admission usually will not interview a prospective applicant. Don't be surprised if the interviewer is a student. While parents may feel they want someone with more "clout" or experience, many schools use highly trained seniors to conduct interviews. Rest assured that more weight is not assigned to one interview over another based on who conducted it. Generally, students love it when they are interviewed by someone closer to their age. When they see a fairly recent graduate walk through the door of the office, they often relax and let who they really are come through. The more relaxed and comfortable the student is, the better she is going to do.

Alumni interviewers, on the other hand, range in age far more broadly than admission office interviewers—they may be recent graduates or octogenarians who haven't been on campus for four decades. In addition, some alumni interviewers may have had fairly little recent contact with their college; others will have completed a rigorous training program.

We'll walk you through what happens in both admission office and alumni interviews.

> You can download Excel and Word documents to keep track of interviews at our website at collegeadmissionbook.com.

WHAT YOU CAN EXPECT AT AN ADMISSION OFFICE INTERVIEW

Once the student has made an appointment for an interview and has arrived at the admission office—on time, please!—here's what should happen.

From the moment they cross the threshold, students and parents should be aware of their behavior and be respectful of the staff and other families present. As in all such situations, the behavior of all parties is easily observed. At this point, the student should take the lead—checking in with the receptionist, filling out any required forms about academic interests, GPA, or extracurricular activities, and making the introductions when the interviewer arrives.

This may seem basic, but it's important: when the interviewer arrives, the student should always stand up, look the interviewer in the eye, shake his or her hand firmly, and introduce everyone in her party. The student isn't trying to win the Miss Congeniality Award, but in the interview, as in most things in life, it is best to make a positive first impression.

At this point, the interviewer will let all those present know what is going to happen. Whether parents are given a role in the interview or not will depend on the college's policy. If there will be an opportunity for the parents to participate, the interviewer will signal that, saying, "Mr. and Mrs. Smith, I am going to take John back into my office. We're going to talk for about half an hour and then I'm going to invite you in to see if you have any questions." Or she may signal that the parents will not have a role, saying, "John, we're going to be about forty-five minutes and then you will be free to go." Finally, the interviewer may say, "John and I will be about twenty minutes and then we're going to come back out and we'll be able to answer any questions you may have." This means that when the interviewer and student return to the waiting room, that will be the time for the parent to ask any questions. Will you know ahead of time which of these scenarios to anticipate? Not likely. It

"It Feels Like Bragging . . ."

Many admission guidebooks will advise students that the college interview is a time to "boast and brag"—in fact, a popular term for a student's extracurricular activities list is "brag sheet." The apparent message in this approach is that the more a student has done, the better a person she is, and the better her chances of being admitted to college.

But that's not the real message. The real message is that you will be better off if you brag. And not only is this bad advice, it's a fundamental misunderstanding of the admission process. Much of that process is focused on determining who is going to be brought into the university community—athletes, scholars, musicians, thinkers, doers, scientists, activists, leaders, followers, and all-around nice people. College interviews are valuable because they provide the admission officers with a glimpse of the student as a real person, a person who may be sitting in the school's classrooms and living in its residence halls the following year. Boasting and bragging hide who you really are—and make you look like a jerk, too.

So students need to make a distinction between bragging and sharing. What admission officers want students to do is think about and reflect on who they are and then let the college know how they spend their time and why, what level of commitment they've had in their pursuits, and any distinctions they've achieved. Most often, an admission officer is much more interested in talking in depth with the student about one or two activities rather than hearing about twenty different things he's done. Some of the best interviews, they say, have been spent talking with a student about why he loved to cook or why she adored her kid sister.

In the weeks leading up to an interview, it's a good idea for students to start a running list of what they've done since 9th or 10th grade. Don't think of this as a "brag sheet." Instead, look at it as a task you need to think through fully, like a school project. The ongoing list is added to as activities or past honors occur to you, so it is thorough and you have the information readily at hand. However, you do not need this information *in* hand—the list should not be taken to the interview.

Students should also keep in mind that admission officers know that self-revelation comes more easily to some than others, and that everyone has good days and bad days. Finally, don't worry if you're asked in an interview to recite a litany of activities and can't remember everything. It's not a one-time win-or-lose proposition. You don't have to convey everything about yourself right then. Information arrives at the admission office in a variety of ways. You can always do a follow-up email to the interviewer that will be included in your application file, and you will list your activities on the application form.

may be determined by something as simple as whether the interview is taking place in an office that has room to seat more than two people. Relax and go with the flow.

The first question in an interview will probably be a softball—for example, "Isn't the summer weather here beautiful today?" It is up to the interviewer to start the conversation. That's proper interview protocol, and the interviewer will be grateful if the student observes it.

As the conversation continues, the questions will require more thought—for example, "If you could learn more about any subject outside school, what subject would that be and why?" Interviewers are frequently interested in what motivates a student. So at this point, the questions are likely to be "why" questions. In fact, the "what" questions are there to get to the "why" questions.

If a student is asked what she likes to read, for instance, she can like to read Nancy Drew instead of Shakespeare as long as she has a good *reason* for it. To take this one step further, when asked by an interviewer what the student likes to read, "books" is not a helpful response. So students should think through questions like those in "Questions for a Student to Think About in Preparation for an Interview" on page 183.

Be alert to the fact that if you get nervous in the interview, you may become overly

What *Not* to Wear

A good general rule is that students headed into interviews should dress as though they are going to dinner with the grandparents. Students—and parents—should be respectful and take the time to look pulled together and as though the interview appointment is important. So girls, don't wear anything too sexy, too revealing, or too short. Boys, do you need to wear a coat and tie? No, but make sure whatever you wear is clean, neat, and pressed.

The guidelines are simple, so why can't people follow them? Admission officers say that, by far, the most frequent interview faux pas are wardrobe malfunctions—blouses that pop open, spaghetti strap tops that are too skimpy, flies that are unzipped, workout clothes that look like you just worked out, makeup more suited to a nightclub, and way, *way* too much perfume for the girls and aftershave for the boys.

Girls are the most frequent transgressors when it comes to what not to wear. But while boys don't have to worry about how to sit in a dress, they should keep in mind that they shouldn't look as though they have just tumbled out of bed. It's not appropriate to get too comfortable (like the young man who took off his shoes and picked at his toenails during an interview), and remove your baseball cap, please.

While we're on the subject, parents should dress appropriately as well. Mothers should not dress like their daughters and fathers should not wear a sweatshirt emblazoned with the name of the college they visited the day before.

Rick Diaz, regional director of undergraduate admission at SMU, offers this advice to students: If you look in the mirror and think to yourself, "I look really good," then change your clothes. You should not look that good. It's an appointment, not a date. You should dress conservatively and look presentable, not "hot."

Parents, Behave Yourselves

There is a place for parents in the college interview, and most will find the happy medium between, on the one hand, being too busy to be bothered to put away the cell phone and, on the other hand, pulling every string on their child's behalf to make sure the dean of admission does the interviewing. Accompanying a son or daughter on a college trip is part of the letting-go process—and at the same time it's an opportunity for Mom and Dad to have their own questions answered. That said, the student should be asking most of the questions. And while it's natural for parents to worry that their child will talk too much (the girls) or not enough (the boys) in an interview, parents need to realize they can't stand in for their son or daughter and need to trust them to speak for themselves.

"OK, maybe it would be better if I interview Anne alone."

When it comes to worries about things like the age and experience of the interviewer or being treated fairly, parents should mentally tell themselves, "Back off!" You are not the ones being interviewed, after all. Your job is to support your child, and the more relaxed the student, the better he or she will do in an interview. So hang back, hang back, hang back. You are there to be the driver and a calming influence. If nerves make your teenager a little cranky, take it in stride.

In general, parents should be aware of their actions and be respectful to everyone around them, treating the student interviewer or the person sitting at the reception desk as they would the dean of admission. And students, if a parent does misbehave, the worst part of it is probably just that it could make you self-conscious. The reality is that admission officers have seen it all, and parental misbehavior usually does not reflect on the applicant.

talkative. Just relax and give the interviewer room to ask questions. Do not take over the conversation, preventing the interviewer from continuing his questioning. Again, remember, this is not an audition, it is a conversation. It's about you sharing your true self with the interviewer so that the college can learn more about why you do the things you do.

When the interviewer says, "What questions do you have for me?" that is the signal the interview is winding down. It is best if you have a question or two. Make sure they aren't questions that can be answered by looking at the college's website or reading its literature. Don't ask, "Do you have economics here?" Instead, ask, "Can you tell me a little bit about what it's like to be an economics student here?" The general rule is to ask questions that cannot be answered via advance homework. (More ideas about what to ask can be found later in this chapter.)

If a student finds herself preparing questions simply to impress the interviewer, she should go back to the drawing board. You should really want to know the answers to the questions you are posing—because you are looking at a place that, if you enroll, will affect your life in profound ways. Former dean of admission at Princeton Fred Hargadon used to get asked how many books there were in the library. His response? "More than you can read in your four years here."

The interviewer will signal the end of the interview by asking something like "Any last questions?" Interviewers are trained to give signals and usually give them very clearly. Again, the student should shake hands, look the interviewer in the eye, and say, "It was a pleasure" or "Thank you very much."

If the parents are going to be brought into the interview, the interviewer may ask the student to bring them back into the office or accompany the student back into the waiting room. No matter what happens, remember that this is not the time to act as if parents are an embarrassment. The interviewer does not think parents are utter buffoons. In fact, interviewers are used to parents who are anxious. Students need to cut parents some

slack—no eyeball rolling, grimacing, or "Oh, Dad, please!"

WHAT YOU CAN EXPECT TO HAPPEN AT AN ALUMNI INTERVIEW

When it comes to alumni interviews, there is no typical experience. Most often, a student will meet with an alumnus one-on-one, but occasionally two or three alumni may conduct the interview together. And an alumni interview may take place at an alumnus' home or the neighborhood Starbucks. So you need to be flexible, and there are several things to do to prepare.

Often the alumna or the admission office will call to set up the alumni interview. When they do, the student can get some important information. You might ask how many people will be attending, what year the interviewer graduated (this may be more delicate if you're speaking to the alumnus directly), where the meeting will take place, and how long the conversation is expected to last.

If the student receives a letter setting up the interview, it's still appropriate to phone the admission office and ask these questions. There are so many variables in an alumni interview that it's fair for the student to ask how many alumni may be attending, or whether the interviewer has twenty minutes or a leisurely few hours.

To return for a moment to scheduling, remember that the interview policy of every school on a student's list must be checked. The school's policy on an admission office interview may differ from its policy on an alumni interview. For example, some schools require that the request for an alumni interview be in by December of a student's senior year. Some schools will get in touch with the student, while others require the student to get in touch with the school.

Most important, the alumni interview, like the admission office interview, is a conversation. The student is there to talk. She is not there to advance her agenda, be grilled, or review her transcript. There are some basic questions that may be asked in alumni interviews—for example, what the student wants to study or what he cares about most outside of class. Think through these questions before arriving. (See a list of questions students should be prepared to answer on page 183.)

But there is one question every student should come prepared to answer: "What about this college is appealing to you?" Alumni expect students to be enthusiastic about their alma mater; if they're not, the interviewer generally will not look kindly on that lack of enthusiasm. So this is not the time for a student to reveal that they're "kind of" interested in University of Chicago but really aren't so sure about it compared to Northwestern. It's not a matter of being insincere—it's just not being impolite.

Students should also be aware that some alumni will Google interviewees or check their pages on Facebook or other social media before the interview. It's helpful to Google yourself and see what comes up so you're prepared to talk about it. You don't want to draw a blank when the alumnus brings up something he saw online.

Students should not always expect alumni interviewers to be able to answer highly specific questions about the schools they represent. But you should have a question or two for the interviewer, such as "How do you think the school has changed?" or "What did you like the most at Lehigh?" The student should invite the interviewer to share his experiences rather than ask him to answer objective questions.

As with the admission office interview, when the interviewer signals the session is over, the student should stand, look him in the eye, shake hands, and thank him for his time.

Thank-You Notes

A thank-you note to the interviewer is not a must for an admission office interview, but it is a nice gesture and will often be added to an admission file. It can be handwritten or sent by email. For alumni interviews, the student should write a thank-you note by hand. A quick note of appreciation for the interviewer's time can also be an opportunity for the student to mention if there was something she forgot to bring up in the interview. But be brief and appropriate! The smaller the college, the more important this gesture is likely to be, because the admission officer is more likely to remember the student clearly and value the personal effort.

OTHER TYPES OF INTERVIEWS

There are three additional types of interviews that are less common but which you may see offered at some colleges: group, off-campus, and online interviews.

Group Interviews

Group interviews usually take place in the admission office and are conducted by an admission officer. Instead of visiting one-on-one with an interviewer, the student may be one of up to a dozen interviewees. Typically, the admission officer will ask the students to introduce themselves and to talk a bit about what they're interested in studying and what characteristics they're looking for in a school. The admission officer will then throw out different questions to the group, such as "What's your favorite subject and why?" Each person in the group will be asked to comment. You should have something to say in response.

Like other types of interviews, the group interview is a conversation. The rule for a group interview is that you should be as aware of your peers in the group as you are of the interviewer. That's because the admission officer is looking as much at behavior within a group of peers as she is at the individual. So, in addition to participating by responding to the interviewer's questions, be polite and generous to your peers.

Off-Campus Interviews

Some colleges routinely send admission staff to "feeder" cities—places where a large number of a college's applicants typically come from. For several days at a time at certain times of the year, regional admission officers meet one-on-one with prospective students. These interviews often take place in a hotel lobby, sometimes at a school, or even in an alumnus' home. The protocol in these interviews is, for the most part, the same as the protocol for interviews conducted in the admission office. A typical exception is that if an officer is interviewing in a hotel suite, one or both parents may be included in the entirety of the interview.

Check each college's website to see if it interviews off-campus. Also, this is another good reason to be on a college's mailing list—you will be informed when the college is doing off-campus interviews in your hometown. (And remember, when you put yourself on that mailing list, make sure you have selected an email address that won't make a statement you may not want to make. A simple johnj@gmail.com is far superior to partyboy@gmail.com.)

Online Interviews

Using a webcam and telepresence technologies such as Skype, an increasing number of admission offices are conducting online interviews. For students who can't afford the expense of traveling cross-country to interview or who live in parts of the world where a college may not have alumni interviewers available, online interviews allow applicants to speak directly to admission offices from their home or school. These virtual interviews are usually allotted the same time and conducted in the same manner as interviews in the admission office.

Senior associate director of admissions at Wake Forest University Tamara Blocker advises students to do a test run if they are unfamiliar with the technology. Wake Forest's admission officers sometimes find themselves interviewing the top of a student's head because the student is looking at the computer screen instead of the camera. But aside from getting used to the technology,

The View from the Other Side of the Desk

Students and parents often feel as if admission officers hold all the cards. They see the admission staff as gatekeepers, dangling the keys to the hallowed halls before them. Keep in mind that even though the interview is about the student, interviews are a two-way street. The interviewer is a real person who is hoping to do a good job in the interview, too. The maxim for both students and parents to keep in mind is: "It's not all about you!"

The best interviewers are skilled at making two things happen. First, they're good at creating a transforming moment in the interview where a student says, "Wow, that was a great conversation." Second, they're good at making a student walk away feeling better than she did when she walked in. The reality is that almost all students have good interviews, because admission officers want the students who pass through their doors to do the very best they can, and will set the stage to achieve that result.

That said, the person on the other side of the desk has a life, with worries and concerns of her own. When a student walks into an interview, she may be the admission officer's first interview of the day or week or her fifth interview of the day and twenty-fifth of the week. If the interviewer seems a little tired or distracted, all is not lost! At that point, the student should lean forward and extend herself a little more, because the admission officer's reticence or distraction may not have anything to do with the student at all.

And while a student should remember to turn off his cell phone and not get so comfortable he puts his feet up on the desk, he should also remember that admission officers have interviewed through it all—fire alarms, a father who fell asleep and snored through his daughter's interview, a blackout that left the dean interviewing by candlelight. Admission officers roll with the punches. A student should, too.

On the other hand, every admission officer has a story that should be an applicant's worst nightmare. There's the student who arrived with her parents two hours late for an interview with the dean—an appointment that had been granted by special request, mind you—and proceeded to chow down on a fast-food hamburger. Meanwhile, the now-ravenous dean, who had skipped lunch to remain at her desk for the interview, pondered the future of the young woman who, moments earlier, she had worried was wandering lost around campus. It hadn't occurred to her the applicant was delayed by a Big Mac. As Rick Diaz of SMU says, "If you're late, don't say you're late because you had to stop and get a latte and the lines at Starbucks were too long—especially if you haven't brought a *grande* for the interviewer." And don't do that either—he was joking. In fact, don't bring chocolate chip cookies, Krispy Kreme donuts, or gifts of any kind.

students should prepare and behave exactly as they would if they were being interviewed on campus, sitting across the desk from an admission officer. And that includes appropriate dress—no avatars involved.

QUESTIONS FOR A STUDENT TO THINK ABOUT IN PREPARATION FOR AN INTERVIEW

The most important thing a student can do prior to an interview is to take the time to reflect on who he or she truly is. Teenagers know a lot about themselves; they just don't always know that they know. Most teenagers know whether they like rap or *Rigoletto,* Dickens or Dostoevsky, art or algebra, *Iron Man* or *Despicable Me.* If students ask the right questions of themselves, they'll have plenty to say.

Here are some questions students may be asked in an interview. You should think about these so you're prepared to answer such questions. In particular, think through the "why" of your answers—why was that teacher so wonderful, why have you enjoyed competitive swimming, why did you choose chemistry over physics?

- Why are you interested in this college?
- What do you hope to get out of college?
- What is your favorite subject and why?
- What is your least favorite subject and why?
- What is important to you?
- What did you do last summer and what did you gain from that experience?
- What are your plans for the coming summer and what do you hope to gain from that experience?
- How do you choose to spend your free time?

- How do you think your friends would describe you if you were not in the room? Your teachers?
- What are you reading for pleasure these days?
- What event going on in the world right now has most caught your interest and why?
- Tell me about your favorite teacher. What makes this person's style good for you?
- How about your least favorite teacher?
- What do you do for fun, just to relax or let off steam?
- Which of your activities mean the most to you? Why did you start? Why do you continue?
- Where do you hope to go with it? Do you see yourself continuing this activity in college?
- What are you really excited about doing in college that will be new to you?
- What are your apprehensions about college?
- Do you have brothers or sisters? What role do you play in your family?
- Do you feel that your grades and test scores are an accurate reflection of your ability? Why or why not?
- Do your studies come easily to you or do you have to work hard for the grades you receive?
- Which subjects come more easily than others?
- Tell me about a class project you have had where you knocked yourself out. Why did you work so hard on that particular project?
- If you had a year off from school and you could choose to do anything at all, what might you do?
- When you think about the "college you," how do you imagine yourself?

When students have done the hard work of learning who they are, the interview should be a positive experience. But it's also helpful to reflect on the process itself. Here are some questions you might want to consider before arriving at the admission office:

- Why am I choosing to interview here?
- What do I want to get out of the interview?
- What do I want to say about myself, if there is an appropriate opportunity?
- What do I want to explain about my background or academic performance, if there is an opportunity?
- What do I want to be sure to ask my parents not to say or talk about?

You may want to write down your answers to these questions in preparing for an interview, but don't bring a "cheat sheet" to the admission office with answers or sound bites. You can pull out a list of questions you have for the interviewer, but that's it.

Never approach an interview like a politician on a TV talk show with a canned talking point—for instance, "I love learning"—and attempt to get that message across no matter what you're asked. Such tactics inevitably backfire. The goal is to go into the interview knowing yourself, having asked yourself questions like those above, and then put all of that aside and have a conversation. That's all there is to it. Do not try to "manage" the interview. The minute you do that, you have given up the opportunity to show who you really are.

QUESTIONS A STUDENT MAY WANT TO ASK IN AN INTERVIEW

In most interviews, the student will be asked if she has any questions, and she should have some at the ready. It's a bad sign to an interviewer when a student shows little or no interest in a school. In addition, the student's questions should not be able to be answered by a quick look at the college's website or its literature. So no questions about the number of undergraduates, majors offered, percentage of students living on campus—nothing about the basic who, what, when, where, and why of a university that can be found on any school's FAQ page.

A good guideline for the kinds of questions you should ask is to inquire about the experiences you might have at a school, not the demographics. Think about it as asking questions that begin with the phrase "What is it like . . . ?" For example, "What is it like to be premed here?" On the other hand, don't try to stump the admission officer. Stay away from anything so specific it requires an answer from the chair of the music department, say.

Here are some questions you may want to ask:

- What kinds of students are most successful here?
- Most colleges have a specific personality that goes beyond its academic offerings. How would you describe the personality here?
- Is there a type of student who is smart and well prepared but who would be happier at a different kind of place? Why or why not?
- Did you go here?
  - If yes: Why did you come and what did you like about it? What would you have changed if you could have? What surprises did you experience? How has the campus changed?

- If not: Why did you choose to come to work here? What kind of opportunities or challenges does this college offer that were not available where you went?

Don't hesitate to ask admission officers what they like about their institutions. You can learn a lot and it feels genuine to make a connection in that way.

Questions Students Should Not Ask in an Interview (Even If the Interviewer Is Young and Hip)

- Don't ask any questions about the interviewer's personal life, including his marital status, living arrangements, or voting record.
- Don't ask the admission officer what the dating scene is like.
- Don't ask if alcohol is easy to obtain.
- Don't ask if classes are "really all that hard."
- Don't ask if there is a lot of reading. And don't follow up that question with "I really don't like to read."
- And once more, with feeling . . . don't ask questions about information that can be found on the college's website or in its literature. Sorry to sound like a broken record on this topic, but this is a pet peeve among admission officers. They expect students to be prepared and courteous enough not to waste their time. Questions about the location of the bookstore and whether the school has a French major make it clear that the student has not done her homework. Such questions take up time better spent by both parties really learning something about each other.

QUESTIONS PARENTS MAY WANT TO ASK

It's fine for parents not to ask any questions. But, if offered the opportunity at the end of the student's interview or within the context of that interview, parents should feel welcome to find out more about the school. Remember, though, this is the time for genuine questions, not an opportunity to speak for your teenager and catalog every achievement in his life since kindergarten.

Here are some common areas of parental concern about which parents might want to ask:

- Can you tell us a little about safety on campus? What type of crime is most common? (Pick one or two questions on this topic; don't dwell on it.)
- How do you feel this college differs—if it does—from the portrait of it in the guidebooks?
- Now that you've met Jane, what should we know about this college that we might not learn from your tour or literature?
- How is roommate matching done?
- What kind of computer support is offered?
- If you were a parent with a child looking at your college—but knowing what you know from working here—what questions would you have?
- Can you tell us a little about financial aid? Merit scholarships? What is your average indebtedness for four-year graduating seniors?
- What do students here complain about?

Also, if your child has a learning difference or a specific health or personal issue, this is a good time to ask about support for those conditions if you and your son or daughter are comfortable doing so.

Finally, the college has selected the admission officer or senior interviewer as representative of the institution, so you can learn a lot by asking general, journalistic questions, such as whether they are from the area and how they like working on campus. You could also ask what their biggest surprise was when they came to the school as a student or an administrator.

Questions Parents Should Not Ask

- Don't ask any questions about issues that are hot buttons for the student. "My daughter struggles with her weight; do you have low-fat food here?"
- Don't ask contrived questions meant to speak for your child. "My daughter is a fabulous singer. Are there opportunities for her to perform on campus?"
- Don't ask about the interviewer's personal life. And don't assume you know his or her age, particularly if the interviewer looks young. You may be talking to the dean.
- Don't ask inappropriate questions. For example, don't ask the Hispanic admission officer about his favorite Mexican restaurant.
- Don't ask if the interviewer minds if you take a phone call. He does mind. Turn off your cell phone before you enter the admission office and keep it off until you leave.
- Don't ask about curfews, about coed bathrooms, or if contraception is available in the dorms.
- Don't ask what the school does for parents so they can stay connected to their children.

This question will be answered in the parent orientation sessions conducted on campus the summer after the student has made her decision.

Questions You May Have

Can a student ruin his shot at admission with a bad interview?

Yes. Appearing to be someone who wouldn't be a positive addition to the college's community can bar a student from that community. And there are many ways that might happen. Chief among them is being rude—not just to the interviewer but to the receptionist, other interviewees, the staff, or the student's own parents. In addition, if a student is uncommunicative with the interviewer or appears contemptuous of the institution that owns the chair he's sitting in, it will work against him. A student should never be obsequious, but should without fail be pleasant and considerate, speak politely to everyone—including the receptionist, the secretary, and his mother—and show up on time.

What if you get an interviewer you feel is biased?

Never assume you will be treated unfairly by either an alumnus or an admission officer. For the most part these people are well trained and their job is to build a community of students that is the strongest and most appropriate for the school's values and mission. Parents may feel that everyone has his or her biases and worry their child is going to get an interviewer who hasn't learned what those biases are and how to filter them out. This is an understandable concern, but it's not something parents can control. Let it go.

Are interviews conducted in the admission office weighted differently from alumni interviews?

It varies from college to college. Most will publicly say they are treated the same, but there are some that will give more weight to an on-campus interview. So, again, if you live within a reasonable driving distance of the school and the school offers on-campus interviews, do the interview on campus. If you can't get to the campus before interviews end that year and the college offers alumni interviews, then take advantage of the opportunity for an alumni interview.

Is it appropriate or advantageous to do multiple interviews—for example, both an on-campus interview and an alumni interview?

For most colleges, one interview will do. There are some schools that will ask the student, even if she has interviewed on campus, to also interview with the local alumni representative. Another exception is that if the student has had an interview with an alumnus before realizing she was able to interview on campus, then she might want to request an interview on campus as well.

Will the interviewer Google the student and the student's family?

Most admission offices do not have time to Google applicants, though they may Google a student who has made a claim they want to verify—for example, if a student claims he discovered a planet (this has actually happened). However, the use of social networking sites and Internet search engines in the application process is on the rise. It's prudent for a student *not* to post anything he doesn't want a college admission office to see. And it's always a good idea to conduct an Internet search on yourself so you can see what comes up and be prepared to talk about it.

What if the interviewer asks the student a "weird" question?

It's not likely a student will be asked an unsettling or odd question—for example, "If you were an animal, what kind of animal would you be?" That said, if an interviewer asks such a question, just roll with it. It's fine to buy time by saying something like, "Wow, that's something I've never quite thought about before." A comment like "Well, that's an interesting question" can buy you a few seconds to think of a response.

What if the interviewer asks an inappropriate or too personal question?

It would be highly unprofessional of an interviewer to ask a student directly about personal matters such as sex, religion, race, or politics. On the other hand, the interviewer does have an interest in knowing what a student is going to be like in a community that is both academic and social. So she may ask questions about what you like to do with your friends or whether you feel most comfortable in large or small groups. And while interviewers will generally not ask a student directly about his politics, it's possible they will ask what issues he has recently read about that most captured his attention.

An interviewer will also probably not bring up sensitive subjects such as family difficulties. Nor should she ask a student a question about the worst experience he has ever had. But be aware that anything the student brings up in the context of an interview is considered fair game to discuss—sensitively, of course.

Finally, the student should remember not to get too familiar with the interviewer. While it's appropriate to ask her whether there's a club for libertarians on campus, it's not appropriate to ask her whom she voted for, what her religion is, or whether she's married.

What if a student is asked where else he is applying?

This is not an appropriate question. While that information may be helpful to the school, it is not necessarily helpful to the student to divulge it. Nevertheless, the question is sometimes asked, so students should have an answer prepared that they feel comfortable with and that is at least responsive and not rude. They could say, "You know, I haven't quite finalized my list, but I do know your college is one I am extremely interested in." Or the student could say, "I haven't finalized my list, but I'm thinking about your college and a few other places." Or the student can make it a joke, "Yeah, my parents want to know that, too!" Finally, if more seems necessary, the student could say, with a smile on her face, "You know, I understand the question, but I'm interested in your school and I'm really still putting the pieces together, so I'm uncomfortable saying more at this point." That should put the matter to rest.

In general, most admission officers will not compare their school to another. It's considered unprofessional. Their job is to tell the student about their own school and leave judgments about other schools to the student and his or her parents.

CHAPTER 12

Recommendations

"Recommendations are important. They tell us how a student might be in the classroom and bring a student to life as a full person."

—Jennifer Rickard, vice president for enrollment, University of Puget Sound

Letters of recommendation can play an important role in the admission decision, particularly at the most selective schools. Required by many colleges, admission offices want them to be written by the people who know the student best in an academic setting—high school teachers and counselors. In shedding light on a student's personal qualities, character, intellect, and motivation, letters of recommendation breathe life into an application and illustrate what can't be captured in grades and scores: what it might be like to have a young person on the college's campus and in its classrooms.

Most private colleges—and more and more public universities—want letters of recommendation from one or two teachers and the high school guidance or college counselor. In this chapter, we'll walk you through obtaining teacher and counselor recommendations, advise you about when additional letters are appropriate (and when they are not), and explain the role these letters play in colleges' admission decisions.

TEACHER RECOMMENDATIONS

Letters of recommendation from teachers tell admission officers how students contribute to the academic and intellectual life of their high school. The Teacher Evaluation of the Common Application asks for a written evaluation of your academic and personal contributions in the classroom, and includes a ratings checklist that compares characteristics such as your motivation, work habits, and intellectual promise to those of other students. Your teachers' input tells the colleges what their faculty can expect from you.

Know the Guidelines

Before you begin thinking about which teachers you will ask to write your recommendations, check the policies of both your high school and the colleges to which you are applying.

Checkpoints ✍

✔ Colleges want recommendations from those who know the student best in an academic setting—high school counselors and teachers.

✔ Ask teachers who know you well and have taught you recently in a challenging class.

✔ Get to know your counselor so she can provide detailed input that helps colleges gain a greater understanding of you.

✔ Waive your access to the recommendations when you sign the FERPA statement.

✔ Check the college's policy about additional letters.

HIGH SCHOOL GUIDELINES

Many high schools will have specific procedures for requesting recommendations from teachers, giving the earliest—and latest—dates students may make their requests, how many teachers students are permitted to request letters from, what materials students should provide, and which teachers are available to write. Find out your high school's policies and follow them.

COLLEGE GUIDELINES

Colleges also have specific policies. Find them on the colleges' websites and on the Common Application website under the individual colleges' information at the College Search tab or under the My Colleges tab in the Assign Recommenders section. Look carefully to determine the number of recommendations required, deadlines for submission, whether recommendations should come from teachers in different academic disciplines, and how they are to be submitted. Colleges'

requirements can change from year to year. Their websites are the authoritative source.

A college's policies may not be immediately obvious. For instance, the Common Application website may note that two recommendations are required, but a student might have to dig more deeply into the application instructions on the college's website to learn the full requirements. For example, it could be that of the two recommendations, the admission office wants one from a math or science teacher and another from a humanities or social science teacher. Always check the website of every college to which you are applying.

When to Ask

Students should begin to think about whom they might ask to write their recommendations at the beginning of junior year in high school. Ask early—but not before the earliest date set by your high school's policy. As a general rule, make your requests in the spring of junior year, especially if you are enjoying a class and connecting with the teacher or if you are going to apply under an early program. (See Chapter 15 for more information about early decision plans.)

If you ask early on in the process, teachers have the opportunity to observe you in class with an eye to writing the recommendation, looking for anecdotes about your participation and intellect—details that make a positive difference in how colleges read these letters. Asking early is also considerate—some teachers like to know in advance how many recommendations they will have to complete in the fall. Finally, if you ask early and a teacher says no to your request, you will have plenty of time to find another recommender.

 ## Best Advice

By the beginning of senior year, there should be two or three teachers—or at least one—who know you well enough to write a recommendation. Participating in the classroom, being friendly and polite, and showing up prepared every day—these things matter, whether or not you think you will need a letter from that teacher.

Whom to Ask

Your most important step in obtaining letters of recommendation from teachers is deciding whom to ask. When admission officers read recommendations, they are looking for what you are like as a person, student, and thinker. Colleges want details about your intellectual energy, work habits, writing ability, attitude, motivation, and academic contribution. Are you an eager learner? Do you bring a classroom discussion to a new place through your contributions? Are you an original thinker? Do you ask interesting questions? Are you able to explain ideas to your classmates in ways that get them excited about a subject? Do you seek opportunities to help classmates who are less able than you? Are you willing to stand up for your point of view?

You probably already have an idea about which teachers can provide the information and anecdotes that will demonstrate these things to admission officers. But here is our best advice:

- Choose teachers who have taught you recently—in the 11th or 12th grade. You experience a lot of growth academically and intellectually from year to year in high school. You want to choose someone who knows you at your strongest—as a junior or senior student. Also, if you are considering asking someone who is teaching you for the first time as a senior, you should be confident that he or she will know you well enough to do a good job before the time when your letters are due.

- Choose teachers who know you well and like you. This sounds obvious, but you'd be surprised how many students don't heed this advice. So think about the classrooms where you've participated, been friendly with the teacher, or even formed a strong bond with him or her. Teachers who know the most about you as a student will be able to write the best recommendations.

- Choose teachers who have taught you in challenging classes where you feel good about how you performed and the grade you got. That doesn't mean that the class has to have been a slam dunk for you. Any teacher who can describe your ability to handle complex or demanding work will add to the understanding an admission officer is seeking.
- Choose teachers who fulfill the guidelines of the colleges where you are applying. Generally, if you're applying to even one college that has a specific requirement—such as recommenders from two different academic disciplines—you will need to choose your two teachers accordingly.

Why Limit the Number of Teachers You Ask to Write for You?

Crafting a strong recommendation letter takes time—often lots of it. We applaud the high schools with strict guidelines limiting students to asking only two teachers to write their recommendations. When students ask three teachers—sending letters from math and history teachers to one college, for example, and math and biology teachers to all other colleges—they have effectively increased the tax on their teachers' time by 50 percent. Pick two teachers and use the same two for all your applications.

This may feel like a hardship to some of you, but it produces much stronger letters because teachers have the time to write thoughtfully when they aren't inundated with unnecessary requests. So be considerate both to your teachers and to your classmates who also need letters of recommendation.

- Choose your recommenders from core academic subjects if the schools where you are applying do not have specific requirements. Core subjects include English, math, science, social studies, or foreign language. Recommendations from music and journalism teachers, for example, are usually not acceptable. We discuss the few exceptions to this for students applying under special circumstances, such as to a conservatory, in Chapter 18.
- Most teachers are happy to help you and will take the time to do a good job in writing your recommendations. You want teachers who will write well about their day-to-day experience with you in their classrooms—not teachers who think, "Why me?" when you make the request.

How to Ask

Writing letters of recommendation is not part of a teacher's normal job duties. Keep that in mind when you are making this request. Your teacher will be devoting hours to something for which she receives no extra compensation. Approach your teachers with a polite, considerate request, not a demand. How do you do that?

- Ask in person. Students are sometimes tempted to ask via email, but our best advice is that a personal request is most thoughtful.
- Ask so that your teachers have plenty of time to complete and send in the recommendations. Go to the trouble to find out when your teacher likes to write—many prefer to write over the summer between junior and senior year.

- Do not ask for more recommendations than you need.
- Say "please" when you ask and "thank you" when the teacher agrees.

Here's what you might want to say:

- "I'm thinking ahead to college applications and wonder if you feel writing a recommendation is something you can do for me."

Phrasing your request this way leaves the opportunity for the teacher to say that perhaps someone else could write a stronger recommendation. Teachers do have the right to say no to you. If that happens—or if a teacher appears hesitant—thank them and move on right away and ask another teacher. You don't want a vague or lukewarm recommendation. Most teachers have your best interest at heart and will want you to have the strongest possible recommender.

What to Provide

Once teachers have agreed to write your letters of recommendation, find out what information they would like you to provide so they can do the job well. Teachers may request three or four of your best papers or an unofficial copy of your transcript, or that you complete a questionnaire for them.

Colleges want teachers to write about their experience with you in the classroom. There's no need for you to provide an activity list or resume unless the teacher specifically requests it. Your extracurricular activities are listed elsewhere in the application and will be covered in the *counselor* recommendation,

which we discuss later in this chapter. Teachers know what they want. Give them what they ask for, not what *you* think they should have.

If your teachers have no preferences about what you provide, but say they would welcome information from you, you could write a short letter—less than a page, even as short as a paragraph—that explains why you are asking them to recommend you. Include information about your growth and experiences in their class. For example, "I'm asking you because when I took your class, math became exciting for me for the first time. It wasn't just getting the right answer. It was thinking about the really interesting problems." You could also consider including a draft of your college application essay.

Once you know what information the teachers want, get organized! Give each of the teachers who are writing for you a folder or manila envelope containing the following:

- Any materials they have requested, such as graded papers, a transcript, completed questionnaire, or a draft of your application essay.
- Recommendation forms—from the colleges' own applications with your personal information completed and the Family Educational Rights and Privacy Act (FERPA) statement waiving your access to the recommendations. See the FERPA sidebar on page 195. (Exception: high schools where recommendations are submitted electronically and colleges and universities that use the Common Application.)
- A list of the colleges where you are applying with each school's deadline, noting whether

you are applying early, whether it uses the Common Application, and if you are applying online or on paper. Also, include on your list any colleges where you are applying that do not require a recommendation letter, and be clear that no letter is needed for those schools.

- For colleges that don't accept online submission of recommendations, provide letter-sized envelopes with adequate postage, neatly addressed to each college's Office of Admission, with the return address of your high school.
- A note thanking the teacher and telling him whom else you are asking to write for you.

COUNSELOR RECOMMENDATIONS

Counselor recommendations fulfill a different, broader function than teacher recommendations. Counselors write about you in the larger context of your high school, not just the classroom. Counselor letters and the School Report (SR), first covered in Chapter 4, explain your transcript, highlight your activities on campus, and illustrate the role you have played in your high school community.

In the SR, counselors are asked to provide detailed information on class rank and GPA calculation, an overall evaluation of you, and a rating of the rigor of your course selection. In addition, counselors are asked to provide a letter of recommendation that should include a detailed and anecdotal—if possible— assessment of your academic, extracurricular, and personal characteristics. Counselor recommendations are most helpful to admission

officers when they provide a picture of who you are as a person, add new information, or explain special circumstances such as a downturn in academic performance due to a particular hardship.

Unlike teacher recommendations, where students can choose those who know them best, students don't get to choose who will write their counselor recommendation. A high school's policies clearly outline who will complete the SR—either the high school college counselor, guidance counselor, or an administrator who knows you well. As we discussed in Chapter 4, that's why it's important to get to know your counselor.

What to Provide Your Counselor

The strength of a counselor's recommendation and ability to present a student fully and accurately can have an influence on the admission decision. Whether or not you are able to get to know your counselor well, you still need to do your part to provide input that can add detail and clarity to the recommendation.

- Ask your counselor if there is any information you can provide. Some counselors may ask you to complete a self-assessment or questionnaire covering personal interests such as your favorite books, jobs you have held, and college goals.
- If your counselor has no preference regarding information you provide, you could create an activity list or resume for her and furnish her with a copy of your application essay.
- Counselor recommendations may also draw on comments from teachers, activity advisors,

coaches, and administrators. If there is no other process for gathering that input, be sure to provide the counselor with names and contact information for those at the school who know you well.

- Provide your counselor with a list of the teachers who are writing your recommendations.
- Sign the FERPA statement, waiving your access to recommendations.
- Parents are sometimes asked to complete a questionnaire or provide a letter about the student for the counselor. These contribute a different and valuable perspective, focusing on areas a counselor might not otherwise know. Parents may fill in gaps about activities and accomplishments that provide a fuller picture, or share stories that illuminate your choices and achievements. It's important for parents to put energy into this, offering insight and anecdotes, rather than simply listing accomplishments.
- Counselors sometimes request a peer statement in which a classmate or close friend comments on your strengths, weaknesses, and uniqueness. These are just another building block for the recommendation. Again, the purpose is simply to learn more about you.

There are two circumstances where it is critical to communicate fully with your counselor so she has the information at hand to fully explain any extenuating circumstances that have

WAIVE YOUR ACCESS TO THE RECOMMENDATIONS!

The Family Educational Rights and Privacy Act (FERPA) is a federal law that protects the privacy of student education records. FERPA gives you the right to have access to your records after you enroll at a college—unless you voluntarily waive your access to certain parts of that record.

You will find the FERPA statement within the Common Application's Assign Recommenders section. For non–Common App schools, the FERPA statement will appear within the application materials. Check the box waiving access to your recommendations and other supporting documents and sign the statement.

Here's why. There is an expectation of confidentiality between your teachers and counselors and the admission office. Admission officers want to know that your teachers and counselors felt free to share their thoughts about you honestly and openly. If you don't waive access, colleges will wonder if your teachers and counselors were cautious in writing—whether there could be something they might have said, or said differently, if they were speaking in confidence. Even if that is not the case, you don't want admission officers to wonder if it is.

had an impact on your high school record in terms of academics or extracurriculars.

- Make sure your counselor understands the reasons for any inconsistency in your academic record. Perhaps you couldn't continue in AP Spanish because of your commitment to the jazz band (or vice versa). Or there was a period of absences due to physical or emotional illness. You may have experienced a drop in grades for a semester due to a family situation such as a parent

Colleges Read Your Recommendations in Context

Admission offices are well aware that the quality of recommendations may vary widely—influenced by the character and size of a high school and the number of students that teachers and counselors are asked to write for. A teacher or counselor evaluation from a school with fifty seniors is going to be read differently than a recommendation from a school of seven hundred seniors. And keep in mind that recommendations provide simply one piece of information in a complex admission decision.

separation or divorce, a death in the family, or a sibling with a health issue. It is important that the counselor be able to explain any anomaly and always beneficial for colleges to have a complete understanding of your circumstances.

- The SR also asks counselors to disclose any knowledge of academic infractions, suspensions, or criminal actions and explain the circumstances, or note that school policy prevents them from responding. Hopefully, the counselor can answer no. But if you have a record of academic or other misconduct, it is best if you initiate a discussion about it with your counselor so he is aware of the circumstances and can offer an explanation to the college. Follow up the counselor's disclosure with your own. We'll talk more about how to handle reporting infractions in Chapter 14.

The time and energy you take with your counselor matter. Do a good job providing input. And one more time: don't forget to say "thank you" to your counselor for his time and effort in writing your recommendation.

FOLLOWING UP

Once you have provided the information to your teachers and counselor, there are still a few things to follow up on.

- Keep your teachers and counselor informed if you make any changes in your plans, such as deciding not to apply to one of the schools on your list.
- Check in with your teachers and counselor a week or so before recommendations are due to make sure they have been submitted.
- A few weeks after the application deadline, check with each college to see if it has received your recommendations. Most colleges will inform you when your application is complete. If the college says it hasn't received your recommendations, check in again with your counselor and teachers. If they say the forms have been submitted, let the college know. Don't stress, just keep checking. They may be in the admission office but haven't yet been registered on the system. Most colleges are not going to refuse to evaluate your application because your teacher recommendations arrive past the deadline.
- Finally, once you have received your acceptance letters, circle back and let the teachers who wrote your recommendations and your counselor know the good news. It's a great courtesy to them, and they truly care about your decision.

ADDITIONAL LETTERS OF RECOMMENDATION

Some colleges—but not all—are happy to read additional letters of recommendation. Students should research the policy regarding additional letters at each of the colleges to which they are applying. Most schools—particularly the most selective—provide clear guidance about whether additional letters are helpful, including how many they will even consider.

If you are applying to a school that will allow you to submit additional letters, there is an important guideline to keep in mind. The letter needs to come from an individual who knows you well and can talk about you in depth. Your recommender should be a person in your life who can write about a dimension of you that is not seen elsewhere in the application—a coach, member of the clergy, employer, or music teacher, for example.

Even if the colleges where you are applying will entertain additional letters, this is an area where less is more. One additional letter is a good general guideline for most applicants. Again, make sure the additional recommender you select can strengthen your application by contributing new and relevant information. Remember, there is a saying in admission offices: "The thicker the file, the thicker the kid."

Letters from major donors, your senator, or a neighbor who is a well-known alum—people who don't really know you well and can't share detailed information about you—are not helpful and may not be well received. The value of these letters is usually inversely correlated with the importance of the person writing because, let's face it, the more important the person, the less well that person probably knows the student. Students are best served by an additional letter when the school has a stated policy that they welcome such input and where the recommender has knowledge of you that is not reflected elsewhere in the application.

For colleges that accept or require them, nonacademic evaluations from peers, coaches, clergy, instructors, or other individuals can now be submitted as part of the Common Application. For other colleges and universities, if you plan to provide an additional letter, check with your high school college counselor about the best way to submit it. And, just as you are not privy to the content of your teacher and counselor recommendations, don't expect to see this one, either!

Parents' Role

Parents, it's fine for you to have a discussion with your teenager about which teachers she might choose to write her recommendations. But the student should take the lead because she will know which teachers know her best. You should *not* call the counselor or teachers writing your son's or daughter's recommendations, or tell them what to say in a letter of recommendation. Also, you will not see any of these letters. As for an additional letter from your second cousin who is a trustee at another university, please see the section above—your insistence on Cousin Bob weighing in may actually weaken your teenager's application.

FROM THE DESK OF THE DEAN

Reading Recommendations

For many schools—particularly more selective colleges—letters of recommendation from teachers and counselors are essential parts of their evaluation of an application. Colleges read the information in these letters carefully, with an eye for the detail and nuance that help them gain a greater understanding of the applicant, whether it's the way a person is in the classroom or the difference they've made in the community. We asked a group of admission deans to talk further about the role of recommendations in the application process.

JAMES WASHINGTON JR.

Director of admissions, outreach and visitor relations, Dartmouth College

➡ The admission process, at heart, is an academic enterprise. We're agents, if you will, of our faculty. So it's important for us to try to consider what students might be like in our classrooms. Are they going to be a dynamic presence? Are they going to be a little bit more reserved and take in information but not have any ripple effect on others in the classroom? Those are the kinds of things that go through our minds when reading teacher recommendations.

You should almost hear and see that person in the classroom when a teacher provides a very helpful recommendation, particularly when they talk about how that student has impacted their own teaching style. Often, teachers will give you a sense of how a student interacts with others in the classroom. What does that student do by way of his or her presence to the level of intellectual discourse? That's, again, an ideal faculty recommendation. It can be very exciting, because you really do get a sense of what it might be like for that person to be in one of your classes. That's what you're trying to envision.

STUART SCHMILL

Dean of admissions, Massachusetts Institute of Technology

➡ We read recommendations in context. We recognize that counselors from schools where there's a very low student-to-counselor ratio may know the students very, very well. And in other contexts, in other schools, with a high student-to-counselor ratio, counselors just can't possibly know the students that well. We don't fault the student for that. It's not a negative. There may not be any overly useful information that comes in from that recommendation, but it's not a negative.

This is important—we get information as part of the application from a number of different sources: from the students themselves, teachers, counselors, and an interview. There are a number of places where information comes in, and not all of it is always useful. That's why we ask for a range of information. So in some cases we will learn something from the recommendations, and in other cases we won't. In some cases we learn something about the student from the essay, and in other cases we don't. But we take this information and try to piece it together to get a picture of the student and her background, motivation, skills, talents, and interests. And if we don't learn something from one particular piece, that's fine.

LORNE ROBINSON

Dean of admissions and financial aid, Macalester College

➡ At a highly selective college, recommendations definitely come into play and their importance in affecting a final decision can range from critical to immaterial, depending on the quality of the recommendation and the qualifications of an applicant.

But interpreting recommendations is certainly more art than science. First of all, how often do people write negative recommendations these days? We just don't see them, and certainly not in the selective college pool, where nearly everyone would be considered a "good" student. There are, however, varying degrees of enthusiasm. So we need to read between the lines a lot, and after you've read a couple hundred recommendations, it becomes pretty easy to tell the difference between a merely positive recommendation and a wildly enthusiastic one.

We do, of course, have to read every one of them in context. So if English teachers tend to write better than physics teachers, we need to be aware of that when we read them. A teacher who clearly knows a student well is going to be able to write a more effective recommendation than a teacher who has merely had the student in class for a couple of weeks in the fall. We factor that all in, and it's part of our filter as we interpret recommendations. This is really where it comes down to the fact that it's not a science. At Macalester, we don't score recommendations. We make comments on them, we interpret them, and we factor them in when they're helpful and ignore them when they're not.

Questions You May Have

Should I ask a teacher to write a letter of recommendation for me in a class where I got a B but I really learned a lot?
Our best advice is that this is usually fine. Students are capable of showing their best academic and intellectual selves when they struggle to achieve. But for students applying to the most selective colleges, we suggest you go with teachers who can speak to your ability to excel in the classroom—that is, in rigorous classes in which you got an A. While many colleges appreciate learning about your academic tenacity, the most selective institutions will want to hear about your ability to be a leader in the classroom and your best intellectual and academic work.

I didn't ask teachers for my recommendations by the end of junior year. What should I do now?
Many students wait until senior year to ask. But some teachers may have already accepted too many student requests to take on another. To be safe, make your requests as soon as possible in the fall of senior year.

The teacher I thought was the best choice to write my recommendation said no. What do I do next?
Ask somebody else. Don't take it personally. Look at any no you get as a favor. You want the strongest recommendation possible. If the teacher doesn't have enough time, doesn't know you well enough, or doesn't think

highly of you, it's better to find someone who will do a better job for you.

Some of the colleges I am applying to ask for a "peer recommendation." Why are they asking for this?
A few colleges—such as Dartmouth and Davidson—require peer recommendations. Others offer these as options. Peer recommendations provide colleges with additional context about who you are and what you would bring to the college community. Again, specific anecdotes and detail are most helpful, so choose someone who is close to you and knows you well. But also choose someone who can write well and who can clearly communicate your strengths, who you are, and what other people appreciate about you. Students most often choose a friend or classmate, but colleges usually regard the definition of "peer" loosely—it could be a best friend, sibling or other relative, co-worker, or teammate. Ask well ahead of the deadline so that your recommender has plenty of time to write a thoughtful letter.

Should I give a thank-you gift to each of the teachers who wrote a recommendation for me?
A gift is not necessary, but a sign of appreciation is absolutely appropriate. Remember, writing recommendations is not part of their official job description. So there are a number of points along the way when a thank-you is appropriate:

- When a teacher agrees to write for you, say "thank you."

- When you drop off any materials, such as your transcript, say "thank you" again.
- When you check with the teacher to make sure the recommendation was sent, say "thank you" again.

- The best thank-you? On the first school day after you get your notification from each college, go to the teacher's classroom and let him or her know your outcomes.
- At the end of it all, send a note of appreciation.

CHAPTER 13

Essays

"The essay is important. . . . It has to be you, and you will be the most compelling argument for yourself."

—Charles Deacon, dean of admissions, Georgetown University

Ah, the terror of the blank page—or, in the twenty-first century, the blank screen. There are no steps in the application process that produce more anxiety and lead to more procrastination than writing the essays. But think of it this way: the essay is the step in the application process where you speak to the colleges directly and tell them who you are and what you care about. Want to be more than a set of grades and scores? This is your opportunity.

We know writing about yourself can be intimidating, maybe even a little embarrassing. Take a deep breath and believe in yourself. Remember, the admission officers at colleges are trying very hard to get to know you, and they will use the essays to gain a deeper sense of your personality and character, an understanding of the how and the why of what you do.

In this chapter we'll show you how to distinguish yourself by taking what you have learned through all the self-examination asked of you in earlier chapters and putting it into an essay that will tell a true story of you—starting with brainstorming topics and on through to the final word count.

WHAT COLLEGES WANT

Don't overestimate the importance of the essay in an admission decision. While colleges differ in the weight given the essay, an essay alone will not get you admitted to a college. An egregiously bad one may keep you out—but that's usually a matter of slipshod effort or questionable taste.

So don't psych yourself out thinking the essay has to do the heavy lifting in an application. It is only one of many pieces. Your academic record—grades and the rigor of your course work—will almost always be the factors given the most weight in an admission decision. Nevertheless, the essay is an important element of the application you can use to help the college see who you are beyond the numbers.

In evaluating the essays, both form and content are important. Specifically, colleges look for two things:

- **Can you write?** They're not looking for Pulitzer Prize–winning prose, but they want to know if your ability to write meets the academic standards of the college. They want to see that you can take a thought and develop it in a clear and organized fashion, using proper grammar. No typos, please. Your ease with language and ability to write in an engaging and thoughtful way shows them that you can express yourself effectively and that you possess the intellectual ability and readiness for college work.

- **Who are you?** Admission officers are trying to get a sense of your beliefs, aspirations, values, or passions. They want to hear your voice and know more about you when they have finished your essays than they did before they started reading them. Above all, they are trying to learn what impact you will have on their community. Will you make their school a better place simply by being a part of it, whether that's in the classroom, chemistry lab, residence hall, or theater program? Colleges look for who you are in the application as a whole, and the essays are one place in particular where this can be seen most clearly.

If you're a better mathematician than wordsmith, rest assured that admission officers recognize that different students have different strengths and not everybody can write beautifully. However, that doesn't absolve any applicant of the responsibility of writing about something important to him or her in a thoughtful, genuine way.

Getting Started

Colleges that require essays in the application process usually ask students to write one or

There's a reason we haven't included sample essays in this chapter. We believe examples limit and inhibit students. The number of ways to approach the essay is infinite. It's very hard to write an essay that truly represents who you are when you have someone else's ideas fixed in your mind.

Our objective is to guide you through finding a topic and developing it for both the long essays and short responses asked for in college applications. We will tell you what colleges are looking for and provide our best writing advice. However, we will not provide you with a template for writing "the perfect college essay" because there isn't one. There is no one-size-fits-all ultimate X-factor secret-ingredient killer-app essay that will result in admission to the school of your choice.

Again, here you must march to the beat of the drum you have heard throughout this book: authentic, authentic, authentic. Colleges want to hear your voice in your writing. Going online or to the bookstore to find examples of "essays that worked" will not serve you well. The only thing you need to find is your genuine voice. The surest path to success here is to be authentically yourself.

two longer personal statements and respond to two or three short-answer questions. The Common Application requires one personal essay. But many schools ask for additional writing in their supplements.

Visit the Common Application website at commonapp.org to see the essay topics and learn the writing supplement requirements of the colleges to which you are thinking of applying. But also visit the websites of all colleges to which you are applying to determine their specific essay requirements, whether they are Common Application schools or not. We repeat: it's your responsibility to double-check individual colleges' websites to be sure you know exactly what is being asked of you.

Your essays will usually be read together as a unit by an admission officer. Each essay—whether it's 650 words or a short paragraph of 150 or 250 words—needs to contribute in a different way to the reader's understanding of who you are. Each is equally important.

When Should You Start?

Start working on your essays over the summer before senior year. The summer will provide you with the luxury of uninterrupted time to reflect, and then to revisit your essays later. Fall of senior year is a busy time, and writing your essays while attending school is like adding a class to your schedule. The more you can get done before September, the better.

 Best Advice

We strongly urge you to have at least your Common Application essay in good shape before senior year begins.

THE PERSONAL ESSAY

The personal essay—or personal statement—with its longer format provides students the opportunity to be reflective and informative. The Common Application specifies an enforced maximum word limit of 650 words and an enforced minimum word limit of 250 words. That is ample space to do a good job telling a college about yourself. And you are not obligated to use all 650 words at your disposal. More is not necessarily better here. Remember, admission officers read thousands of essays every year. You will make a stronger impression if you tell your story without excess verbiage. Think one page, single-spaced— that's about 650 words, ideally.

Selecting a Topic

Start by reading through all the essay topics or prompts on the Common Application and the applications of the schools to which you are applying. Take your time and consider each one's potential. Give each one a chance. If, as you read through them, one leaps out at you, that's great! You have a starting point and can move on to developing it into an essay. Finding a topic can be the most difficult aspect for some students. No idea where to start? We're here to help.

Remember, the real topic is *you*. Whatever the essay is about on the surface, colleges care what the essay says about you. You could write about your fascination with the musical *Grease,* robotics, being bullied, babysitting your younger siblings, playing video games, studying viruses, your collection of vinyl records, or your family's holiday rituals. There is no single "right" topic. Any topic that reveals your true self, in your own voice, is right.

Every student has had some experience that has been meaningful. The hard part is

figuring out what it was, because it is not usually something *big*. You probably shouldn't even be writing about big subjects that require grand terms. Write about a specific incident or subject, a little thing that was really meaningful to you—not the whole massive subject

KNOW THE JARGON . . .

Prompt

A prompt is a statement or question designed to get students to think about and respond to a topic in depth. A prompt from the Common App: "Some students have a background or story that is so central to their identity that they believe their application would be incomplete without it. If this sounds like you, then please share your story."

of "my childhood" or the huge challenge of "how I want to change the world"—and do it in a way that is personal and authentic.

Admission officers' favorite essays are often about subjects you might consider trivial. It's all in how each student handles what he or she says—how he uses the fact that he adores his baby brother to tell about his values and dreams, how she talks about her love of Quentin Tarantino films to illustrate her interest in telling truth through dark humor, how he describes his research in the rat lab to make a point about the use of animals as test subjects, how she writes about acquiring her first telescope, looking in depth at her first starry night and discovering a deep interest in astronomy, how he took a computer personality test and discovered he was a Yoda and decided that was just right.

Also, don't start out strategizing about some way you want to portray yourself—as "a good friend" or "funny" or "a thinker"—and then go in search of a topic you think accomplishes that in an effort to tell colleges what you think they want to hear. It's a waste of time trying to figure out exactly what they're looking for because the list is endless and ever-changing. It might be niceness or a sense of humor, an interest in algorithms or activism, the boy who is fluent in French or the girl who raises pigs in 4-H. No college is saying, "We must have a cook." They are looking for the way students come across when they write about why they like to cook. Simply be genuine so they can see for themselves who you are.

Here are two strategies to help you find a topic:

- **Put a microscope to your life.** Take a look at the little things around you. Go to your room and look at what's on the walls, what's under the bed, and the things you've kept since second grade, or consider the thing you threw

> The Common Application is subject to change from year to year, including the essay prompts. Please check our website at collegeadmissionbook.com for real-time updates on all aspects of the Common Application and the college application process.

away that you really miss now. Where in the house do you spend the most time? Look for inspiration right under your nose. Ask yourself some of these questions:

- How do I spend my time?
- What do I like to do?
- What do I think about most of the time?
- What are the things that truly matter to me?
- What is my family like? Do we have any interesting rituals about dinners or board games or TV shows?
- What would I say about myself if I had to omit any mention of my extracurricular activities?
- When I think about who I am or what I care about, is there a particular day, moment, or event that was important in shaping that?
- If I, like Tom Sawyer, had a chance to eavesdrop at my own funeral, what would people say about me?
- What do I like best about my school?
- If I had a day to do anything I wanted—no school, no work, no homework, no chores—what would I do?
- What do I want this college to know about me?
- What keeps me up at night?
- What drives me, makes me tick?
- What am I most proud of?

- **Brainstorm.** Brainstorming is a great way to generate ideas. All you need is a piece of paper and a pen—or a keyboard. If you want company, invite a friend you trust. Or schedule a fifteen-minute appointment to talk with a teacher whose class you enjoy. In the meantime, try these exercises:
  - Make lists. Pick one of the following and free-associate, listing anything and everything that comes to mind. There is no right way to answer these. Follow the trail of what comes to mind and see where it leads.
    - I am really good at . . .
    - I hate . . .
    - I used to think . . .
    - I think it's hilarious when . . .
- Imagine you have five minutes in a room with someone you've never met before and in those five minutes you have to tell him or her everything you feel is crucially important about you. Set a timer. Are you panicking? That's okay. This is just for five

What *Not* to Write

While we have said repeatedly in this chapter that colleges don't require that you write about certain topics, there are some topics you should definitely avoid. Here are some guidelines:

- Young love. Don't write about your first sexual experience, sex life, or love life. In admission offices, these are known as the "too much information" essays.
- Drug-free zone. Colleges are looking to admit students who will keep their campuses safe communities. Don't write about the use of recreational drugs, alcohol, or any illegal substance.
- Resumes in prose. Don't list your activities and achievements here—it's a wasted opportunity. That information can be found elsewhere in the application.
- Health check. Be careful with health issues. Choosing to write about your struggle with childhood cancer may be appropriate, but writing about lactose intolerance as a hardship you overcame is not.
- Me, myself, and I. Yes, you do need to tell the college about yourself, and you'll likely write in the first person. But if your twenty-seven-sentence essay has twenty-seven sentences that begin with the word "I," start over.
- The rap sheet. No essays about illegal activity, even if it's a misdemeanor or prank—like tipping over portable toilets (we kid you not). Remember, admission offices are trying to imagine the role you will play on a campus.
- My way or the highway. There are ways to write about capital punishment or being a Christian that will tell a college something important about you. But be judicious. Colleges seek students with strong opinions but open minds, those who are eager to engage in an exchange of ideas

What *Not* to Write (continued)

and willing to listen to others as well as share their own beliefs. A narrow worldview will work against you, especially if you act as though your way is right and the rest of the world is wrong.

- The complaint. Don't whine or complain about your life, your parents, your teachers, your coach, ethnic food, or anything else.
- The excuse. Don't attempt to explain away shortcomings such as a bad SAT score or grade in a class—there's a place for that, and this isn't it.
- Bad taste. Pass up any topic that calls attention to deep personal biases, disrespect for your parents, pomposity, contempt for groups of people, sexism, negative stereotypes, racial slurs, or profanity. Also, no bathroom humor or vulgarity.
- The stand-up routine. Go ahead and be funny if you really are a funny person, but do so in a way that reveals who you are and what you value. You, not the humor, should be at center stage.
- The term paper. Don't get lazy and submit one of your American literature assignments! Your treatise on *Heart of Darkness* or Lincoln's first inaugural address may have been brilliant, but colleges want a first-person essay about you.
- The travelogue. This is another area where you need to be thoughtful. Don't write an essay about Chile—you are supposed to write an essay about what Chile meant to you. And it's best to avoid play-by-play accounts of luxury vacations or exotic adventure holidays.
- Community service. If community service is truly central to who you are, it may be a good essay topic. But proceed in a way that shows great respect for all you met along your path. The "it made me a better person to build latrines in Country X" essay is difficult to write well, calling for a nuanced understanding of issues such as class, social justice, and economics.
- The lie. Do not lie. It has been tried, it doesn't work, and you won't like the consequences. When one young man wrote his Stanford essay about his father dying of cancer, not only did his father not appreciate it, but when the truth came to light, neither did the admission office. We'll talk more about the importance of representing yourself honestly later in this chapter.

minutes. And sometimes a little panic can help clarify what's really important and the extraneous falls away, leaving room for some insights to move in. Write them down.

- List values, issues, or experiences that have been important to you. Then go back and sketch out the stories in your life that describe what you have experienced around those issues.

- List all the people who have inspired or influenced you—historical figures, family, friends, people in your community, fictional characters.

Don't get caught up in finding the "perfect" topic. There is more than one thing in your life you can write about that will tell a college a lot about you. If you have one or two topics in mind, you're ready to move on to the next step—developing the topic into an essay.

Developing the Topic

You've done the most important thing—found something in your life that you can write about in a way that will tell the college something important about you. Once you have your topic, it's all in the execution. While there are numerous prompts on the Common App, they're all basically asking you for the same two things: "write something" and "tell us about yourself."

The process of turning your topic into a finished essay—writing, revising, proofing—may be different in its details for each student. But, in general, what you're going to do is pretty straightforward—you're going to tell a story straight from your heart in your authentic voice and then work on it until it is clear, organized, and vivid in its detail.

As with all such things, getting started can be difficult, even if you know what you want to write about right away. It's not rocket science—just hard work. To get an essay ready to be sent off to a college, it will have to go through as many as ten drafts and some feedback from readers. No kidding. Don't freak out about it. Sometimes a draft will take a couple of hours, other times twenty minutes, depending on where you are in the process and what you're trying to accomplish.

Some of you won't believe you need multiple drafts and will think you can just sit down a few nights before your applications are due and whip out an acceptable essay in a couple of hours. Not so, even if you are the next Ernest Hemingway or Langston Hughes.

Here's what the draft process might look like, including advice on form, content, and style.

Draft 1

Writer Anne Lamott coined a term for this— "the sh*#@ty first draft." We highly recommend that you Google this and read her essay. It will make you feel a lot better about the process you are about to set out on. All writers are intimately acquainted with the sh*#@ty first draft. So, college applicants, let us introduce you.

You've got your best idea. Start writing! You are going to sit down and put pen to paper or your fingers on the keyboard and just go at it. Are you writing yet? Good. Get it out there on the page. Tell us the story. It's not English homework. It's a true story about who you are. Pour everything that comes to mind about your topic onto the page.

If this sounds completely intimidating, set a timer for twenty minutes and don't stop moving your fingers until it goes off. The topic you write about in your first couple of rough drafts may not be the essay you end up submitting, but you won't know that until you try to write it. Keep writing. Think of this as practice. It doesn't have to be good. It's okay if it's sh*#@ty!

Just keep writing. Don't slow down to find the perfect metaphor or most apt adjective. More careful writing happens later. Keep typing; don't stop. Tell us more of the story. Focus on what happened. What was important?

Why? How? Keep typing. Beware of well-loved methods of distraction and procrastination (also known as Candy Crush, getting a snack from the kitchen, or checking your Tumblr). Keep writing. Tell the story the way you would tell it to a friend. Don't worry about length. Write five or six pages if you have to. We know you only need 650 words. Editing comes later.

Finished? Next step: do nothing about it until tomorrow.

Draft 2

It's the next day. Read your sh*#@ty first draft. *Oh, man . . .* We know just how you feel. But it's okay. Take another look.

First, do you think this is the right topic for you to write about? Is it a story only you can tell?

Second, is it about you? Even if it's about apartheid, robotics, the Magic School Bus, your coach, *Game of Thrones,* or anything else, *you* need to be the focal point.

Third, is it written straight from your heart? Is this truly your voice?

Writing an essay is a process of self-discovery. Dig past the big-picture clichés about hard work and passion and inspiration and leadership. Get to the "who, what, how, and why" of you. If you are writing about your brother, the story in the essay is not as much about your brother as it is about the impact your brother has had on you—how he has shaped who you are, what you value, and how you see the world. Ask yourself some more questions:

- Why is this important to me?
- What did I learn from this?
- How did it shape my beliefs and values?
- What was the biggest stumble?
- When did I first learn how to do this?
- What was it like before this was in my life?
- How did it change me or who I think I will become?
- What was I feeling?
- What was I experiencing in my life at that time?

Now rewrite the sh*#@ty first draft using these questions to make it completely your own story. And then don't look at it for a couple of days.

Draft 3

Read Draft 2 with fresh eyes. Now it's time to consider whether your essay tells a story. The most memorable essays tell a story. Stories have a beginning, a middle, and an end. Does yours?

Look at the essay's structure. Does it start out with something that will bring the reader immediately to attention? Does it reach out and grab you in the first sentence?

Are there things here that don't really support the story you want to tell? Take them out. What is missing? Fill it in.

Is the story shaping up like a story that you'd enjoy hearing? Does it move from the general to the specific? Does it flow? Are there good transitions tying one paragraph to the next? Does it make sense?

How did you get from point A to point B? Constantly ask yourself "how" and "why" questions as you read through your essay. Where is the evidence for what you are saying? Does the story come full circle in the last paragraph? Does the conclusion return to the introduction?

If you are having trouble with the structure, try outlining your essay. But remember that the story doesn't have to be linear or chronological. It just has to tell the story so the reader can understand and be moved by it.

Finish your rewrite, print it out, and stick it in a drawer for at least a week or so. Time for a vacation.

Draft 4

Pull out Draft 3 and reread it. Looking at it with fresh eyes will give you a chance to see holes in your story that need to be filled or places to say more about yourself. At this point, you also need to think about the "voice" of your essay.

Voice—the tone, the style, the attitude of your essay—is extremely important here because it is about writing from the place of "Who am I?" Writing with voice gives a sense of the author's personality—it makes your writing sound different from anyone else's. The voice can be humorous or serious, formal or casual, objective or subjective, so long as it's yours. You may have to undo some of what you have learned in English class—in particular, using the passive voice and writing in the third person.

In essay writing, the passive voice is taboo. Look at the difference:

- **Active.** "I crossed the road."
- **Passive.** "The road was crossed."

Passive voice deprives the reader of color, emotion, and a feeling of intimacy with the writer.

Writing in the first person—writing so that you refer to yourself just as you speak, using terms such as "I," "me," "myself," and "mine"—allows you to tell a story that is closer to your speaking voice and captures your spirit. It may reflect your quirky vocabulary, the rhythms of your speech, and the energy of the way you speak. An example? Think of Holden Caulfield in *The Catcher in the Rye* or Maya Angelou in *I Know Why the Caged Bird Sings*. These books are each written with an unmistakably personal point of view with no pretense of being anything else. That's why they work. Want to know more about what first-person writing sounds like? Check out our list of books written in the first person on page 214.

Finding your voice is simply finding a more natural way of expressing yourself. One way you can find your voice is to read your essay out loud. Does it sound like you? Does it sound the way you sound when you talk with your best friend at 2:00 a.m. about something you're excited about? Try reading into a recorder and playing it back. Does it sound stiff, or as if you're trying to impress someone? Does it make you wince? Relax and you'll find your authentic voice.

Rewrite your essay to capture your voice as perfectly as you can. Save the document and take a break from it for a few more days.

Draft 5

In this round, you're going to go through Draft 4 and apply two maxims that we cannot emphasize enough:

- **Details make a story come alive.** Meaningful, well-observed details. Not "the mountain I climbed was high." Instead, the name of the mountain, the time of year you were there, its elevation, the shoes you wore, the Indian paintbrush and bunchberry growing along the paths. Go through your essay and make sure you have taken every opportunity to provide vivid examples that are yours and yours alone. Everyone has interesting details to their life; they may just not realize it because they live it every day. Think about the food and drink at family dinners, the furniture in your piano teacher's home, or the contents of your closet. Detail makes it personal. Use your grandmother's name instead of just calling her "my grandmother." Be specific. Look for little details that tell the big story—the heft of your first cello and the faint pine scent of the bow rosin paint a picture of what it felt like to "make music on a day in the spring eight years ago." Having a hard time coming up with details? Make lists—take a key word from your essay and free-associate, writing down everything that comes to mind. The details you're looking for will emerge.

- **Show, don't tell.** An essay comes alive when you show the reader yourself. Don't tell the reader you're "a leader." Show it by describing how you held a group of screaming five-year-olds together at summer camp, stopping two in one corner from pulling each other's hair and three in the other corner from hitting one another over the head with shovels. Don't tell the reader that your participation in a sport shows your "dedication." Show it by describing the alarm going off at 5:00 a.m. every morning so you can get to water polo practice, how it feels to jump into a cold pool at that hour, why you have to log miles in laps year-round, and how hard it was to read your calculus textbook in the dark of the van on the way home from a meet. Let the reader experience your story along with you.

Rewrite your essay so the reader will see it, feel it, smell it, and hear it. Then put it away in a drawer for a few days or a week—or longer, if you've gotten an early start and time is on your side.

Draft 6

Take out Draft 5 and make sure it's taking you where you want to go.

Ask yourself these questions:

- Did I answer the prompt? Failure to do so is a particular complaint of admission officers.
- Did I convey the information I wanted to?
- Did I convey my enthusiasm and passion?
- What has the reader learned about me?
- What impression am I leaving?
- Is this who I really am?
- Have I made myself vivid?
- Does this sound like someone other than me?
- If someone who had never met me read this, what impression would he get?

Now it's time to check your word count. If you've been writing long, you need to start cutting. Can you answer the questions above using 650 words? The best essay will. That doesn't mean it's easy. There is some disagreement about who said it—Mark Twain or William Faulkner or Lillian Hellman—but it's an apt description of editing your writing: "killing your darlings." That perfectly crafted sentence you love? Turns out it doesn't add much to the narrative. Get rid of redundancies, unimaginative writing, anything extraneous to the storytelling, and anything not in your authentic voice.

Cut and rewrite.

Draft 7

Get some constructive input from a teacher, peer, parent, or family friend. Run your essay by someone who knows you well—and then someone who doesn't, for yet another perspective.

There's no need for paranoia about someone stealing your ideas if you show your draft to your peers. If the essence of your essay is who you are—which it should be— no one can steal that. So do a round robin with fellow students where each of you reads your essay aloud. Ask your listeners these questions:

- Does the opening draw you in?
- What do you think I'm trying to say?
- How do I come across as a person?
- Is there any point where you were confused?
- Is it clear why this story is important to me?
- Where do I need more detail?
- Where were you bored?
- Which parts did you like best?
- Could anyone else have written this essay?

Regardless of how you solicit feedback, there should be no editing by committee. Trust your instincts. If someone is telling you to change something but it feels right to you, go with your gut. See the sidebar on acceptable/unacceptable feedback.

Also, you don't have to wait until this

Getting Feedback

Feedback can be very helpful as you develop your essay topic, but too much interference can erase your individual stamp on the essays. Here are some guidelines for how to tell if the feedback you're getting is constructive:

Acceptable feedback:

- I think you might want to clean up your grammar in this paragraph.
- It's hard for me to know what you're saying in this section.
- This sentence doesn't really sound like you.
- Think about whether your essay really needs this paragraph.
- This is repetitive; go back through and think about how and where you could say it once, with impact.

Unacceptable feedback:

- I have a better way for you to say this. Say it like this . . .
- This sentence is awkward. Let's rewrite it together.
- Let's cut this.
- You say you were "hungry." How about saying "ravenous"?

point in the process for feedback. If you feel it would be helpful sooner, go ahead and search out some readers. But don't invite others in before you've got a good head start.

Draft 8

You've revised, revised, revised. It's time for a final polish on the content.

Author and writing teacher Ellen Sussman recommends this four-part exercise:

1. Go through the essay word by word to see if there is a better way to say what you want to say. A better word is not a fancier word—stay away from the thesaurus. A better word is often a very simple one that creates a more vivid picture.

2. Reread and look for any opportunities to make the writing richer, or where a good metaphor or simile can underline a theme. An oboist described her first efforts as "the sound of dying geese."

3. Look one more time for opportunities to add details and specifics. "The Radiohead poster on the wall" tells the reader so much more than "the poster on the wall."

4. Look to see if you have used more than one of the five senses. Don't just be visual. Remember to include smells and tastes and sounds and textures.

Rewrite until your essay is totally smooth and rich in detail but with no excess fat. Walk away from it for a few days.

Draft 9

Pull out Draft 8 and look at the mechanics—grammar, punctuation, and spelling. Check and recheck. Remember, your computer's spell-check isn't always right. As Albuquerque Academy director of college guidance Ralph Figueroa notes, "Spell Czech is knot yore friend and it will betray ewe." Look for problems such as switched tenses and slang. No text shorthand like "LOL" or "IMHO"! See where your Microsoft Word software has underlined the essay in red or green—that might mean misspelling or bad grammar. Fix it, if the software really caught a mistake. Proofread again for typos that weren't picked up by spell-check. Note the colleges' specific instructions about headings, length, and extra pages and comply with them.

Make all corrections and edits.

Writers Who Found Their Authentic Voice

We strongly recommend you avoid books hawking application essays that "worked." You won't find the story that says the most about you in someone else's work. You're much better off investing your time—and money—in some good writing. Here are our recommendations of engaging, first-person essays:

- David Sedaris: *Santaland Diaries* and *Dress Your Family in Corduroy and Denim*
- Sloane Crosley: *I Was Told There'd Be Cake*
- Gayle Pemberton: *The Hottest Water in Chicago*
- Julia Alvarez: *Something to Declare*
- Calvin Trillin: *Feeding a Yen* and *Family Man*
- Anne Lamott: *Bird by Bird: Instructions on Writing and Life* and *Operating Instructions*
- Caitlin Flanagan: *To Hell with All That*
- Mark Salzman: *Lost in Place: Growing Up Absurd in Suburbia*
- Amy Tan: *The Opposite of Fate*
- Tim Cahill: *Hold the Enlightenment*

Draft 10

Almost done.

Your essay is organized, focused, polished, vivid, personal, and meaningful. It's time for a final proofreading. Even if you have forgone feedback from others, it's important to let at least one other person proofread your essays before you submit them. Ask someone you trust who has a good grasp of grammar and spelling. You'll be amazed what errors will be picked up instantly by someone else even though you've read the essay a hundred times and still missed them. Make any necessary final edits.

Save, print a copy for your records, and congratulate yourself on a job well done.

SUPPLEMENTS

Many colleges have their own writing supplements, which can require multiple short-answer and additional essay-length responses. The prompts on the colleges' individual supplements are often unique to that school. They may ask you to describe a creative work that has had an influence on you, discuss an international issue, or describe your favorite place to get lost. Many colleges include a "Why us?" essay on their supplement, and we discuss this specifically in the box on page 216.

Colleges are trying to get to know you a little better with these supplemental essays—how you think, what's truly important to you in a college—and to project the type of impact you may have as a student on their campus. Believe us: admission officers do not lack for reading material, and if they have asked you for a supplemental essay, they believe they need it to make the best decision possible. So do it and do it well. The draft and writing process for these essays is the same as for those on the Common Application. It is usually not a good idea to try to shoehorn a response to one college's prompt into that of another. That's why an early start is a good idea. The supplemental essays require time and energy if you want to make yourself memorable to the schools to which you are applying.

Assume until proven otherwise that every school you're applying to has a supplement. It's your responsibility to find out exactly what is required and make sure it arrives safely at the admission office. The college will not consider your file complete until the supplement is received.

Additional specific supplements that may be required for applicants with special talents in the arts are discussed in Chapter 18.

SHORT-ANSWER ESSAYS

Short-answer essays should be approached just like the longer personal statement essay—they are just as important. The writing process is the same. You need to write well and in your own voice, keep it personal by being honest and open, use specific details to make yourself distinctive, and revise, revise, revise. Don't get stymied by the shortness of the responses called for—usually 150 to 250 words or less. Stay focused, strive for clarity, and don't try to cover too much.

Remember that colleges are looking to know you better, and the longer essays are read along with the shorter essays by admission officers. They are all of a piece. So balance the content among all of the essays—on both the Common Application and the college's individual writing supplements—to paint the fullest picture of yourself.

For example, the college supplements frequently ask students to elaborate on an extracurricular activity or work experience in a short-answer essay. Portraying an extracurricular activity or work experience in a way that is both accurate and evocative can be hard to do. Irena Smith, a former Stanford application reader and writing teacher who works with high school students applying to college, advises them to focus on what they learned and how their participation changed them. Try to describe the essence of your extracurricular activity or work experience. Look back on your history with the experience so you can come up with a story that accounts for where you were when you started and where you are now. Above all, explain why the activity or work experience you choose to write about is so important to you. But don't write your short essay on the same subject you covered in a supplemental long essay or the Common Application essay. Don't waste the opportunity to tell the college something more about yourself.

Finally, there is no correlation between the word "short" in "short-answer essay" and the amount of time required to spend to produce a good response. In some ways, it can be trickier to express yourself in a few words

The "Why Us?" Essay

Many colleges ask students to respond to a "Why us?" question. Variations include: "Why do you wish to attend College X?" and "Which aspects of our curriculum or undergraduate experience prompted your application?" Students often think that what the college is asking for is a "suck-up" essay. It's not. Admission officers want to see that you're a good fit for their school, you've done your homework, and you have a real understanding of their institution.

Don't even think about using the same "Why us?" essay for multiple schools by simply swapping out the names of the colleges. It's insulting to the college and suggests you're not that interested in the school. If you write, "I want to be in a great city at a college with a really strong academic reputation and terrific professors," you're talking about hundreds of colleges. Some colleges may also be considering your likelihood to enroll when they read this essay. Don't just drop the name of the college, the U.S. News and World Report ranking, or the city where it's located—that doesn't show any understanding of the specific institution to which you are applying.

Think back to your visit—real or virtual—and remember what excited you about the school. Why did you like this particular college? Don't just spout stuff from the college's home page. Remember what you liked about that school's programs, campus organizations, and academic and social environment. If after you finish you can go back through and plug in the name of another college, you haven't taken your best shot at explaining your interest.

Submission of Graded Papers

Some colleges want to see an additional example of students' writing and will require submission of a graded paper from a class—either at the time the application is submitted or partway through the application reading if they believe additional writing would be helpful in reaching a decision.

While their reasons for this may vary from college to college and student to student, in general colleges are looking for the following:

- To confirm the impression of the strength or weakness of a student's writing. In some cases, an admission office might want to admit a student and needs additional evidence that a student's writing is strong enough for that student to succeed at their college.
- To confirm that the application essays are the student's own work. An admission officer might compare the writing on your academic paper to the writing on your essays to see if the style and level of writing are consistent.
- To provide a better understanding of the academic expectations at a student's school. The grading scale, teacher comments, or complexity and challenge of the assignment might show, for example, that a student with a strong writing sample who earned a B attended a demanding school, or at least was enrolled in demanding courses.
- To illuminate the quality of teaching a student has had. Teacher comments may be helpful, supportive, encouraging, or nonexistent. They may be from an English teacher whose comments are eloquent or whose grammar in the comments is faulty. This adds to the admission officer's understanding both of a student's abilities and of the context of their high school.

If any of the colleges where you are applying require or request submission of a graded paper, you should submit a photocopied copy of a returned paper that shows the grade and teacher comments (if any).

Here are some further guidelines:

- Use a paper from junior or senior year.
- Have mercy. You can send in a twenty-page paper, but all things being equal, the three-pager is preferred.
- Choose a paper you believe shows your strongest work. Unless specifically stated otherwise by the college, assume this should be a text paper written in the English language. No in-class essays, tests, calculus problem sets, or chemistry lab reports.
- If possible, choose an assignment that shows your thought process, including some analysis of the subject and some of your own conclusions or opinions, rather than a paper that is solely a recital of facts.

Plagiarism

Plagiarism is the act of representing someone else's words or ideas as your own. You will be signing a statement on the application form that certifies that all elements of your application, including the essays, are your own work.

Don't underestimate how easy it is to figure out if someone has plagiarized material. Admission officers read thousands of essays. They know what high school students sound like and they're expert at homing in on discrepancies in the application—a middle-of-the-road teacher recommendation, for example, for an applicant whose essay boasts prose that sings. In addition, the college where you're applying may be submitting their essays to Turnitin or some other Web-based plagiarism detection service. Colleges won't necessarily tell you they're using such technology, so if you decide to test it, you might not know until it's too late.

"I ran the essay through Turnitin just to be sure, but when it began with 'Four score and seven years ago...'"

But know this: colleges can withdraw their offer of admission at any point if they learn you misrepresented yourself on the application, even if you are about to graduate from that college. We'll talk more about this in Chapter 14.

---

than in many. And even though these essays are short, don't assume that they don't matter as part of your application—they do. So put your short-answer responses through the same draft process you used for the long essays.

Questions You May Have

What if I don't have an extracurricular activity to talk about in a college's writing supplement?

Think about how you spend your time when you're not in class. Do you have a job, care for younger siblings, read Siddhartha, tutor, or skateboard? Colleges just want to know what you do with your time and why you do what you do.

Is it important to submit the optional essays in the supplements?

Yes. These are the essays that used to be on the colleges' own unique application forms. The colleges agreed they could receive some information—asked by all colleges—through a shared application form. They then placed additional questions and essay prompts they cared about as individual schools on

How Much Help Is Too Much?

Good writing involves getting feedback. But there is a difference between feedback and coaching—whether it comes from your aunt who works for the newspaper, your English teacher, your mom or dad, or your best friend. Appropriate feedback occurs when a reader makes suggestions, points out faulty grammar and punctuation, and informs you of any glaring omissions or errors. Inappropriate coaching occurs when content is directly altered by someone other than the student. (See some examples in the box on page 213.) Keep this in mind: a clear line is crossed when the essay ceases to be the student's exclusive work in either thought or words.

Also, parents, don't send the message to your teenager that you don't trust his ability by doing too much doctoring of the essay. This needs to be the student's process and colleges can see when it's not. Admission officers can tell exactly how many proofreaders a student had in their household. As Kenyon associate dean Jennifer Delahunty says, "Do you think I don't know what a forty-five-year-old investment banker sounds like?"

The bottom line: even one thought, sentiment, piece of content, or expression that is not originally the student's should not be in the essay. If it is, the line has been crossed.

So what about essay coaches? We know that sometimes families may think hiring an essay coach is a good idea. Perhaps the student's writing skills are not as strong as her aptitude in math and science. Maybe the student attends an underresourced school. Or perhaps the parents are too involved and the student needs an outsider to mediate.

This is a tough call, but we advise you to avoid essay coaches. There are simply not enough good ones out there. And bad coaches don't understand what colleges want and interfere too much with a student's writing. The bottom line is that you don't need a personal coach. The vast majority of students who apply to college don't use them. It's fine to seek some help if you feel you need it. But look for it from a writing teacher, or a teacher with a strong writing background. And if no teacher is available to you, other possibilities are a family friend, parent, peer, or academic advisor who knows you and will respect the line between feedback and coaching.

their supplements. Bottom line: these essays matter—a lot. Give them your best effort.

? Should I repeat the prompt at the beginning of my essay?

The Common Application asks you to check off the prompt to which you are responding.

If you are working on a supplement in an individual college's application, find some way to indicate the prompt to which you are responding—either by flagging the question on the form or repeating it at the beginning of the essay. There is no need to "name" or title your essays.

FROM THE DESK OF THE DEAN

Advice on Your Essays

STUART SCHMILL

Dean of admissions, MIT

➡ The essay is one piece of many in an application. It's more information for us about the student's personal qualities, motivation, interests, and talents. We ask very specific questions, and generally if students answer those questions, we'll learn what we're trying to learn about them. One of the mistakes students make is that they don't answer the question we ask. They have some essay they wrote for some other school and they try to fit that into one of our questions. That tends not to work, because then we're not learning what we're trying to learn about them.

And some students try to be what they think we want rather than who they are. They think we're looking for a certain type of student, so they're trying to be that. Here's an example. One of the essay questions—it's a short essay—asks students, "Tell us about something you do for fun." What we want to learn is how students balance their lives. We don't want students who are just working all the time. But some students are afraid. They think it's a trick question, and they're afraid to actually answer and tell us that they like to goof off and hang out at the mall or play video games or whatever it is they like to do. They think that they can't project that image to us, so they tell us how they love to clean bedpans in the local senior center, that kind of thing. And that is not what we're looking for. We want to actually learn how they achieve balance and have fun.

KITTY McCARTHY

Vice president for enrollment management and student affairs, West Virginia State University

➡ Most students don't need to stretch to look for essay material. They're surrounded by it. I always recommend to students that they take a thoughtful approach. The best essays cannot be rushed to meet a deadline. If you read the questions, walk away, and mull them over, an essay topic will often come to you when you least expect it—at a soccer game, during a conversation with family, or on your way to school. And then have some fun with it. Take the question, think about it, and make it your own.

Students should remember to use the essay to share something that isn't conveyed elsewhere in the application. The best essays are absolutely the ones that tell me something I don't already know about the student. Over the years I've seen students who provide perfectly acceptable writing samples—perhaps something they've used in a class—and they're good writers. But they haven't told me anything about themselves, and they might not have addressed one of the questions we put forth. That's a missed opportunity.

Be sure to read your final response once and then again and then ask a trusted friend or family member to take a look.

YVONNE M. ROMERO DA SILVA

Vice dean, director of admissions, University of Pennsylvania

➡ As we're sitting in committee, we often use the phrase, "What is the student's voice?" What are they saying about themselves? How are they articulating their interests? A complete application (and by complete I mean everything that the student submits: testing, transcript, teacher recommendations, interview, counselor recommendation)—should answer three questions. The first question is, "Who are you?" So that's the context. That's the history of the student. That's what has driven them to the point where they are at that stage. The second question is, "What do you want to do?" That speaks to their aspirations. It should link to their passions. And the third question is, "Why will this institution get you there, toward your dreams and toward your goals?" And it's not that every component of the application needs to answer each of those three questions, but collectively the whole application should succeed in answering those three questions. And that's where the essay can shine a light. Essays can be incredibly important because they give us that glimpse into the individual. And the more sincere and down to earth and honest and truthful, the more engaging the essay.

We're very much interested in finding those very active students who are going to make our community come to life. And we'll look for that in multiple places in the application, but we particularly want to see it or hear it or read it in the student's voice. And that can come through in the essays.

RICHARD NESBITT

Director of admissions, Williams College

➡ The essays are an opportunity for students to let colleges know what they're passionate about. The best ones use personal anecdotes to really show the reader what the student values, and do that in an articulate way. Part of the goal of the student should be to find his own voice, not to try to be someone else, not to try to anticipate what the admission officer is expecting him to be. Instead, be yourself, be honest and direct, and write in a way that sounds like you. Don't use the thesaurus to gild your essay; just use your own voice, your own vocabulary.

You don't have to pick an earthshaking experience to write about. Your topic can be a very day-to-day kind of thing, but something that had an impact on you that helped you define yourself and define what's important to you. That's what the personal statement is: a window into who you are that the admission officer may not otherwise see from the rest of the application.

MICHAEL BESEDA

Vice president for enrollment and university communications, Willamette University

➡ When students sit down to write the college essay, they're being asked to say something about themselves. It's this existential moment: "Who am I?" They're asked to think about what matters to them and then make choices about communicating that in ways that are more powerful and more impactful than maybe other things they've done in their lives. So it's really daunting. And they learn a lot from it. They're tested, and they grow and develop. So ultimately it can be a great experience. Along the way, it feels terrifying and overwhelming and frightening. But at the end of the day, it can be a great experience for that young person. If the parents just stay out of the way enough, support their children when they need it, but let them struggle and fail and do the things they have to do to get through it, they'll find that students get a lot out of the process.

CHARLES DEACON

Dean of admissions, Georgetown University

➡ The essay is important. In some cases, it is the only chance for a student to have his own voice in the process. Our view is that, offered the chance, probably most of our applicants would like to meet personally with the admission committee and tell them their story. And since they don't have that chance, the essay becomes an opportunity for their voice to come through. That's why we keep hearing, "Let your natural voice come through," "Don't have your parents look it over," "Don't have someone else write it for you." It has to be you, and you will be the most compelling argument for yourself.

If the college where I am applying offers the option of submitting a supplementary video, how important is it to do that?

Some schools offer students this option. It's an opportunity to provide one more piece of information to a college. If it's a medium you're comfortable with and you feel it would add something to your application, go ahead. And don't be concerned if you don't have sophisticated equipment. Deans of admission say these video essays are just as likely to be shot with a camera phone as with a high-end video rig. Also, keep in mind that the operative words are usually "option" and "supplementary"—you will still have to submit written essays as well.

Do you recommend using an online editing service for my essay?

No. They are expensive and there is no guarantee that the person editing your essay knows anything about what a college is looking for. These services may also attempt to interfere too much with your writing. Don't forget that the college expects your essays to be your work, honestly presented.

The Application Form

—Binding certification students must sign, from the Common Application[23]

Copyrighted portions of The Common Application® are used with the permission of The Common Application, Inc.

Filling out the application form may seem like the simplest—and most tedious—step in the admission process, but it plays a crucial role. The information colleges ask for in the application form serves as the foundation of the admission file. Providing your biographical data, academic record, testing, extracurricular activities, and future plans—accurately, completely, and on time—tells a college who you are. Do not underestimate the power you have over how an admission officer will view you, based simply on how you complete the application form.

As you begin this step in the process, go to the website of each school to which you are applying and see what applications they offer or support—whether that is the college's own unique form, the standardized Common Application, or a form from another electronic application provider, such as the Universal College Application or XAP. Also note whether they accept online submissions, paper applications, or both.

THE BASICS, STEP BY STEP
MEET THE FOUR TABS

We suggest you begin by going to the following: commonapp.org. After you create an account, you will see four tabs across the top of the page:

Dashboard. Here you will monitor and keep track of your application, including

Checkpoints ✍

✔ The application form is the foundation of your admission file. Your job is to make sure it is complete, accurate, and submitted on time.

✔ The information you provide in the application provides further context for the admission officer and is yet another opportunity to show who you are.

✔ The application must be the student's own work at all times.

✔ Completing the application is, in part, an exercise in following directions. Let your individuality show, but follow the rules set by the colleges.

✔ The student's signature on the application pledges he has upheld the highest standards of honesty, character, and moral and ethical principles. Take it seriously. Colleges do.

Each year, nearly one million students file their applications using the Common Application, which is accepted by more than five hundred colleges and universities. Many other schools, most notably public universities, have their own applications, and there are also a number of other electronic application providers colleges may use. For the purposes of this chapter we will use the Common Application as our template. The information colleges request in their application forms is, in most cases, broadly similar and serves a common purpose for all schools. You should be able to easily adapt our advice about the Common Application to the application of any other college to which you are applying or any other application supplier you are using.

The Common Application may experience changes from year to year, so please check collegeadmission book.com for real-time updates.

deadlines, requirements, and progress for each school to which you are applying.

My Colleges. This is where you will find and complete the college-specific questions and supplements for each college to which you intend to apply. You must add a college to your My Colleges list (which you'll find on the College Search tab) before you will be able to use this screen.

Common App. This is the infrastructure of your application. It includes six sections:

1. Profile
2. Family
3. Education
4. Testing
5. Activities
6. Writing

We will explain section by section what information is being requested, why colleges want this information when relevant, and our best advice for how to provide it.

College Search. Under this tab, college searches can be performed a variety of ways—including by city, state, distance from a specific zip code, and specific college name—and using multiple search terms. Information such as phone numbers, deadlines, fees, and recommendation requirements can be seen by clicking the school name link from the "results list." You can also simply enter the names of the colleges to which you already know you'd like to apply. Once you add a school, it will appear in My Colleges.

The Common App Tab

Profile
The Profile consists of eight sections: Personal Information, Address, Contact Details, Demographics, Geography, Language, Citizenship, and Common App Fee Waiver.

Personal Information
- **What:** Name, birth date, phone number, sex.
- **Why:** This section is the framework for your application, allowing the admission office to accurately identify you.
- **How:**
  - Use your full legal name as it appears on your Social Security card and make sure it is consistent with your high school records and the name you used for your SAT or ACT

testing. It will also need to match the name on your financial aid application. (FYI, for financial aid, your name *must* be the one used on your Social Security card.)

Address
- **What:** Your permanent home address, as well as any temporary or alternate addresses. The Common App will check your address during registration and if unable to verify the address will alert you.

Contact Details
- **What:** Email and phone numbers.
- **Why:** This information provides the details that allow the admission office to communicate with and deliver information to you quickly and easily.
- **How:**
  - Make sure your email address is appropriate. If you're using loves2party@ hotmail.com, create a new email account.

Demographics
- **What:** This section asks for information about religious preference, military service, and race; responding is optional.

Note that the Common App uses "smart questions" technology. Questions are presented a few at a time and appear only if they are applicable to you. For example, if you select your parents' marital status as "Divorced" in the Family section, that will prompt new questions, such as "With whom do you make your permanent home?" Also, as you navigate the application, help topics directly relevant to the section you are working on appear in the right column of the page.

- **Why:** Many colleges believe it is important to enroll a class that is diverse on a number of dimensions. Colleges can choose to "suppress" or blank out information on some questions such as SSN, test scores, religious preference, and disciplinary history.
- **How:** We strongly recommend you answer all optional questions. You will be best served by giving admission officers as accurate and clear a picture of who you are as you possibly can.

Geography

- **What:** Birthplace, countries lived in, and number of years in and out of United States.
- **Why:** Your answers to these questions provide context for admission officers so that they can evaluate your application with a better idea of who you are. If you live in Manhattan but were born in El Centro, California, or now reside in Des Moines but were born in Vietnam and lived there until you were ten, this background adds to the admission officers' understanding.

Language

- **What:** Number of languages, proficiency.
- **Why:** Again, this information provides context for the admission officers evaluating your application.

Citizenship

- **What:** Citizenship status and Social Security number (SSN).
- **How:**
  - Providing your Social Security number on the application form is required for U.S. citizens and permanent residents applying for financial aid via the FAFSA.

- In providing citizenship status, undocumented students should select "Other" from the online menu.
- If you do not have a SSN, leave this entry blank.

Common App Fee Waiver

- **What:** Guidelines for eligibility for application fee waivers and certification that you will qualify.
- **Why:** While the Common Application is free, colleges may require submission of an application fee. Colleges realize application fees may present a financial hardship for some families, and fee waivers are available to students who meet eligibility requirements.
- **How:**
  - If you think your financial circumstances might qualify you for an application fee waiver, check "Yes" to certify that you meet the eligibility criteria. Your school counselor must confirm and verify your eligibility for the fee waiver. Once confirmed, the fee waiver will be applied to all colleges to which you apply and payment will be waived when you submit the Common Application. More information about fee waivers appears later in this chapter.

Family

- **What:** Background on your household, parents or legal guardians, and siblings (if applicable); includes contact information, marital status, occupation, and education. This section also includes questions about the applicant's spouse or child if applicable.
- **Why:** The particulars of home life are useful for colleges trying to get to know who you

are. The student who lives with her father has a home life different from that of the student who lives with both parents, as does the student who is in a foster home or the applicant who is married or has a child. Colleges want to take into account circumstances that may have an impact on how they view an applicant's grades or activities—for example, a student who reports that a parent is deceased, where the date of death indicates it occurred during the junior year in high school.

- **How:** Respond in full to every question. This level of detail may seem irrelevant, but it helps round out the college's picture of you. For example, the colleges attended by parents and siblings and the level of education attained tell the school whether there was a college-going culture in the home. Having a college-going culture in and of itself is neither a positive nor a negative, but knowing what a student's home life is like provides admission officers with context.

Education

- **What:** Information about high school attendance, additional school experiences, contact details for your guidance or college counselors, your current academic record—GPA, current courses, and honors—as well as your career interests and the highest degree you intend to earn is self-reported in this section.
- **Why:** Providing this information to colleges allows them to begin evaluating your application even if they haven't yet received official transcripts. The current courses section is particularly important for students

whose high schools do not include senior-year courses on a transcript until grades are available. Information about your counselor is important because if the admission officer has questions or concerns, you want her to be able to reach out to the person most likely to have answers—your high school counselor—as quickly and easily as possible. In addition, details such as the circumstances of an interruption in your high school education provide valuable context.

- **How:**
  - Enter your guidance counselor or high school college counselor's information (name, phone, and email) correctly! The college wants the name of the person who completes the School Report (SR). Check with your high school if you are unsure about whose contact information to include.
  - If your schooling was interrupted by illness, a displacement due to a natural disaster, military service, travel, disciplinary issues, or other circumstances, note it here and follow up with an explanation in the Additional Information space in the Writing section. You can request that your high school counselor include an explanation, but that will not substitute for your own.
  - List every high school, college, or enrichment program you have attended or participated in. If you don't feel proud of your record at one of the schools you attended, report it anyway. Failure to do so can have serious consequences.
  - Obtain class rank, size, and grading information from your high school college counselor or guidance counselor.

- Many high schools do not rank students. If your high school doesn't, simply select "None" from the menu.
- Note that the form asks for any organization that provided you free assistance with your application. Examples might include the Posse Foundation or Questbridge. The dropdown menus provide lists.
- The credit value of your current courses is important for the admission office to know, so include it.
- By entering your current courses here, you are committing to completing them. See the questions at the end of this chapter for more information.
- "Honors" in this section refers to academic honors only—not sports or citizenship awards.
- Colleges want to get a sense of your interests, goals, and intentions in order to build a picture of who you are at this moment in time. In many cases, your answers do not commit you to anything—if you write down "Neuroscience" as an academic interest, you are not committing to that course of study.
- If you don't see the academic area you are interested in pursuing in the menu, select "Other."

Testing

- **What:** Information about college entrance testing—the SAT and ACT; academic subject tests, including AP, IB, SAT Subject Tests, and A-Levels; English testing for non-native speakers, including TOEFL, IELTS, PTE Academic; and optional reporting for any

other relevant testing done in grades 9 through 12.
- **Why:** This information allows colleges to begin evaluating your application even if they haven't yet received official scores. You will still need to follow up and ensure the colleges receive all official reports from testing agencies.
- **How:**
  - Check with each college to which you are applying for their testing reporting requirements by going to their website, or you may find the requirements within the college-specific supplements under My Colleges on the Common Application.
  - On SAT/ACT testing, provide your highest scores in each area even if those scores are from different test dates.
  - Answer "Yes" if you have scheduled future testing, so that the admission office can anticipate receiving further score reports. The colleges want to see your best scores, so making them aware that there may be additional testing reported will help them track this.
  - For AP, IB, and SAT Subject Tests, report your best scores. You do not have to include scores you wish to withhold, unless the college requires you to submit them.
  - If you are applying to test-optional schools, you can choose not to self-report or choose to report a different set of tests. (Some colleges will require you to submit AP or Subject Tests though not the ACT or SAT, for example. Check the website of every college to which you are applying to make sure you understand their testing requirements.) If you are applying to

schools where testing is required, as well as test-optional schools, most of the test-optional schools will have the test scores suppressed on the applications. However, if you want your scores to be considered by a test-optional school—for example, to be eligible for merit scholarships—official scores will need to be submitted.

- Some colleges allow submission of AP scores under flexible testing policies, but while AP scores may be self-reported here, official scores are not usually sent as part of the admission process.

Activities

- **What:** Activities and work experience, including the number of hours per week and per year, positions held, honors, employers, and your plans to participate in these pursuits in college.
- **Why:** Admission officers are interested in how you spend your time, both to see who you are now and to understand how you may participate in the community at their college. Your list may include sports, volunteer activities, school clubs, part-time work, hobbies, or caring for your siblings. If you are uncertain about what to include, look back at Chapter 6 to see the many ways in which colleges anticipate students spend their time outside the classroom. The goal here is simply to reflect the day-to-day reality of your life.
- **How:**
  - More activities are not necessarily better. The form asks for your principal activities—those that have the most meaning for you or where you have spent a lot of time. Plenty of space is provided to give you

flexibility, but admissions officers don't expect you to fill every line.
- Prioritize your activities and work experience. The form instructs you to list items in order of their importance to you. Use a piece of scratch paper to do a rough draft before your enter the information. You can also reorder activities using the up and down arrows in each activity reading pane.
- Don't overstate your hours. Admission officers know how many hours there are in the week.
- Describe activities in a way that reveals as much as possible. Some positions and honors are self-explanatory—for example, "Quarterback" or "MVP. "
- Other activities require more explanation—for example, fly fishing. Select "Other club/activity" from the menu and write "Fly fishing" in the space under Position/ Leadership. Sentences won't fit here, but phrases will. For example, "Fly fishing, Fished major rivers in 12 states." In the Details, Honors and Accomplishments section, you could add, "Expert at tying flies, business selling woolly bugger ties to sports store."
- If you care for your siblings every day without pay, you would select "Family Responsibilities" from the menu and enter, for example, "Caring for siblings, 6 years, 5 days a week, walk to school, evening meal preparation, homework supervision until parents return from jobs."
- For each of your activities, you have two lines to work with: "Positions/ Leadership" and "Details, Honors and Accomplishments." Don't feel confined by

the titles of those headings—use both areas to tell the school what you want them to know. If that is still too confining, you can submit additional information, but check the directions on the Common Application page of the college or the college's website first to see if they will accept it and it will be read. If it is still unclear, check with the college.

- If you have a lot of activities, group them by type—such as student government, community service, or work. For example, under the heading Work (Paid), list "Babysitter, Gap retail, housesitter, and tutor" on the Position/Leadership line if there isn't enough room to list each separately.
- If you group activities, separate out any national or international participation and recognition.
- While you may need to abbreviate to fit your text into the box provided since there is a limited amount of space, especially in the field for "Details, Honors and Accomplishments" (allows for 50 characters), don't save space by using abbreviations the admission officer won't understand.
  - *Under Position/Leadership don't enter:* AISF participant
  - *Enter:* Artificial Intelligence Science Fair participant
  - *Then, under "Details, Honors and Accomplishments," enter:* Invitation-only robotics competition, sonar systems, paper considered for publication.
- You may also utilize the Additional Information area in the Writing section to include anything that will not fit in the Activities section.
- If your activity type is not listed, select "Other club/activity" from the drop-down list. You can specify in the box for Position/Leadership and Details, Honors and Accomplishments.

Fee Waivers

While the Common Application is free, colleges may require submission of an application fee. Colleges realize application fees may present a financial hardship for some families, and fee waivers are available to students meeting eligibility requirements. Eligibility guidelines are listed on the Common Application in the Profile section under "Common App Fee Waiver" and can be viewed on the websites of the National Association for College Admission Counseling (NACAC) at nacacnet .org; ACT, Inc., at act.org; and the College Board at collegeboard.org.

Check the box on the Common Application (in the Profile section) indicating you feel your financial circumstances might qualify you for an application fee waiver. Your school counselor must confirm and verify your eligibility for the fee waiver. Once confirmed, the fee waiver will be applied to all colleges to which you apply and payment will be waived when you submit the Common Application.

Fee waivers may also be available from some state governments and the Expanding College Opportunities program. Non-need-based waivers based on unique criteria specified by individual colleges may also be available from those schools. Check the college websites for this information.

Writing

There are three sections here: the Personal Essay (Chapter 13 covers essays in depth), Disciplinary History, and Additional Information.

The Personal Essay

- **What:** Students can choose from five essay prompts, which may change from year to year. Each essay will have an enforced maximum word limit of 650 words and an enforced minimum word limit of 250 words.
- **How:**
  - You should not customize your essay or make it college-specific because the Personal Essay in the Writing section of the Common Application will go to all of your schools.
  - See Chapter 13 for a full discussion of essays, including how to get started and what the colleges are looking for.

Disciplinary History

- **What:** This section features affidavits requiring students to disclose any academic or behavioral misconduct or any criminal conviction, whether misdemeanor or felony.
- **Why:** Colleges want to understand your stumbles as well as your achievements—and they want to see what you have learned from them. You can count on fair treatment if you are a student who has made mistakes.

Additional Information

- **What:** The Additional Information section provides an opportunity for students to explain any special circumstances or qualifications not reflected elsewhere in the application.

- **Why:** It can be used to elaborate on an activity or family situation that is not self-explanatory or is not explained elsewhere in the application. For example, to clarify academic issues such as a drop in grades or a scheduling conflict that required a student to choose between physics and calculus.
- **How:**
  - Use the Additional Information section if you wish to explain an important activity you didn't address in the essay or college specific supplement or an activity, family situation, or work obligation that is not self-explanatory. Don't write an additional essay or repeat information that is already covered in the application or supplement.
  - If you answered "Yes" to any Disciplinary History question, you must include further information. The explanation should show that you understand what happened, take responsibility for it, regret the lapse in judgment or behavior, and have clearly moved forward.

The My Colleges Tab

- **What:**
  - All colleges that accept the Common Application require students to answer a series of questions unique to their school. These college-specific questions are found under the My Colleges tab once a school is selected through the College Search function. The landing page for each college details application fees, decision plans, and recommender requirements. Under Questions, each college may feature a wide-ranging set of questions covering academic and career interests, including whether

you will apply for financial aid or merit scholarships, as well as whether you wish to enroll under an early admission plan. The questions asked in this section are unique to each college.

- Schools may also require—or include as optional—a Writing Supplement of additional short answers or essays. For example, this is where students are often asked to write the "Why us?" essay (see Chapter 13). This is also where colleges may request additional materials such as resumes, research papers, or graded assignments if they are required in the school's admission process.

- In this section on the Common Application, you will also find a tab for assigning recommenders through which you will access the FERPA release authorization, teacher evaluations, and school report forms.

- **Why:** Colleges want to get a sense of your interests, goals, and intentions in order to build a picture of who you are at this moment in time. Again, in most cases your answers do not commit you to anything—if you write down "American studies" as an academic interest, you are not committing to that course of study. Nevertheless, some of your answers here help colleges in their planning process—for example, your intent to live in campus housing. For some students, the information provided here may also play a larger role in the college's decision. For example, if a student's interest is in an area such as engineering or science, the admission office may want to confirm an ability to perform math and science at a certain level.

Your answers here will also trigger later responses in the Common Application. For example, if you are applying under an Early Decision program, once you select the Early Decision term option for one school, the ED Agreement will be available in the Questions section of the individual school under My Colleges.

- **How:**
  - Give the Questions and Writing Supplements the same time and attention you gave the essay and information gathering called for in the regular application form, whether you are asked to write full essays or short answers, and whether they are required or optional. This information and these essays can be among the most important to an admission staff. Trust us when we say that most admission officers are not begging for more reading material. If it's here, it's here for a reason. Take it seriously. Pay attention to the word count in the directions on the supplementary essays, since each school may have different requirements and word counts for their questions.
  - Be honest about your need for financial aid. There are very few students who can afford

The Meaning of Your Signature— Even When It's Electronic

Your signature says that you pledge to have upheld the highest standards of honesty, character, and moral and ethical principles. By signing, you are saying that you have told the full truth. You will be held to that standard.

to pay full college tuition, so by checking "Yes," you put yourself in the majority. Colleges generally ask this question so they can coordinate communication among the admission office, the financial aid office, and the applicant. Also, the information in this section may or may not be taken into account. Need-blind colleges (see Chapter 16), for example, may deliberately suppress the information in this section for application readers.

- In this section, you may also be asked to indicate whether you will apply for merit aid, and you will find information about specific scholarship opportunities. Pay attention here. Merit scholarships are often awarded out of the admission office, so your response acts as a trigger to let them know you are interested.

- If you don't see the academic area you are interested in pursuing in the menu, select "Undecided." And welcome to the club! The most popular intended major at many colleges is "Undecided." Does this give you an advantage? Not at all. But it is not a disadvantage, either. It's most important to be honest.

- Read the instructions carefully for execution and submission of the ED agreement. You must inform your school counselor, who will also read and sign an ED agreement. A parent or legal guardian must read and sign the agreement as well.

When Does the Clock Strike Midnight?

If you insist on taking it down to the wire, check to make sure you understand how the colleges time-stamp their applications. For example, if the college's time stamp is set as 11:59 p.m. in the United States Eastern Time zone, this means that if you are filing from Seattle on January 1, with a January 1 deadline, you will need to submit your application no later than 8:59 p.m. Pacific Time. The Common Application instructs applicants to submit by midnight of the student's local time. Whether you are using the Common Application, a college's unique form, or another electronic provider, check to see how they time-stamp their applications and submit accordingly.

 Best Advice

Submit each of your applications well before the clock strikes midnight on the due date.

Submission

The Common Application, College-Specific Questions, and application fees are submitted together. The college-specific writing supplements are submitted after the application. If a school accepts or requires an arts supplement, it may be a separate form available directly from the school, or it might be integrated into the Common Application with SlideRoom (slideroom.com). The deadline for an arts supplement can often come sooner than the application deadline. Check the information on the college-specific landing page for each school to which you are applying for information about deadlines, or go to each college's website. If it's not clear when the application and supplements are due, call the admission office.

Submission of the Common Application,

Deadlines: When Should You Submit the Application?

College deadlines generally cluster around the same time, depending on the type of school and the decision plan a student has selected. You will need to check the website of every college to which you are applying, since deadlines can vary from school to school and may be confusing. And if you receive emails or letters urging you to send in the application earlier than the stated official deadline, don't worry. Take your time and do a good job. However, be aware that many colleges shut down completely between Christmas and New Year's. If you run into problems, the admission office will not necessarily be open to advise you. Plan accordingly.

 Best Advice

Don't wait until the due date to file your application. But there is no need to be the first to submit. It's better to dedicate adequate time to the application. Submit early enough so that if anything goes wrong, you will have time to remedy it.

Also be alert for special circumstances that may affect when you submit your application. For example, you may want to file earlier if receipt of your application determines where you fall in the queue for an alumni interview. And at some large public universities, submitting earlier may give you greater access to housing or scholarships.

Deadline information can be found on the individual landing pages of the schools under the My Colleges tab or on the websites of the colleges to which you are applying. We suggest you develop a method for keeping track of deadlines that works for you—whether that's a piece of paper on your bulletin board or an Excel spreadsheet. Find sample worksheets in Appendix III or on our website at collegeadmissionbook.com.

Keep track of deadlines with the Application Deadline Organizer available in Appendix III, which you can download as an Excel and Word document by visiting our website: collegeadmissionbook.com.

College-Specific Questions, and application fees occurs in three steps.

1. Final PDF Review
• **What:** This is your last chance to check for errors and make any changes or edits. When all required questions have been answered and you're ready to begin the submission process, a preview PDF is generated automatically once you click on the "Start Submission" button. This is your only opportunity to print out the Common Application prior to submission. While colleges rarely lose things, they might. We strongly advise you print out a copy for record keeping.

2. Application Fee Payment.
• **What:** Payment is submitted at the same time that you submit the Common

Application and College-Specific Questions. (College-specific writing supplements can be submitted separately.) Students must submit an application fee or fee waiver to any college where such payment is required. Application fees can range from no charge to upward of $100 per college. Fee information can be found on the Common App's college-specific pages for each school to which you are applying or on colleges' official websites.

- **How:** For the Common Application, payment is made using any major credit card or by providing bank account information that allows for submission of an electronic check. Application fees are nonrefundable. If you have qualified for a fee waiver, payment will be waived.

3. Applicant Signature

- **What:** This section of the application requires you to certify that all information and materials in the application are your own work and that all documents become the property of the college to which they have been submitted; to acknowledge that all offers of admission are conditional; and to affirm that you will send an enrollment deposit to only one institution.
- **Why:**
  - This section covers a lot of territory. Primarily, it is here to remind students of and reinforce the requirement that the application needs to be a student's own work. It is also here to enable the college to enforce these provisions. For example, a college may rescind an offer of admission

Supplementary Materials

Some colleges encourage submission of supplementary materials by any student who wishes to do so. Such materials may include a website URL that documents a special project, an academic paper, a short story, or a YouTube video.

Don't submit supplementary materials unless the school indicates on the application or its website that they welcome or require such a submission. If the school's website isn't clear, call or send an email to the admission office and ask if they will entertain additional material.

Filling out an application is in part an exercise in following directions. For example, if a college invites students to submit a one-minute video, that's an opportunity for you to showcase your originality if you choose to do so. But that doesn't mean your video can be two minutes, and it doesn't mean you can send that video to other colleges—unless those colleges have specifically invited you to do so.

Neither should you spend any time devising some flamboyant way to get recognized by the admission office. The application process is not about who yells the loudest, dreams up the most creative contraption, or can pull off the wildest stunt. Let your individuality show, but follow the rules set by the colleges.

if a student is found to have sent an enrollment deposit to more than one college that accepted him. Admission may also be rescinded if a student is found to have misrepresented any facts or work in the application. Misrepresenting oneself on a college application is so serious that whenever it comes to light, your admission can be rescinded— whether that's three years later or thirty.

- Think of these certifications in this way: in signing these statements, you are saying, "This is who I am and what I stand for, and I stand by it." That's something to be taken very seriously as a matter of personal honor. Colleges require it, and rightly expect it.

- **How:**
  - Read *every word* and understand exactly what you are signing.
  - Be scrupulously honest. If your personal honor isn't enough, then know that if you present someone else's work as your own or fail to honestly provide any information, it is likely to be discovered. More and more schools are conducting audits of applications, including the University of California, Harvard, and Stanford.
  - Note the instructional statement requiring applicants to inform the colleges to which they are applying of any changes in the information in the application, including disciplinary history. Failure to do so can have serious consequences.

ADDITIONAL FORMS

- **Early Decision Agreement.** If you are applying under an Early Decision program, you must complete an ED Agreement. It is discussed further in Chapter 15. In the Common Application, once you select the Early Decision term option for one school, the ED Agreement will be available in the Questions section of your Common App account.

- **Nonacademic Evaluations.** For colleges that accept or require them, nonacademic evaluations can now be submitted by peers, coaches, clergy, instructors, or other individuals as part of the Common Application. These will be found in the Assign Recommenders section. A number of colleges permit or specifically ask for character references and peer recommendations. The colleges will indicate whether they wish to receive these supplemental evaluations. This is not—*not!*—an invitation or expectation to send more recommendations. Always check with a college before sending anything not specifically required.

- **The Teacher Evaluation and the School Report (SR).** These forms have been addressed in Chapter 4 and Chapter 12. On the Common Application, these forms are found on the college-specific pages under Assign Recommenders in My Colleges and can be submitted online or printed out and mailed by your teachers and counselor.

> Parents, the application form is hands-off, eyes-only. It's fine to proofread the form—but that's it. You're not an administrative assistant (or a ghostwriter!). What's more, admission officers have multiple means of detecting inappropriate involvement. At the end of the application, your student will be signing his name attesting to the fact that the application is his own work. Make it so.

Arts Students

Students with interest and talent in the arts should check to see if the colleges to which they are applying require an arts supplement. This supplement may be a separate form available from the school or be integrated through the Common Application with SlideRoom (slideroom.com) on the landing page of the individual schools in the My Colleges section.

- **The Midyear Report.** This is a midyear status report covering a student's grades, courses, activities, and disciplinary and criminal history that must be completed by the high school college counselor or guidance counselor. Students should request that it be sent to all colleges to which they are applying, either at the end of the first semester or when they submit their official transcript requests. Check the websites of the colleges to which you are applying for the deadline for submission of this report, and follow up to make sure the colleges received it. This form may also be submitted online through the Common Application.
- **The Final Report.** This is a status report like the Midyear Report, but it will verify end-of-year grades and graduation date. It is sent only to the college to which the student has made a commitment to enroll. Colleges usually want this information by no later than early July after high school graduation, so students should check in with their high school counselor before graduation. It is the student's responsibility to make sure the colleges receive both the Final Report and an official final transcript.

FAST APPS

"Fast apps"—also known as "snap apps" or "priority apps"—are fast-track applications that, depending on the college, waive application fees as well as requirements such as the essay or letters of recommendation—and promise quick decisions.

Selected students may receive an email or letter bearing headings like "Advantage Application," "Preferred Applicant," or "Distinctive Candidate Application." You may be flattered to think you've been preapproved for admission when you receive such a letter. But that's not the case. Fast apps are, in fact, more like Chase or American Express notifying you about a promotional offer you can apply for but might not get.

Fast apps are controversial because skeptics believe they are first and foremost marketing tools—colleges employ them to boost the number of applications they can report receiving, which allows them to reject more applicants, heightening the appearance of selectivity and in turn boosting the college's status in rankings such as *U.S. News and World Report*'s "Best Colleges" list.

Because fast apps waive fees and make the application process easier, responding to a fast app may be a good idea for some students. But remember that the application process is about finding the right match between student and college. Don't compromise that goal just because it's easier to apply with a fast app.

Our best advice: send the fast app only to colleges you already are interested in attending. And if you choose to use a fast app, make sure you inform your high school college or guidance counselor, who must submit

To-Do List

There are a lot of moving parts to consider in completing your applications. Here's a checklist of tasks and advice to help you do the best job, again using the Common Application as a template.

- Follow directions.
- Keep track of deadlines.
- Be sure to use the most up-to-date version of each application. The Common Application changes from year to year, and the colleges' unique applications may change as well. For up-to-date real-time changes in the Common Application, please visit our website at collegeadmissionbook.com.
- Add the email addresses for the Common Application and all colleges to which you are applying to your email address book and safe senders list, so that important messages aren't treated as spam.
- Sign the FERPA waiver, waiving your access to the recommendations. On the Common App, you will find this under the Assign Recommenders tab. See more about the FERPA waiver in Chapter 12.
- Make sure you complete the college-specific supplements for all the colleges to which you are applying.
- Use the same name on all materials you submit.
- Proofread the application before submitting. Errors of omission, sloppiness, and spelling mistakes can make it difficult for admission officers to do their job.
- Use spell-check, but make sure you proofread the application yourself, because spell-check is not always right. "Coarse" doesn't mean the same thing as "course." As high school counselor Ralph Figueroa says, "Spell Czech is knot yore friend and it will betray ewe."
- Double-check everything. Make sure that you have completed each section. Small errors in your name, date of birth, or email address can cause big problems.
- Have someone else proofread the application before you submit it. (Notice a pattern here?)
- Request official test scores to be sent by testing agencies such as ACT and the College Board.
- Follow up with your teachers and high school college and guidance counselors to make sure recommendation letters and reports have been submitted. (If your school submits through the Common Application, you can view this on the Dashboard.)
- Request that official transcripts and the midyear report be sent to all colleges to which you are applying. Official transcripts must be submitted from all schools where you have taken classes, such as local colleges, summer schools, or a previous high school.
- Read the signature affidavits carefully and think them through before you hit "Submit."
- Pay the application fee or request a fee waiver.
- Print a hard copy of all documents and forms before you hit "Submit."

- Submit your applications on time. Don't wait until the due date—websites can get overloaded and run out of processing capacity. So hit "Submit" before the final hour.

  Congratulations! You're almost done. There are just a few more things you will need to do.

- Complete your alumni or admission office interviews at the schools offering them.

- Follow up to make sure all forms and documents have been received at every college to which you are applying. Use the Common App dashboard or check the status pages available online for many colleges. If you can't check online, send an email or place a phone call to the admission office several weeks after submitting your application. Respect that the admission office is busy at this time; don't call every day. In most cases, the school will inform you if your file is incomplete.

transcripts and other materials. Please note that colleges cannot access school forms for the applicant unless he or she submits a Common Application or the school's own unique form (not a fast app) to that college. Remember, these offer no guarantee of admission—and you still have to provide all the information necessary for the school to make a decision.

RESUMES

Resumes are for adults applying for jobs, not teenagers applying to colleges. In principle, the application form provides students with all the space needed for whatever information colleges seek.

So should you attach a resume to an application? Only if the college specifically requests it.

Jeannine Lalonde, senior assistant dean of admission at University of Virginia and author of the well-known blog *Notes from Peabody,* has this advice:

➡ Students overthink the "Activities" section of the application. I fear that people are spending way too much time crafting an elaborate answer to a really simple question. What are you involved in? What do you like to do?

Unfortunately, students sometimes go over the top. Instead of just listing their activities, they write four-page resumes. This should be the no-brainer, the easy part to fill out.

Fill in the chart. And in the text box you can expand on something that's really important to you. You don't need to explain what Girls State is. We know what it is. If you've got a leadership position, we know what that means. It's fairly standardized.

It's an energy drain when students really should, at this point, be spending more time crafting the essays.

Colleges ask for information about a student's activities in a specific format because it works for their database. For schools that are "paperless," properly formatted data are essential to an efficient admission process. Remember, at some schools they are reading as many as thirty thousand applications. They don't have time to figure out each student's methodology for listing activities.

Make every effort to use the format provided through the Common Application or, if using another electronic provider or a college-specific application, their format. The Common Application will not allow students to upload a resume if the college has not specifically requested it. If a school specifically requests or allows it, students will upload the resume as part of the college-specific writing supplement.

If you feel you have a distinctive or un-usual activity to portray and there is not space on the application, check with the admission office about how to disclose it. You also can use the Additional Information section in the application.

Questions You May Have

Can I submit a paper version of the Common Application?
No. The Common Application is online only. Other schools may have their own unique application forms or use another electronic provider. Check the websites of the colleges to which you are applying to see which forms they prefer and/or accept.

Can I print out my Common Application?
The Common Application is completely paperless at this time. This means that there is no printable version that you will be able

to download. A "print preview" copy of your application will become available to you right before submission since it is intended for record-keeping purposes only. After submission, a PDF of your submitted application is available in the Dashboard.

The questions for one of the colleges to which I'm applying ask for the names of all other schools where I am applying. Do I need to provide these?
You do not. Go ahead and list some of the schools you're applying to if you like, or leave it blank if that's what makes you most comfortable. The college is not going to deny you admission just because you do or do not tell them where else you are applying—they may be curious for any number of reasons, but it's not going to affect their decision.

My parents are divorced and I spend equal time at both my mom's and dad's homes. Should I include both addresses on my application?
Many college admission offices are set up to mail to only one snail-mail address at a time. For this reason, you need to pick one home as your primary address, just for the application process.

Why does the application form ask for an "alternate address" when they already have my permanent home address?
The colleges want to be confident they can communicate with you in a timely fashion. Your alternate mailing address may be different if your family uses a post office box, for example, instead of receiving mail at home.

Other circumstances may include a student using a temporary residence or spending a semester overseas.

? What if my legal name is the same as someone else's who is applying?

Don't worry. That's why the application form asks for other information, such as your birth date. In addition, once you have begun the application process, the Common Application will assign an identifier number; other schools may assign an institutional bar code. Whatever the school uses, make sure it is on every document you submit.

? If a college gives me the option of using its own application or the Common Application, is there an advantage to filling out one over the other?

There is no advantage to filling out one over the other. Colleges that use both have all their admission officers sign a statement saying that the applications will be treated the same.

? One of the colleges to which I am applying accepts the Universal College Application. What is this?

The Universal College Application (UCA) is an online application similar to the Common Application. You may also see the Common Black College Application, XAP, or forms from other electronic providers. If a college offers the UCA, Common Application, its own unique application, or another form, use whichever is easiest for you. If the cost of applying is a consideration, you may want to compare the application fees as well.

? I have heard there are quotas at some schools. Should I leave blank the section that asks about race?

No school has quotas. It's against the law. We advise you to answer the questions about your ethnicity. It provides additional context for the admission officer when evaluating your application.

? There isn't room to list all my AP, IB, or SAT Subject Test scores. What do I do?

The Common Application allows you to list up to ten tests. If you have more than ten, give priority to the scores you have already earned, followed by SAT Subject Tests you intend to take. Colleges can use your transcript to discern which AP and IB tests you will take later this year. If you still need more space, you may report the remaining scores for any tests in the Additional Information section.

? I am going to be taking the SAT again in the future. How do I let the colleges know this?

In the Testing section of the Common App you will find the following prompts:

- Do you wish to self-report Standardized Test Scores? Answer "Yes" to this question.
- Indicate all tests you have taken or expect to

take. A drop-down will offer the SAT as an option

- Number of times you have taken the ACT. Answer appropriately
- Number of future sittings you expect. Answer appropriately
- Date. Indicate the month and the year

❓ I don't have a lot of academic honors to report. Will that hurt my chances for admission?

Not every student has received academic honors, and colleges know that. Remember colleges are not just seeking students with academic distinctions. They are building communities—seeking tuba players and point guards and writers.

❓ Does answering the question about my academic interests tie me to a specific major?

In most cases, the answer is no. However if you are applying to a particular school within a university—for example, a college of education, architecture, engineering, or business—you should check the website to see if students are admitted to a specific college and that college only, or whether their admission is good across that university.

❓ I want to drop a class that I entered on my application as a current course. What should I do?

If you have not yet received your admission decisions, you may drop a class so long as you send each college a note or email saying you have done so, and explaining why. If you have already been admitted, we advise you to call the college and discuss this with them before deciding to drop the class or not. You may find they are not willing to honor your offer of admission if you do not take a specific class they think you will be taking.

❓ Why do all my materials become the college's property?

Many colleges receive too many supplemental materials to return all of them to their rightful original owners. It is simply a matter of volume.

PART VI

TIMING

CHAPTER 15

Decision Plans

"The first question is, 'Where would I really like to be next year? And where am I best prepared to be? Where is it realistic for me to go?' That's the starting point."

—John Latting, dean of admission, Emory University

Students not only have to make decisions about which colleges to apply to; they also have to make decisions about decision plans.

Decision plans fall into three major categories: regular, rolling, or early. Then there are additional variations of the early

Checkpoints ✍

✔ Students may apply to colleges under regular, rolling, early action, early decision, and restrictive early action decision plans.

✔ Colleges offer different decision plans based on their size, mission, philosophy, and enrollment objectives.

✔ The vast majority of students apply to college under regular decision plans.

✔ Early decision plans are binding and appropriate only for those students who are in a position to use properly.

✔ The decision plans that may be appropriate for you depend on a number of factors. Most important are the plans offered at the colleges on your list, especially the ones that have emerged as your top choices.

✔ Other factors that you must consider: your own goals, your grades and test scores, and your family's need for financial aid.

Decision Plan Definitions

- **Nonrestrictive plans.** These decision plans place no conditions on students. Applicants are free to apply to other colleges and are not required to commit to a school until May 1, the National Candidates Reply Date.
  - **Regular decision (RD).** Students apply by a specified date, usually sometime in January, and receive decisions on a specified date, usually sometime from mid-March to mid-April.
  - **Rolling admission (RA).** Students' applications are reviewed by the college as they are submitted. Some colleges send students a decision as soon as possible, usually within four to eight weeks, depending on the school and the size of its applicant pool. Other colleges release decisions on a few specified dates. Check each college's website for specifics.
  - **Early action (EA).** Students apply by a deadline that is earlier than the RD deadline and receive a decision earlier than the regular response date.
- **Restrictive plans.** These decision plans place conditions on students, restricting them from applying to other schools or committing them to enrolling.
  - **Early decision (ED).** Students apply to only one ED college, and sign a binding commitment to enroll if accepted. Applications are submitted early, usually in November, and notification usually occurs in December. If the student is admitted, applications to any other colleges submitted under regular decision, rolling admission, or early action must be withdrawn immediately.
  - **Restrictive early action (REA).** Students are restricted to applying early to only one college. Think of this as early decision without the commitment to enroll. Applications are submitted early, usually in November, and students are notified early, usually in December. Students are not bound by the acceptance and have until May 1 to decide. This decision plan is offered by very few schools.

options—early action, early decision, and restrictive early action. This abundance of choice raises a lot of questions for students and their families: "What are the advantages of regular decision over early decision?" "My first-choice school offers an early decision plan, but is it right for me?" "Does applying early to some of the schools on my list help or hurt my chances?" "How does applying under these different plans affect financial aid at the schools on my list?"

In this chapter, we will define each of the decision plans and provide you with guidelines, tools, and advice so that you can determine which decision plans offered by the colleges on your list may be appropriate for you.

REGULAR DECISION

Regular decision (RD) is what most people think of when they think of applying to college. The vast majority of students apply this way. Typically, under RD, students must submit all application materials by sometime in early winter and are notified of decisions around April 1. Students should check the deadline and notification dates for each school to which they are applying since these can vary. For example, deadlines and notification dates for public universities can fall earlier or later than the standard dates for private colleges. There are three possible outcomes in RD: acceptance, denial, or waitlist (we discuss these further in Chapter 17). Accepted students must respond by May 1, the National Candidates Reply Date.

As you think through the decision plans offered by the colleges on your list, regular decision is the default application option. If there is not a compelling reason for you to apply under another option, this is the decision plan you will use.

ROLLING ADMISSION

Colleges offering rolling admission (RA) often do not offer other ways to apply, so students are not necessarily *choosing* a rolling plan when applying to these schools. With RA, there is no one set deadline for submitting an application. Students are invited to apply within a large time frame that can begin as early as August. Colleges review applications as soon as they are submitted and notify students either within weeks or on any one of several predetermined dates. Applications continue to be accepted as long as spaces are available in the class. Admitted students usually have until May 1 to let the college know if they will attend.

Many public colleges and universities, and a number of privates as well, employ rolling decision plans. These schools believe they can render good decisions as they go and don't need to compare one applicant against the rest of the pool in order to know whether a student should be admitted. These colleges may be less holistic in their review of applications and may rely more on objective criteria.

While there is not a deadline in the usual sense in rolling admission, there is a caveat with respect to timing. If a school on your list offers RA, consider applying earlier rather than later. Since a school with RA makes decisions as applications arrive, spaces in the class can fill up, resulting in qualified applicants being denied as time goes on. In addition, find out whether access to housing, financial aid, scholarships, or special academic programs is influenced by the date when you apply or accept an offer of admission.

The typical outcome when applying under rolling admission is simply acceptance or denial. Occasionally, a college with RA may defer its decision about your application until they can see your first-quarter or first-semester senior-year grades. If you are going to take full advantage of RA by applying early in the cycle, your junior-year academic record and testing should be strong (relative to that college's profile) since your senior-year grades and scores may not reach the school before a decision is made.

EARLY ACTION

Under early action (EA) plans, students apply by an early deadline and receive an answer by an early notification date. EA plans are non-binding, and students may continue to apply to the other schools on their list. (But check the websites of each college to which you are applying to research any specific requirements.) If accepted, students have until May 1 to inform the college whether they will enroll.

There are three potential outcomes under early action plans: acceptance, denial, and deferral. If deferred under EA, students are placed in the regular admission pool for later consideration. You will want to send the college updated information, including first-semester grades, scores from any retaking of the SAT or ACT if they are higher, SAT Subject Test scores the college hasn't seen, or any significant academic or extracurricular achievements. In some cases you may request an interview. In their notification letter, the college will usually be clear about what additional information should be submitted.

Some schools offer two rounds of early action. The deadline for Round I is usually in November, and for Round II it is usually January. For students who would benefit by having a college consider November test scores or first-quarter or first-semester grades, applying during the second round may be a better choice.

Restrictive Early Action

This option is offered by only a handful of colleges, but if a school you are interested in happens to be one of them, then you need to understand it.

Pay Attention When Early Plans Are Discussed

You may hear early action and early decision lumped together and discussed under the single heading of "early programs." This is appropriate at times. For example, depending on the colleges on your list, your consideration of whether to apply early may encompass early action *and* an early decision option. But EA and ED are very different plans, with distinct rules, requirements, deadlines, and notification dates. Each has advantages or disadvantages depending on the applicant.

"I'm an early decision bird. I get the worm the day before."

In addition, the schools to which you are applying may offer both EA *and* ED plans. And deadlines and notification dates can be different from school to school, with some schools offering both EA and ED or even multiple rounds of EA or ED. Pay close attention to the designation of the plan being discussed and the specific details of the decision plans at each college on your list as you consider where, when, and if you will apply under an early plan.

Restrictive early action (REA) is a non-binding plan where students apply to a first-choice school early and receive an early decision. Students have until May 1 to respond to an offer of admission. You may apply to other colleges under regular or nonbinding rolling admission plans but may not apply to any other school under early action, early decision, or REA. Students should check the website of any college where they are applying REA to understand if there are further restrictions.

There are three outcomes under restrictive early action: acceptance, denial, and deferral. If accepted, the student has until May 1 to respond. If deferred, the student's application is moved to the regular decision pool for later consideration. If you are deferred, you should follow the advice on

You Don't Have to Jump on the Early Bandwagon

"I want to apply early—I just don't know where." If that's how you're thinking about this, think again. Students report a lot of pressure to apply early. It comes from peers, parents, and newspaper headlines—and sometimes it comes from the students themselves. In October of senior year, it may seem like everyone is jumping on the early bandwagon. But there is nothing wrong with sitting out this round and opting for more time and the greater choice it allows. There are distinct advantages to waiting and applying regular decision. Before you jump on the early bandwagon, seriously consider whether it's right for *you*. We've provided a list of questions to help you figure that out on page 254.

Does Applying Early Improve My Chances?

Whether applying early improves your chances is the wrong question. The better question is: "For the colleges on my list, am I a suitable candidate for an early program and do I want to take advantage of that option?" After all, it's not really an advantage to be accepted early at a school if you haven't decided you really want to go there.

That said, we know you would like us to try to answer this question. Unfortunately, the answer is that it's situational and complicated—and involves a lot of inside baseball about the college admission office. Here it is.

Whether or not there is an advantage to applying early will vary from school to school and from applicant to applicant at each school. At schools that want to fill their classes with students who have made a commitment to the college through early decision or who have made it clear that they are sincerely interested by submitting their application through early action, there may be an advantage. But at other schools, applying early will make no difference. You just apply earlier and find out earlier. For some schools, the early plan may be the most competitive part of the admission cycle; at others, it could be the least competitive.

> **KNOW THE JARGON . . .**
>
> ## Admit Rate
>
> The admit rate is the percentage of applicants admitted by a college among those who applied. The admit rate is calculated by dividing the number of students admitted to a college by the number of students who applied to that college.

For example, when the admit rate for early applications is higher than the admit rate under regular decision, you can't necessarily conclude that there is an advantage. It may be that the candidates were stronger statistically, or that they just happened to meet other institutional priorities of the college. Students who apply early are often statistically among the strongest students a college will admit—these students are not relying on first-semester senior-year grades and November scores to boost their candidacy. Also, special-circumstance groups—such as athletes or legacies—may be steered toward the early pool, which can skew the statistics in a way that is difficult to sort out without a lot of inside information.

One thing is for sure: applying early is no solution for weak grades or other problems a student may have. As Wesleyan dean of admission Nancy Meislahn has said, "Applying early does not have a Rumpelstiltskin effect: you can't spin C's into A's."

As you can see, for every generalization about applying early creating an advantage, there are many exceptions. Because of this, it's important that students and families *not* use an early plan merely to game the system. Applying early as a strategy works only if you know it's your first-choice school and if you definitely want to go there—and then it's not a strategy but a natural outgrowth of your interest.

page 250 for students who are deferred under early decision plans. If you are denied under REA, you cannot reapply for consideration under RD.

EARLY DECISION

Early decision (ED) plans require careful consideration, because they are binding. Students apply to one school early, are notified of a

Students: Do the Right Thing

You have applied under early action, rolling admission, or restrictive early action and you're in. Congratulations.

We now encourage you to do the right thing. If you know you will not enroll at some of the other colleges on your list, don't apply to them. Go back through that original list and cross off those schools. Or if you've already sent in your applications, let those colleges know your plans. Don't collect trophies in the form of admission letters from colleges you will never attend.

There are some exceptions to this rule. Some colleges very much want to make their case to you even if you have been admitted to another college under rolling admission, early action, or restrictive early action. If there are schools on your list you can still imagine you might attend, feel welcome to keep your options alive *provided you are open to the case those colleges will make.* And if you need to compare financial aid or merit scholarship awards, you will definitely want to proceed with applications to the other schools on your list.

As you can see, this isn't simple. But matters of integrity rarely are. Think carefully, and for any school where you would just be collecting another acceptance letter, let that college know your decision as soon as possible so they can offer your seat to another student who wants to attend.

decision early, and agree to enroll if admitted. If you are applying ED, you are saying that you are positive that this school is your first choice and that you will enroll if accepted.

There are three possible outcomes in early decision: acceptance, denial, and deferral. If you are accepted ED, you must immediately withdraw any applications you have submitted to other schools. You can notify the colleges by email, but make sure your email is acknowledged. If it is not acknowledged, follow up your email with a letter and save a copy for your records. If you have been accepted at a school with rolling admission in the meantime, let that college know immediately that you will not enroll.

If you are deferred under early decision, you will be reconsidered with the regular pool of applicants. You do not have to reapply. Our best advice if you're deferred: update your application. Colleges will typically have a form that requests any new information on grades, testing, extracurricular activities, or achievements. You should also send an email or letter indicating that you are still very interested in attending the college, highlighting for the admission office anything new in your life. If the college says it will welcome additional information, consider sending in an additional essay or a class paper you're proud of.

If you are denied early decision, you will not be reconsidered. This may seem harsh, with the denial coming right around the holidays. But accept it as valuable guidance. The school is sending you a strong signal early on that you're not in the running and will be best served by placing your attention elsewhere—on your applications to the other wonderful schools on your list.

An early decision plan is a great alternative for those students who are in a position to use it properly. Because it is binding, you will need to carefully consider the following:

- Have you fully investigated your options by researching the schools on your list early, and spent a significant amount of time on at least several of their campuses?
- Is the college to which you are applying ED your first choice? In other words, of all the places that you are applying, would you definitely enroll here even if you got in everywhere? And have you felt this way for a period of time, not just a couple of days?
- Have you visited the college, observed classes, and had an overnight stay, if possible?
- Do you change your mind easily about what you like and what is important to you?
- Do you understand how your grades and test scores fit into the college's academic profile?
- Do you understand how the college implements its ED plan? For example, of the students they are seeking who have a strong desire to attend, are they focusing on those who are the most competitive academically or on those who are at the bottom of their academic profile?
- Do you and your parents agree that if you are given a reasonable financial aid package, you will attend the ED college even if other schools offer you a better financial aid package or a merit scholarship?

Some colleges offer two rounds of early decision. Applying to a college ED II can be a good idea for students whose performance in

ADVANTAGES Early Decision

- Colleges want students who will be thrilled to be there. Applying ED lets the college know you have decided it's the one you most want to attend.
- Cost savings. If you are accepted ED, you've filed just one application and paid only one fee (although you will want to have your other applications ready to go, just in case).
- A less stressful senior year. ED frees students from the anxiety of waiting to hear from multiple schools.
- Once you are admitted, you can start getting to know the school where you will spend the next four years—bonding and networking with the college and your classmates via social media and admitted student visits.
- You are done! Enjoy your senior year.

If you are applying early under any decision plan, you should proceed with preparing your applications to the other schools on your list as though your early application did not exist. But you may want to wait to press "Send" on your regular decision applications until you learn whether you've been admitted early.

Does Early Decision Fill Most of the Seats in the Freshman Class?

"The college you're applying to has filled half its freshman class with early decision applicants!" You may have heard things like this and worried there won't be enough room left if you apply under regular decision. But this is a case where the numbers are deceiving. Let's do the math.

The question is not how many seats are being taken up in the class by applicants who applied under early decision. The question is, what percentage of the school's total admission offers is already gone? It may sound incredible, but even when half the seats are filled with ED applicants, fewer than half the acceptances have been given out.

Here's how it works. Say a highly selective college can only enroll ten students in its freshman class, and five are accepted early decision. Because the ED process required their prior commitment to attend if accepted, the college knows for sure they are coming. Yes, that leaves five spots to be filled in next year's class under regular decision. But remember that the dean of admission knows that students accepted through the regular decision process haven't precommitted to actually

Does Early Decision Fill Most of the Seats in the Freshman Class? (continued)

attend. In fact, on average for this hypothetical but not untypical college, only about half will. The college can admit ten students under its RD process to fill the remaining five seats.

So the college will actually admit fifteen students total. When five acceptances were given early decision, that wasn't half the fat envelopes—it was only one-third. Two-thirds are still left for the regular decision process. No reason to panic.

The Early Decision Agreement

If you apply under an early decision plan, you must submit an Early Decision Agreement. This form can be found as part of the Common Application, with any other electronic application provider's form, or as a part of a college's unique form. The ED Agreement is a contract whereby the student agrees to enroll if accepted and to immediately withdraw all applications submitted to other colleges. The ED Agreement is signed by the student, a parent, and the high school counselor. It is usually submitted by the high school counselor. But pay careful attention to instructions for submitting this form, which may differ from high school to high school.

Colleges take this contract seriously. Read it fully and make sure you understand what you are committing to by signing it. If you fail to abide by its terms and, for example, apply to more than one college early decision, your acceptances at both schools may be rescinded. Note that you have agreed to let the college to which you're applying share your name and ED Agreement with other institutions.

Students sign a similar agreement when applying under a restrictive early action plan.

Financial Aid

Colleges handle financial aid differently under each type of decision plan. Some schools release financial aid decisions beginning on a specific date, typically around March 1. Other schools provide families with either a financial aid award or an estimated financial aid award with the offer of admission or shortly thereafter. This award will be updated and confirmed in the spring. If your information remains the same, you can assume the award will remain the same. Students should check each school's financial aid website carefully for deadlines and notification dates. Take advantage of any opportunities to ask questions of admission or financial aid officers at each school so you can understand how financial aid is handled under each decision plan. We've provided some questions for you on page 260. See Chapter 16 for further information on financial aid. Also, note that the early decision plan presents a special case where you will receive an award only from the ED college and there will be no opportunity to receive or compare aid packages from other colleges.

How Do Your Grades and Scores Figure into Your Decision to Apply Under an Early Plan?

Much of the advice you will receive about applying under an early plan—early action, early decision, or restrictive early action—will be to apply *only* if your grades and test scores place you in the top half of that college's academic profile. For many of you, this is great advice. But for some of you, it's not. Whether or not this is good advice will depend upon the schools on your list and the goals those schools have for their early plans.

In order to understand how your grades and scores should figure into your decision to apply early, you will need to understand:

- Where your grades and scores fit into the college's academic profile.
- The pattern of your grades. Are they going up, going down, or staying the same?
- The college's philosophy and practice with regard to its early plan.
- How your grades and test scores fit into that philosophy and practice.

What does all that mean?

Here's an example. Every class has a bottom group of students. Some schools may want that group to be made up of the students who most want to be there, not those who would have been just as happy at another college. So applying early to such a school might make sense for a student whose grades and scores are not in the top half of that college's academic profile. On the other hand, if the college's approach is to select their strongest students during an early plan cycle, then you might want to wait and apply during the regular decision cycle if your grades are on an upward trajectory with your strongest marks yet to come.

You know how to evaluate your grades and scores and where you fall in the academic profile of the college (remember, it was in Chapter 8). But where do you find out how the colleges on your list implement their early plans? Your best bet is to discuss it with your high school counselor. Or call and talk to the admission officer at the college—tell her your grades and scores and ask for her best advice about applying under an early plan.

You may not be able to obtain a definitive answer. But don't worry about this too much. There are many factors that you may want or need to take into account to determine whether applying early is an appropriate decision for you. This is simply *one* of those factors. This is not a way to game the system. You should do what feels right for you and what works best for your family.

Is Applying Early a Good Idea for Me?

To help you decide what might be right for you, consider the following questions in order. The more yes answers you can give, the more applying early might be your best approach.

- If you're considering early decision, start here and work your way through all the questions below:
  - Of all the colleges on your list, is this the school where you would unquestionably enroll?
  - Is your first-choice school an environment that fits you well, but also a place where you can change and grow?
  - Have you felt the school where you are going to apply early decision is your first choice for more than a few days or weeks?
  - Do you and your parents agree that if you are given a reasonable financial aid package, you will attend the school even if other colleges were to offer you stronger financial aid packages or a merit scholarship?
- If you're considering early action or restrictive early action, start here:
  - Do your junior-year grades and classes support an early application, relative to the philosophy and practice of the college to which you're applying?
  - Have you completed all standardized testing by October of your senior year?
  - Considering your commitments to extracurricular activities or work, will you be able to complete your application by November?
  - Are you a student with a special talent, such as an athlete, or a special circumstance, such as a legacy applicant? If so, see Chapter 18 or 19.

high school is improving and who are doing their best work in senior year. Those students are going to be stronger candidates in the second round of ED, which has a deadline in January or February.

Questions You May Have

What happens if my financial aid is not what I expected at the school where I was accepted early decision?

This is one of the few circumstances under which a student may be released from the early decision agreement. If your financial aid

package from the school where you've been accepted ED is inadequate for your family, let the college know immediately. Alert both the admission office and the financial aid office. When you talk with financial aid, let them know what you thought the package might be, and explain your current financial circumstances to see if they want you to put anything else in writing. (For some tips on how best to talk to financial aid offices, be sure to see Chapter 16.)

If the financial aid office tells you there is nothing they can do to improve your award, you must decide whether you can live with that award or let the admission office know

Why Colleges Offer Different Decision Plans

There are many reasons colleges employ different decision plans. A school that offers rolling admission may choose to do so because it helps them spread out the task of reviewing the thousands of applications they receive. On the other hand, a school that chooses to offer early decision might want to offer an early option but lacks the staff to complete a holistic review for everyone who can get their application done by a certain deadline. So they offer an early plan *only* to students who know the school is their first choice. For everybody else, there's regular decision.

Colleges are always listening to the messages they are getting from their applicants. For example, schools that have instituted an early plan may have been hearing that students would have welcomed an option that would have allowed them to have a more fulfilling senior year in high school, with the admission process wrapped up early.

Different decision plans benefit both colleges and students. For example, early plans unclog the admission pipeline. With an early acceptance, students can withdraw applications to the schools where they know they aren't going to enroll, decreasing the number of applications filed at second-, third-, fourth-, and fourteenth-choice colleges.

Everybody gains when the number of applications is reduced, because colleges are better able to forecast how many students will enroll (admission professionals call this their "yield"). When it's more difficult for colleges to predict who may enroll, the admission office may send out fewer acceptance letters and create larger waiting lists. Then they wait until after May 1, when candidates have replied, in order to see if they came in high, low, or on target for the number of spaces available in the class. But that means the decision process for students stretches into the summer, creating more uncertainty and anxiety for both the students and the colleges—and potentially a good number of far more somber high school graduation ceremonies.

Parents May Need to Weigh In on This Decision

Parents, choice of a decision plan is a step where your input may be required. The plan your child selects may influence your ability to compare financial aid packages. Be candid with your college-bound teen about your family's need for financial assistance and be proactive in investigating the financial aid policies at the schools your son or daughter is considering. We have included here a list of questions you and your teenager may want to ask admission and financial aid officers.

Applying early also means completing all the necessary steps—writing multiple essays, preparing the application, requesting recommendations—within a much tighter time frame. Your teenager may need your support and advice in managing the stress and day-to-day particulars. Just remember to *offer* your help before you jump to the rescue.

you are regretfully withdrawing and will go elsewhere. If they tell you they may be able to make an adjustment to your award, find out what date they will be in touch with you about that adjustment, and call the admission office back to request an extension to a few days after that date. In the meantime, do not withdraw your applications from other colleges—and if you have other college deadlines coming up, be sure you are getting those applications ready to submit, just in case.

What is early notification?

This is another name for a "likely letter," in which a college lets you know before the official notification date that you are likely, but not guaranteed, to gain admission. Recipients of early notification letters are usually strong candidates. But the operative word here is "likely"—this is not a *firm* offer of admission. Very few colleges send out likely letters.

I was denied admission under an early decision program. If there is another school that is high on my list and offers two rounds of ED, should I apply for the second round?

It's fine to do this, provided you meet all the other conditions we've outlined that show early decision is right for you. If—once you take away the ED I school from your list—you are certain of your next top choice and that school offers ED II, by all means apply. If you were deferred from your ED I school and then apply to a second school ED II, you will need to attend if you are admitted to the second school, and must then withdraw all other applications, including your application to the ED school you applied to in the first round.

What does it mean for me if I'm applying to a college that denies a significant portion of its early applicants?

If you are an "improving" student, you may want to wait and apply during the regular decision cycle. If you apply and are denied, you will not have the opportunity to present your (stronger) senior-year grades. The same holds true if you plan to retake the SAT/ACT and get stronger scores. Once you are denied, that's it. Our best advice? Call the admission office and ask to speak with an admission counselor, who can help you understand your options.

FROM THE DESK OF THE DEAN

Decision Plans

Whether a college offers early decision, rolling admission, regular admission, early action, or some combination of any of the above depends on the college's size, mission, philosophy, and goals. There is tremendous diversity in what colleges offer and what they think about these programs. And you will find disagreement among the deans who share their thoughts here. Why? Because each admission dean is speaking about what is best for his or her college and the students it serves. No one decision plan is best for every student or college in the country.

WILLIAM FITZSIMMONS
Dean of admission and financial aid, Harvard University

➡ Harvard University offers restrictive early action and regular decision.

Early admission appears to be the "new normal," and more of the nation's and the world's most promising students apply early to college.

For four years, from 2007 to 2010, Harvard did not offer early admission due to concerns that such programs advantaged students who attended secondary schools that had more resources and better college counseling—while putting pressure on all students to make premature college choices.

But in the wake of the global financial crisis it became clear that many students from low-income backgrounds were looking for the certainty provided by early admission and early financial aid awards.

That said, applying early is not an advantage at Harvard, and students should take the entire senior year to make the best possible college choice. When a student applies—either early or regular—has no bearing on whether he or she will ultimately be admitted.

If we are 100 percent certain that we would admit the person later, we will do so early. We have no quotas in our minds for the number admitted early or for anything else. Regular decision offers important practical advantages in a later application deadline (January 1) with more time for students to edit and proofread portions of the application and more time for teachers and counselors to become familiar with students before they write on their behalf. Students may also want to consider whether their application would be strengthened by senior-year extracurricular achievements or improved academic performance.

But if your record and accomplishments have been consistently strong over time, early action may be an attractive choice. You do not have to commit to coming to Harvard until May 1, but you will learn earlier if it is an option for you.

KITTY McCARTHY

Vice president for enrollment management and student affairs, West Virginia State University

➡ West Virginia State University offers rolling admission.

The upside to rolling admission is that students learn earlier than they otherwise would that they've been admitted. They can do some more exploring, visit or revisit the campus, and just get in the mind-set of WVSU. They can figure out, "What more do I need to know? What questions do I have?" They can move on from the conversation about "Can I get in?" to "What are the other opportunities I'm interested in?" At WVSU, that might be honors or research or choosing a particular residence hall, and they will have time to explore these areas over time rather than having to pack it all into four to six weeks in the spring. With rolling admission, students have more time to have those conversations about student experience with WVSU students, faculty, staff, and alumni.

The upside of rolling admission for WVSU is that it gives us an opportunity to have more contact with students before they're likely to hear from other schools they've applied to, particularly from the non-rolling-admission schools. It gives us an opportunity to express the strongest level of interest possible in students we very much want to be a part of this community, and then it lets us set up a whole path of communication to continue to reinforce that interest. Our hope is that by the time a student hears from their other schools, they feel connected to WVSU—we want them and they want us.

JOHN LATTING

Assistant vice provost for undergraduate enrollment and dean of admission, Emory University

➡ Emory University offers two rounds of early decision and regular decision.

We make an assumption that students who come in through the early pathway raise the bar when it comes to energy and enthusiasm, and that's a great foundation on which to build a class. I think we see it as the core of the freshman class. So there are these two pathways through which people can come to Emory. It's not necessary for everybody to come through early decision, or even most students. And in the end it's all one freshman class.

Is there an advantage to applying early at a given school? If you haven't really been thoughtful about that, if you haven't really researched colleges and visited some and really considered the options, then all of these other strategic issues are really not that important. What's the use of getting a leg up on a school that really is not a good place for you? So let's focus on the appropriate question. Not "How can I increase my chances of getting in?"—that's not the first question. The first question is, "Where would I really like to be next year? And where am I best prepared to be? Where is it realistic for me to go?" That's the starting point.

NANCY HARGRAVE MEISLAHN
Dean of admission and financial aid, Wesleyan University

➡ Wesleyan University offers two rounds of early decision and regular decision.

Even when you're looking at a place that has a pretty heavy investment in early decision, there are still lots of places open in the regular decision cycle. So the notion that if you don't apply early there are no seats left is a false assumption. At Wesleyan, even when we've taken 38–40 percent of our class early, given our yield in the spring, that's only about 15–16 percent of our total number of offers of admission.

At Wesleyan we believe early decision serves some students as well as the institution. We think of early decision as being the heart around which we build a class. In the über-competitive, highly selective admission process, we're always splitting hairs. In the regular cycle we are often making assumptions and judgments and choosing one student over another very similar student. So why wouldn't you want to maximize the process for the students who most want to be at your institution?

STEVE THOMAS
Director of admissions, Colby College

➡ Colby College offers two rounds of early decision and regular decision.

There's a lot of unpredictability in college admission, more so all the time, and this causes both the colleges and the students to act in their own selfish interests. And what the colleges do is take a higher percentage of their class early, because they're going to effectively get 100 percent yield, so there's less exposure in the regular round. What kids do to protect themselves is they apply to more colleges, which creates more uncertainty, which makes the colleges pick a higher percentage of the class early. So the whole thing goes back and forth, and we're kind of stuck right now. But if a student can know where he or she wants to go, they can avoid all of that back-and-forth and take advantage of it, actually. Colleges are excited to have kids who want to go there. So if you've got a student who wants to go to your school, why would you not want to take that student instead of waiting to admit one who maybe wants to go somewhere else?

TOM DELAHUNT
Vice president for admission, Drake

➡ Drake University offers rolling admission.

Early decision programs work great for institutions, but we do not think they work so well for the students. The pressure to apply early is just too intense for the sixteen-, seven-teen-, and eighteen-year-olds that we're working with, and that's really who we're supposed to serve. The students are pushed to make decisions earlier about what they want to study and where they want to pursue it. We know that many students change majors once they get to college, which often leads to extending the length of time toward their undergradu-ate degree, and we think one of the reasons is that they're making their college decisions without fully considering all their options. Early decision essentially eliminates any college and career exploration from taking place in the senior year and pushes it into the junior and even sophomore years. We're asking them to make enormous financial and educational decisions that have an effect on their lives without really having all the information. At Drake, we have opted to give students and their families an opportunity to fully investigate their options, and we believe it is one of the reasons we have so few students transfer.

PART VII

PAYING

CHAPTER 16

Financial Aid

"Don't be afraid to reach out and have a personal conversation with your financial aid officer. It could literally change your financial future."

—Angel B. Perez, vice president, dean of admission and financial aid, Pitzer College

"Will our family qualify for financial aid? Will we be able to get any merit aid? Which colleges will we actually be able to afford? What happens if my financial aid award isn't big enough? How can I possibly finance this?"

Paying for college is a concern for most families. Very few can foot the bill for one year of college up front, much less four. In this chapter, we will help you figure out the bottom line—that means the "sticker price" of tuition and all the other expenses, minus the financial aid and scholarships you may receive.

GETTING STARTED ON FINANCIAL AID

As you begin to think about paying for college, keep the following in mind:

- Many families mistakenly assume they aren't eligible for aid. You may be eligible and not even know it.
- You could get more aid than you may think. There are no guarantees and every college is different, but you might be pleasantly surprised.
- Expensive schools may be cheaper to attend because of strong financial aid programs.
- The biggest mistake students and families make is to dream too small. Dream big—apply for financial aid at colleges you wouldn't otherwise be able to afford. But make sure you cover yourself by having affordable colleges on your list, too.

As we've discussed earlier, students and their parents should have a frank conversation early on in the college search about what the

Checkpoints ✍

✔ Start investigating financial aid as soon as you start thinking about the colleges to which you will apply.

✔ Net price calculators can provide an early understanding of what you will be asked to pay at individual colleges and what your aid award might look like.

✔ Assume you are eligible for aid and take the time to apply.

✔ All students applying for financial aid must complete the Free Application for Federal Student Aid (FAFSA). Several hundred colleges also require the CSS PROFILE form or their own institutional form.

✔ Aid comes in many forms—grants, loans, scholarships, and work-study.

✔ A family's ability to pay—the Expected Family Contribution (EFC)—is calculated differently from college to college.

✔ Deadlines matter. Track them carefully.

✔ Carefully compare your aid awards to understand which combination of price and student aid is most advantageous.

family can afford. Start thinking about financial aid as soon as you start thinking about which colleges will be on your list. Just as you ask yourself questions about who you are and what you value in order to help you visualize which colleges will be best for you, you need to understand your financial realities, what you can afford, what each college can offer in financial assistance, and what your possibilities will therefore be.

Applying for financial aid can be an intimidating process. But if even one college on your list seems unaffordable, apply for financial aid.

It's important to understand that most aid is need-based. It is awarded on the basis of a family's ability to pay,

not its willingness to pay. In other words, the federal government or an individual college computes what it thinks a family can afford. But that may be very different from what *you* think you can afford.

HOW TO USE THIS CHAPTER

There are many differences in financial aid policy from college to college. This chapter provides general advice and will serve you well overall. It cannot possibly take into account the precise way financial aid works for every individual college. What does this mean for you? Understand the concepts in this chapter—and then read each college's financial aid information with care. We're your starting point for all the basics, but the colleges themselves are your authoritative source for the critical details.

TYPES OF AID

Need-Based: Aid Determined by Your Calculated Ability to Pay

Grants

Grants are gifts and do not have to be repaid. They come primarily from three sources: the federal government, state governments, and individual colleges.

FEDERAL GOVERNMENT

- **Federal Pell Grants.** Awarded to undergraduate students in lower income brackets.
- **Federal Supplemental Educational Opportunity Grant (FSEOG) Program.** Awarded to students with exceptional need through participating schools; priority is given to Pell Grant recipients.

Eligibility for each of these programs is determined through the Free Application for Federal Student Aid (FAFSA), discussed on page 276. The federal government also sponsors some specialized grant programs—for example, grants for students whose parents serve in the military.

STATE

Many states have financial aid programs that offer grant assistance to residents who attend a college in that state. In addition, some states have reciprocity with neighboring states, enabling the grant to "travel" with a student. Information can usually be found at the website of your state's higher education authority. The U.S. Department of Education publishes a complete list of state higher education commissions, as well as other helpful resources, in the Education Resource Organizations Directory at ed.gov.

COLLEGE-FUNDED

Colleges have different amounts of grant aid available and different policies with regard to how their funds are awarded—see the explanation on page 273. In addition

---

Forms of Financial Aid

Financial aid takes many forms and is accessible for many different kinds of students.

Need-based aid. Your family's resources must be determined to be insufficient to cover college costs through an analysis of your financial situation. Need-based aid includes:

- **Grants**
  - Federal
  - State
  - College-funded
- **Self-help**
  - Loans
  - Work-study

Merit-based aid. Awarded on the basis of special talents or skills, such as athletic or academic ability.

- **Scholarships**
  - College-funded
  - State
  - Private organizations

Gaining an Early Understanding of What You Can Afford

Many families are eager to understand how much financial aid they may receive. While there is no way to know in advance the *exact* amount of aid that will be awarded to attend a specific college, or for college in general, families can gain a preliminary understanding of the amount of aid they can expect to receive from the federal government and also from a specific college by using some basic online tools.

All colleges are required by law to have a net price calculator (sometimes referred to as a financial aid calculator) available on their website. This gives you a quick estimate of your bottom-line cost of attending college—your net price.

Cost of Attendance − Grant Aid = Net Price

With most net price calculators, your estimated net price is the cost of attendance (COA) for one year minus the estimated grant aid—scholarships or other outright gifts—you are likely to receive for that same year. Cost of attendance includes tuition, room and board, fees, and allowances for books, personal expenses, and transportation. Net price calculators compute your estimated net price for a single and specific year of college (for example, the year you will enter college) by considering student and family income and asset information as well as other factors, such as the number of dependents in the family and the number of students from that family in college in any one year. See the full discussion on page 275.

But the calculation doesn't end here, because grants aren't the only form of aid. The number that will be of most interest to you is the "estimated remaining cost."

Cost of Attendance − Grant Aid − Self-help = Estimated Remaining Cost

The estimated remaining cost is the net price minus self-help, which includes loans and work-study. This figure will give you a good idea of the amount you may be expected to spend out of pocket. (See our hypothetical net price calculator result on page 271.)

Your net price and estimated remaining cost may differ significantly from college to college. So will the exact composition of your financial aid package, which will be a mix of grants, scholarships, loans, and work-study. Why? Because each college uses its own formula to determine your family's ability to pay. Some colleges are able to meet the full amount of what they calculate you need, while others are not. Some colleges have the funds to provide students with assistance consisting completely of grants and scholarships, while most colleges must include loans in their aid packages.

Use the net price calculators at the schools you are considering to help you figure out what the colleges offer, as well as to start thinking about what you will need to do to make your choices work financially. The federal government posts a calculator—the FAFSA4caster—on the website for the Free Application for Federal Student Aid (FAFSA) at fafsa.gov. This calculator generates an estimated Expected Family Contribution based on the information provided and will estimate the total federal aid you may be eligible for, including grants and loans—though not what you may receive from the colleges themselves.

For a more complete picture of the financial aid you might receive at the colleges you are considering, go to the net price calculators on the financial aid section of each college website. The College Board offers a calculator at collegeboard.org as well as links to specific colleges (both public and private) that use the College Board's calculator as their own. You can also use a calculator on FinAid's website at finaid.org to determine your Expected Family Contribution (EFC).

Just to see how things compare, try out the calculators at a few less expensive colleges and some more expensive ones. It can often be as affordable to attend a more expensive college that offers a strong financial aid program. Find out now, so you can select the colleges that work best for you while factoring in price, but not ruling out options that might initially seem unaffordable.

As you use financial aid calculators, be aware of the following:

- The calculators provide only an estimate.
- The calculation provided is for one year only.
- The more accurate the information you put into the calculator, the more accurate the information you will get out.
- Calculators do not include professional judgment that a college financial aid officer may apply to your family circumstances. Your actual award may be different from what you see on the calculator.
- When you use the calculator, you are not filing an application for financial aid. The information you submit there does not go to the colleges' financial aid offices. *You* will need to file the appropriate forms separately. We'll show you how later in this chapter.

SAMPLE PRINTOUT FROM FINANCIAL AID CALCULATOR

Estimated Cost of Attendance

Tuition	$ 42,295
Room and board	$ 10,544
Books and supplies	$ 1,692
Transportation	$ 500
Personal expenses	$ 2,000
Total	**$ 57,031**

Estimated Grant Aid

Pell grant	$ 1,500
Federal grant	$ 1,200
Institutional grant	$ 25,633
Institutional scholarship	$ 10,000
Total	**$ 38,333**

Estimated Net Price	**$ 18,698**

Estimated Self-Help

Student loan	$ 5,500
Work-study	$ 2,000
Total	**$ 7,500**

Estimated Remaining Cost	**$ 11,198**

to financial need, some programs may have other eligibility criteria. Check the financial aid section of the websites of every college to which you are applying to understand their policies and, most important, the deadlines.

Loans

The federal government is the major source of loans for college. Some colleges have their own loan programs in addition to federal programs. Check college websites to see what financing options are offered. Other sources of borrowing for families may include private lenders and state programs. For state programs, check the website of the higher education authority in your state to see what is available.

FEDERAL LOAN PROGRAMS

The federal government sponsors several federal loan programs, under which loans may be subsidized, resulting in lower interest rates or more favorable repayment terms. Each federal program differs with regard to eligibility requirements and criteria for disbursement and repayment. Depending on the program, the student or parent may be the borrower. Funds come directly from the U.S. Department of Education and are disbursed through the individual colleges. There are usually annual maximum loan amounts. For more detailed information visit studentaid.ed.gov. Federal loan programs include:

- Federal Direct Loans
  - **Federal Direct Subsidized Loans (formerly Stafford Subsidized Loans).** Variable-rate loans with favorable interest rates for students with financial need. While the student is in school, the federal government pays interest and repayment is deferred until six months after leaving college.
  - **Federal Direct Unsubsidized Loans (formerly Stafford Unsubsidized Loans).** Variable-rate loans for students awarded without consideration to financial need. Interest rates are the same as those for Direct Subsidized loans. Interest is not paid by the government while the student is in school, but may be accrued and added to the principal until repayment begins, six months after leaving college.
- **Federal Perkins Loan Program.** Fixed-rate, low-interest loan offered to students with the greatest need through participating schools. The amount received depends on need, any other financial aid received, and the availability of Perkins funds at that school.
- **Federal PLUS Loans.** PLUS loans enable parents to borrow annually at a favorable fixed rate the entire cost of a student's

"OK, your grant, your loan, your scholarships and your work study are all taken care of, but would you mind telling me where you got this 10% off coupon?"

education minus any financial aid received. PLUS loans are provided without regard to financial need to parents who do not have an adverse credit history.

Work-Study

Employment opportunities for students on financial aid are often subsidized by the federal government through the Federal Work-Study Program, which provides funds directly to colleges to help pay for student wages, incentivizing them to hire you. During the course of the school year a student will likely work eight to ten hours a week, usually on campus. The paycheck comes directly to the student, who can typically expect to earn about $2,000

to $3,000 per year, roughly the amount anticipated for books and personal expenses.

Merit-Based: Aid Awarded on the Basis of Your Talents and Abilities

Merit-based aid—also called scholarships—comes from individual colleges, state governments, and private groups and institutions.

College-Funded

Many colleges offer merit-based aid. These scholarships or merit awards may be conferred in recognition of a student's academic strength, special talents including those in athletics or the performing arts, or special circumstances, such as students who are the first in

To Borrow or Not to Borrow?

Some colleges with significant endowments have made a commitment to not require students to borrow to finance their educations. These schools are able to do this both because they have a strong commitment to financial aid and because they are fortunate to have large endowments that permit them to use their funds this way. These colleges are also some of the most selective in the country.

Generally loans will be part of most aid packages, which means that students will be expected to borrow each year as an investment in their own education. Only you can decide how much debt you are willing to live with. Remember that an education is very valuable in today's world—a good education can increase your lifetime earning power substantially. So a loan is truly an investment in your future financial success. For some perspective, consider that a total indebtedness of, say, $20,000 at graduation is less than most loans for new cars.

Since students can borrow only a set amount through federal programs, parents may have to take out loans toward the cost of a college education as well—for example, Federal PLUS loans or private loans. Some banks also offer private student loans, but they often have variable rates and usually require a parent as a co-signer. We strongly suggest that students and parents pursue federal loans first, because interest rates usually are lower. In addition, some federal loans for students don't accrue interest while the student is in school and can even be forgiven if the student pursues certain careers.

Our best advice: federal loans are by far the best option and should be applied for before considering private loans.

their family to attend college. This assistance may be part of a need-based student aid package, it may be on top of any need-based aid given, or it may be awarded to students who do not demonstrate any financial need at all.

Check with each college to understand what merit-based aid you might be eligible for, how to apply, and what special deadlines there may be. Pay particular attention to the eligibility and application requirements for scholarships offered through colleges; they may involve a competition, submission of a project, a campus visit, or interview. Some colleges have an additional scholarship application for those applying for a merit scholarship, or require an additional essay on the regular admission application.

State

Some states have scholarship programs based on merit as well as on need. These awards may be applicable only if you are attending an in-state college or university. Check with your high school college counselor about state merit aid available, or visit the website of the higher education authority of your state. (The FAFSA must be filed to be eligible for most state scholarships.)

Private Groups and Institutions

Some private organizations, foundations, and businesses award scholarships directly to students to help pay for college—for example, the Rotary Club, the Boy Scouts of America, IBM, or a church. There are also national competitions sponsored by private organizations that award scholarships—some of the best known are the National Merit

Scholarship Foundation, the Gates Millennium Scholars program, and the Coca-Cola Scholars program.

Check with your high school college counselor about these opportunities. You can also search for private scholarships at the following websites:

- College Board Scholarship Search at collegeboard.org
- Fastweb's free scholarship search at fastweb.com
- FinAid: The Smart Student Guide to Financial Aid at finaid.org
- Scholarships.com's free scholarship search at scholarships.com

The above search engines are all available free of charge. Note: never use a scholarship search organization that charges a fee. See the "Scams" box on page 285.

Read all scholarship information carefully, paying particular attention to eligibility, requirements, deadlines, and renewability.

ELIGIBILITY FOR NEED-BASED FINANCIAL AID

The guiding principle of need-based financial aid is that families—parents and students—are the primary source of funding for a student's college education and need to pay as much as they are able, up to the full price. The difference between what a student's budget will be at a specific college (the student's cost of attendance) and what a family will be expected to pay based on the application of a financial aid formula to their circumstances (the Expected Family Contribution or EFC)—is called "financial need."

Cost of Attendance

− Expected Family Contribution

= Financial Need

Financial aid (grants, loans, scholarships, and work-study) is what covers the need—the amount remaining between what your family will be expected to pay and a college's full cost. "Need" is a variable term. If your family is expected to pay $20,000 a year and you will attend a college with a cost of attendance of $20,000 or less, your need is zero. If the college you attend costs $50,000, your family's need is $30,000.

Cost of Attendance

In order to understand whether you can afford a specific college, you first have to understand the full cost of attendance:

Tuition

+ Room and Board

+ Fees

+ Books and Supplies

+ Personal Expenses

+ Transportation

= Cost of Attendance

Check the financial aid sections of the websites for each of the colleges to which you are applying—look for "Student Budget" or "Cost of Attendance." In most cases, you will be looking at costs for the current year—not the year when you expect to enter—and will need to anticipate cost increases. For tuition, room and board, and fees, estimate a 5 percent increase for the coming year. Costs may increase more or less than the 5 percent estimate we use in this exercise, but this will give you a starting point.

How Colleges Handle Outside Awards

Check with the colleges about how they handle scholarships from private groups and organizations—known as "outside awards"—in their calculation of their financial aid award. Different colleges calculate their impact differently. Some colleges count half an outside award toward grant aid and half toward student self-help, lowering the student's work-study or loan amount by the equivalent of half the outside award. Others count the entire outside award against loans and work-study, and only lower the institutional grant portion of an aid award if self-help is brought down to zero. Still others count the entire outside award against institutional gift aid. Why? Because colleges are legally prohibited from overawarding federal aid. In other words, the total amount of aid a student receives cannot be greater than a college's cost, and usually not more than a student's overall calculated financial need. Also, colleges only have so many resources to award based on student need. If a student is suddenly less needy by $10,000 from an outside scholarship, the college must responsibly reassess the situation and award that student less so it can help other students with more need.

Here are some additional guidelines for estimating costs.

- **Tuition.** Tuition is generally the largest part of the total bill to attend a school, but it's only a part of it. Don't make the mistake of considering only tuition in your understanding of cost.
- **Room.** If a variety of housing options are offered with different prices, use the cost of a double room.

- **Board.** If a variety of meal plans are offered, select—for this exercise—21 meals a week. You can always go down from there, but even if you do, your total food costs will likely approach this number.

- **Fees.** Fees are listed when they apply to every undergraduate at the college—for example, a student activities fee.

- **Books and supplies.** Check the financial aid website to see the amount the college recommends budgeting. This figure does not cover crucial learning tools such as personal computers.

- **Personal expenses.** Personal expenses are meant to include spending money for gas, pizza, subway tickets, movies, hiking boots, toothpaste, and the dorm ski trip. Warning: the amount a student will spend will usually be higher than you think. If you think you will spend less than the budgeted amount, think again.

- **Transportation.** International students are typically budgeted for one round trip per year, domestic students for two. While a student may return home more than this, it is unusual for a financial aid award to cover additional trips. In addition, colleges may also allow for local transportation costs.

Expected Family Contribution (EFC)

Different colleges determine a family's ability to pay—the Expected Family Contribution (EFC)—differently. Colleges awarding federal student aid ask families to fill out the Free Application for Federal Student Aid (FAFSA), which determines your eligibility to receive federal assistance. The FAFSA is also the form used by most states for state grants and by many colleges as they determine eligibility for financial aid awarded directly from the college's own funds.

In addition, many colleges—particularly those with strong need-based financial aid programs—also ask families to complete the CSS PROFILE (College Scholarship Service PROFILE), available from the College Board at collegeboard.org, in order to determine their eligibility for aid awarded directly from the colleges. Some colleges also require additional forms—for example, divorced parents may be asked to submit a Noncustodial PROFILE, or self-employed parents to submit a Business and Farm Supplement. And finally, some colleges, either instead of or in addition to the PROFILE, request their own specific form.

FAFSA

The formula used by the FAFSA to determine your Expected Family Contribution and your eligibility for federal aid is called Federal Methodology (FM) and takes into account annual income, certain assets, family size, reasonable nondiscretionary expenses, and other factors such as the number of students in college and parental age (the older the parent, the more the formula adjusts to allow money to be set aside for retirement).

CSS PROFILE

The CSS PROFILE and college-specific forms enable schools to apply their own Institutional Methodology (IM) to determine Expected Family Contribution. For example, the CSS Profile takes into account additional information the FAFSA does not, such as home ownership, regional differences in cost of living, K-12 private tuition, and extraordinary medical expenses. This can produce results very different from those produced by the FAFSA, and exists to help colleges disburse their institutional gift aid wisely and be most responsive to your needs.

Typically, the lower your Expected Family Contribution, the more aid you can expect to receive. But the EFC on your FAFSA or PROFILE isn't the amount of money your family will necessarily be expected to pay for college. It is a number used by your college to calculate the amount of federal and institutional student aid you are eligible to receive. You may end up paying something more or less than your EFC, depending on the resources and policies of the individual college (see more on this below).

FILLING OUT THE FORMS: FAFSA AND CSS PROFILE

Even if you have input information into a financial aid calculator, you have not filed your student aid application. You will need to separately fill out and submit the FAFSA, CSS PROFILE, and any other forms that may be required by the schools to which you are applying or by other providers of financial aid—for example, to apply for a PLUS loan or a private scholarship.

All students and families applying for financial aid complete the FAFSA. In addition, several hundred colleges and universities, as well as some states and private groups or institutions that award outside scholarships, require the CSS PROFILE. You already have an understanding of how the FAFSA and PROFILE calculate your EFC. Here is some additional information to help you navigate the application process.

Why Do Some Colleges Require Both the FAFSA and the PROFILE?

The federal formula for determining your Expected Family Contribution is set by law and is used by all colleges to determine the amount of aid a family qualifies for from the federal government. Many colleges dedicate tens of millions of dollars of their own funds to student aid. Collecting additional financial information enables them to disburse their funds in accordance with their policies and philosophies and give some families much stronger aid awards than they could without this information.

Alison Rabil, assistant vice provost and director of financial aid at Duke University, explains,

➡ People ask, "Why do I have to fill out basically the same form twice? Why do I have to tell you my adjusted gross income again?" Well, the reason you have to tell me again is because we're using it for two different sources of funding. We're not allowed to use the PROFILE to give out federal funding, and the government form (the FAFSA) doesn't give us enough information to give out our own funds. So we use two forms to do the same thing, basically, or to calculate how much from each of these sources you're going to get. Two sources of funding, two forms.

Documents You'll Need

You will need tax returns for you and for your parents for the most recent year, as well as other financial information, in order to complete your FAFSA and CSS PROFILE. That information may include:

• Social Security number
• Driver's license (if any)

- Student and parent W-2 forms and other records of money earned*
- Student federal income tax return*
- Parent federal income tax return if you are a dependent*
- Untaxed income records, such as child support, workers' compensation, and veterans' benefits*
- Current bank statements
- Current business and investment information, if any, including mortgage records, business and farm records, stock, bond and other investment records, and retirement account information
- Alien registration or permanent resident card (if you are not a U.S. citizen)

Failing to disclose assets or misreporting information is a criminal offense, subject to the U.S. Criminal Code. Penalties can be severe. The United States Department of Education and the IRS have authority to compare information, and FAFSA conducts random verification audits. See page 279.

* Documents with an asterisk should be from the most recent year, unless otherwise noted by the form instructions.

FAFSA

Here are some things to keep in mind as you file the FAFSA.

- January 1 of the year you will enter college is the first day you can file the FAFSA. File as soon after that as possible. Don't yet have your W-2s? If you or your parents work for organizations that have a payroll or human resources office, call and ask for your W-2 information and then plug those numbers in.
- Families who are eligible can access and transfer tax information directly onto the FAFSA via the IRS Data Retrieval Tool after their tax returns are filed. A valid Social Security number and a FAFSA PIN are required. Eligible applicants will be prompted to use the tool while filling out the FAFSA.
- The FAFSA is only available online at fafsa.ed.gov. Do not use any other website to complete this form.
- There is no fee for submitting the FAFSA.
- You will require detailed information from your and your parents' federal tax returns, but you do not have to have filed your income tax returns in order to complete the FAFSA. It's best to meet deadlines and submit the FAFSA

Who's Applying for Financial Aid, Anyway?

Even though in most families it is up to the parents to provide the bulk of the money for college costs, it is the student who applies for student aid. Many parents will do the paperwork, but even so, most college financial aid offices will insist their communications be with the student. Financial aid offices can take in information from any number of sources, but they can give some information only to the student. There is a law—the Family Educational Rights and Privacy Act (FERPA)—governing what information can be shared and with whom. Many colleges have a website where students can log on to view their account. Parents, you may want to ask your students to share their password so you can access the account in order to streamline this step in the process and ensure that no important documents are forgotten or deadlines missed.

with the closest possible estimates of the figures that will appear on your completed tax return. You will correct these forms as soon as your tax forms are filed.

- If your parents are divorced or separated, the FAFSA is completed by the parent with whom you lived the most in the previous twelve months.

- Male students must show evidence they have registered with the Selective Service Administration if they are eighteen or older. If you have not yet registered, you can register by checking the appropriate box on the FAFSA and your information will be forwarded to Selective Service.

- There is no place on the FAFSA to explain special circumstances, such as financial support of relatives beyond those in the immediate family. If your family has a special circumstance that isn't reflected on the FAFSA, first complete the form, and then write or email the financial aid offices at the colleges to which you are applying to discuss your situation.

There are many free resources available to help you complete the FAFSA, including the Federal Student Aid Information Center at studentaid.ed.gov. More resources are listed in Appendix III of this book. First and foremost, remember that the FAFSA is free. No one should charge you for help in completing it.

The Student Aid Report (SAR)

Once you complete the FAFSA, a Student Aid Report (SAR) is automatically generated. You should receive an email within forty-eight hours after submitting the FAFSA on-line. If you don't receive the SAR in that time frame, check the status of your application by going to the "FAFSA on the Web" home page at fafsa.ed.gov or calling the Federal Student Aid Information Center for assistance at 1–800–4FED-AID.

The SAR summarizes the information you provided on the FAFSA and provides the Expected Family Contribution. (If there's an asterisk next to the EFC figure on the SAR, it means your FAFSA has been selected for verification. See below.)

At the same time the Student Aid Report is sent to you, an electronic version is sent to the colleges you indicated on the FAFSA. Each school's financial aid office—for those schools that don't require a PROFILE or their own form—uses that information to compute an Expected Family Contribution and subtracts that amount from their school's cost of attendance, resulting in your financial need for that school. If your EFC is equal to or exceeds the cost of attendance that means you are not eligible for need-based aid, but you could still qualify for loans or merit scholarships. Cost of Attendance (COA) can vary wildly among schools, so you could have need at a high-cost institution but no need at a lower-cost institution.

Because the Expected Family Contribution is such a crucial number in the process, review your Student Aid Report carefully to make sure it is correct in all details. If you find errors, check fafsa.ed.gov and with the financial aid offices at the colleges to which you are applying to find out how you should make corrections.

Verification

Verification is a process to confirm the accuracy of the information the student provided in the application for financial aid. The U.S. Department of Education selects up to 30 percent of FAFSA forms for verification. Some selections are random, but many occur through a series of audits conducted by the Department of Education. Also, if the information you submitted was inconsistent or incomplete, your FAFSA may be selected as well. Students who find an asterisk next to their Expected Family Contribution on the Student Aid Report have been selected for verification and will be asked to provide additional documentation to the schools where they have applied.

If you are selected for verification by the federal government, the financial aid office of the college you will attend will contact you—usually by email—to collect the necessary documentation. Typically you will be required to complete a verification worksheet and submit federal tax returns or other supporting documents, such as W-2s or information on Social Security benefits or tax-deferred pension plans. If eligible, you can submit your tax data using the IRS Data Retrieval Tool. Schools typically withhold financial aid until students complete the verification process.

The financial aid offices of some colleges may have separate verification processes of their own requiring submission of tax returns and other documents. Selection may be random or due to discrepancies in the data. In addition, some private colleges require all financial aid applicants to submit tax returns and other documentation as part of the application process.

Many colleges handle the collection and verification of financial information themselves; others have a partnership with IDOC (the Institutional Documentation Service, a service of the College Board) that collects verification documents for the schools. If any of the schools to which you are applying employs the services of IDOC, you will receive a notice from the College Board instructing you to visit the IDOC website and complete various forms.

CSS PROFILE

The CSS PROFILE asks many of the same questions FAFSA does, but delves deeper into a family's finances with more customized questions. Here are some things to keep in mind as you complete the PROFILE.

- Available beginning October 1, the PROFILE is often required to be submitted within several weeks of the colleges' application deadlines. Check all deadlines for the colleges, state aid, and private scholarships. Pay particular attention to colleges' priority deadlines and file as early as possible.
- The PROFILE is available online at profileonline.collegeboard.org.
  - There is a registration fee as well as a processing fee for each college that requires the PROFILE. A limited number of fee waivers are granted automatically to students with low or no assets from low-income families, based on the financial information provided.

KNOW THE JARGON . . .

Priority Deadlines

Some colleges have priority deadlines for submitting applications for financial aid. Priority deadlines exist because some aid programs have limited funds and those funds are awarded on a first-come, first-served basis.

- If your parents are divorced or separated, a college may request that the noncustodial parent submit a Noncustodial PROFILE that includes information about his or her income—and that of their spouse if they have remarried—and assets for the college's evaluation. If you cannot provide a Noncustodial PROFILE, contact the financial aid offices requesting it and explain your circumstances.
- If your parents are self-employed or own a farm or business, a college may request you submit a Business/Farm Supplement.

After submission, the CSS PROFILE data are analyzed and reported back to the colleges and scholarship programs. The colleges and other aid programs then apply their own formulas to determine your family's ability to pay.

If you discover errors on your CSS PROFILE, you must notify the colleges that required it. It cannot be updated online.

Additional Forms

Some colleges have their own specific forms that must be filed in addition to the FAFSA and/or CSS PROFILE. For example, some require a separate form for families that own their own business or farm instead of the PROFILE supplement. In addition, most state aid programs use the FAFSA, but they may require additional forms or have different deadlines. Go to your state's higher education agency on the Internet. (The U.S. Department of Education publishes a complete list of state education agencies, as well as other helpful resources, under the Education Resource Organizations Directory at ed.gov.) Finally, many private scholarships require the FAFSA but use their

You can download Excel and Word documents for the Financial Aid Deadline Organizer at our website at collegeadmissionbook.com.

own unique application forms as well. Read the instructions carefully for each source of aid and carefully track all submission deadlines.

YOUR FINANCIAL AID AWARD

Your financial aid will be in the form of a package that may consist of aid from federal, state, college, and private sources, in the form of grants, scholarships, loans, and/or student employment. Your financial aid award letters, which come from the colleges to which you have been admitted, will usually arrive with your letter of acceptance or soon thereafter. There is no standard award letter format. Each college has its own way of reporting and itemizing your aid package. But the aid is usually categorized as follows:

- **Grants.** Money in the form of grants and scholarships, effectively gifts that do not have to be repaid or earned by working.
- **Self-help.** Money in the form of loans that will have to be repaid, or work-study that you will have to earn by working.

As we've noted, the composition of the award package will differ from college to college.

Comparing Financial Aid Awards

Different colleges cost different amounts, present their costs in different ways, and offer you different amounts of financial aid in different combinations. This can make it difficult to understand which combination of price and student aid award is best. While the amount and composition of your aid award may not be the deciding factor in where you attend college, all students should be wise consumers and understand what they are being offered and signing on for.

We will walk you through the process of evaluating and comparing aid packages using the case of Joe, an imaginary high school student with awards from five fictional colleges.

1. Start by noting the total COST OF ATTENDANCE for each college—the amount Joe would have to spend without any aid at all. If you cannot find this easily in each college's aid award letter, go to the college websites and find it in the financial aid section. Make sure it includes all relevant expenses.

	Atchue University	Callahan State	Kleeman University	University of Luskin	Alamb College
Cost of Attendance	$50,000	$20,000	$58,000	$15,000	$35,000

2. From the award letter, find for each college the total amount of GRANT AID—that is, grants and scholarships, *not* loans or work-study—in the award letter.

	Atchue University	Callahan State	Kleeman University	University of Luskin	Alamb College
Grant Aid	$26,500	$8,000	$54,000	$11,050	$7,000

3. Calculate the NET PRICE Joe will pay to attend each college for his first year, by subtracting GRANT AID from COST OF ATTENDANCE.

	Atchue University	Callahan State	Kleeman University	University of Luskin	Alamb College
Cost of Attendance	$50,000	$20,000	$58,000	$15,000	$35,000
− Grant Aid	$26,500	$8,000	$54,000	$11,050	$7,000
= Net Price	$23,500	$12,000	$4,000	$3,950	$28,000

4. Now, from the award letters, find out for each college how much Joe is expected to borrow in the form of LOANS, and how much he is expected to earn through WORK-STUDY. Add up the loans and the work-study—that's total SELF-HELP.

	Atchue University	Callahan State	Kleeman University	University of Luskin	Alamb College
Loans	$20,000	$2,250	$2,000	$0	$7,250
+ Work-Study	$2,000	$2,000	$2,000	$2,250	$2,250
= Self-Help	$22,000	$4,250	$4,000	$2,250	$9,500

5. Now add the GRANT AID and the SELF-HELP, to get TOTAL AID. At this point you can make a quick comparison of the dollar amount of support that each college has offered you. But as we'll see, that amount really won't allow you to make your choice until you put it in context.

	Atchue University	Callahan State	Kleeman University	University of Luskin	Alamb College
Cost of Attendance	$50,000	$20,000	$58,000	$15,000	$35,000
− Grant Aid	$26,500	$ 8,000	$54,000	$11,050	$ 7,000
= Net Price	$ 23,500	$ 12,000	$ 4,000	$ 3,950	$28,000
Loans	$20,000	$ 2,250	$ 2,000	$ 0	$ 7,250
+ Work-Study	$ 2,000	$ 2,000	$ 2,000	$ 2,250	$ 2,250
= Total Self-Help	$22,000	$ 4,250	$ 4,000	$ 2,250	$ 9,500
= Total Aid	$48,500	$ 12,250	$58,000	$13,300	$16,500

6. Now let's put it all together and head toward the bottom line. Subtract TOTAL AID from COST OF ATTENDANCE, and we get Joe's REMAINING COST at each college.

	Atchue University	Callahan State	Kleeman University	University of Luskin	Alamb College
Cost of Attendance	$50,000	$20,000	$58,000	$15,000	$35,000
− Grant Aid	$26,500	$ 8,000	$54,000	$11,050	$ 7,000
= Net Price	$ 23,500	$ 12,000	$ 4,000	$ 3,950	$28,000
Loans	$20,000	$ 2,250	$ 2,000	$ 0	$ 7,250
+ Work-Study	$ 2,000	$ 2,000	$ 2,000	$ 2,250	$ 2,250
= Total Self-Help	$22,000	$ 4,250	$ 4,000	$ 2,250	$ 9,500
= Total Aid	$48,500	$ 12,250	$58,000	$13,300	$16,500
REMAINING COST	$ 1,500	$ 7,750	$ 0	$ 1,700	$18,500

Now to a decision. First look at the REMAINING COST. That's the out-of-pocket amount Joe would spend to attend each college. It looks like a three-way tie between Atchue, Kleeman, and Luskin, the ones with the three lowest REMAINING COSTS. We've highlighted them on the table above.

But all is not as it seems, because the REMAINING COST isn't the full story. Now Joe has to look deeper inside the package. He is going to be paying particular attention to how much of the package is in the form of GRANT AID and how much is SELF-HELP.

Remember GRANT AID is made up of outright gifts, not LOANS you have to pay back, or payment for WORK-STUDY you have to earn. At Kleeman and Luskin, GRANT AID covers almost the entire COST OF ATTENDANCE (COA). At Atchue, GRANT AID covers roughly half the COST OF ATTENDANCE. You can tell this easily by looking at the NET PRICE. That's the difference between COST OF ATTENDANCE and GRANT AID.

Now look at the LOAN amounts. If Joe attends Atchue, he will incur $20,000 in LOANS for his first year alone. Some students might decide taking on that kind of debt is worth it, but that's not the case for Joe. He crosses Atchue off his list.

But let's not necessarily count out Callahan or Alamb. Why are their aid packages so much less generous than those from Atchue, Kleeman, and Luskin? Could there be an opportunity to ask them to reconsider? To find out, we'll need to take an additional couple of steps in our exercise.

1. Now, under the REMAINING COST you calculated, enter from the award letters from each college the amount of your EXPECTED FAMILY CONTRIBUTION. Remember, this is the amount that the college's aid formulas calculated Joe's family should pay. Note: the colleges might not report an EFC on the award letter. Remember, the EFC is the difference between Cost of Attendance (COA) and total aid.

	Atchue University	Callahan State	Kleeman University	University of Luskin	Alamb College
Remaining Cost	$ 1,500	$ 7,750	$0	$1,700	$18,500
Expected Family Contribution	$ 1,000	$4,000	$0	$1,400	$ 1,400

2. Now subtract the EXPECTED FAMILY CONTRIBUTION from the REMAINING COST. The result is Joe's UNMET NEED—how much of a gap in financial aid each college left Joe's family.

	Atchue University	Callahan State	Kleeman University	University of Luskin	Alamb College
Remaining Cost	$1,500	$ 7,750	$0	$1,700	$18,500
− Expected Family Contribution	$1,000	$4,000	$0	$1,400	$ 1,400
= Unmet Need	$ 500	$ 3,750	$0	$ 300	$ 17,100

Two gaps stand out—Callahan and Alamb both left Joe with the biggest UNMET NEED. We've highlighted them in the table above.

Why the gaps? It could be because these colleges just don't have the financial resources to offer as much aid as the others. But there's something else, too—at Callahan, Joe's

Scams

Applying for financial aid can be complicated, and the stakes are high. You will see offers of help in the mail, on the Web, and in magazines. Some of these are legitimate. Others are from individuals or companies trying to make money off unsuspecting students and parents. Don't fall for come-ons like these:

- "This scholarship is guaranteed or your money back!"
- "Attend our seminar to understand how to get more financial aid."
- "We guarantee you'll get aid."
- "The scholarship requires a small fee."

Never pay a fee to locate scholarship or aid information. And avoid any organization or service that either guarantees a reward or charges a fee for completing the FAFSA or applying for or receiving a scholarship.

Information on legitimate financial aid and scholarships is easily available at no cost at:

- The FAFSA website at FAFSA.ed.gov
- The U.S. Department of Education at studentaid.ed.gov
- College Goal Sunday at collegegoalsundayusa.org
- The College Board at collegeboard.org
- Fastweb.com at fastweb.com
- FinAid at finaid.org
- Your local library
- Your high school college counseling office
- The websites of colleges and universities

EXPECTED FAMILY CONTRIBUTION is much larger than at any of the other colleges.

So Joe calls the financial aid office at Callahan, just to make sure that an error wasn't made in calculating the EXPECTED FAMILY CONTRIBUTION. As it turns out, Joe and the financial aid office are able to determine that there was an error. So they recalculate the EFC, and it comes out $2,000 lower. As a result, Callahan increased Joe's LOAN by $2,000, reducing the REMAINING COST to $5,750.

Next, Joe calls Alamb. There's nothing unusual about Alamb's EXPECTED FAMILY CONTRIBUTION, but compared to the others, Alamb's aid package isn't very generous. Joe explains that Alamb's package is substantially different from the other offers, and asks if anything else is available to him. Alamb is not able to adjust his award, and he crosses it off his list.

So Alamb is out—and Joe decides that Callahan's improved REMAINING COST still isn't good enough compared to the

Deadlines

Deadlines are important and can be confusing. There are federal deadlines, deadlines for each state, deadlines for each college, and deadlines for private scholarship sources. And they are usually different from one another.

- Federal deadlines. The FAFSA can be submitted as early as January 1 and no later than June 30 of the academic year for which aid will be received. We advise you to file it as soon after January 1 as you can.
- State deadlines. Each state has a different deadline. Check the FAFSA website at fafsa.ed.gov for a full listing. Be vigilant about state deadlines. State aid is often need-based, and typically, a state agency does not have unlimited funding. They may run out of money before getting to the end of the applicant pool. Get your application in on time, if not early.
- College deadlines. Each college has a different deadline. Check the websites of each college to which you are applying.
- Private scholarship deadlines. If you are applying for scholarships from private groups or organizations, make sure you add these deadlines to the list.
- Priority deadlines. Some colleges have priority deadlines for submitting applications for financial aid. Priority deadlines exist because some aid programs have limited funds available and those funds are awarded on a first-come, first-served basis. At schools where financial aid is limited, the demand is often greater than available funds. If you want to receive maximum consideration for financial aid, meet the priority deadline. If you don't, you will still be considered for financial aid, but you may not receive as generous a package as those who meet the priority deadline.

Our best advice? Apply as soon as possible after January 1. Anytime you don't have the exact information requested on a form, do your best to find it, but if you just can't, give your best estimate and follow up immediately upon receiving your W-2 forms or other information.

Track all financial aid and scholarship deadlines with care. They matter. See our Financial Aid Deadline Organizer in Appendix III or go on our website at collegeadmissionbook.com.

alternatives. Joe had already rejected Atchue because LOANS made up such a large portion of its package.

So Joe's choice is between Kleeman and Luskin. He has been offered generous grant aid and will be expected to take on a modest loan at Kleeman and no loan at Luskin. Joe ultimately decides to attend Kleeman because he believes they have the strongest engineering program. While he is not thrilled about having to borrow, he believes he will be able to afford the monthly payment he will need to make beginning six months after he graduates.

Financial Aid Awards for Those Applying Under Early Action and Early Decision Plans

If you are applying under an early action (EA) or early decision (ED) plan (see Chapter 15 for more information about decision plans), some colleges have established procedures for obtaining an early estimate of your financial aid. Such colleges may request you file the CSS PROFILE at an earlier deadline, using best estimates for your financial information if specifics are not available. You would then receive an Estimated Financial Aid Award at the time you receive your acceptance or shortly thereafter, based on your best estimates and the college's cost of attendance for the current year.

If you receive an estimated award, you will still have to complete a FAFSA after January 1 like all other applicants, and you will receive a revised award that takes into account any changes in your finances, as well as changes (usually upward) from one year to the next in that college's cost of attendance. Check each college's website for its policies.

Do colleges give early decision and early action applicants less appealing financial aid awards because they know they have committed or are likely to enroll? Not necessarily. Many colleges feel compelled to offer the same award whether a student has applied early or regular. Ask the college about its policy, listen carefully to the answer, and make your best decision from there. Lots of financial aid applicants apply early and generally they are not disappointed by their awards.

Remember that applying under an ED plan requires serious consideration if your family will require financial aid. You may not want to apply ED if any of the following are true:

- You want to be able to compare financial aid offers from a number of institutions prior to deciding where you will go.
- The college you are interested in advises financial aid applicants to wait for the regular decision round.
- The college you are interested in says its financial aid is most favorable for regular decision applicants.

Appealing Your Aid Award

Can you appeal an aid award? In other words, can you ask for a better aid award? There are usually two scenarios where students might find themselves contemplating doing so.

You Weren't Awarded the Amount of Aid You Need

If you did not receive the aid you need, ask yourself if there is some aspect of your financial situation you haven't yet shared with that financial aid office. Are your uncle and his children living with you, for example, and your parents find themselves helping with his children's expenses and footing all the grocery bills? Did your family have an unusually large medical bill four years ago that you are still paying off? Did your mother lose her job two years ago and so your family had to put things on credit cards for a while, and even though

How Can the Financial Aid Award Received from Two $65,000 Colleges Look So Different?

Financial aid programs reflect the fact that colleges each have different endowments and different operating budgets, and therefore different amounts of money for aid and different philosophies about using it. In addition, some colleges receive greater funding from government sources—for example, some state college systems. That's why some colleges are able to meet a family's full demonstrated financial need while others are not.

Some colleges may be able to offer a financial aid package that consists primarily of grants and scholarships. For example, at Harvard, at one end of the spectrum, students whose parents are middle-income (earning $65,000 to $150,000 annually) are asked to pay between 0 and 10 percent of that income and are not asked to assume any loans. At the other end of the spectrum would be a college that has considerably less endowment or other funds at its disposal. Such a college might ask students to rely solely on federal and state aid, or to borrow, work, or otherwise provide additional funds on their own. (See the explanation of "gap" on page 289.)

Colleges also have different goals in filling their classes. While some colleges try to meet need similarly for students with similar financial profiles, others meet need more generously for some students than others, giving greater grant amounts to some students based on a variety of factors including family ability to pay, academic strength, and personal qualities such as leadership. (This is called "preferential packaging.") Still others factor in what they believe is a student's likelihood to enroll.

she found new work a year ago, your family still carries the credit card debt? You won't get aid to make up for overspending on luxuries, but these examples are all circumstances financial aid officers at many institutions could factor into their professional assessment of your situation.

If your situation involves these or other circumstances, call the financial aid office and introduce yourself as an admitted student (or

"Need-Blind" Versus "Need-Aware"

"Need-blind" and "need-aware" are terms used to denote how a college makes admission decisions, not how financial aid is awarded. At a college that has need-blind admission, a family's ability to pay does *not* factor into an admission decision. Need-aware or need-sensitive colleges factor a family's ability to pay into *some* of their admission decisions. Colleges with the strongest financial aid programs are need-blind and also meet the full demonstrated need of all admitted students. Other colleges—whether need-blind or need-aware—can sometimes award students significant amounts of financial aid but may not be able to meet the entire demonstrated need of a family.

the parent of an admitted student) and ask to speak with someone about the award. Here is what you might say: "I've been admitted to your school and really hope to be able to come. I'm concerned about my financial aid award, though, and there are a few family circumstances I would like to explain." Be respectful, but there is no need to plead. This is a working professional whose job is to help you. At the end of the call—no matter how it goes—thank the aid officer for her time, concern, and help.

A few colleges have a form for students to fill out if they are appealing their financial aid award. If you are hoping to attend a college that uses such a form—check their website—that is the place to start.

If there are no circumstances you can think of to add to the picture but the amount of aid you've been awarded is still not enough, call the financial aid office, begin your conversation in the same way, and ask if there are any additional resources the officer can recommend.

You Want to See if Your Top-Choice College Will Match a More Favorable Award from Another School

There are some circumstances where it is appropriate to let the college know that another institution gave you a more favorable package. These include:

- **Your Expected Family Contribution at one college looks significantly different from your**

KNOW THE JARGON . . .

Gap

Some colleges are unable to meet the full need of all students who are admitted. At colleges that do not meet a family's full demonstrated need you may hear the difference between the amount of a family's calculated need (that college's cost of attendance minus grants, self-help, and the Expected Family Contribution) and the amount of the student aid award referred to as "unmet need." Unmet need means there is a gap between what a family qualifies for in financial aid and what that family is awarded. So the term used when a college leaves some need unmet is "gapping."

EFC at another. There may be a perfectly good reason for the difference—remember, every school's approach to aid is unique. But a big difference may be an opportunity to open a fruitful conversation. Call the financial aid office, explain that the EFC the college computed is significantly larger than the EFC at the other schools that have awarded you aid, and ask how that might have happened and whether there are any potential adjustments that could be made to bring them closer together.

- **You have been admitted to a university where specific colleges have scholarship funds they can award.** At a number of

Summer Earnings

Many colleges expect all students to contribute *something* to the financing of their education, both by working on campus for ten hours or less per week during the school year and by working over the summer and contributing a portion of their summer earnings.

See Appendix III for a Financial Aid Package Evaluator worksheet to help you compare your awards. Download Excel and Word documents for the Financial Aid Package Evaluator at our website at college admissionbook.com.

universities, a central financial aid office will calculate need and eligibility for both federal and need-based institutional aid. But specific colleges or departments—such as a school of music or a college of business—may have their own funds for merit scholarships. If this is the case and a merit award could help you afford that university, call the individual college or department, request to speak with someone who works with admitted students, explain your situation, and ask if you could be considered for additional merit aid.

In general, most financial aid officers are not receptive to an invitation to enter a bidding war. Colleges don't hold back aid in anticipation of a negotiation. They make what they believe is their best offer.

Yet every spring, financial aid officers anticipate the week where the television talk shows feature "experts" who tell America's college applicants not to accept the initial aid award they've been given, and go back to the colleges and ask for more.

As Diane Stemper, director of The Ohio State's Office of Financial Aid, explains:

➡ **Financial aid staffs are in financial aid because they want to help families afford their college. Approach a conversation with financial aid as**

We Don't Qualify for Financial Aid. Now What?

Even if you didn't qualify for financial aid, the financial aid office can still be helpful to you. Students from families who apply for aid by filing the FAFSA and do not show calculated need are eligible for Federal Direct Unsubsidized Loans, which have more favorable terms than private commercial loans. For example, payment on the principal does not begin until six months after the student leaves college (though interest accrues).

Unlike the Federal Direct Subsidized Loans available to students with demonstrated financial need, on unsubsidized loans the government does not pay the interest while you are in college. Unsubsidized loan terms specify that students begin payment on the interest immediately, even if they are in school. Most students get around this by deferring the interest and adding it to the balance owed—they begin payments following the six-month grace period after leaving college. Federal Direct Unsubsidized Loans are awarded through the financial aid office of the college you will attend and can be awarded only to students who submit the FAFSA.

Families who did not qualify for aid should also consider reapplying in subsequent years, even if they think they won't qualify. There are many factors affecting eligibility for financial aid, and some can change from year to year.

Special Situations

Financial aid policy and requirements are different for students in the following situations:

International students. Financial aid is extremely limited for students who are not U.S. citizens. You will need to plan accordingly, which will likely mean applying only to colleges that offer financial aid for international students. See Chapter 20.

Students without Social Security numbers. A Social Security number is required to apply for federal student aid. U.S. citizens who cannot locate their Social Security numbers should do what is necessary to find them. Students who do not have a Social Security number may still be eligible for aid directly from the colleges or for state aid in states that have passed their own form of Dream Act and should see Chapter 19.

Transfer students. Some colleges award financial aid to transfer students while others do not. Policy, requirements, and deadlines can differ from those for first-year students. Check the websites of the colleges to which you are applying.

Waitlisted students. Some colleges have financial aid for students on the waitlist, while others do not. If you find yourself on a waitlist and will require financial aid to attend that college, check your waitlist materials carefully to see what is said about financial aid.

a partnership. Come in to the office and say, "Here's what I can afford to do, and here's what we've saved, and here's what we think we can pay. And with the aid you've given us, we're close but still this far away from it being an affordable decision for us." That's a way to approach the conversation that most aid directors would consider acceptable and appropriate. You might say, "We can only come up with this much; are there any other resources we can look at? Are there any other scholarships we can apply for? Reasonable loans?"

I've had families show up with a chart of every aid award they've received and say, "If you want me, here's what it's going to cost you. You need to beat this one over here." That's absolutely the worst approach you could take. My guess is you're not going to meet with a good response in those cases. Parents shouldn't put their children on an auction block and sell to the highest bidder.

That said, some colleges do have a policy that they will not lose a student due to a stronger aid package from a similar institution. For example, both Cornell and Dartmouth state that if a student receives a more favorable aid package from another Ivy League college, that student should let them know so they can consider adjusting their offer to match it. Colleges that have this policy will usually let you know this—either on their financial aid website, in their award notification, or both.

If you are appealing or negotiating your award, always let the *admission* office know that you are working with the *financial aid* office on your aid award. If there is a specific admission officer you have come to know, call or email to keep him in the loop. Let him know that you are excited about being admitted but that you are concerned about affordability and are working with the financial aid office to see if anything else can be done. If you have not gotten to know any of the admission officers, call the office and ask to be put in touch with the person responsible for applicants from your city or for admitted students.

Accepting Your Aid Award

Some colleges will ask you to formally accept the aid award you receive with your acceptance letter—or shortly thereafter—in order to receive funds. To finalize your award, sign the notification and return it to the financial aid office. Be sure to follow the instructions and meet all deadlines. Other schools will automatically accept your aid awards when you pay your enrollment deposit for admission. Read your award letter carefully and call the financial aid office if the method of acceptance is unclear to you.

Renewing Your Award

It's the last thing you're thinking about now, but you need to know that students must apply for financial aid each year. Family income and assets and college costs can change up or down. Applying every year takes such changes into account.

In addition, the federal government's and college's policies on providing aid can change after a student's first year. For example,

juniors and seniors are allowed to borrow more under some programs. Why? To protect students who may attend college for only the first or second year. They will likely not earn as much as their counterparts who continue on and graduate. The closer you get to graduation, the more you can borrow.

The good news? Applying in subsequent years is much easier than applying the first time around. If you filed your FAFSA online, for example, you will be able to access a version that has much of your information prepopulated, and you can then make any necessary changes and adjustments. Many colleges also have later deadlines for returning students, so it is more likely that you won't have to estimate.

Ways to Pay Your Bill

There are a number of ways to pay for college, whether you are paying $500 once your financial aid award is factored in or $50,000. Check with your college to see which payment plans they offer.

- **Lump-sum payment.** Some colleges have one date when payment is due, usually over the summer. Other schools allow families to make two or three payments, depending on whether the college is on a quarter or semester system.
- **Payment plans.** Some colleges offer monthly or quarterly payment plans.
- **Payment in advance.** Some colleges accept payment for all four years at the tuition for the year in which payment is made. Other Cost of Attendance items will change and cannot be prepaid.

Veterans

Veterans are eligible for a variety of financial aid benefits under the GI Bill, and can often graduate from college debt free. Financial aid benefits for undergraduate student veterans include the following:

- Grants up to the highest public in-state undergraduate tuition rate plus books and fees for those with thirty-six months or more of active duty since September 11, 2001.
- For some private colleges, grants exceeding the highest public in-state undergraduate tuition. These colleges have committed to participate in the Yellow Ribbon Program, a private university provision in the GI Bill in which private schools split some or all tuition costs with the U.S. Department of Veterans Affairs.
- Enhanced benefits that include additional funds for education, a living allowance, money for expenses such as books, and the ability to transfer unused educational benefits to spouses or children.

The definition of a veteran for financial aid purposes is a person who has served in active duty (including basic training) in the U.S. Armed Forces and was discharged with honorable or general status. Veterans should check the websites of both the individual colleges to which they are applying and the Veterans Administration at va.gov. The level of a student's benefits varies with the length of active-duty service. Most are able to apply for financial aid as independent students, meaning that parental income is not considered in assessing the need for financial aid.

Questions to Ask Financial Aid Officers

- Do you meet the full calculated need of all admitted students? If not, can you tell us a little more about how you package aid?
- Do you gap?
- What is your average total aid award?
- What is your average institutional grant?
- What is the average amount of debt for your graduates?
- Do you have merit aid available? If so, what constitutes merit?
- Do you package early decision or early action admits any differently than regular admits?
- How do you calculate outside awards in the financial aid package?
- How is the first-year financial aid package going to compare to packages for the sophomore, junior, and senior years, so we can understand what our four-year investment may be?

Interacting with the Financial Aid Office: How to Behave and Why

Financial aid offices are not set up like admission offices. They are often less well staffed, and they have the college's existing student body to care for, as well as applicants and their families. Financial aid officers walk many tightropes simultaneously. They are charged with meeting the demonstrated need of each family in a way that is consistent with their institution's guidelines. Typically they have an institutional aid budget they must stay within, and the pressures related to this can be significant. They must also disburse federal and state funds in accordance with law. They must keep up with an ever-changing array of rules and regulations. They are audited annually, and the stakes are high—if they have not done their jobs well and kept excellent records, their college can lose a great deal of money that will then not be available for students who need aid.

What does this mean for you? You cannot ask a financial aid officer to hold your hand. You need to do as much as you can to master the process, and call him or her with specific and informed questions. That is how you will obtain the best guidance.

Look for opportunities such as financial aid nights at local high schools, any "open office hours" a financial aid office might hold for prospective students, or programs such as College Goal Sundays. February is "Financial Aid Awareness Month," and there are usually numerous initiatives to educate families during this time. Try to attend at least one of these educational programs during a student's junior year of high school to start understanding the details, then attend again in senior year to be sure you've done everything possible.

Check the website of each college to learn their policies, programs, and deadlines. Take any remaining general questions about financial aid to the admission office, which is set up to respond to questions from prospective families. If an admission officer then directs you to the financial aid office, that is the time to engage them.

The vast majority of aid officers do their jobs because they care about helping families afford higher education. Many were able to get through college themselves because of financial aid. They want to make this work for you as well—within the legal and institutional guidelines under which they operate. So treat your financial aid officers well. And don't forget to say thank you!

Bill estimators are available on the Financial Aid or Student Business Office/Bursar sections of some college websites. These show estimated charges as well as payment options available. Note: Bill estimators are about payment options and do not fill the same purpose as financial aid or net price calculators.

Questions You May Have

What if our household income varies significantly from year to year?

The financial aid formulas are based on actual income rather than what families think they will make, so use the prior year's income.

Financial Planning

Colleges expect students and parents to contribute to their education. Advance financial planning can make a huge positive difference for a family.

When colleges calculate your aid award based on your need, they look at lots of information about your financial situation, including your income, some assets, and some fundamental family expenses. What they don't look at is your cash flow—that is, the amount of money you need every month to pay all your bills, which may include interest on consumer debt. If your family hasn't saved much but instead has spent a significant amount of income on consumer goods or debt service, you may find that colleges consider you richer than you feel you are. Such families will have to confront the fact that colleges are not going to give them more aid because they chose to save less and spend more. Our advice?

• Start thinking about reducing expenditures as soon as possible so you will have the ability to save.
• If at all possible, start saving or investing—the sooner the better.

The "Savings Myth"

There is a myth that families applying for financial aid are penalized for saving—that they will receive less aid because they are expected to dip heavily into savings to pay for college.

Your Expected Family Contribution typically does not go up significantly if you have saved; neither does it go down significantly if you have not. The federal formula—and most school formulas—assumes some savings for college by including a portion of assets in the calculation. However, the formula includes only a small fraction of a family's assets, often excluding from consideration equity in the family's home and retirement savings among other assets. Furthermore, the formulas that determine need for financial aid evaluate parent assets at a much lower rate than student assets. The formula allocates just over 5 percent of parent savings as part of the EFC—and 20 percent of student savings.

Beyond this, there is simply a general principle guiding financial aid formulas that families that have had the luxury of discretionary income—those families that are upper-middle-income and higher, for example—should be saving for college. These families might find their Expected Family Contribution a stretch if they have not saved, and may be compelled to borrow. The conclusion? You are always better off saving.

529 Plans

All states and some colleges offer 529 plans—named after the section of the IRS code that defines these plans. There are two basic types: a savings plan and a prepaid tuition plan. Both plans are ways to save for college and offer important tax benefits that effectively reduce the cost of attending college. Plans differ from state to state and college to college. Enrollment is through a 529 plan manager or a financial advisor. For more information, check the 529 Plans section of the Securities and Exchange Commission website at sec.gov.

Advice on Financial Aid for Students and Families

SALLY DONAHUE
Director of financial aid, Harvard University

➡ First of all, plan ahead and apply for financial aid. Use the net price calculators on websites and familiarize yourself with the various kinds of financial aid that are available. There are a variety of federal financial aid loan programs and a couple of federal grant programs; there are institutional grant and loan programs; and then there are outside sources of scholarship funding from organizations such as the Gates Foundation or the National Merit Foundation or Coca-Cola or your local Kiwanis Club. So families think, "Oh my gosh, this is so confusing!" But it's actually easier to understand than families know, and they don't have to understand everything completely before applying for financial aid, because schools will help families in guiding them through the various sources of aid for which they are eligible.

Also, if families can save anything at all toward education expenses for their children and grandchildren, they should do it. There's sometimes a misconception that if you save, schools will take 100 percent of what you save, so why save? Why not just spend it, right? But that's not true. The need analysis relies much more heavily on income than on assets. Financial aid programs in general assume that paying for education is a family financial priority. If you don't save for education, what's going to happen, at Harvard for example, is, if you're earning $150,000 a year and your assets are fairly typical, we're going to ask you to contribute about $15,000 toward the expenses of your son or daughter. If you're living up to your income, you're going to have to take out a loan to cover that. But if families can try to save, it helps. And if they can't save, which is completely understandable, they should probably prepare themselves to take out some loans to help cover the cost of education. In order to be able to take out loans, families need to have good credit histories and be fiscally responsible. Families need to plan ahead.

DIANE STEMPER
Director, Office of Student Financial Aid, The Ohio State University

➡ Students should be investigating financial aid as soon as they start thinking about what schools they want to apply to. People sometimes wait until after they've narrowed down their list, and that's a mistake. It's smart to be very proactive about this process. You want to find out early on what kinds of programs a school has, how you apply, and what the deadlines are. You should be doing that in your junior year so that by the time you're in your senior year, you've got yourself really ready to go.

For some loan and work programs, you have to show that you don't qualify for need-based student aid before you are eligible for a different kind of aid. So students who think they will not qualify for need-based aid do themselves a disservice when they don't complete the FAFSA or other required student aid forms. My advice is that it's generally a good idea to apply for need-based as well as merit aid. If they're both available, apply for both and see what happens.

ANGEL B. PEREZ

Vice president, dean of admission and financial aid, Pitzer College

➡ While financial aid can be one of the most confusing aspects of the college application process, there are many ways to prepare for success in this area. Asking the right questions and meeting every single deadline can help students get the most financial aid possible. In all my years overseeing financial aid, fear is what I believe holds most students back from maximizing their potential. If a student receives a financial aid package they feel does not work for them, they can always call the financial aid office and speak to the counselor that has been assigned to their file. Sometimes financial aid offices are able to adjust financial aid packages based on new information families provide. While financial aid forms are formulaic, financial aid counselors take personal family circumstances into account. Don't be afraid to reach out and have a personal conversation with your financial aid officer. It could literally change your financial future.

MAUREEN MCRAE GOLDBERG

Director of financial aid, Occidental College

➡ Families need to understand that there is a complexity to financial aid, and you can't start learning about it in January before your child graduates from high school. Financial literacy is so low in our country. Literacy about financial aid is just as important as literacy about what college a student is going to go to. And parents need to have a hand-in-hand process with their child about paying for college. There's a complete disconnect between the conversations that parents are having with their child about going to college and the conversation they're having about paying for college. Students need to be just as involved with the financing as they are with the application for college itself. Starting to talk to your child about paying for college and applying for scholarships needs to happen in freshman year of high school.

Financial aid officers do recognize that some professions have incomes that can vary a lot from year to year, such as salespeople on commission. But they will still need to work with actual earnings from prior years. If your parents experienced one unusually strong year, talk with the financial aid office to see if you can submit documentation from other years to help explain the situation, but expect that you might be asked to stretch. Ask if your financial aid award will be adjusted upward for the following year if you in fact do not earn as much.

What if a parent has lost his or her job after the student has applied for aid?

Most colleges have emergency aid funds reserved for families who experience sudden and dramatic financial changes midyear. If there is a death in your family or a job loss and your financial picture changes in the middle of the year, contact the financial aid office or go in and see them as quickly as possible to explain the situation. They are there to help.

If my parents are divorced, which parent files the FAFSA?

If your parents are separated or divorced, the custodial parent is responsible for filing the FAFSA. But the custodial parent is not necessarily the parent with legal custody. FAFSA is concerned with the parent with whom the student lived most during the previous twelve months (the twelve-month period ending on the FAFSA application date, not the previous calendar year). Child support and alimony received from the noncustodial parent, however, must be included on the FAFSA.

I have two parents of the same sex. Whose information should be provided on the FAFSA?

Pay close attention to the definition of "parent" in the FAFSA directions. When same-sex parents are legally married in a state that recognizes same-sex marriage, both parents provide information on the FAFSA—whether or not they now reside in the state where they were married. However, all "legal" parents may have to provide information. So in addition to your same-sex parents, the biological parent or stepparent may also have to provide information in some instances. For more specifics about who must provide information, check the FAFSA website at fafsa.gov and the financial aid sections of the websites of each college to which you are applying.

My parents never married, but we all live together. Whose information should be provided on the FAFSA?

If you reside with your legal parents, both must complete the FAFSA, regardless of their legal relationship to each other.

The FAFSA asks me to list the colleges I'm thinking of attending. Does the admission office use this information?

Most admission offices do not routinely use this information, but some colleges may view the order in which the colleges are listed as an indication of the application preference of the student. Best advice? Be aware that there is a possibility this might happen and list the schools in order of preference, with your first-choice school listed first.

? One of my colleges requires the Non-custodial PROFILE, but we don't know how to find my father. What should I do? Contact the financial aid office of that college and explain your situation. They will tell you how to document your situation.

FINANCIAL AID GLOSSARY

Award See "Financial aid award"

Calculated need The difference between the cost of attendance at a specific college and the expected family contribution. In other words, your calculated need is the amount that college could potentially offer you in need-based aid.

> Cost of Attendance
> − Expected Family Contribution
> = Calculated Need

COA See "Cost of attendance"

Cost of attendance (COA) The total amount it will cost a student to attend; includes tuition and fees, on-campus room and board (or housing allowance for off-campus), books, supplies, fees, transportation, and personal expenses.

> Tuition
> + Room and Board
> + Fees
> + Books and Supplies
> + Personal Expenses
> + Transportation
> = Cost of Attendance

CSS Profile The form required by many private colleges and universities and some private organizations to determine eligibility for the institution's own grants, scholarships, loans, and/or work-study programs.

EFC See "Expected Family Contribution"

Expected Family Contribution (EFC) The amount the financial aid office calculates a family should be able to contribute for one year of college.

FAFSA (Free Application for Federal Student Aid) The application used to apply for federal student aid, state aid, and institutional aid. The FAFSA may also be required by some scholarship organizations.

Federal Direct Loan (Formerly called a Stafford loan) A fixed-rate federal loan for students. See "Federal Direct Subsidized Loan" and "Federal Direct Unsubsidized Loan."

Federal Direct Subsidized Loan A need-based, fixed-rate federal loan for students. The Department of Education pays the interest while the student is enrolled in school, with repayment deferred until six months after the student leaves college. See also "Federal Direct Unsubsidized Loan."

Federal Direct Unsubsidized Loan Non-need-based federal loan for students made at favorable rates. Students are responsible for paying the interest on Direct Unsubsidized Loans beginning immediately after the loan is disbursed, but may choose to add it to principal until repayment begins six months after leaving college. See also "Federal Direct Subsidized Loan."

FEDERAL METHODOLOGY (FM) The formula used to determine eligibility for federal funds.

FEDERAL PLUS LOANS Non-need-based federal loans made to parents of dependent undergraduates through the U.S. Department of Education. Parents may borrow at a variable rate up to the full cost of a student's attendance minus any financial aid received, depending on their credit history.

FEDERAL SUPPLEMENTAL EDUCATIONAL OPPORTUNITY GRANT (FSEOG) A federal grant awarded to students with exceptional need, with priority given to Pell Grant recipients. Not all colleges offer FSEOG, and funds are limited.

FINANCIAL AID AWARD The total amount of financial aid (grants, scholarships, loans, and work-study) a student is offered by a school.

FINANCIAL AID CALCULATOR See "Net Price Calculator"

FM See "Federal Methodology"

FSEOG See "Federal Supplemental Educational Opportunity Grant"

GAP The difference between the family's calculated need and what that student is awarded.

GRANT Financial aid that does not have to be repaid.

IM See "Institutional Methodology"

INSTITUTIONAL FUNDS Student aid awarded from an individual college.

INSTITUTIONAL METHODOLOGY (IM) A formula employed by an individual college or university to determine eligibility for institutional funds.

LOAN Borrowed money that must be repaid, usually with interest.

MERIT-BASED AID Scholarships given students for academic, artistic, athletic, or other talents, achievements, or circumstances, generally irrespective of need.

NEED See "Calculated need"

NEED-AWARE A college that considers a family's ability to pay in some or all of their admission decisions.

NEED-BASED AID Aid given students based on calculated financial need, using the family's financial circumstances.

NEED-BLIND A college that does not consider a family's ability to pay as it makes its admission decisions.

NEED-SENSITIVE See "Need-aware"

NET PRICE The cost of attendance minus all grant aid a student will receive.

> Cost of Attendance
> − **Grant Aid**
> _____
> = **Net Price**

NET PRICE CALCULATOR A federally mandated Web-based calculator required of every institution used to estimate a student's net price for a single year of college, based on information provided by the family.

OUTSIDE AWARD Educational funding not provided directly by or through the college or university you plan to attend. The main sources of these scholarships are private foundations or organizations.

Pell Grant (Federal Pell Grant) Need-based federal grants made to low-income undergraduates.

Perkins Loan Fixed rate, low-interest federal loans made to students with financial need. Interest is paid by the federal government while the student is enrolled in school, with repayment deferred until nine months after the student leaves college. Not all colleges offer Perkins Loans, and funding is limited.

Preferential packaging The students a college would most like to enroll may receive the most advantageous financial aid packages; for example, students with strong academic records or special talents may receive a financial aid package with more grant aid than self-help.

PROFILE See "CSS PROFILE"

SAR See "Student Aid Report"

Scholarship See "Merit-based aid"

Self-help Aid that is not an outright grant, such as loans and work-study.

Student Aid Report Summarizes the information from the FAFSA, including providing the EFC.

Unmet need The gap between a family's calculated need and what that family is awarded.

Verification Procedure by which a college checks the information reported on the FAFSA, CSS PROFILE, or a college's unique financial aid forms, usually by requesting copies of documents such as signed tax returns.

Work-study A federally subsidized program in which students earn money, usually through part-time on-campus jobs.

PART VIII

DECIDING

CHAPTER 17

Notification and Making the Decision

Congratulations! You're in!

We hope there is much celebration in your home! Take some time to enjoy your good news—and share it with your family, teachers, counselors, and any others who have been there for you, particularly during these last few months.

Now it's time for you to make your decision. For some of you, the choice will be straightforward—if you have an acceptance from your top-choice school or applied early decision and were admitted. For others, with more than one admission letter and no clear first-choice school, or a waitlist offer, choosing will require further thought.

In this chapter, we will walk you through this almost-last step on your path to college, covering everything you need to know about saying yes, hearing no, waiting out maybe, and thanking those who made all of this possible.

MAY 1

May 1 is the National Candidates Reply Date, the deadline for formally notifying *one* college that you are accepting its offer of admission and sealing the deal with a deposit check. This date is non-negotiable, and failure to comply will have serious consequences—you may forfeit your admission. There are exceptions to this deadline for some schools, so read all the materials that arrive with your acceptance letters carefully and pay particular attention to additional deadlines for housing or scholarship awards.

There is no need to wait until May 1. If you have reflected on your offers of admission and know where you would like to be next fall, first accept that offer and then inform the other schools as promptly as possible. It is good form to take yourself out of the running at any college where you have been accepted

Checkpoints ✍

✔ Congratulations! Now it's your turn to decide . . .

✔ May 1 is the National Candidates Reply Date, the deadline for notifying one college you will enroll.

✔ Admitted-student visits, reflecting back on your original list of priorities, and comparing financial aid awards will help you decide where to enroll.

✔ Students must send a nonrefundable deposit to the college they plan to attend. Double-depositing—sending a deposit to more than one college—is unethical and may result in both colleges rescinding your admission.

✔ If you are offered a position on the waitlist, consider carefully and accept only if there is a good chance you will attend if admitted.

✔ Stay immune to senioritis. A college's acceptance is conditional on completing your senior year at the same level of performance you have shown thus far.

✔ As you share your good news, be thoughtful and kind to your fellow students.

but know with certainty you will not enroll. That way the college can offer your seat to another student who may want to enroll.

ACCEPTANCE

Where Do You Start?

Take Time to Reflect!

Go back to the beginning of your college search, revisit your list of priorities, and see what is important to you *now*. Think about the best fit, as you did when you started this process. Take your time, because there's no need to rush—unless it's late April. Make a list of pros and cons, or journal about the qualities you are looking for in a school. Talk it through with friends, parents, or your high school guidance counselor. But keep in mind that you don't have to talk about it with everybody. There can be a lot of noise at this point, with everybody weighing in on your decision. Don't be afraid to tune it out. Remember, *you* are the expert about what you want and need—not your cousin, your boyfriend, your mom and dad, or the alumna who lives next door.

Your news may arrive by snail mail, express, or email. Most colleges now offer a Web lookup option. But think carefully about when and where you want to sign in to get your news and whether you want to have a friend or family member with you. Whether that news is good or bad—and no matter how it comes—finding out can be an emotional experience that may impact you and distract you more than you think it will. Be cautious.

We're not suggesting you actually make the decision this way, but try a thought experiment where you toss a coin to make your choice of colleges. Say you're trying to decide between College A and College B. Now flip a coin. If it lands on College A and you say, "Oh, I want to flip it one more time," think about the message there. If it lands on College B and you think, "Great!" you have another strong signal about your choice. It's a way of listening to your gut. For most students, ultimately this decision is going to come down to some combination of affordability and what your gut tells you about the community you want to be a part of for the next four years.

Make a Return Visit

Once you have an acceptance in hand, the view from the middle of the campus may look and feel different. Many colleges offer admitted-student days—on-campus programs that allow you to visit with current students and faculty, attend a class, a performance, or a sporting event, eat in the dining hall, or even stay overnight in the dorms. The colleges will be wooing you, hoping you will enroll. So make sure you veer off on your own for a while without the college representative curating your experience. But, aside from feeling the love, you will also get a good sense for the students who may be your fellow freshmen. That may tell you a lot about where you want to be next year. Listen to your heart and your gut as well as your head.

Underresourced students should do whatever they can to visit the schools they are considering. Call or email the admission office to see if assistance is available. Some colleges sponsor fly-in programs for students who need financial assistance to visit. Some high schools also provide assistance, so speak to your high school college or guidance counselor. If assistance isn't available, ask about any programs or events for admitted students in your hometown, so you can get a better sense of the people who may be your classmates. In the meantime, start to get to know the college communities and your potential classmates through social media.

Compare Financial Aid Packages and Scholarships

Financial aid can be a determining factor in deciding where to attend college. If paying for college is a concern for your family, evaluate your financial aid packages and any scholarship awards to make sure the college you choose will be affordable for you and your family. If there are schools on your list you would like to attend but from whom you haven't received an aid package that meets your needs, let them know. Start looking at your other options very seriously, but also talk to any schools you really want to attend but cannot afford. Chapter 16 explains how to have that conversation and how to compare financial aid packages.

Rest assured that at some point you will get off the fence. You'll make a decision, and you'll feel good about it.

The Early Acceptance

What steps do you take if you applied under an early plan?

If you have been accepted under an early action (EA) or rolling admission (RA) plan, you have received notification long before March 1. But you still have until May 1 to inform the colleges of your plans, so you will follow the same steps as those recommended for regular decision applicants who are making their final decision. Refer to Chapter 15 for further advice.

However, if you have been accepted under a *binding* early decision (ED) plan, you will need to take certain steps immediately upon notification in December. Your financial aid package may arrive with your acceptance or shortly thereafter. After making sure it will work for you, you must withdraw any other applications you have submitted. Your acceptance notification will typically include a form for you to sign acknowledging your intent to enroll, as well as the deadline for submitting a deposit check. Depending on the college, there may be additional information, such as about financial aid, so read your notification letter carefully and respond promptly.

If you have been deferred or denied under an early plan, please see Chapter 15 for further advice.

Deposits

A nonrefundable deposit will be due with your response to the school where you will enroll. Read your notification letter carefully and follow the instructions with regard to the deposit.

Keep in mind that you have signed a

"Can you believe this school only sent me an admit letter? Where's my swag?!"

certification on your application form promising you will send a deposit to only one institution. You also have an ethical obligation. Double-depositing—sending deposits to two or more schools in order to keep your options open—takes places away from other students.

Remember, your acceptance letter is conditional, and it's easier than you think for the colleges to find out if you have deposited at more than one institution. You run the risk of both colleges rescinding your admission.

Waitlisted students should take care not to double-deposit as well. Suppose you are accepted at College A and waitlisted at College B, but your first choice is College B. You would enroll at College A and send a deposit. If you are later accepted at College B, you can also enroll and send a deposit there. This is not double-depositing provided you inform College A immediately and *in writing* that you will not be enrolling. (You will forfeit your deposit with College A.) If you fail to inform College A and also make a deposit at College B, that is double-depositing. Don't do it—it is irresponsible and you could end up with your acceptance rescinded by both colleges.

Parents, Here's How You Can Help

Parents, your job here is to be a sounding board and help your teenager feel confident about making this decision. Hopefully you have been upfront about certain parameters, such as cost and location, right from the beginning. At this point, then, you can give students the space to make the final call.

Do be available to help them think it through. Sit down and listen to what they have to say and reflect back what you are hearing. Sometimes you may hear them saying something they don't realize they're saying. For example, you might point out that all their positive remarks were made about College B, while they had nothing similar to say about Colleges A and D. Just make sure it's what *they* are saying, not *your* opinion.

Try not to use value-laden terms. Don't talk about "good schools" and "bad schools." Students will pick up on it and easily interpret the subtext. And don't push your own agenda. If it's blatant, it can backfire. Teenagers are probably going to do what they want anyway, whether in spite of you or because of you. And all the worse if they don't, because this decision is about them, not you. Badgering, pushing, or prying will make them uncomfortable, and the result will be that your teenager will very likely not want to talk to you about what's going on in this very

important year of their lives—and their last year in your home.

So honor them as young adults and allow them to make this decision. Again, it's not about you. You're not going to college next year, your teen is.

Waitlists

If you are placed on a waitlist, you haven't been accepted and you haven't been denied. You're in limbo, and that can be stressful. Students rarely anticipate they will be placed on a waitlist at one of the colleges where they have applied, but they very well may be.

Respond

If you receive a waitlist letter from a college, pay close attention to what it says. Usually you aren't actually placed on the waitlist—the letter is telling you that you can choose to be on it if you want. In order to be placed on a waitlist you will need to respond by submitting a form or emailing the college. Typically, you are asked to respond by a set date. If you don't respond or if you miss that deadline, you will not be placed on the waitlist. Follow instructions and respond accordingly.

If you have been admitted to your first-choice school and would not attend the college that offered to put you on their waitlist, *immediately* inform that college that you do not want to be placed on their waitlist. Waitlist spots are not a trophy-gathering opportunity.

◉ Best Advice

Accept a waitlist spot only if there is a strong possibility you will attend that college if admitted.

There are several factors you may need to consider in deciding whether to accept a spot on the waitlist:

- **Uncertainty.** You may not know if you have been admitted off the waitlist until sometime during the summer.
- **Cost.** You will need to make a firm commitment to another school and send in a deposit to ensure a seat in the fall. If you are accepted off the waitlist, you will forfeit the deposit made to that first school.
- **Financial aid.** Make sure the school where you are waitlisted will still have aid available when you hear about your acceptance. Some colleges may have already awarded most of their aid or scholarships.

- **Pressure.** Your continued achievement—a particularly successful second semester both academically and in your extracurricular activities—may be a fundamental factor in a college's decision about whom to admit off the waitlist.
- **The hard truth.** Be realistic about the low acceptance rate for most waitlists. It is statistically much less likely that you will be admitted from the waitlist than from the regular applicant pool.

Your waitlist letter may also include information about whether the waitlist is prioritized or ranked, which tells you a lot about your chances of being admitted. If the letter is unclear, you could ask the admission office the following questions as you try to decide whether to remain on a waitlist.

- How many students do you anticipate will be on your waitlist?
- Do you rank or tier your waitlist? And if so, where do I fall?
- What is the likelihood of being admitted from the waitlist?
- Will financial aid still be available if I am admitted from the waitlist?
- Will housing still be available?
- Is there anything I can do to improve my chances of being admitted?
- When do you expect to inform students you are admitting from the waitlist?

Send in a Deposit to a School Where You Have Been Accepted

If you decide to accept a spot on the waitlist, look over your acceptances, decide which college you will attend if you are not admitted at your waitlist school, and send in a deposit so that you are guaranteed a spot in the fall.

Then embrace the college where you *have been* admitted. Get to know that school, starting with social media to meet your fellow classmates, and begin picturing yourself on campus. You can sit back and relax, secure in the knowledge that you will be attending a wonderful college in the fall. And if you are admitted off the waitlist elsewhere, you will have the pleasure of deciding if you want to accept that offer or stay with the college to which you originally committed.

Follow Up

When you receive a waitlist letter, it will often outline specifically what information should be submitted or what additional materials may be sent, such as the most recent grade reports or additional letters of recommendation. In some cases, the letter will tell you the college has all the information they need and nothing additional should be sent unless it is specifically requested. Colleges usually give clear directions. Follow them.

The two most important things you can do are:

1. Show the strongest possible next grading period. Your final grades will need to demonstrate consistent progress and an upward trajectory.

2. Write a letter to your admission officer or the dean of admission thanking her for the opportunity and telling her why the college is a good fit for you. In that letter, bring her up to date with any accomplishments, awards, or

extracurricular activities that provide *new* information. If in fact this is the one college for which you would drop everything else and enroll in a heartbeat, then state that if offered admission you will enroll. This is important to some schools.

What about submissions that have not been specifically requested by the college, such as additional recommendations or letters from those who have special connections with a school, such as major donors? This may be a time to speak up, but think carefully. A shower of letters from illustrious alumni or major donors is ill-advised. One more recommendation will not usually make a difference. Being admitted off the waitlist isn't about bringing pressure to bear. It's about whether there is room for you and what you will bring to that college.

The most impressive students are those who advocate for themselves in an articulate and clear manner. The college is going to look with fresh eyes for what it needs as students are admitted off the waitlist. There is no way for a student to know what the priorities might be from year to year. Our best advice? Continue to present yourself authentically and consistently.

Getting Admitted off the Waitlist

If you are notified that you've been accepted at the school that waitlisted you, you may not have the luxury of time to make up your mind. The college will likely want to know your response as soon as possible so that if you decide not to accept their offer of admission, they can give it to another student.

If you decide to enroll, you will need to

Waitlist Advice

The waitlist works in different ways from college to college. A school's approach to its waitlist may depend on the size of its student body, its philosophy and mission, the number of applications it receives, or all of the above. The best advice for students may vary accordingly, so read any waitlist letter with care. Most colleges will come right out and tell you what they want from you.

We asked a group of admission deans to address how the waitlist works at their schools and provide some advice for students who find themselves on it.

WILLIAM FITZSIMMONS

Dean of admission, Harvard University

➡ Predicting yield is much more art than science. Because of this, colleges expect to take students off the waitlist every year. At Harvard there are some years where we are able to admit more than a hundred students off the waitlist, and there are other years when we can admit zero.

We expect that a significant number of people we put on the waitlist will decide to withdraw from further consideration. But for those who remain, we reconvene our committee in the same way we do for the regular admission process. In some instances, in the time after we sent out the waitlist letter, we have significant amounts of new information about students that can help them be admitted. Waitlist meetings begin a little after May 1, the common reply date. And we have a firm rule that we finish our waitlist process by the end of June.

The best thing students can do, if they are sincerely interested in being admitted off the waitlist, is to send an email or letter expressing that interest and updating the college on any particular accomplishments or changes that have taken place in the meantime. It's also perfectly appropriate for a teacher or counselor or someone else to add an additional letter of recommendation or two. But good judgment is important. It is possible to be in touch too much, and it's certainly not a good idea to start sending daily or semi-daily emails or letters or phone calls to colleges. What you don't want to do (whether it's in the regular process or in the waitlist process) is to mount what could appear to be a "campaign" with barrages of emails, letters, and phone calls from various people. That can be counterproductive.

CHRISTOPHER WATSON

Dean of undergraduate admission, Northwestern University

➡ At highly selective schools, our applicant pools are quite deep with talent. The students on the waitlist are those we simply don't have room for but would love to have if space becomes available. Every university has a freshman class target they are charged with meeting. At Northwestern, it's 2,025 every year. We use the waitlist to make sure we hit that target of 2,025 without going over. We are a residential community, and as a residential community, we only have so many beds. If we go over, we don't have places for our students to sleep.

We do not mind, at Northwestern, if a student writes to us and says, "I'm on the waitlist, and Northwestern is my top choice." They should wait for all their decision letters to arrive and find out where else they've been admitted. Once that's happened, they should take some time to think about their choices. And if Northwestern is still the number one choice, they should, by all means, write a letter to the admission office saying that. At that point they don't need to submit anything else. The fact that the student was put on the waitlist to begin with means we would love to have them here—we just didn't have room. So no additional letters of recommendation, no additional academic materials or anything like that. Simply a letter saying, "Northwestern is my top choice" is more than sufficient.

In the meantime, students who are waitlisted should get absolutely 100 percent excited about one of the schools to which they've been admitted. Do not sit around and be disappointed. Go to the admitted-student program at the school where you've been accepted. There is a very, very good chance that that's the school where you're going to end up.

VINCE CUSEO

Vice president for admission and financial aid, Occidental College

➡ Fifteen or twenty years ago, waitlists were smaller and, frankly, students had a greater chance of being admitted from the waitlist at that time. From the point of view of an admission office, there is now a greater capacity for variation on yield from year to year. Students currently are each applying to many more colleges than students did twenty years ago. So the yields on those students—the percentage of students who will accept an institution's offer of admission—have shrunk. The way an institution can meet its enrollment target is to build a waitlist, and given this day and age, likely a larger waitlist than twenty years ago, to ensure they'll be able to meet the enrollment target of the institution. Particularly at a relatively small institution like Occidental, if you're above or below your enrollment target by fifteen or twenty students, it has a fairly significant impact—that's another writing seminar class, for example, that the college must offer in the first year.

The waitlist also allows the institution some leverage. For example, if an admission office and a financial aid office has X number of committed students on May 5, and that total is twenty students fewer than the enrollment target, yet they have overspent in their financial aid, that's when there is some engineering that may have to go on. So they may turn to the waitlist for students who can pay a greater portion of their freight. Or the first-year class appears to be less diverse than they expected it to be, so they may turn to the waitlist to add greater diversity. In other words, the waitlist may serve a more particular need than merely meeting the ultimate enrollment goal.

immediately submit a deposit and inform the other college where you originally enrolled of your withdrawal *in writing*. You will lose the commitment deposit at the school to which you originally responded.

DENIALS

It can be hard for students when a college says no. And for most students, there will usually be some disappointment when the colleges' decisions are received. If you've made your list wisely, some will say yes—but usually some will say no, too, no matter how well qualified you are.

There are many reasons a student may receive a denial letter. Understand that while the application process is all about you and showing colleges who you are, the decision process is often more about the colleges and their priorities. Don't take it personally. You weren't denied—your application was.

Probably the last thing you want to hear is that it's important to learn to deal with

rejection, but it is a valuable life lesson. Life isn't fair and neither is the college admission process. The majority of students who apply to selective colleges are qualified to attend, but there simply isn't room.

If you have been denied at a college on your list, let yourself feel disappointed. Don't pretend it didn't happen. Talk with your parents and friends about it—or not. The choice is yours. Where you have been accepted or denied is your business and no one else's unless you choose to share that information. And don't worry that you may have disappointed your parents, teachers, or others in your life. They want what is best for you, which is to move on and be happy about the choices you do have. So allow yourself to feel sad, but don't wallow in feelings of disappointment for too long.

When you started this process you set out to make a list full of top schools for yourself. The good news is that if you have done the hard work recommended throughout this

Advice for Students and Parents from Rosalind Wiseman

During this step in the process, as students receive news from the colleges to which they've applied, there is a lot of talk. Inquiring minds want to know if you've heard from the colleges, what you heard from the colleges, where you will be going to college. Oh, and how about your friends, the class president, the quarterback, and the kid down the street? Some of this is genuine interest in you, some of it is nosiness, and the rest is thinly veiled status competition.

We asked Rosalind Wiseman, author of *Queen Bees and Wannabes*—the inspiration for the hit movie *Mean Girls*—and an expert on teens and parenting, for her advice about talking the talk during this step in the college admission process.

Students

Students, by the time you're a senior you should have at least two or three friends with whom you can share your experiences and feelings. Be aware of the feelings of others—even of close friends—as you discuss your options with one another. It can be hard, because you've got friends who may not have the choices you do. So you can say, "Yes, I got in, and I'm really proud," but that's all you need to say. You don't need to have extended conversations. Be sensitive. Support each other, but respect one another's privacy.

When other parents ask questions, be polite, but you don't have to respond at length. "Yeah, I got in, I'm really proud of it. I am looking forward to next year. And thank you so much for your good wishes." Saying "And thank you so much for your good wishes" tends to politely close that conversation down. If the person continues to ask questions or compares your experience to other students', say, "Thanks for your interest, but I don't feel comfortable talking about where others got in. It can be a sensitive topic for a lot of people, so I want to respect that."

What if an adult is going on and on about your good news by saying things like, "That's incredible! How did you get in? I heard that there were twenty-four thousand applications for four spots!" That entire conversation needs to be nixed immediately by both student and parent. And of course the parent should be the person to take the lead on that. But an eighteen-year-old can say, "I'm glad I got in, but a lot of people who are just as worthy as I am didn't." And then change the subject to something like an upcoming event at school.

Parents

Parents, your ultimate responsibility is to help your child make this decision with integrity. But you won't be able to guide your child with authenticity and integrity if your higher thinking processes are hijacked by inane, anxious conversations with other parents. And no matter how sane you are, you can get caught up in this.

It's totally appropriate to share your concerns and your feelings—and even positive feelings, good experiences—with your friends. But there is no place for social banter with other parents. Nothing good is going to come of it. However, if you get stuck in one of these conversations, there are different ways you can handle it. You can say, "You know, I just don't think talking about who got in where is fair to our kids because it really contributes to their anxiety." You can make a joke of it: "Hey, c'mon, we're really not going to be those parents, are we?" and then talk about something else, like your favorite restaurant. Have some backup conversation in mind, ready to go.

It's also important to admit how difficult going through this experience can be—but just with one or two close friends who know your kid, who have been there before as you've struggled with other parenting challenges. These are the ones to whom you can admit, "Wow, this is hard. Watching him get rejected is breaking my heart," or "I can't believe how much this is impacting me. I'm a nervous wreck!" On the other hand, you also should have someone who's good at telling you when you need to think about something differently—such as when you need to back off your kid.

Don't have those same conversations with your teenager. You can say to your child, "Wow, this is tough. I went to a cocktail party, and man, was it tough for me not to get in that conversation!" You're just telling her you're a part of this process, too. And she knows that anyway. But it's important to maintain that boundary, for kids to know what you're going through in a limited way so that you are still a support system for them.

When your teenager gets good news, it's fine to be enthusiastic and happy within your family. You want your child to be proud of his hard work and the accomplishment of being recognized for that hard work, but also be clear that once the moment of euphoria is over and you have a wonderful dinner to celebrate, think about how you're going to share the news with other people in a way that is mindful of their experience.

book, you now get to make a choice among several schools from your list that said yes.

BEYOND THE DECISION

Thank-yous

While it may be inappropriate and unkind to spread the news loud and clear among your peers, there is a list of people you need to talk to about the outcomes of your applications. Once you have your letters in hand, take the time to inform all the people in your life who had a hand in your admission process about the results.

That includes the teachers who wrote recommendations, the high school college counselor who loaned you her College Board *Handbook*, the guidance counselor who advised you to take AP calculus, the English teacher who proofread your essays, the coach who wrote a letter to the athletic department, and the faculty advisor for the newspaper who encouraged you to write an editorial about the stress of applying to college.

Postponing Your Freshman Year

Taking a "gap year"—deferring enrollment for a year once you have been admitted to the school you plan to attend—is a choice more and more colleges are encouraging. It's already a common experience for students in the United Kingdom, Australia, and Canada. Admission officers believe that students who take time off gain maturity and experience that benefit the college community.

Once you know where you are going to go to college, it's a great way to spend a year de-stressing or pursuing an activity, travel, or other interest you've been dreaming about—whether that's mountain climbing, carpentry, the study of viruses, cattle ranching, a job with the Forest Service, playing oboe in a professional orchestra, community service in Cape Town, an internship in computer animation, or learning to pilot a plane.

Middlebury College encourages students to consider a gap year, describing it in its offers of admission and providing the opportunity for students to pursue a semester off and enroll in February. Robert Clagett, Middlebury's former dean of admissions and now director of college counseling at St. Stephen's Episcopal School in Austin, Texas, shared his thoughts and advice on taking a gap year.

➡ As the tensions that surround the admission process continue to grow, it can cause students to lose sight of what their education is all about. And the college admission tail has come to wag the education dog in so many ways. A gap year is a way of allowing education to wag the education dog again, the opportunity for students to step off the treadmill and reacquaint themselves with what their education should be about. That's the main purpose of a gap year. And the fact that it leads possibly to a greater sense of direction once students get to college, a greater maturity, a greater knowledge of what they want to do with their education—those are all positive effects. It's just a big win-win for everybody.

It doesn't matter what students do—not that we would encourage them to sit around their homes and eat bonbons. But it can be work, volunteer experiences, going to school as long as it's not in a degree-granting program, travel for those who can afford it, community service, working at a salmon-canning factory in Alaska—virtually anything to break up the lockstep mentality that too many people take toward their education, that you graduate from high school in May or June and trot off to college in August or September for four years. It doesn't have to be that way.

Several years ago, we did some research comparing the academic performance of incoming students in a variety of ways. In that particular year, the best predictor for higher academic performance at Middlebury was enrolling in February. Now, it's not to say there is a huge difference, but it was statistically significant.

So keep a really open mind to the possibility of doing a gap year and then just let your imagination flow about all the fascinating things you could do with a year to yourself. In the long run, one year isn't going to make any difference, and could, in fact, improve the quality of your education and what you derive from it in myriad ways. It will likely lead to an even more positive college experience, as students gain maturity and focus. And it gives students the opportunity to remind themselves what their education is all about.

If you decide a gap year is a good idea, you will need to accept an offer of admission from the school where you plan to enroll, send in your deposit, and then—if it is a school that will consider deferrals—request a deferral of admission from the college. Check the college's policies on its website or talk to an admission officer about any specific requirements that school may have; for example, some schools may request that you check in with them midway through your gap period or send them a letter about how your experience is going.

Let them know where you have decided to enroll and thank them for all they did to help you get there. And don't forget a big thank-you for the people who have helped you get to this point for the last eighteen years . . . your parents.

A Final Word: Don't Mess Up

At this point in the admission process, students can become susceptible to "senioritis," a malady characterized by a lack of motivation that may present as falling grades, missed classes, or a propensity for goofing off in the classroom and on the playing field.

Know this: your senior year is important to colleges. Acceptance letters are contingent on your finishing the year at the same performance level as when you were admitted. If slacking off gets out of hand, it can have serious consequences, including having your admission rescinded.

What might make a college reconsider? A significant change in your academic record, such as a notably lower grade in one or more classes; increased absences; dropped classes; or a lapse in judgment or integrity, such as cheating, plagiarism, suspension for drug or alcohol use, or any disciplinary action for behavioral issues. If you do experience a decline in your GPA or a disciplinary issue, let the college where you have been accepted know about it with a phone call—the sooner the better.

 Best Advice

Don't mess up. Stay fully engaged in your high school classroom and on campus—not just because you might have your acceptance rescinded but also because it's important that you model good behavior for the junior class following in your footsteps.

A Final Checklist

- Go back and thank all the people who made this possible for you.
- Accept the offer of admission and submit a deposit by May 1 at the school where you will enroll.
- Inform all other schools where you have been offered admission that you will not be

enrolling. Remember you're holding on to someone else's spot.

- Start getting to know the school you will attend for the next four years by forming relationships with classmates via social media.
- Complete financial aid documentation by the designated deadline. See Chapter 16 for more information.
- Send your final transcript.

Questions You May Have

What are "likely letters"?

Likely letters are sent to students by some colleges before official notifications are mailed. These letters typically tell a student how much the admission office enjoyed reading their application and that they are "likely" to receive good news. Does that mean an acceptance is a done deal? No. It means your application is promising as long as your grades don't fall. But likely letters are not offers of admission. These are sent primarily to athletes and superior students; the vast majority of students will not receive a likely letter.

Can I appeal a denial?

Most private colleges and universities do not reconsider their admission decisions. A number of public universities do have an appeals process. Check the college's website to see if it has an appeals process. If they do, feel welcome to use it.

I have been offered admission at midyear. What does that mean?

It means that you will have a place at that college provided you stand ready to begin your freshman year in the spring semester rather than the traditional fall start. If you are considering this, find out about any transition or orientation programs the college may have and how spring enrollment may affect your housing options, so that your adjustment to college life goes smoothly.

If I know another student at my high school has turned down a spot at the college where I am waitlisted, will I be offered that seat?

No, a notification of admission does not belong to a particular high school, nor to a student to give to another as he or she sees fit. Only the admission office can do that.

Do I need to tell the college where I am accepting a spot that I have been waitlisted elsewhere?

There is no need to inform a school that you are waitlisted elsewhere unless they specifically ask for this information.

What if I am denied admission at all the schools on my list?

For students who followed this book's advice, this is unlikely. But what if it nevertheless happens? Depending on the reasons for your denials, there are some courses of action for you to consider:

- NACAC publishes a "college openings update" on its website at nacacnet.org listing colleges that still have space for applicants after May 1.

- Enrolling for a postgraduate year at another high school and reapplying next year.
- Attending community college and transferring later to a four-year college. See Chapter 21.

? Can I accept a waitlist offer at more than one school?

Yes, but we advise doing so only if you would attend either one over the school to which you are committing.

? When is it appropriate to call a college and ask about my chances of getting admitted from the waitlist?

If the college does not let you know when you are likely to hear from them either in your notification letter or online, feel welcome to call them in early May—before that time, they will not have an answer—to inquire as to whether they intend to go to the waitlist, and what your chances might be.

PART IX

SPECIAL CIRCUMSTANCES

CHAPTER 18

Students with Special Talents

For students with talent and interest in athletics or the arts, applying to college will require extra preparation and planning. This chapter will address the additional steps you will need to take, along with how your talent will be considered in the colleges' admission decisions.

ATHLETICS

"Listen to what the coaches are telling you objectively, without projecting your own wishes onto what a coach might say."
—Stuart Schmill, dean of admissions, MIT

There are six primary ways to participate in sports at the college level: NCAA Division I (D-I), NCAA Division II (D-II), NCAA Division III (D-III), NAIA, club, and intramural. As student athletes put together their initial list of colleges, they may consider schools with athletic programs at each of these classifications. For the purposes of this chapter, however, we will address student athletes considering participating in NCAA D-I, D-II, or D-III sports.

For those students with the desire and talent to play NCAA athletics, the process of applying will be different in two ways:

- Your timing may be significantly earlier. You may start to look at colleges and talk with athletic departments as early as your sophomore year of high school, test as early as possible, or make a commitment to a school much earlier than your peers who are not athletes. You will need to plan well in advance for meetings with college coaches and the recruitment process.
- Creating your list of schools will require research that is deeper and wider.
  - In addition to understanding the kind of college you want to attend, you will need to ascertain how your skills and athletic talent fit with each of those schools and programs.

Checkpoints ✍

✔ Athletes have an earlier timetable for applying to college.

✔ Athletes' lists of prospective schools should include schools they love, as well as schools whose teams they'd love to play for.

✔ Make sure you have a thorough understanding of NCAA rules, including regulations about visits, eligibility, and National Letters of Intent.

- You will want to understand the differences among the NCAA divisions, including eligibility requirements, the availability of scholarships, and the influence of your athletic ability on an admission decision.
- You will want to understand the nature of the different athletic conferences, such as Big 10, NESCAC, Centennial, Ivy League, etc. The conference in which a college participates will have an impact on the commitment of time and effort required of you, the level of competition, and the availability of scholarships and financial aid.
- You will need to have a firm grasp of the particulars of applying as a student athlete at each school on your list. There is great variability—deadlines, additional materials the coaches want, scholarships—and the rules governing recruiting and academic eligibility can differ from division to division, conference to conference, and sport to sport.

Information about a student's athletic achievements is collected on the Common Application and available to athletic departments and coaches where the college admission office chooses to forward that information. If you are not being actively recruited by a D-I or D-II school, you may also want to reach out to the athletic departments at the schools in which you're interested.

In this section, we will provide an overview of NCAA D-I, D-II, and D-III programs, as well as specific advice about researching and applying to the colleges on a student athlete's list.

NCAA Division I and II

Divisions I and II of the National Collegiate Athletic Association are made up of the most athletically competitive schools. Division I schools are generally considered more athletically competitive than the universities and colleges in Division II. D-I schools also have more scholarship funds, though most—but not all—schools in both divisions do offer scholarships. An exception is the D-I Ivy

League Conference, whose schools do not provide athletic scholarships.

Rules and policies governing scholarships—as well as eligibility and recruitment—differ between the two divisions, and within those divisions between individual colleges or conferences. You will need to check the NCAA website at ncaa.org and the websites of each school to which you are applying.

If you are considering participating in a sport at a D-I or D-II school, here are some steps you will need to take:

• Visit the NCAA website to understand the rules regarding recruitment and eligibility. Check both D-I and D-II policies, since their certification of eligibility requirements are different. Download the Guide for College-Bound Student Athletes for the most recent year at ncaa.org. Register online at the NCAA Eligibility Center at ncaa.org by the end of junior year. NCAA eligibility is based on a sliding-scale calculation using your grades, test scores, proof of graduation, and other academic information. You need to be proactive and follow through with your high school and the testing services to make sure your transcripts and scores are submitted.

• Submit the application fee for the Eligibility Center. If you received a fee waiver for the SAT or ACT (see Chapter 7), you may be eligible for an Eligibility Center fee waiver. Check with your high school counselor or coach.

• Check the website of each school to which you are applying, or call the athletic department, to determine their policy regarding eligibility. For example, the Ivy League Conference uses its own formula, known as the Academic Index (AI), to determine whether you are eligible to be recruited.

Students who have the talent to be recruited for D-I or D-II schools will usually begin receiving correspondence from coaches during their junior year. Prior to that time, many prospective student athletes may participate in summer camps to sharpen their skills. At the more selective of these camps, college coaches are often in attendance to have an opportunity to evaluate upcoming talent prior to the senior year of high school competition. Participation in these camps can occur as early as freshman year in high school.

However, coaches can directly contact a student by phone or in person only after his junior year. While the coaches can't reach out to you prior to that time, you can and

Even if you have exceptional athletic talent, when you are creating the list of colleges to which you will apply, it should be among your top priorities to select "broken-leg schools"—colleges you would want to attend even if things didn't work out for you on the playing field. This is because things can change: you could be injured, your coach could move or resign, or your program could be eliminated. So as you go through this process, make sure you pick a school you love as well as a team you can see yourself being happy spending a lot of time with and a coach you like.

should feel welcome to initiate contact yourself as you conduct your research and make any unofficial visits. See the NCAA website to fully understand NCAA recruitment regulations. Coaches at D-I and D-II programs often have meaningful input into the admission decision and will provide a list to the admission office of the athletes they are most interested in recruiting. As you visit schools, you should ask coaches whether they have input into the admission decision and whether you will be someone for whom they will actively advocate. At the more selective colleges, the coach often will have input but will not determine who is admitted. Be sure you are doing your best work academically as well as athletically.

The National Letter of Intent

At the end of the recruiting process, a student may commit to participate in a sport at a D-I or D-II college and, if she will receive a scholarship, be asked to sign a National Letter of Intent (NLI). The NLI is a binding agreement between the college or university and a prospective student that she will enroll and receive an athletic scholarship. It will be accompanied by a scholarship agreement and may include an estimated financial aid award.

When you sign an NLI, you will likely not have a definitive letter of admission in hand. You may have a letter from the admission office telling you that admission is likely, or simply an assurance from the coach that you will probably be admitted. This can be disconcerting, but it is very rare for the

> If you are fortunate enough to be recruited and sign an NLI, be mindful that your classmates typically do not yet know where they may be admitted to college. Please be respectful of that as you share your good news.

admission and athletic offices to be out of sync. If you are not admitted, you can be released from the agreement.

If you fail to enroll after signing a NLI, there may be a substantial penalty. There are different signing periods and rules governing signing periods for each sport. Check the NCAA website. If you're not receiving scholarship money, you will not sign an NLI.

Official Athletic Visits

Official athletic visits—paid for by the colleges or universities—occur in the senior year. These may be offered at D-I and D-II schools, less often at D-III schools. Check with each school about its policy. Prior to that time you may make unofficial visits and meet with coaches at schools to which you are considering applying. Some schools also have recruiting events such as Junior Days with facilities tours and presentations by coaches, athletic trainers, and financial aid representatives.

When you make an official visit you are being recruited, and you may have little contact with anyone outside of the athletic department. If you want to do anything unchaperoned by a coach, such as the regular admission office tour or a meeting with a faculty member, you should expressly request this as your visit is being planned. We recommend you do so. See our advice about "broken-leg schools" on page 325.

NCAA Division III

D-III colleges and universities do not provide athletic scholarships. Eligibility, financial aid, and competition at D-III schools are governed by rules and policies set by the individual colleges, conferences, and the NCAA. You will need to check the websites of each school and conference as well as the NCAA.

- Recruitment is handled differently in D-III, so you may or may not be contacted by a coach. If you are interested in playing for a school that is not recruiting you, you should initiate contact. Let the coaches know of your interest with a phone call or by arranging to meet when visiting colleges. Describe your athletic accomplishments honestly, and ask for candid feedback about whether you are strong enough for their program.

- At D-III schools, your timing will be closer to that of applicants who are not being recruited as athletes. Check with the coach to see if applying early decision or early action (see Chapter 15) will prompt extra consideration of your athletic ability in the admission process.

- D-III is not scholarship-driven, but need-based financial aid is available for those who qualify. At some D-III schools there may also be merit scholarships awarded for qualities not related to athletics. If you are a student who has need and/or qualifies for a merit award, you will go through the regular admission and financial aid process. Depending on your qualifications and the strength of the financial aid or merit

Scholarships for Athletes

You will have a good idea of the terms of your scholarship before you sign your NLI. Be aware that many scholarships awarded at D-I and D-II schools are not full scholarships. Mostly the "head-count sports"—such as football, basketball, and volleyball—provide full scholarships, and even then not in every case. The majority of college sports are "equivalency sports" with partial scholarships. (Information about this can be found on the NCAA website.)

Awarded annually, athletic scholarships must be renewed each year and are not guaranteed for more than one year at a time. You will be informed of your scholarship for subsequent years during the summer before each new school year. If you are injured and can no longer participate, athletic departments will work with the college and the NCAA to help you retain your scholarship and aid as long as you remain in good academic standing. Athletic scholarships may be supplemented by financial aid in the form of grants or loans. Make sure you are in the process of applying for regular financial aid. Find out how to get an estimated financial aid package, and take care to understand the breakdown between your scholarship and financial aid package. See Chapter 16 for more information.

program at the colleges on your list, your financial aid or merit award at a D-III school can potentially be stronger than your athletic scholarship at some D-I or D-II institutions. See Chapter 16 for more information about financial aid.

Dos and Don'ts

Don't assume when you get mail from a coach that the college is necessarily interested. But it does mean that the coach is interested in talking with you.

If a coach calls you, it means you are someone she wants to get to know. From there, you may or may not become one of her recruited athletes.

Interest from a coach doesn't guarantee admission—or playing time if you are admitted.

Don't make assumptions about your scholarship award until you have signed your National Letter of Intent.

Think hard before making even an informal verbal commitment, especially prior to the start of your senior year. You could change your mind. Or if you are injured or fail to develop as a player, the coach may change his mind.

Applying Early

If you are applying to D-III schools, or applying to D-I or D-II schools but not being considered for athletic scholarships, you may be urged by the coach to apply early decision or early action. As you research schools, inquire about their policy with regard to when student athletes should apply. And go back and read Chapter 15 as you contemplate your timing. If you're considering a school with early decision, make sure it's a college you really want to attend. If you're considering a school with early action, make sure you're following all the rules as you complete your other applications.

Questions to Ask Athletic Coaches

If you're interested in participating in a sport at a particular college, here are some questions you may want to ask as you research schools and make unofficial visits:

- What is your policy about official visits?
- What is the time commitment and schedule you ask of your team? What are the off-season commitments?
- What is your policy about allowing time at home during the summers or holidays?
- How much playing time will I get? Will you guarantee playing time?
- What is your graduation rate for athletes in this sport?
- What is your four-year graduation rate for athletes in this sport?
- Do you have a student athlete code of conduct?
- What type of community involvement do you expect your student athletes to participate in?
- What kind of academic support is provided to student athletes?
- If there is a conflict with a class schedule, is there any flexibility or will I have to delay taking a course due to practice or competition?
- What are your policies on medical care?

Additional questions for those considering D-I and D-II schools:

- How many scholarships do you have available for next year? Do you anticipate that might change?
- What's your policy on renewing scholarships?
- What happens if I'm injured?
- Does your conference have any additional

regulations governing scholarships or financial aid?

As you narrow your list of schools:

- What positions do you need to fill for next year?

- How many spots do you have available for next year?

- Where am I on your list? (Don't just ask if you're on the coach's list. That list may have twenty-five students and he's going to get seven—so where you are on the list is important.)

FROM THE DESK OF THE DEAN

Further Advice About the Application Process for Student Athletes

STUART SCHMILL
Dean of admissions, Massachusetts Institute of Technology

➡ MIT hosts both Division I and Division III sports, and its primary league affiliation is with the New England Women's and Men's Athletic Conference (NEWMAC).

Often, in some families' minds, there's a belief that playing a sport at a Division III school means there is less emphasis or less of a commitment asked or required of students. That's not always true. A lot of Division III athletic programs are every bit as intense in terms of commitment and time and energy as some Division I programs. So students really need to get a feel for whether there's a good fit between the intensity and the commitment level that the coaches will expect and what the student is interested in putting forward.

Otherwise, it's important for students to get to know the school beyond what their connection is with the coach. Any athlete needs to really get a full picture of the academic environment and the social environment on the university campus beyond just what he's hearing from the coach. On top of this, he needs to make sure that he listens carefully and objectively to what the coaches are saying so that there is no miscommunication.

MONICA INZER
Dean of admission and financial aid, Hamilton College

➡ Hamilton College competes in NCAA Division III and is a member of the New England Small College Athletic Conference (NESCAC).

There is so much confusion about the role of athletics in admission. Families are ramping up the pressure and trying to shoehorn their kids into places they might not have gotten into otherwise, instead of stepping back from the process and saying, "Where does my kid belong?" It's hard to get at the culture of each conference or each program, and it's tricky to navigate. High school coaches will help. They often have contacts with college coaches, but they don't always understand the admission process. Students should communicate early with lots of coaches, but also with the admission office.

ROB MULLENS

Director of intercollegiate athletics, University of Oregon

➡ The University of Oregon competes in NCAA Division I and is a member of the Pacific-12 (Pac-12) Conference.

At the University of Oregon, student athletes are considered based on the same admission criteria as all applicants to the university: high school grades, course work, grade trend, academic motivation, and more. Early communication between the prospective student and the recruiting coach ensures a clear understanding of the documentation required with the institution as well as the NCAA eligibility center for evaluation. As the point of contact with the prospective student, the coaching staff works closely with the Athletics Compliance Office to collect the required information for the admissions staff to move the process forward.

RICHARD SHAW

Dean of admission and financial aid, Stanford University

➡ Stanford University competes in NCAA Division I and is a member of the Pacific-12 (Pac-12) Conference.

At Stanford, we work with the coaches and the coaching staff and the department of athletics to help them understand clearly what our expectations are. There are no shortcuts. The coaches wait for our decision and we know of their interest. No student is given any kind of offer to Stanford without full consideration in the admission process. So there has to be a completed application.

We consider all the same characteristics we do in the general applicant pool. We promote the same preparation, such as a curriculum that's rigorous. At the same time, we acknowledge student athletes' commitments in terms of pursuing athletic excellence. We try to understand context, but we're not interested in admitting students we don't believe have the full capacity to be successful at Stanford.

Our goal is to say "scholar-athlete," and the "scholar" part is critically important. Those kids are students. We spend our time thinking about them as students. We're not going to dismiss the responsibility they have as students.

DOUG TIEDT
Associate athletic director for student services, University of Wisconsin

➡ The University of Wisconsin competes in Division I of the NCAA and is a member of the Big Ten Conference.

First, finish high school strong. Regardless of whether you are already admitted to an institution, have applied and are waiting for an admissions decision or are still in the process of selecting a school, it is imperative that you enroll in challenging high school courses your entire senior year and complete these courses to the best of your ability. Many students make the mistake of thinking that it's acceptable to "coast" in their seventh or eighth semester of high school because they are already an NCAA qualifier, have the necessary core requirements, and in many instances, have already been admitted to the institution of their choosing.

The danger in following this approach is that the courses you enroll in your senior year are the foundation for all future college course work. When speaking to parents and students, I like to compare one's academic endeavors to the importance of eating breakfast. Without a solid nutritional foundation to start the day, one cannot perform at his or her peak. High school course work is the breakfast of your educational career. Without a solid educational breakfast, which includes challenging high school courses in the senior year, which prepare you for future college work, attainment of your educational goals and aspirations will be much more difficult.

Second, thoroughly research the institution and make the most of your campus visit. The school of your choosing should be a good fit academically and athletically. The two experiences are synergistically connected and the only way to truly understand the best fit for you is to get the most out of your campus visit experience. During your visit, attend a class, go to the student union, visit the campus library, develop an understanding of the academic support systems that are offered, and explore campus on your own. Create a list of predetermined questions that should be answered before the visit is complete. During your visit, get feedback from students, professors, coaches, and staff as to their thoughts of the strengths and weaknesses of the campus, the athletic program, and the community.

The four to five years you spend in college will lay the groundwork for the next forty to fifty years of your life, so the time spent in preparation is vitally important.

Checkpoints ✍

✔ Students with talent in the arts may decide to make arts the focus of their studies or simply elect to have their talent considered as part of the admission decision.

✔ Fulfilling requirements for auditions and submission of portfolios requires significant time and effort. Students must plan ahead.

THE ARTS

"Experiences in music and other arts will translate in many, many ways because of the training involved, especially at a college that has a broad-based liberal arts component to the education."

—*Dennis Craig, vice president, enrollment management, Purchase College*

For students with talent and accomplishments in the arts, strength in music, fine arts, design, film, dance, or other disciplines may play one of two roles in the application process. For some, the arts may be the focus of your studies and you may pursue either an arts degree as part of a liberal arts program or admission to a specialized program such as a conservatory of music or film school. Others may simply want colleges to consider their arts experience as part of the overall admission decision.

For most students with significant involvement in the arts, the process of applying will begin earlier and be more extensive, in two important ways:

1. Submission of supplementary materials demonstrating your talent, such as an art portfolio, film, PowerPoint presentation, DVD, or CD, will require thought and planning.

2. Additional requirements for auditions, portfolio review, and interviews can necessitate significant additional preparation and attention to scheduling and deadlines.

In this section, we will discuss what you need to know, whether the arts are your major course of study or a distinguishing interest.

Students Pursuing the Arts as Their Major Course of Study

As you research schools and compile the list of colleges to which you may apply, you may be considering whether to apply to a specialized program, such as a stand-alone conservatory or design school, or to an arts school or arts major within a college or university—or to several of each. Carmina Cianciulli, assistant dean for undergraduate studies and student affairs at Temple University's Tyler School of Art, offered her perspective on the contrasts between these two alternatives.

➡ **A student seeking a sense of community in the visual arts will find it either in a private art**

Submitting Arts Materials

Regardless of the depth in which you will study the arts, there are some constants. Anyone submitting additional materials will need to carefully study each college's requirements, paying particular attention to:

- Arts supplement. A separate form may be available from the school or the supplement may be integrated through the Common Application with SlideRoom (slideroom.com found on the landing page of the individual schools in the My Colleges section).
- Submission of additional materials, such as performance DVDs or CDs, fine arts/architecture/design portfolios, or resumes. Most colleges have detailed requirements for the creative portfolio or other submissions, and these requirements vary from school to school. Some schools of visual arts or design, for example, may request a PowerPoint slide presentation; others may want digital images on a DVD or CD. Film programs may want film clips or may request an entire film and a copy of the original script. Some art schools and colleges may invite students to bring in their portfolio for review after the application has been received.
- Auditions. Check the repertoire requirements, if applicable to your artistic pursuit, of each school. Such requirements will vary from school to school and, like the supplementary material requirements, are often quite specific. Vocalists may be asked to perform an eighteenth-century Italian art song at one school, an aria in French at another, and a number from a Broadway show at yet another. Dates, times, and locations for auditions or reviews will also vary from school to school. Check the websites and plan ahead. Also, note that some schools have a prescreening round that must be completed before a student is invited to audition.

school or in an art school or art department within an academic university. The intensity of an arts-based curriculum encourages community, as artists look to learn from each other as much as they do from their faculty and from the professional art world. An art school or art department within a university will generally offer a more diverse academic complement to the art curriculum, and will give art students the opportunity to take academic courses with students in other majors. Students who attend an art department or art school within a liberal arts college or university will also have access to a more traditional college experience if they want it—the opportunity to play sports, participate in Greek life, and join student clubs and organizations that are not arts specific. Students who seek art schools look for a totally shared experience and a total arts community, and generally feel that the studio art course work is more important to them than the opportunity to take a more varied academic curriculum.

For students who make the arts the focus of their studies, your talent and accomplishments will play a major role in the admission decision. Nevertheless, you will be required to present your full self—not just yourself as an artist—through the application process. So, artists, take note: the rest of this book still applies! Most arts programs want thinking and even entrepreneurial artists. All the other steps in the application process will be relevant, including essays, grades, and testing.

Students applying to art colleges and conservatories may use the Common Application, a school's unique application, or another form, such as the Unified Application for Music and Performing Arts, a form similar to the Common Application used by a group of conservatories. In addition, for many art schools or conservatories that are part of a larger university you will apply both to the university as a whole and to that arts college specifically. Students pursuing an art major in a liberal arts program will follow a process similar to what is outlined in this book and should pay particular attention to any additional requirements for recommendations from arts instructors, arts supplements, or auditions at each college to which they are applying.

The scope of requirements for submission of supplementary materials, as well as auditions and interviews, is much more comprehensive for students for whom the arts will be the focus of their studies. Colleges' guidelines for submission for such students will be rigorous, detailed, and specific. The websites of colleges with specialized programs have many resources to help you understand what the school requires for admission. Visit them early, read carefully, and follow directions. If you have any questions, call or email the admission office. Your application will not be considered without all of these requirements being properly fulfilled.

Questions to Ask

- Does the school offer the major or concentration I'm interested in?
- Is the degree a Bachelor of Fine Arts or a Bachelor of Arts? If both are offered at the same institution, what are the programmatic differences between the two?
- What is the academic component of the program?
- Is your faculty made up of working artists?
- What are the support services for careers?
- What are students doing after graduation?

Students Who Want Colleges to Consider their Arts Experience as Part of an Overall Admission Decision

Students who have made a substantial commitment of time and energy to the arts and wish to have their talent and accomplishments considered as part of their application should check the policies regarding arts submissions at each college on their list. Colleges will differ in how accomplished a student should be in order to submit supplementary materials—from Stanford ("applicants with extraordinary talent") to Occidental ("If you're passionate about music, theater, or visual art and plan to pursue it at Oxy, we welcome you to submit a fine arts resume with your admission application").

Some schools specify that if you submit arts materials, you should plan to at least participate in that art while in college. Other colleges are clear that a submission neither obligates you to participate nor guarantees that you will be able to participate.

In general, think carefully before submitting an arts supplement to your application or seeking an audition. Ask yourself if your talent and experience truly distinguish you. For example, in music, you might be studying privately and working on a solo repertoire—that says something about you. But simply participating in a chorus would not warrant submitting an arts supplement or auditioning, as the experience isn't unusual and doesn't illustrate the kind of commitment that would impact an admission decision. In such a case, you would simply list chorus as an activity on the application form.

It takes a lot of time to prepare an arts supplement, and if your experience is not at a distinguishing level, your time may be better spent in the classroom and preparing a good basic application. Your arts teachers, whether private or at your high school, can be good sources of guidance and can give you honest feedback on the level of distinction in your work. Typically, arts submissions are evaluated not by the admission office but by the relevant department. If the faculty of that department believes your talent will add to that college's program, they will let the admission office know. Arts talent alone will not get you admitted, but the admission office may positively factor your talent and accomplishments into their evaluation.

The requirements for submission of supplementary materials for students who want their talent considered as part of the admission decision likely will be less exhaustive, but in some cases they will be just as specific. Pay scrupulous attention to the individual

> **DEADLINES**
>
> Pay attention to deadlines when submitting arts supplements, supplementary materials, or applications to specialized programs. Colleges may require art portfolios or performance DVDs to be submitted weeks or even months earlier than the application deadline. At some colleges, you may need to submit not only supplements and materials by that earlier deadline but the entire application.

colleges' instructions. Requirements will vary from college to college, from art to art, and even within an art. For example, there may be one set of requirements if your music talent is composition and another if it is string bass. Make sure you go to the website of each college well enough in advance to shape your audition or portfolio accordingly.

Guidance provided for submissions considered as part of the regular admission process is often less comprehensive than guidance for students applying to specialized programs. If a school's policies are unclear on the website, call or email the admission office. In general, do not send original work—send copies only. Many schools will not return your submissions. Also, be sure to label submissions clearly with the medium of your art, your full name, and your Common App ID number (if you are using the Common App) or other identifier.

If art is important to you and a college to which you are applying does not accept supplementary materials, consider writing about your interest in the arts somewhere in the application in addition to your list of extracurricular activities.

Questions to Ask

- What is your policy on submission of supplementary materials?
- Are your deadlines for submission of an arts supplement different from regular decision deadlines?
- Are my supplementary materials evaluated by the relevant department faculty or just noted in my admission file?
- Are opportunities for participation in plays and concerts, for example, reserved exclusively for students majoring in music, film, theater, and so on?

Resources

Performing and Visual Arts College Fairs
The National Association for College Admission Counseling (NACAC) at nacacnet.org sponsors national college fairs specifically for students who are interested in pursuing serious study in the performing or visual arts,

FROM THE DESK OF THE DEAN

Advice for Applicants Interested in the Arts

DENNIS CRAIG
Vice president, enrollment management, Purchase College

➡ It's very important for students and parents to have—as best they can—a mature understanding of what life would be like after graduation, the ideal life they want to have as an artist. How much money will you be making? What's the mix of glamour and hard work? How much will you be valued and appreciated by society? The life of professional artists is very different, and they need to have a firm understanding of what is really important to them with regard to family, personal time, personal wealth, benefits, and how much they're willing to compromise art being a major component of their life in some way. It's tough. Everyone has to decide at the end what success is going to look like.

I'm an advocate for arts education because I think you can be a musician, to use one example, and end up being very successful working for Apple. Experiences in music and other arts will translate in many, many ways because of the training involved, especially at a college that has a broad-based liberal arts component to the education. The creative mind is a huge resource for any industry, especially if someone has a respect and appreciation not just for the arts but for an interdisciplinary approach to thinking and problem solving.

KEN ANSELMENT
Dean of admissions and financial aid, Lawrence University

➡ I have to tip my cap to students who are applying to arts programs—especially music programs, in Lawrence's case—because not only do they have to be diligent, capable students with strong music potential, they also have to be fairly accomplished project managers, where each of them is the project to be managed.

Colleges are going to help students through the process, but the student is the one who has to spend the energy registering for auditions, tracking down additional documents like music teacher recommendations (in our case), and practicing a repertoire, which even if the pieces being played for each college are the same, each college has different expectations and procedures for their own auditions. And if you're planning on completing auditions on campus, you have to be a travel agent as well, making sure you get yourself where you need to be so you can perform at your best. By the way, that audition season usually happens during the winter, so you also have to be a bit of a meteorologist and be able to plan accordingly to allow for weather-related travel issues. For the students who go through the whole conservatory audition process, the good news is that if they manage to complete all of their applications, hit all the deadlines, and perform their repertoire to the colleges' specifications, college will probably seem easy by comparison! It's a great crucible they get to fire themselves in.

And I'd also add that students, as much as they are being evaluated by the colleges, should remember that they have some power and agency in this process themselves, because they are also evaluating the colleges as they're going through the process. I think students sometimes forget that there is power in being a prospective student.

CARMINA CIANCIULLI
Assistant dean for undergraduate studies and student affairs, Tyler School of Art,
Temple University

➡ Each art school has a unique set of admission requirements. Some schools weigh the portfolio review heavily and will admit students with weaker grades and test scores who have strong portfolios. Schools with more competitive admission will review the academic component more carefully. Liberal arts colleges and universities with art schools or art departments generally hold art students to the same academic requirements for admission to the university as all other students, despite the results of a portfolio review. In some cases a borderline student may gain admission based on strong portfolio work, but at other schools, like Tyler, students must meet the same academic standard as regular admission to the university.

We strongly recommend a personal interview whenever possible as part of the process. An interview helps us evaluate how a student articulates ideas, gauge a student's passion and enthusiasm, and ask questions about materials, educational experience, and ideas/inspiration that went into the portfolio of work. The portfolio and academic credentials, rather than recommendations, extracurricular activities, or any supplemental materials, are the best gauge of a student's preparation for a professional arts school.

such as design, theater, creative writing, and other disciplines. Typically held in the fall, these events allow students to meet one-on-one with admission officers from colleges, universities, art schools, and conservatories to learn about their programs, entrance policies, financial aid, and audition requirements. Check the NACAC website for schedules and lists of participating schools, and also see our advice on attending college fairs in Chapter 8 for tips on making the most of the experience.

National Portfolio Days

Whether arts will be the focus of your studies or simply considered as part of a regular application process, take advantage of help along the way. For example, visual artists—at any point during high school—may want to participate in National Portfolio Day Association events (see portfolioday.net). Covering a wide range of disciplines from architecture to animation and photography to Web design, these events feature representatives from art schools and college or university art departments who review student portfolios, offer feedback, and are available to discuss your work and plans for further study. High school sophomores and juniors are encouraged to attend in order to learn how to strengthen their portfolios.

Additional Resources

- The National Association of Schools of Art and Design at nasad.arts-accredit.org
- The National Association of Schools of Music at nasm.arts-accredit.org
- National Unified Auditions at unifiedauditions.com
- National Association of Schools of Dance at nasd.arts-accredit.org

CHAPTER 19

Students with Special Circumstances

Some students applying to college have special circumstances that may impact the admission process. In this chapter, we discuss the extra considerations required of students in the following situations:

- Students with learning differences or physical or emotional challenges
- Home-schooled students
- Undocumented students
- Legacies and children of major donors

STUDENTS WITH LEARNING DIFFERENCES OR PHYSICAL OR EMOTIONAL CHALLENGES

For students with a learning difference or physical or emotional challenge, making the right match with a college is particularly important. In the application process, these students must ensure that the colleges on their list provide the support and accommodations they require, as well as determine when and how to disclose any need for services.

Selecting a College

When creating the list of colleges to which you may apply, a student's learning difference or emotional or physical challenge should not be the primary criterion for determining the best fit. First, look for fit in general—for example, curriculum, campus culture, or geography—and then make sure the colleges on your list have the programs that will offer the support you need.

Some schools provide only the minimum services and accommodations necessary to conform to the law. Others see providing assistance as part of their mission and go a step further with comprehensive programs designed to support students. Some of the schools with highly comprehensive programs charge a fee for services. In addition, schools with very structured programs require students to submit a separate application. All schools are governed by the Americans with Disabilities Act, but each school has its own policy regarding the criteria students must meet to receive accommodations.

In determining if a specific college offers the support you need, you will use some of the same tools and strategies we recommended in researching an initial list of colleges—the college websites, campus visits, and talking with current students.

One sign of a school's resources and commitment to students with learning differences or physical or emotional challenges is how easily information can be found on their website. Such information can usually be found under "student services," "academic services," or "accessible education." Look for lists of services and special technologies, such as Kurzweil readers, as well as documentation requirements. At each college to which you are considering applying, you should visit the office that oversees assistance, often called the Office for Accessible Education or Office of Disability Services, and any dedicated facilities such as learning centers or handicapped-equipped dormitories.

Here are some questions you may want to ask, if this information is not available on the website:

- **Learning differences**
  - What type of support is available for students with learning differences?
  - What technologies and equipment do you have available for students with learning differences?
  - Is there a learning resource center and what are its hours of operation?
  - Is the program supported by a full-time professional staff?

- Can students with learning differences obtain counseling for registration and course selection?
- What kind of tutoring is available and who does it—peers or staff?
- Must the student request tutoring?
- Is there a separate application required to obtain services?
- Is there a fee for services?

- **Physical challenges**
  - How many physically challenged students attend the college?
  - What technology and equipment do you have available for physically challenged students?
  - Are classrooms accessible for the physically challenged?
  - What living arrangements do you have for physically challenged students?
  - What are the hours of the Office for Accessible Education?
  - What kind of medical care is available?

- **Emotional health**
  - What kind of mental health staff is available through the student health center?
  - Is individual counseling available?
  - Is medication evaluation provided?
  - What are the fees for services?

Resources for Students

The following reference guides provide detailed information about colleges that provide services for students with learning differences:

- *K&W Guide to Colleges for Students with Learning Disabilities or Attention Deficit/ Hyperactivity Disorder,* by Marybeth Kravets and Imy Wax

- *The College Sourcebook for Students with Learning and Developmental Differences,* by Midge Lipkin

In addition, preliminary information about whether a college provides services for learning differences, physical challenges, or emotional challenges can be found here:

- *The College Handbook,* issued by the College Board

Disclosure

A student's decision to disclose a physical challenge, learning difference, or matter of emotional health in the application process will depend on a variety of factors, including her own wishes, whether the challenge has affected her grades or extracurricular participation, and whether accommodations will be required during the application process or once enrolled at college. Colleges cannot deny a student solely on the basis of her learning difference or physical challenge. A student will be denied if she does not meet admission criteria or is unable to be successful at the college even with accommodation.

Disclosure is voluntary and confidential. It is up to you. Disclosing a disability or psychological issue can be an emotional matter for a student and his family. Not all students are comfortable talking about the challenges they face. But we advise you, in general, to disclose any learning difference, physical challenge, or psychological issue if it is essential to a college's understanding of your academic and/or social and extracurricular background. You will almost always benefit from being

Testing Accommodations

Both the ACT and SAT provide special accommodations for students with learning differences and physical or emotional challenges. The testing services require documentation to determine eligibility. Check their websites at act.org and sat .collegeboard.org for information about applying for special accommodations, such as wheelchair-accessible facilities or extended time. For more information, see Chapter 7.

Some students may decide to apply to schools where they don't have to submit test scores. A list of these schools can be found at fairtest.org.

honest and forthright about your life in the application process.

It is always better to disclose than to have a college guessing about a change in high schools or performance gaps such as a drop in grades. For example, if your grades dropped because you experienced an episode of depression, disclosing and explaining it will help the college understand that you weren't just goofing off that semester but were struggling with some problems you have since mastered. As we've stressed throughout this book, the colleges are most interested in understanding your authentic self—who you are in the context of your life.

Our best advice? Disclose a physical or emotional challenge or learning difference in your application if:

- It has caused a disruption in your education.
- It affected your academic record.
- It has impacted your involvement in social or extracurricular activities.

- You believe it has influenced who you are as a person in a way that you want admission officers to understand.

You may choose to explain such circumstances in one of your essays or the section on the Common Application titled "Additional Information." Disclose what your challenge is, when it was diagnosed, how it impacted you, and what you have done in order to be as successful as possible throughout high school. The tone can be matter-of-fact—along the lines of "This is something else you should know about me when you review my application."

If you choose not to disclose during the application process, we urge you to disclose as soon as you've accepted an offer from a college and sent in your deposit, and no later than June 1. You cannot obtain services until you disclose, and a college must be prepared in order to serve you well. Accommodations, such as sign language interpreters, tutor assignments, or scheduling classes

Documentation

Documentation is not usually required for admission unless a student is requesting special consideration in the application process or applying to a program that requires a separate application. If a student discloses a learning difference, physical challenge, or emotional challenge that has had a particular impact on her test scores or grades, the admission office might request testing or diagnostic documentation. Guidelines for additional documentation should be available on the colleges' websites.

in handicapped-accessible buildings, will be accomplished most easily with plenty of advance notice. Medical referrals and emergency protocols for students with serious illnesses are likewise best planned early. And many times it's helpful to a student's transition to meet with someone from the college over the summer, before arriving on campus.

HOME-SCHOOLED STUDENTS

Colleges recognize there is more than one path to obtaining a high school education. Students who are home-schooled should follow the advice in previous chapters of this book about courses, testing, recommendations, and other steps in the application process. In addition, you will need to take further action at certain stages of the application process so that admission officers can understand the framework and context of your academic life and social experience.

In this section, we will explain how home-schooled students can best provide that background in the application process. For each step listed here, you will want to both review the related chapters in this book and check the websites of colleges you are interested in to understand their recommendations and requirements.

The Academic Record: Grades and Courses

The lack of a conventional high school transcript can present a challenge for colleges in determining the rigor of your classes and assessing your grades. Your curriculum must meet or exceed the preparatory course requirements of the schools to which you are applying. Your transcript, whether or not it is from a home-school "umbrella" program, should include a detailed outline of the classes you have completed—with grades and credit summaries—as well as any classes in progress. We highly recommend providing a brief descriptive summary of the content for each course, as well as an explanation of the curricular approach, grading philosophy, and additional materials such as course bibliographies and/or syllabi.

If you have been enrolled in individual classes at a local high school, college, or university, report that on the application form itself and send official transcripts from those schools or colleges.

Extracurricular Activities

Colleges understand that extracurricular opportunities are different for home-schooled students. Admission offices don't have specific requirements, but they do want to see that you have made use of whatever opportunities you've had to add to your personal growth and participate in the community beyond your home environment.

Options for home-schooled students may include:

- Activities at the local high school, such as band or debate
- Part-time employment
- Volunteer work at a church or in politics
- Community organizations, such as Scouting
- The arts, including community theater or orchestra
- Sports via club teams or through organizations such as the YMCA

Testing

Some colleges place increased emphasis on testing for home-schooled applicants or may even require further testing, such as additional SAT Subject Tests. Check the testing requirements carefully for each college you are interested in.

Interviews

Interviews are a way for the admission office to get to know a home-schooled student better. On-campus or alumni interviews are often recommended and may be required. We encourage you to schedule an interview if it is offered.

Recommendations

Letters of recommendation provided by teachers at traditional public and private schools have the ring of objectivity because those teachers are able to compare a candidate to others they have taught. Since recommendations from home-schooled students usually come from parents as the primary instructors, they may be seen as lacking objectivity. As a result, we strongly advise you to send at least one recommendation from someone other than a parent—and preferably from someone in a teaching or learning environment. If you have taken a class at a secondary school or college, we encourage you to ask the teacher of that course to be one of your recommenders. You may also want to provide a letter from a coach, employer, clergy member, tutor, or volunteer coordinator.

The Application

Home-schooled students may apply to schools using the Common Application, another electronic application, or a school's unique form. The Common Application collects additional information from home-school supervisors on the School Report (see Chapter 4). Colleges and universities that have their own unique application form may require a supplement to be filled out by the home-school supervisor. Information asked for may include an explanation of the home-schooling philosophy, a summary of instruction, an explanation of how the student was evaluated, and why home schooling was chosen.

In addition, it is our best advice that home-schooled students submit a brief statement along with the application that explains their reasons for and experience with home schooling, including:

- How and why your family chose home schooling
- Your learning approach and process
- What, if any, choices you had to make in opting for home schooling

"Undocumented" students are students who are foreign-born and entered the United States without legal documentation or have overstayed their visas.

Because of these additional considerations, home-schooled students may want to start early to understand which schools might be a good fit so they will have time to plan for additional requirements the colleges may have, such as scheduling an interview. Check the website of each school to which you may apply or call the admission office and ask them about their policies for home-schooled students.

◉ Best Advice

Mary Chase, associate vice provost for enrollment, Creighton University, has this advice for home-schooled students.

➡ **The biggest concern for a home-schooled student is often "Are we home-school friendly?" We try not to treat home-schooled students any differently in the evaluation than if they were attending a private or public accredited high school. We want to understand what they're able to do academically but also socially. We want to make sure they're going to fit in. The best advice we can give them is to have a solid group of recommenders and follow an established curriculum.**

UNDOCUMENTED STUDENTS

If you are an undocumented student, you can attend college in the United States. There is no federal law that says you cannot attend college. You will have additional challenges, but these challenges should not deter you from applying to and attending college.

Undocumented students will have to be especially committed to preparing themselves for college. Follow the advice in previous chapters of this book about grades, classes, activities, testing, and all other steps (paying particular attention to tips for underresourced students). In that way, the application process is the same for undocumented students as it is for any other student. But there are some additional challenges you will need to be aware of:

- You will need to know how to complete the application without a Social Security number or with the Social Security number provided to you if you are a Deferred Action for Childhood Arrivals (DACA) beneficiary. (DACA grants temporary administrative relief from deportation and a work permit to undocumented youth who meet certain requirements. Information can be found at uscis.gov.)

- You should be informed about your state's residency policies with regard to undocumented students. You may be eligible to pay in-state tuition.
- Undocumented students, even those who have been granted deferred action status under DACA, do not qualify for federal government aid, but you may be eligible for state aid and many private scholarships.

Build a Network

All students need to be advocates for themselves in the college admission process, but this is particularly important for undocumented students. You will need to get comfortable asking for help and start early to build a network of individuals you can call on.

Reach out to people you feel at ease with and who you believe will be strong advocates for you. For example, start with a teacher or counselor who is familiar with your academic record, commitments, and interest in college. At the same time, reach out to other undocumented students who are now attending college. They've made it work, and their experience and advice can be invaluable.

Keep in mind that not everyone is aware of the circumstances and legal rights of undocumented students. So if you do encounter an individual who is negative or discouraging,

There is no federal or state law that prohibits the admission of undocumented immigrants to U.S. colleges, public or private. You do not need to worry about revealing your immigration status when filling out admission or financial aid applications. It is crucial that you do not lie about your citizenship status on any application form.

don't let that be a barrier that stops you— even if that person is a counselor, teacher, or admission officer. Move on and find somebody else who can help you. There is a great deal of misinformation out there. Also, the situation for undocumented students is in a state of flux; information can change from week to week or month to month. You have the right to go to college. Be persistent. Stay optimistic. Make it happen.

Researching Your Possibilities

Information about a college's policies on undocumented students may be available on the school's website. Private colleges may classify undocumented students as "international," so check that section of the website for any additional information. If a school's policies are unclear, call the admission office and ask to speak with an admission officer in charge of diversity or multicultural recruitment. And ask your high school counselor about other resources, such as local organizations that provide counseling for first-generation college students.

You will need to work closely with your high school counselor and the schools you are interested in to understand the laws and policies of your state and each school to which you may apply. In most states undocumented

Virtually all college admission officers will value and be sensitive to diversity. Usually one or more are assigned specifically to coordinate the work of the office in understanding and being responsive to the unique issues of students from underrepresented racial or ethnic backgrounds. These admission officers will be particularly attuned to challenges faced by undocumented students of all backgrounds.

students can attend public colleges or universities, but in some the schools may have policies that bar students without documentation from attending. Undocumented students in those states will want to look at private colleges—in their own state and in other states—and public colleges in states where undocumented students can enroll.

Completing the Application

You do not have to worry about revealing your citizenship status specifically when filling out college applications. The confidentiality of your educational records—application and financial aid forms—is guaranteed by the Family Educational Rights and Privacy Act (FERPA), which covers both high schools and colleges.

Information about your citizenship, Social Security number (SSN), and immigration status can be requested, but it is not required for your application to be considered. When completing your applications, leave this information blank. Do *not* lie or misrepresent yourself by providing a false SSN or claiming citizenship.

You will also need to know how to answer questions about residency, which, for example, may influence your eligibility for in-state tuition. The information colleges require regarding your residency will differ from school to school, so you will have to talk to the college directly. Some states have passed laws providing undocumented students with a path to citizenship that includes their eligibility for in-state tuition rates under certain conditions.

Call the admission office and ask to speak with the admission officer who works with diversity or multicultural recruitment. Once you have been connected with that person, you might say, "I am a high school student who has grown up in the United States, but I was born in another country and immigrated here." The admission officer should be able to address questions about residency, tuition, financial aid, and the college's general policies about undocumented students.

These inquiries are absolutely appropriate, and most knowledgeable admission officers will respond candidly and sympathetically about their requirements, your options, and any other information you need. If you are nervous about sharing information with the colleges, you could ask someone who knows your situation, such as a teacher or counselor, to make these phone calls with you.

The decision as to whether to disclose your undocumented status in the application is an important one. Many students feel their status is central to their identity and wish to share that story in the personal essay. It is recommended that you talk with the college about whether or not they recommend doing so. Some colleges offer scholarships specifically for undocumented students, so disclosure would be necessary, but it is not a decision to be taken lightly. Students who have been granted deferred action status may feel more comfortable in disclosing.

If, during the application process, an undocumented student is coded as an international student, it can then generate a list of additional forms needed for application completion, such as a Verification of Finances. These forms are necessary in order for a college to issue a student visa. However, as an undocumented student, you are ineligible for a student visa and therefore not required to submit this extra documentation. Do not assume that this means you cannot be considered for admission. Contact the director of diversity or multicultural recruitment to assist you in getting your application back on track. If you encounter difficulty, enlist the help of your high school counselor.

Paying for College

Federal and state aid are not generally available to undocumented students. So you will need to think carefully about cost—and not just tuition but room and board, travel, books, and other expenses.

At public colleges and universities in most states, undocumented students must pay the higher tuition charged to out-of-state students, even though they are in-state residents. Some states *do* allow undocumented students to qualify for in-state tuition if they reside in the state, have attended high school in the state for a specific period (one to four years), and graduated or received a GED in the state. Also, in addition to providing in-state tuition, some states—for example, California, Illinois,

Five Secrets to Success for Undocumented Students

From Katharine Gin, co-founder and executive director of Educators for Fair Consideration (E4FC):[24]

1. Get comfortable asking for help. You can't do this alone.
2. Find older students who can be role models and mentors. They may just be a few years older than you!
3. Form strong relationships with teachers and mentors with whom you can speak honestly and openly about your challenges.
4. Be creative. Be entrepreneurial. Don't take no for an answer.
5. Believe in yourself. Know that you have value to your family, your community, your classmates, and your country.

and Texas, currently—provide undocumented students access to state financial aid. For further information about state policies check the websites of the National Immigration Law Center at NILC.org or the uLead Network at thenationalforum.org.

Private colleges and universities set their own financial aid policies for undocumented students, so some will offer aid and others will not. You will need to check with each school. Your high school college or guidance counselor can help you do this. Also check the website of each college in which you are interested. If financial aid for undocumented students is not addressed, call the admission office and ask to speak with an admission counselor responsible for diversity or multicultural recruitment.

The process of applying for financial aid—forms, deadlines, and other requirements—will be different at each school, both public and private. Talk with each of the colleges to which you are applying about what is required for submission. Some colleges may ask you to fill out the Free Application for Federal Student Aid (FAFSA) in writing and mail it to them for the purpose of determining scholarship eligibility. This is not recommended and you should ask the college if it is permissible to complete an institutional financial aid application. Also, some states, such as California, may ask undocumented students to fill out a separate financial aid application to determine eligibility for state aid. See further advice about paying for college in Chapter 16.

Explore your immigration case

Undocumented students often assume their immigration status cannot be changed. In fact, many qualify for an immigration remedy and might not even know it. On June 15, 2012, Deferred Action for Childhood Arrivals (DACA) was announced. DACA calls for a two-year temporary administrative relief from deportation for certain undocumented young people who came to the United States as children and have pursued education or military service. Those who qualify can obtain a Social Security number, a driver's license, and a work permit. DACA is just one of many immigration remedies that you may qualify for. Find out more about DACA at immigrationequality.org. Also, since the announcement of DACA some states have changed their laws to grant in-state tuition to DACA recipients, and DACA has also widened the number of scholarships available to undocumented students.

Resources

Here are some websites that offer good guidance and helpful information for undocumented students preparing for college, including listings of scholarships available to students without SSNs:

- Educators for Fair Consideration (E4FC) at e4fc.org
- National Immigration Law Center at nilc.org
- Mexican American Legal Defense and Education Fund at maldef.org
- Asian American Legal Defense and Education Fund at aaldef.org
- The Illinois Association for College Admission Counseling at iacac.org/undocumented

 Best Advice

Vince Cuseo, vice president for admission and financial aid, Occidental College, offers this advice to undocumented students:

➡ **Undocumented students should begin preparing for the possibility of college early in high school, with the same intent that their fellow college-bound students sitting to the left and right of them would approach the process. Be optimistic, but recognize that you will have to do a bit more front-end research to gain an understanding of what your possibilities may be.**

It's not simple to do, particularly since you may not have easy access to the information, resources, and expertise to understand what the possibilities are at both public and private

colleges and universities. But there is quite a bit of information available on the Internet about your rights, scholarship opportunities, and financial aid. Also, keep in mind that the options and possibilities available to you may change on a yearly basis. Keep current about what these opportunities may be as you apply to college.

LEGACIES AND CHILDREN OF MAJOR DONORS

Being the child of alumni or a major donor can play a role in an admission decision at some colleges and universities.

Legacies

"Legacies" are what colleges and universities call the offspring of alumni, and some schools give special consideration to such applicants. These schools value the long-term relationships and loyalty that arise from attendance by multiple generations of a family.

Other schools explicitly state that legacy status provides no special consideration in the admission process. Colleges that do not recognize legacy status have a number of reasons for taking that stance. For public colleges and universities, in particular, there can be a mandate of public accountability that calls for an egalitarian approach to the citizens of that state overall, without regard to family history.

Among colleges and universities that do recognize legacy, each school has its own policy for determining such status. Usually it's limited to the son or daughter of a graduate. At some schools, however, applicants will be considered legacies if a parent or grandparent is an alum, or if a sibling already attends. Typically, alumni need not be donors for an applicant's legacy status to be valued in the admission process.

You may not be aware of the details of your immigration status. If you have questions about this, have as candid a conversation as possible with your parents so that you know where you stand. Your family may wish to get a comprehensive analysis from a reliable immigration attorney. You may decide to share details about your status with your high school guidance counselor, college counselor, or teachers. Your counselors and teachers cannot legally inquire about your immigration status, but you can choose to discuss it with them at your own initiative. You will need to decide what you feel safe sharing and with whom.

Furthermore, some colleges and universities grant legacy status to those with degrees from either the undergraduate college or a graduate or professional school. At others, only an undergraduate degree confers legacy status when the student is applying as an undergraduate. It is policy at a few colleges that for a legacy to receive extra consideration in the admission process, that college must be the student's first choice and the student must apply under an early decision or early action plan.

In the colleges' admission decisions, legacy status can confer anything from a slight benefit to a more significant advantage. The influence legacy status may have at some schools is often called a "legacy tip"—all things being equal, being a legacy will tip you in. In other words, of students who are similarly strong in that school's applicant pool, a legacy will be preferred. Another way to understand this is that being a legacy may—if you are sitting on the fence within an applicant pool—tip you over into being admitted. But whether it's a light nudge or a heavy shove off the fence, it will not place you on that fence to begin with; only your grades, scores, essays, character, and all other aspects of your application can do that.

That said, there are some colleges and universities (and it is a small number) that value legacy status a great deal and will weigh it more heavily in the admission decision. At those schools, the advantage created by legacy status can actually cause a student to be considered for admission when he wouldn't have been otherwise. But even then a legacy would not be admitted if the admission office believed he would not thrive on that campus.

Legacy status never ensures acceptance or rules out rejection. It would be a significant error to assume that all legacies at an institution are there because of a legacy tip, or for that matter that being a legacy factored in the admission decision at all. The reality is that many legacies have a natural affinity for the school where their parents went. They've been brought up knowing the place and its values and have been aware for many years of what it takes to go there and have been working toward that.

Only the college or university itself can tell you how legacies are treated in the admission process. You should ask them about their policy if you are a legacy.

Major Donors

Colleges depend on philanthropy for support, and being the child of a major donor can carry weight in the admission decision at many schools. But, parents, you need to understand that the definition of "major donor" usually means you've made a highly significant gift—on the order of having donated enough to have a building named after you, rather than just giving a sum of money each year, even if that sum has been quite generous. This is not to dismiss the importance of the annual gift to your alma mater. Such donations are the lifeblood of schools. But in the context of admission, in most cases a donation must be unusually substantial to have an impact.

If you believe you fall into this category, typically the parents—not the student—would initiate contact with the development office. If you are in fact a significant donor to that college or university, there is usually a member of the development staff with whom you have already been working. Start with that person and ask them whether there is anything you or they can do to help bring your student's application to the attention of the admission staff.

The development office itself cannot offer you admission—only the admission office can do that. But the development office can sometimes weigh in on a small number of applicants each year. How much difference this makes, a lot or a little, depends on the college and—to be realistic—the amount you have given.

Because it is rare for universities to receive the kind of donations that really make a difference in the admission decision, the number of students on campus who are there because of such donations is quite small. And as with legacies, it would be unwise to assume that all students who happen to have their last name on a building are there only through some sort of favoritism; most are not.

However this process may look from afar, it is in fact a reciprocal valuing of those who have valued the college. It is not a barter transaction or a quid pro quo, and it is unseemly and counterproductive to treat it as such if you intend to make a significant donation. It is typically unwise to give a large amount the year your student is applying, or to suggest that if your student is admitted you will put up the school's new science center. Most development officers, should you try to make a gift the year your student is applying, will ask that you wait until an admission decision has been made. Better yet, wait to even bring up the subject until after the admission decision is made—and even then, wait a reasonable amount of time so that there is no possible intimation that your gift and your child's admission were linked.

CHAPTER 20

International Students

"Students learn as much from their peers as they do from their professors. We really want our students to be exposed to the ideas, thoughts, and opinions of students who come to study here from abroad and who have experienced a very different view of the world than the one our U.S. students might have."

—Kelly Walter, associate vice president and executive director of admissions, Boston University

International students are actively recruited by many U.S. colleges who value the global worldview they bring to a campus, adding richness and diversity to the experience of a school's community. In this section, we will discuss what students applying from abroad need to know.

NON-U.S. CITIZENS APPLYING FROM OVERSEAS

Non-U.S. applicants must understand two important distinctions between American colleges and universities and those in most other countries:

- American colleges are dominated by the liberal arts rather than professional training. While there are a small number of professional programs for undergraduate students, including schools of design, architecture, and engineering, most U.S. undergraduate colleges and universities offer a liberal arts education. This means that students study broadly across a variety of disciplines while concentrating on one—and sometimes two—particular fields of study. Students are encouraged to explore and experiment before deciding on the course of study they will pursue in depth. The goal is to gain the

Checkpoints ✍

✔ U.S. colleges are distinguished by the emphasis on a liberal arts education and the holistic process of admission.

✔ The process of applying to U.S. colleges begins earlier than the process in most other countries.

✔ Understanding why a college is a good fit is as important for international students as other applicants.

✔ International students will have to complete some additional steps in the application process—in particular, testing, supplements, translation of documents, and certification of finances.

✔ There is limited financial aid for international students, which may constrain your options.

ability to reason critically and analytically, communicate powerfully in both writing and speaking, understand how to examine a question within multiple frameworks, and prepare for a lifetime of learning and growth.

- There is no national standard for applying to college in the United States. In many other countries, a national exam plays a definitive role in the admission process. This is not how admission decisions are made by American colleges. The SAT and ACT are important, but they are not part of a national college placement plan under which you will be admitted if your score is sufficient. There is a wide array of requirements for admission, including letters of recommendation, essays, extracurricular activities, school reports, and testing. Each college and university typically asks for slightly different information from applicants. You will have to be vigilant in learning what each college will ask of you.

International applicants apply for admission basically in the same way as U.S. citizens applying from American high schools. Read the previous chapters in this book carefully and follow their advice. The major difference in your application process is that there is limited financial aid for international students, so your options may be fewer if cost is an important factor. In addition, you will need to take further steps at several stages of applying. We'll walk you through these steps, emphasizing what international students most need to know.

Researching

Finding colleges that are a good fit is as important for international students as it is for American students. While there are a handful of U.S. colleges and universities you will have heard of because they are well known around the world, there are hundreds—thousands—of excellent colleges in the United States. Keep an open mind as you conduct your research. You will need to learn enough about yourself and the colleges to identify schools that are a good fit, and then convey that fit in your applications.

Research is particularly important for international applicants because you will likely be choosing a college sight unseen, relying, for example, more on the Internet than personal visits to understand what a campus is like. Check into opportunities to talk by phone or video conference with international students on campus, as well as admission officers. Many colleges can arrange this for you. Not only will this type of interaction help you determine if the college is right for you, but it can also have an effect on the admission decision, because it is a welcome demonstration of interest.

In addition to the resources discussed in Chapter 8, EducationUSA offices are a good resource for international applicants. Operated by the U.S. Department of State, these offices provide advice and information about applying to American colleges. They are affiliated with the offices of U.S. embassies or the United States Information Service in most major cities in the world. Information can be found at educationusa.state.gov.

Academic Record

In addition to transcripts of your grades and courses, U.S. colleges may require copies of school diplomas or certificates, results of any national examinations, or lists and descriptions of your course work. Check the website of every college

to which you are applying to understand exactly what transcripts and school reports are required and how they should be submitted. For example, American colleges typically require that documents be sent directly from the schools you have attended.

If your documents were not originally issued in English, they should be accompanied by a notarized or certified translation. Most colleges have staff responsible for international students who are familiar with the educational systems and academic credentials of countries around the world. But colleges may require that your credentials be translated and evaluated by an approved service that converts education credentials to U.S. standards by describing each certificate diploma or degree and its academic equivalency. Again, check with college websites for referral to the translation or certification services they recommend.

Testing

Although standardized tests do not play the same decisive role in admission at U.S. colleges that they do elsewhere in the world, they are still an important factor in the admission decision. International applicants should therefore plan—and plan early—for testing. The SAT and ACT may not be offered as

GET AN EARLY START

The timeline for applying to U.S. colleges typically starts much earlier than the timeline in most other countries. Start thinking about preparing to apply to U.S. colleges as early as three years before you plan to attend.

frequently in some countries, and you may have to travel to take the tests.

As you sign up for the tests, check with the websites of every college to which you will apply, in order to understand their testing requirements. Requirements will vary from college to college—some may require additional SAT Subject Tests or the writing section of the ACT. Others may not require standardized testing at all. Note: Some colleges that are test-optional nevertheless require testing for international students, so check each website with care.

If neither the SAT nor ACT is offered in your country, most colleges that require testing will still consider your application, but they will have less information with which to work. If there is a way for you to take the test, our best advice is to do so. In some countries just one of the tests—either the ACT or SAT—may be offered, and you should take whichever it is.

Colleges need to feel confident that your English-language speaking and writing skills are strong. If English is not your first language or if you are unable to take the SAT or ACT, testing in English proficiency may be required. Colleges will usually recommend a testing service such as the Test of English as a Foreign Language (TOEFL), International English Language Testing System (IELTS), Pearson Test of English (PTE), or another approved service.

Interviews

A college may or may not offer interviews for international students. If an interview is offered, it may be conducted by college representatives or alumni in your home country or with a college admission officer in the United States via a video conferencing technology. Check the college websites for their policies.

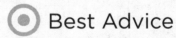

Best Advice

If an interview is offered, do it.

Recommendations

In some countries, teachers rarely write recommendations and may not be familiar with what American colleges require in a strong letter of recommendation. Students should become familiar with the Teacher Evaluation form on the Common Application and then schedule an appointment to speak with the teacher who will write the recommendation to clarify what it must accomplish. It may also be helpful for the student to provide the teacher with a written summary of the student's intellectual interests and an explanation of why the student is requesting a letter from that teacher. Certified translations must be included with letters of recommendation that were not originally written in English.

Decision Plans

Check each college for its specific requirements with regard to when international students should apply under various decision plans (see Chapter 15). Some schools have separate decision plan deadlines for international applicants or restrict decision plan options for international applicants. For example, a college may not permit applicants who are not U.S. citizens to apply early decision.

Application Forms and Supplements

Most colleges do not have a separate application for international students—they ask for the Common Application, or their own unique form. We strongly encourage you to apply online even when a college accepts a paper application, to avoid any delays with international mail. Application fees for international applicants are sometimes slightly higher than for U.S. citizens. Check the college websites.

Counselors for international applicants using the Common Application and applying from a school with a non-U.S. educational system will be asked to complete the School Report. If you don't have a counselor or an advisor for students applying to college, you could ask a tutor, housemaster, principal, or comparable school official to complete these forms. If you or your counselor has questions about the School Report, email or call the college to which you're applying. They will work with you to help you understand the application and identify who at your school might be in the best position to complete it.

Financial Aid

There is limited financial aid available to international students. Since international students are not eligible for U.S. federal aid or state grants, all scholarship monies they receive must come from private sources. Some colleges have funding available for this purpose. Many do not. Each college sets its own policies and rules regarding financial assistance. Some may offer need-based or merit aid, with some having greater amounts of funding available than others.

Obtaining aid can be a competitive process for international students at colleges that have limited funding. Keep in mind those colleges that are need-blind for international students tend to be the most competitive or highly selective schools. Therefore, while these colleges have more aid available, they are often the most difficult schools to be admitted to, whether one is applying from inside or outside the United States. Note: some colleges that are need-blind for U.S students are not need-blind for international students and may have little aid available. Check the website of each college carefully.

If you are applying for financial aid, you will be asked to submit either the CSS PROFILE application or the International Student Financial Aid Application (ISFAA). Both are available at collegeboard.org. See Chapter 16 for more information on the CSS PROFILE; the ISFAA is similar in content. Carefully research every college's website to understand their policies and requirements for eligibility, application, and deadlines.

How American Colleges Make Admission Decisions

It is important for international applicants to pay particular attention to how U.S. colleges make their admission decisions, since it is likely to be very different from the way they are made in your own country. This will require you to think differently about how you present yourself in your application. Keep in mind that the colleges want to understand not just your testing and academic ability but also your overall level of achievement, how you will participate in the classroom and with peers, how you spend your time outside of school, your leadership abilities, your writing skills, and who you are as an individual and how that will contribute to and enrich the college community. Keep this firmly in mind as you write your essays and request your recommendations.

Jean Lee, associate director of undergraduate admission at Yale University, explains:

➡ It's important for an international student applying to Yale to understand that when you come to Yale you are not only a student but also a roommate and a teammate and a participant in a discussion group. Hence our application process, though it might seem terribly drawn out and multifaceted and complicated—all those pieces are crucial in our evaluation process. We get calls from students wondering what went wrong when they weren't offered admission even though their credentials—the grades and testing—are flawless. But they need to understand the overall concepts behind our evaluation. For example, if a student is more used to the U.K. system, where an essay is a statement of academic intent, they may write an essay of that nature, which might be perfectly fine for Oxford. But for our purposes it's not a personal essay that reveals what we want to know about a student. So knowing those differences can, again, allow students to make a better application, one that reveals to our admission committees how they might fit in on our campus.

Additional resources about the financial aid process at U.S. colleges or colleges and universities that offer financial aid for international students include:

- The Association of International Educators (NAFSA) at nafsa.org
- eduPASS: The Smart Student Guide to Studying in the USA at edupass.org

Certification of Finances

If you will not be receiving financial aid, certification of your ability to pay may be required. A form for this purpose is available from the colleges and may be called an Affidavit of Financial Support or a Certification of Finances. Some colleges will require this form be completed and submitted before your application can be reviewed; many will require it only if you commit to enrolling. Once again, check the colleges' websites.

Use of Agents

Some U.S. colleges may use agents in your country to help recruit international students.

Be aware that while these agents may have your welfare in mind, they are paid based on the number of students placed at the schools with which they have contracts, so they may not be providing entirely disinterested guidance. Our best advice? If you find yourself working with an agent, be sure you do research on your own as well as listen to the agent. Make sure all schools to which you apply—whether with the assistance of an agent or on your own—are a good fit. Find out as much as you can about a college by talking to other international students who attend and making your own connections with the admission office.

U.S. CITIZENS APPLYING FROM OVERSEAS

The process of applying will be largely the same for you as it is for noncitizen international students, with one exception: as a U.S. citizen, you are eligible to receive federal financial aid. For all other steps, follow the advice in the chapters of this book. Also check the websites of the colleges to which you will apply, in order to understand what they may require.

FOREIGN NATIONALS APPLYING FROM U.S. HIGH SCHOOLS

Foreign nationals applying to U.S. colleges from U.S. high schools will apply as American students would. However, you will be treated as an international student for the purposes of financial aid and will not be eligible for state or federal aid. In addition, be sure you understand your visa or green card status prior to beginning the admission process (if relevant,

see the section on undocumented students in Chapter 19).

Follow the advice in other chapters in this book while applying. In addition, we encourage you to take the SAT Subject Test in your primary language, since this may underscore your ability to add to the global experience of a campus. And if English is not your primary language, think about taking one of the English-language proficiency examinations such as TOEFL, IELTS, or PTE.

QUESTIONS INTERNATIONAL STUDENTS MAY WANT TO ASK

- What is your admit rate for international applicants?
- What is your admit rate for international applicants from my country?
- Do you have financial aid for international applicants?
  - How many international students will you be able to fund in the coming year?
  - Do you cap the amount of aid offered an individual international student?
- What support services do you offer international students?
- Do you have supplementary English-language courses?
- Is there a special orientation for international students?
- How active is the international student organization on your campus?
- Where do international students go on school holidays?
- Would it be possible for me to Skype with an international student from my country?
- When international students leave or transfer out, what are the reasons?

FROM THE DESK OF THE DEAN

Advice for International Students

CHRISTOPHER WATSON

Dean of undergraduate admission, Northwestern University

➡ International students bring a wonderful perspective to a college campus—where they're coming from can drive an intellectual conversation, an extracurricular activity, or a social event in a direction that many U.S. students aren't used to. When we recruit and admit international students, we are looking for students from diverse backgrounds—from different parts of the world, different countries, and different continents. Just think of the conversations in the dorms late at night when you have students not only from Chicago and Texas but also from Brazil and South Africa. The different perspectives international students bring to campus make Northwestern a far more interesting place.

KELLY A. WALTER

Associate vice president and executive director of admissions, Boston University

➡ We recognize that an international applicant's experience is different from that of an American student. It's therefore important to review their application in the context of their experience, their culture, their country, and their educational system. They may have a perception that what is valued in their country may not be understood or valued in our admission process, and that couldn't be further from the truth. We value the experience they have and what they will bring, and we will make sure we evaluate their credentials as such.

It's important for an international student to understand that an admission decision is primarily an academic decision. Therefore, we are most interested in a student's overall level of academic achievement. We are looking for students who are highly motivated to succeed and who we feel confident will thrive in our classrooms. We are also looking for students we feel confident will enrich our community and will be successful, and this decision will be driven by their secondary school transcript.

We are very knowledgeable about the educational systems throughout the world. We understand that an international student's course work may not parallel exactly what we might typically see in an American school transcript. If a student is applying from a country and an educational system we're not familiar with, then we will seek outside advice to make sure that we are making fair and thoughtful and informed decisions.

PAMELA HORNE

Associate vice provost for enrollment management and dean of admissions,
Purdue University

➡ One of the most important things for international students is to do their homework early—to make sure they've taken the TOEFL in plenty of time to get the information to the schools they're applying to, to carefully understand if other test scores are required of international students or not. There are some schools that will not waive SAT/ACT requirements for international students. There are others that don't necessarily require it but would recommend it.

Similarly, depending on how a school works with family financial statements and financial-resource statements, begin gathering that information sooner rather than later. We have literally thousands of international applicants at Purdue, and I would say that those at the most serious disadvantage are those who don't have all their credentials together and in our hands by January. Planning ahead is extremely important.

International students are also not as likely to have counselors and access to advisors who know about the hidden gems, as it were, in American higher education. A greater proportion of international students are more likely to just go down the list in *U.S. News* and not understand the diversity of institutions in the United States that deliver a really high-quality education. So I think international applicants need even more information to understand fit, opportunities for engagement, and moving beyond only the few most well-known American universities.

JARRID WHITNEY

Executive director of admissions and financial aid, California Institute of Technology

➡ International students need to plan ahead, especially with regard to requirements and deadlines. Our requirements are very specific at Caltech. It doesn't matter where you're coming from in the world—you're expected to meet those requirements, especially in the math-science core and testing expectations, coming out of high school. We don't bend at all on them. So international students have to hit those requirements by the time they apply or at least while in the process of applying.

And if you have to get your information and records translated, work with a resource that is already recommended by the schools you're applying to. You shouldn't be scrambling after the deadline to try to get your documents translated.

International students should also always ask early on the front end of the process about financial assistance, if any, offered by the schools. Sometimes students apply, and if the school doesn't ask about their financial situation on the front end, students hope that they can get in and then figure out the finances afterward. Don't wait until you've been admitted to figure out this important aspect of attending college.

Finally, my best advice for international students is the same as my advice for all domestic students. We preach so much to our domestic students about finding the right fit. But I'm not sure if this fit conversation or philosophy comes up as much for students coming from abroad, and it should.

REBEKAH WESTPHAL
Associate director of undergraduate admission, Yale University

➡ The most important piece of our evaluation process in general is context. And that's no different for international students. The context of their schooling, the context of their background, the context of their home country—they're all important. International students can sometimes, on the surface, look quite different from the domestic students we admit. But we spend a lot of time digging into how they've progressed through school and what kind of hurdles they had to get over to get to the point of even applying to Yale.

Likewise, it's important for international students to understand our evaluation process and how the university works in terms of admission and the style of education. If they really understand what liberal arts is, if they really understand what a residential college is, that will be reflected in their application. They'll be able to make a much more successful application to us if they have a good sense of how things actually work here.

CHAPTER 21

Transfers

"Transfer students bring a different seriousness to their education and lifelong goals. These students infuse the campus, every year, with change. They have new ideas. They bring a little bit more experience."

—Tom Delahunt, vice president for admission and student financial planning, Drake University

The admission process is generally the same for transfer students as it is for first-year applicants. So if you are applying for transfer admission, most of the advice elsewhere in this book still applies to you. In this chapter, we'll explain what students who are considering transferring need to know about the application process the second time around.

In general, colleges and universities value the diversity of background and experience that transfer students bring to a campus, and specifically allot space in their enrollment plans for them each year. In addition, many public colleges and universities have a mandate to enroll transfer students, particularly those from two-year colleges.

THE DECISION TO TRANSFER

There are a number of good reasons for transferring from one college to another. Some students may be looking for a more challenging curriculum or a specialized major. Other students may have chosen to start at a two-year college for financial reasons or for the opportunity to develop academically, and are now ready to move on. Still others may be at a school that turned out to be a poor fit, or perhaps they didn't get into their "dream school" and want to try again.

Push yourself hard to understand why you are thinking of transferring. You will be a stronger candidate if you fully understand your reasons for making a change. You will be more capable of selecting a college that is a

Checkpoints ✍

✔ Push yourself hard to understand your reasons for transferring. It will make you a stronger candidate.

✔ Look for signs of "transfer-friendly" colleges, such as articulation agreements and significant numbers of entering transfer students.

✔ The admission process is generally the same as it is for first-year applicants, with the admission decision based largely on your college academic performance.

✔ As you write your application and essays, articulate clearly and thoughtfully your reasons for transferring.

✔ Pay attention to how your course work will be evaluated for transfer.

better fit and better able to convey your reasons for making a change in your application.

When Should You Transfer?

Some colleges accept the majority of their transfer students after the freshman year of college, others after the sophomore year. Still others do not have strong policies regarding when you transfer but will try to ensure that if you are accepted, it will be possible for you to graduate in four years (including your years at your first college). Most colleges will not accept students for transfer in the senior year. You will need to check the transfer policy of every school to which you are applying.

Keep in mind that if you are transferring to a school where you were denied admission for freshman year or if you had a less than stellar academic record in high school, you might want to wait to transfer until you've established a track record that shows at least three semesters of strong performance in college.

Researching

As you research the schools where you may apply for transfer, look for those that are receptive to transfer students. Signs of a "transfer-friendly" college include:

• College outreach or programming specific to transfer students, such as a transfer orientation program.

• A significant number of entering transfers each year. There will be exceptions, but in general a significant number would be at least 5 percent of the size of the incoming freshman class. Having others who transfer in with you can be helpful as you adjust to your new home.

• Articulation agreements with other colleges that allow students to transfer with little or no loss of credit.

• A transfer student graduation rate that is close to the institution's overall graduation rate. This information is available from the admission office or on the college's website.

Is Transferring the Right Answer?

Sometimes students hit on the idea of transferring for reasons that may be short-lived or ill-advised—homesickness, romance problems, roommate issues, or general feelings of dissatisfaction. These issues often resolve with time or when a student seeks out the academic and social services colleges provide. Consider these steps before you move ahead with making a change.

- Reach out to resources at your current school—your advisor; someone in the office of the dean of students, dean of studies, or dean of freshmen; someone in the admission office; a peer mentor or residential advisor; or all of the above. Explain that you are wondering if you should transfer and why, and ask for their opinion.
- Talk to your parents about your situation.
- Try to gain a sense of the patterns or rhythms of the freshman or sophomore year. Is this a time when nearly everyone is struggling a bit? Would it be a good idea to see if you still feel this way in a couple of weeks? Or does this seem to be something specific to you? Consider alternatives to transferring—junior-year programs at other colleges and universities and overseas. If you transfer, you probably will not have these opportunities.
- Remember that wherever you go, you take yourself with you. Try to be sure you have done all you can to be happy where you are.

- Guaranteed housing for transfer students for their first year.

When researching the colleges where you may apply for transfer, pay particular attention to the schools' eligibility requirements. For example, most colleges require you complete at least one full academic year of course work before your anticipated enrollment at the transfer school. Colleges are usually very clear about such requirements, and that information can be found on the transfer section of their websites.

Also keep in mind how your course work meshes with the requirements you will face when you get to the college to which you're transferring. Check the websites of the schools you're considering to understand their graduation requirements, particularly with regard to general education and your intended major.

KNOW THE JARGON . . .

Articulation Agreements

Articulation agreements are formal arrangements that some colleges have with other colleges—typically with nearby community colleges—specifying which courses taken will be accepted for credit. Be aware that some universities change transfer requirements periodically. Stay up to date and check each school's website to see their current articulation agreements.

APPLYING . . . AGAIN

The process of applying to transfer is generally the same as it was applying the first time around. As with the regular application process, admission officers are seeking to understand who you are. They are looking for students who will succeed and stay at their college—that is, not transfer again!—and will want to see evidence of that throughout the application. Colleges are going to be most interested in understanding your motivation to transfer. Every transfer student has a story. Be sure you convey your story clearly, emphasizing why you wish to leave the school you're attending and why the college to which you're applying is a good fit. Your reasons should be compelling, well defined, positive, and mature, and they should suggest that you have done the self-reflection required to know yourself well and understand what is in your best interest.

Colleges' policies and requirements for applying as a transfer may vary from school to school, and you will need to understand the transfer process at each of the schools to which you are applying. Here are some things to keep in mind.

The Application Form

Colleges may use the Common Application, another electronic provider, or the college's own unique form for transfer applications. When you create an account for the Common Application, you will identify yourself as a transfer applicant. Check for college-specific supplements on the Common App website and the colleges' websites. Note that some colleges have a separate supplement for transfer applicants in addition to their college-specific supplement.

The Common Application will also require the following:

- **The Registrar Report.** Must be completed by your college/university registrar or appropriate dean/college official who can verify your enrollment and academic standing.
- **The Academic Report.** A recommendation form for professor, instructor, advisor, dean of students, or other official.
- **The Mid-Term Report.** It will be completed with input from each of your current college instructors, including the grades you are currently earning and general comments on your performance.
- **The Final Report.** It will be completed by your former high school counselor, principal, or other administrator.

If a college uses another form, its application packet for transfers will likely include equivalent evaluations and reports.

Time Management

As you begin the transfer application process, keep in mind that this can take a considerable amount of your time. You will need to keep track of deadlines, obtain letters of recommendation from your college instructors, and visit the dean's office to request completion of application forms. Make sure you are aware of the time management component of transferring and plan for it.

The Transcript

Your course work and GPA will likely be the most important factors in the transfer admission decision. As with freshman applicants,

Deadlines

Transfer application deadlines for students seeking to enter in the fall sometimes occur later in the year than those for freshman applicants. Expect to see deadlines beginning as early as the fall and running through the academic year, depending on the college. Schools that accept transfers for both fall and spring semesters will have separate deadlines for each. Carefully check each college's website to understand when your application is due.

a college's decisions are based largely on academic performance. For some schools, if your college academic record is strong enough, they will not weigh your high school record heavily in an admission decision. Other schools will consider both your high school and college record. The Mid-Term Report you will file with the Common Application will likely be one of the most important aspects of your application; how you are currently performing in your classes counts a great deal.

Letters of Recommendation

Most colleges want two letters of recommendation for transfer applications. You will want to ask your college professors, instructors, dean, or advisor for recommendations. Additional letters from employers or coaches may be welcome as well. Letters from former high school teachers are usually not acceptable. Check each college's website for guidelines and requirements.

Essays

The Common Application asks for a personal statement addressing your reasons for transfer-

ring and the objectives you hope to achieve. It is important to portray honestly and positively why you are transferring to a particular college and why you believe you can have the experience you seek at that school. If the college's own unique application does not request such a statement, consider sending an additional essay outlining your reasons for transferring and why you will be a good fit for that school. Remember, the colleges on the Common Application may have additional essay questions on their school-specific supplements under the My Colleges tab. If the school is using its own specific form, check for additional essays with any transfer supplement.

Interviews

Some schools offer interviews to transfer applicants, and we encourage you to take advantage of this opportunity if possible. Much of your interview will have the feel of the regular admission interviews described in Chapter 11, but there may also be some differences. Be prepared to talk about why you want to transfer and how you have grown since you applied to college as a freshman.

A few colleges *require* that prospective transfer students interview, especially those students who have had an interruption in their studies—for example, those who have completed military service. Again, check the transfer section of the website for every school to which you are applying to see what the requirements and opportunities are.

Testing

Requirements for standardized testing will vary from college to college. Some schools

Transfer of Credit

An important aspect of your transfer process will be the evaluation of prior college credits. You will need to have your course work and credits assessed to see if you will be awarded credit for your previous work. Be sure that you will be able to graduate in four years, if that is important to you.

Try to get a preliminary assessment of the colleges' policies for transfer of credit as early as possible in the application process. Guidelines and information about articulation agreements are usually available on the colleges' websites. Pay attention to major requirements, core curricula or general education requirements, and the overall number of credits required to graduate from that college, as well as specifics such as how the courses you've taken will be evaluated and how credits from quarter systems transfer into a semester system, or vice versa. If you are visiting a campus for an interview, ask your interviewer for an informal read on how your course work might be evaluated.

Some colleges send transfer students a credit assessment with the notice of admission. Other colleges might take longer to provide an evaluation but should be able to tell you which credits will be transferable prior to your sending in an enrollment deposit. Still others leave it up to you to look at their general policies, figure out whether it is possible for you to graduate in four years, and then weigh your options. If you receive an assessment from the college, read it carefully and call the admission office if you have questions.

will require you to submit scores from the SAT or ACT as well as Subject Tests. Other schools will not. You should not have to retest if your scores were reported within the last five years. Check the transfer section of the websites at each school to which you are applying to understand their testing policy.

Notification

Notification dates will vary from college to college. Some schools have rolling admission for transfer applicants, while others have definitive dates, usually in late spring.

Waitlists for Transfer Applicants

Some colleges will keep a transfer waitlist in the event that they have room to admit more students than they initially planned. There is a great deal of variation on waitlist policy from college to college. If you find yourself on a transfer waitlist, carefully read all the information the college sends you, and check with the admission office if you have further questions. See our advice on waitlists in Chapter 17.

Questions for Transfer Applicants to Ask (if Answers Cannot Be Found on the Website)

- How many transfer students apply and are admitted each year?
- What GPA do you look for in a transfer student?
- When will I find out which courses I have taken will transfer?

Financial Aid

Many colleges have financial aid for transfer students, but not all. At some schools, aid for transfer students is available but limited. Check with each school in which you are interested. If you intend to apply for financial aid, make sure you answer yes to the financial aid question on the application form. Also, pay attention to all deadlines for qualifying for financial aid. For more information, check the colleges' websites and Chapter 16.

- Can I schedule an interview during the application process?
- What is your policy on financial aid for transfer students?

- Do you have articulation agreements, and if so, with which schools?
- Do you have an orientation program for transfer students?

FROM THE DESK OF THE DEAN

Advice for Transfer Applicants

TOM DELAHUNT
Vice president for admission and student financial planning, Drake University

➡ There was a time when many college enrollment officers viewed transfer applicants as being less worthy than prospects coming directly from high school. Thankfully, that day has passed! Often, students initially choose a community college because they really do not know which area of study suits them best or they do not have the financial resources necessary to explore and experiment at a more expensive institution. Students usually come to us as transfer applicants with a singular purpose: to finish their degree and go on to whatever comes next, whether it is to further their studies at a graduate or professional school or to finally begin a career. Due to this, transfer students bring a different seriousness to their education and lifelong goals. These students infuse the campus, every year, with change. They have new ideas. They bring a little bit more experience. Chief enrollment officers are charged with shaping the campus community. When you can build a community that's diverse—in thought and actions—it creates a wonderful environment to be associated with, both as a student and a faculty/staff member. There is no doubt that transfer students bring a unique perspective to campus and are a vibrant part of our community.

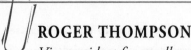

ROGER THOMPSON
Vice president for enrollment management, University of Oregon

➡ The admission process for transfer students is much more transparent. And the transfer process for publics is often less competitive—far less competitive—than the initial application process. It's much more rote—it's about your GPA and how many hours of credits you have. But the biggest issue for transfer students is assessing why it is they want to transfer and finding the right match.

Transfer students need to really assess why it is they're not happy at the school they originally chose to attend. Generally that unhappiness falls into one of three categories: academic, social, or financial. So assuming it's not financial but social, what is it that went wrong? As an example, if they're at a small liberal arts school and they feel it is confining for them, well then, a bigger university such as the University of Oregon might make some sense. So that's the first thing they need to do: assess why it is they want to transfer, and make sure that the things they're looking for in an institution are things that the transfer-in institution offers.

For the student who wasn't qualified at first, it's a little different. Those students typically don't have to assess their reasons for leaving the previous school as much. Those are kids who perhaps really wanted to go to the University of Oregon, and now they've got themselves to a level where they can make that happen.

NANCY HARGRAVE MEISLAHN
Dean of admission and financial aid, Wesleyan University

➡ Our evaluation of a transfer student is very much about "Where is this student now?" We are much more forgiving about his high school record—although some of that is dependent on how close he is to that high school record. We are much more interested in the academic work he's doing now and what he's doing extracurricularly, in terms of what he would bring both to the classroom and to the overall campus community. So there's a different mind-set with regard to a less-than-perfect record in high school for a transfer student but an expectation that a transfer student is more mature and can articulate why he wants to be at Wesleyan at a greater level of substance than an applicant in the first-year pool.

SHAWN BRICK
Associate director of admissions, University of California

➡ Students choose to go to community colleges for a variety of reasons, one of which is to either reinvent or find themselves academically. But the moment they step onto that community college campus—or even before they step onto the community college campus—

they should start narrowing their focus, in terms of what they want to study. Because transfer admission is very different from freshman admission in the sense that transfer students are arriving at our campus roughly halfway through their degree, and so by that point, we really want to see them having completed some of what we call the lower-division major preparation.

Also start to focus on campuses that you're interested in. Depending on the state you live in, you may need to prepare differently for different institutions. For example, in this state, if you're not sure you'll be admitted to the University of California campus of your choice, you may want to make sure you've done what you need to do to be admitted to a California State University campus. So prepare broadly, but do so in a way that is conscientious about the different requirements at the schools you're looking at for transfer.

JOHN LATTING

Assistant vice provost for undergraduate enrollment and dean of admission, Emory University

➡ A transfer student is, by definition, already a college student, so you know how colleges work, where the resources are. That's a luxury and you should take advantage of that. Go ask questions and get the information you need to make a good decision. For example, it's really worthwhile before committing to enroll, to have at least a phone meeting with somebody in an academic advising capacity. Put your current college transcripts in front of that person and have a conversation about where you fit in, what courses are going to be accepted for transfer, and what their forecast is for your time to degree. The decision on course acceptability varies across colleges and universities.

PART X

APPENDICES

Timeline:
The Path to College

There are many paths to college. But all of them, especially the ones leading to the more selective colleges, require preparation. Here are some general recommendations and a timeline of steps you should take.

These steps are important for all students—and all families. But the earliest steps are especially important for underresourced students, particularly those who are the first in their families to go to college. Better-resourced families are already probably doing many of these things. Whatever your background, once you've missed the early steps, it's very hard to go back and make up for them. Remember, you are your own best resource. Here's what it takes to make the most of your opportunity to apply to college.

9TH GRADE

- Parents and students, over the summer before 9th grade, browse through the first three chapters of this book. Then look ahead and read through the first few sections of Chapter 5.
- Start talking about the college search process. Think broadly about the kinds of colleges the student may consider.
- Talk about finances, so you can start thinking about paying for college and applying for financial aid.
- Students, give your best effort in all your classes.
- Get to know your high school college counselor. If you think you want to attend a selective college, make sure your counselor knows.
- Do at least one hour of homework a night. If you do not have at least one hour of homework a night, talk with your counselor and enroll in more advanced courses.
- Become involved in a couple of extracurricular activities or one activity in depth.
- Start a file where you save items such as

report cards, awards and honors, certificates, ribbons, and trophies. Keep a list of all school and community activities you participate in, including any offices you hold in these organizations, and any jobs or volunteer work.

- Visit your counselor to plan your 10th grade course schedule. Be sure you are on the college preparatory track, taking advanced or honors courses when available.
- Plan to do something productive over the summer—a summer job, volunteer work, sports, summer school, or travel. There are many options.
- Parents and students, over the summer, read Chapters 4 through 6 of this book. Also take a look at the information on Subject Tests in Chapter 7.
- Read, read, read.

10TH GRADE

- Students, if the PSAT and the ACT Aspire are offered to sophomores at your school, take them as practice.
- Do at least two hours of homework a night. If you are not doing this much, talk with your counselor and enroll in more advanced courses.
- Give your best effort in all your classes.
- Sign up for or continue your involvement in at least two extracurricular activities, or one in-depth. The number of activities you do is less important than finding one or two things you really enjoy.
- Form study groups with friends. It's fun and much of your work in college will be done in groups and teams.
- If you are struggling with a subject, sign up for peer tutoring, ask a teacher for help, or

work with a friend who excels at that subject. If you are doing well, reach out to friends who might appreciate help.

- Read Chapter 7 of this book. Start to create your testing plan.
- Research colleges on the Web to get an idea of what may interest you.
- Students, if your parents have yet to show much interest in your college plans, go to the websites of a couple colleges you like and sign up for their mailing lists. Leave a couple of brochures lying around the living room. Start a conversation.
- If there is a possibility you will be seriously engaged in music while in college, begin thinking about building an audition repertoire.
- If you want to play intercollegiate sports in college, familiarize yourself with NCAA (National Collegiate Athletic Association) requirements and policies.
- Keep updating that file of grades, awards, and so on—and keep listing your jobs and other activities.
- Visit your counselor to plan your 11th grade course schedule. Be sure you are on the college preparatory track, taking advanced or honors courses when available.
- If your school does not have a summer reading list, create your own. Need ideas? Google "summer reading lists for high school students."
- Plan your summer. Consider a job, volunteer work, sports, summer school, travel, or participation in a special precollege program. Don't forget to include some fun and downtime.
- Over the summer, read Chapters 8 and 9 of this book and the first half of Chapter 16.

Ask your parents to read the first half of Chapter 16.

- If you are thinking of participating seriously in intercollegiate athletics in college, familiarize yourself with Chapter 18 of this book over the summer.
- Read, read, read. (Did we mention this?)

11TH GRADE

- Students, do at least three hours of homework a night. If you are not, talk with your counselor and enroll in more advanced courses.
- Give your best effort in all your classes.
- Take the PSAT or ACT Aspire.
- Revisit your testing plan and make sure you are on track. Revise as necessary.
- Continue your involvement in extracurricular activities. Start new ones if something excites you. Take the initiative and consider a leadership position.
- Do a test-run visit at a local college.
- Continue to research colleges by browsing online. Enter the email addresses of any college of interest in your address book so their emails get through your spam filter.
- Attend at least one college fair.
- If a college representative of a school that interests you visits your high school or your area, sign up and attend, if possible.
- Register for the SAT or ACT in the winter or spring of junior year.
- Register for SAT Subject tests.
- Create a preliminary list of schools (fifteen to twenty). See Chapter 8.
- With your parents if possible, try out a net price calculator (see Chapter 16) to begin to understand financial aid.
- Meet with your college counselor to discuss a preliminary list of colleges. Discuss your list's range of selectivity and cost.
- Save samples of your best work for your academic/extracurricular file.
- Begin planning college visits, perhaps for over spring break.
- Read Chapters 10 and 11 of this book.
- Start thinking about summer plans. Investigate and apply for an internship, job, camp, or other program.
- Narrow your preliminary list of schools— based on visits, test scores, finances, and other factors.
- Interview at a college that is not a first-choice school for you.
- Read Chapter 12 of this book.
- Meet with your counselor to plan your senior-year course work. A fourth year of math and a laboratory science as well as a fourth year of foreign language are strongly recommended (see Appendix II for a recommended course of study). If your school does not offer an AP, IB, or other advanced curriculum, consider enrolling in a course at a local community college or university.
- Consult with your counselor about your college list and the teachers you would like to write your recommendations.
- Ask two teachers to write recommendations.
- If you do not have a summer reading list from your school, develop one. Need ideas? Ask at your local library. Bookstores often have the summer reading lists for all local high schools.
- Visit colleges over the summer if possible. Schedule interviews when possible.
- If you plan to study one of the arts in college,

complete any audition tapes, art portfolios, theater audition pieces, or other special materials required for admission to the programs you are considering. Read Chapter 18 of this book.

- If you hope to play Division I or II sports in college, register with the NCAA Eligibility Center.
- Over the summer, read Chapter 13 of this book. Begin work on your college essays. Try to have at least your Common Application essay in good shape prior to the beginning of senior year.
- Over the summer, read Chapters 14, 15, and 16 of this book. Parents, be sure to read Chapter 16—the one about financial aid.
- Once more, with feeling: read, read, read!

12TH GRADE

Fall

- Finalize your list of the eight to ten schools to which you will apply.
- Decide if you will be applying under an early decision or early action plan at any schools.
- Begin to keep track of deadlines, required essays, and financial aid requirements for the schools to which you're applying. Use the Application Deadline Organizer and the Financial Aid Deadline Organizer in this book.
- Think through the best timing for your college applications if you are considering any colleges that have rolling admission.
- Visit the rest of the colleges on your list. Schedule any interviews.
- Reread Chapter 12. Provide the teachers who are writing your recommendations with a

list of the colleges to which you're applying, deadlines for the recommendations, and any required forms.

- Provide your guidance counselor with your list of schools and deadlines for submitting transcripts, the School Report, and midyear grades.
- Finish your college essays.
- Take the SAT or ACT again, if needed.
- Register for CSS PROFILE in early fall if you are applying for financial aid.
- Reread Chapter 14. Fill out your applications—and don't wait until the last minute.
- Submit your test scores for the SAT or ACT to schools.
- Print out and save a copy of each application. Keep all copies of records, test scores, essays, and applications until at least the end of your first year in college.
- Submit applications, supplements, and fees (or, if applicable, fee waiver documents) for all colleges with fall deadlines.

Winter

- Apply for your FAFSA PIN number in December.
- Submit applications, supplements, and fees (or, if applicable, fee waiver documents) for all colleges on your list.
- Fill out and submit FAFSA, CSS PROFILE, and any other required financial aid forms. Print out copies before you press "Send."
- Review your Student Aid Report (SAR) when it arrives. If necessary, make any corrections. See Chapter 16.
- Confirm that all application and financial aid materials have been received.

- Complete college scholarship applications.
- Confirm that midyear grades are sent to the colleges.
- If accepted early decision, withdraw your applications to other schools.
- Over winter break, read Chapter 17 of this book.

Spring

- Celebrate your acceptance letters.
- Visit any college where you may enroll. Stay overnight if you can.
- Think about your summer plans. If you are expected to earn money for college over the summer, start applying for summer jobs.
- By May 1, notify your school of choice that you will attend.
- If applicable, review your financial aid offers.
- Accept those parts of the financial aid offer you will use for the school you will attend. Remember to decline other schools' offers.

- Choose the college's payment plan you will use.
- Reread Chapter 17 on "senioritis." Don't mess up.
- Confirm that the final grade report is sent to the college where you will enroll.

Summer

- Follow up on any remaining financial aid details.
- Look for summer mailings from your college about housing, orientation, course selection, and other subjects. If you will be away for a significant part of the summer, be sure the college knows where to send your mail, or arrange for your mail to be forwarded. A response from you may be required.
- Make your first payment on time.
- Complete the summer reading assigned by the college.
- Pack for college. Have a wonderful freshman year!

A Recommended Course of Study

The best preparation for success in college is taking a challenging curriculum in high school. Highly selective colleges will expect to see course work that reflects the recommended course of study below.

FOR ALL STUDENTS

- **English**—four years
  - Choose courses that give you continued practice in academic writing.
  - Look for courses that teach critical or analytical reading.
- **Mathematics**—minimum of three years, four years preferred
  - At least two years of algebra, one year of geometry, and one year of trigonometric functions.
  - Select courses that include puzzling over mathematical relationships and include word problems.
- **Foreign language**—three years of one foreign language, four years preferred.

- If you reach the AP level prior to your senior year, colleges will consider that sufficient.
- If you are fluent in a language other than English, colleges still want to see you study language in high school. Studying a language is different from speaking with friends and family.
- **Sciences**—minimum of two years of two laboratory sciences, three years preferred. Best advice: four years.
  - If four years:
    - One year each of biology, chemistry, and physics.
    - One year of advanced work in one of the above or a challenging science elective.
  - If three years:
    - One year each of biology, chemistry, and physics.
    - Or one year each of biology, chemistry, or physics and one year of advanced work in one.

- If two years:
  - Minimum one year of biology, chemistry, or physics.
- **History**—minimum two years; three years preferred.
  - If three years or more, must include at least:
    - One year of European history.
    - One year studying the history of a country or area outside Europe and the United States.
  - If two years: must include one year studying the history of a country or area outside of the United States.

- **Arts**—minimum two semesters of course work in the visual arts, music, dance, or theater.

For Students Intending to Study Engineering or the Physical Sciences

All of the Above, Plus . . .

- **Mathematics**—course work should include calculus.
- **Sciences**—course work must include one year of math-based physics or higher-level physics, and one year of chemistry.

Worksheets

It's important to get organized at the outset when applying to college—and stay organized. In this appendix, we'll give you some tools to help you so you don't get mixed up.

- For every school where you are applying, write down every deadline on the Application Deadline Organizer.
- For every school where you are applying for financial aid, write down every deadline on the Financial Aid Deadline Organizer.
- For every school where you have been offered financial aid, compare your award packages using the Financial Aid Package Evaluator.

You can download Excel and Word documents for these forms at our website at collegeadmissionbook.com.

HOW TO USE THE APPLICATION DEADLINE ORGANIZER

Fill in a column for each school that has offered you a financial aid package.

- In line A, fill in the decision plan you intend to use—regular, rolling admission, early action, early decision, or restrictive early action.
- In line B, fill in the application deadline appropriate for your decision plan.
- In line C, fill in the deadline to sign up for an interview, if necessary.
- In line D, fill in the date of your interview, if any.
- In line E, fill in the deadline for submitting college-specific writing supplements, if required.
- In line F, fill in the deadline for submitting supplementary materials, such as arts portfolios, if required.
- In lines G and H, note any other deadlines particular to your situation.
- Once you are done, transfer these deadlines into your personal or college calendar.

Application Deadline Organizer

Schools you are applying to >	Callahan State
A. Decision plan	Regular
B. Application deadline	Jan 15
C. Interview sign-up	Jan 31
D. Interview	Feb 12
E. College-specific supplements	Jan 15
F. Supplementary materials	Feb 15
G. Other notes	Audition Sign-up Jan 31
H. Other notes	Audition Feb 28

Application Deadline Organizer

Schools you are applying to >					
A. Decision plan					
B. Application deadline					
C. Interview sign-up					
D. Interview					
E. College-specific supplements					
F. Supplementary materials					
G. Other notes					
H. Other notes					

HOW TO USE THE FINANCIAL AID DEADLINE ORGANIZER

Fill in a column for each school where you are applying for financial aid.

- In line A, fill in the FAFSA deadline—remember, it can be different from school to school, but we recommend getting it in as soon after January 1 as possible.

- In line B, indicate whether the CSS PROFILE is required.
- In line C, if the CSS PROFILE is required, fill in the deadline—and note whether this is for regular admission or one of the early options.
- In line D, indicate whether other forms are required, and what they are.
- In line E, if there are other forms required, fill in their deadlines.
- In line F, indicate whether merit aid is offered.
- In line G, if merit aid is offered, fill in the deadline.
- In line H, indicate if the school has a need-blind admission policy.
- In line I, indicate if the school has a policy of meeting full calculated need.

Financial Aid Deadline Organizer

Schools where you are applying for financial aid >	Callahan State
A. FAFSA deadline	Jan. 1
B. CSS PROFILE required?	Yes
C. CSS PROFILE deadline	March 1 Regular
D. Other form required?	Yes Profile
E. Other form deadline	April 15
F. Merit aid offered?	Yes
G. Merit application deadline	February 1
H. Need-blind?	No
I. Meets full calculated need?	No

Financial Aid Deadline Organizer					
Schools where you are applying for financial aid >					
A. FAFSA deadline					
B. CSS PROFILE required?					
C. CSS PROFILE deadline					
D. Other form required?					
E. Other form deadline					
F. Merit aid offered?					
G. Merit application deadline					
H. Need-blind?					
I. Meets full calculated need?					

HOW TO USE THE FINANCIAL AID PACKAGE EVALUATOR

Fill in a column for each school that has offered you a financial aid package.

- In line A, fill in the cost of attendance.
- In line B, fill in the grant aid you were awarded.
- In line C, subtract grant aid from the cost of attendance to get your net price.
- In line D, fill in the total loans you were awarded.
- In line E, fill in the total work-study you were awarded.
- In line F, add the loans and work-study to get your total self-help.
- In line G, add the grant aid and total self-help to get your total aid.
- In line H, subtract total aid from cost of attendance to get your remaining cost.
- In line I, fill in the Expected Family Contribution (EFC) from your award letter.
- In line J, subtract the EFC from the remaining cost to get your unmet need.

- Review the discussion on page 281 in Chapter 16 to see how to compare packages across different schools.

Financial Aid Package Evaluator

Schools that offered you a financial aid package >	Callahan State
A. Cost of attendance	$20,000
B. Grant aid	$8,000
C. Net price A − B	$12,000
D. Loans	$2,250
E. Work-study	$2,000
F. Total self-help D + E	$4,250
G. Total aid F + B	$12,250
H. Remaining cost A − G	$7,750
I. Expected Family Contribution	$4,000
J. Unmet need H − I	$3,750

Financial Aid Package Evaluator

Schools that offered you a financial aid package >				
A. Cost of attendance				
B. Grant aid				
C. Net price A − B				
D. Loans				
E. Work-study				
F. Total self-help D + E				
G. Total aid F + B				
H. Remaining cost A − G				
I. Expected Family Contribution				
J. Unmet need H − I				

Resources

The following list of books and websites includes resources that we believe will be helpful to you in applying to college. Some of these resources are data-driven, such as the College Board's *College Handbook*. Others are anecdotal—for example, Unigo. Both have value. Use each appropriately.

OBJECTIVE REFERENCE GUIDES
Books
College Handbook, The College Board
Four Year Colleges, Peterson's
Four Year College Admissions Data: Index of Majors and Sports, Wintergreen Orchard House

Websites
University and College Accountability Network at ucan-network.org

National Association of Independent Colleges and Universities at naicu.edu
College Results Online at collegeresults.org

SUBJECTIVE REFERENCE GUIDES
Books
The Best 371 Colleges, Princeton Review
Big Book of Colleges, College Prowler
Colleges That Change Lives: 40 Schools That Will Change the Way You Think About Colleges, Loren Pope

Visit our website at collegeadmissionbook.com for an updated list of resources.

Colleges with a Conscience: 81 Great Schools with Outstanding Community Involvement, Princeton Review

Fiske Guide to Colleges, Edward B. Fiske

The College Finder, Steven R. Antonoff

The Insider's Guide to the Colleges: Students on Campus Tell You What You Really Want to Know, Yale Daily News Staff

Student's Guide to Colleges, edited by Jordan Goldman and Colleen Buyers

Websites

Unigo at unigo.com

College Prowler at colleges.niche.com

SUBJECTIVE MATERIALS ABOUT THE ADMISSION PROCESS
Books

College Unranked: Ending the College Admissions Frenzy, Lloyd Thacker

The Gatekeepers, Jacques Steinberg

Harvard Schmarvard, Jay Matthews

I'm Going to College—Not You!, Jennifer Delahunty, editor

Less Stress, More Success: A New Approach to Guiding Your Teen Through College, Marilee Jones and Kenneth Ginsburg

Going Geek: What Every Smart Kid (and Every Smart Parent) Should Know About College Admissions, John Carpenter

Websites

Class Struggle, blog by Jay Mathews at voices.washingtonpost.com/class-struggle

GENERAL ADMISSION INFORMATION
Websites

College.gov at college.gov

College Board at collegeboard.org

High School Counselor Week at Hscounselorweek.com

KnowHow2Go at knowhow2go.org

National Association for College Admission Counseling at nacacnet.org

The Common Application at commonapp.org

International Baccalaureate at ibo.org

Advanced Placement at collegeboard.org

College Fairs Online at collegeweeklive.com

Collegiate Choice Walking Tours Videos at collegiatechoice.com

Campus Tours at campustours.com

NACAC National College Fairs at nacacnet.org

The Campus Safety and Security Data Analysis Cutting Tool at ope.ed.gov/security

COLLEGE DATA
Websites

College InSight at college-insight.org

College Navigator at nces.ed.gov/collegenavigator

National Survey of Student Engagement at nsse.iub.edu

TESTING INFORMATION
Websites

ACT at ACT.org

SAT at sat.collegeboard.org

Fair Test at fairtest.org

TESTING INFORMATION FOR INTERNATIONAL STUDENTS
Websites

International English Language Testing System at ielts.org

TOEFL at ets.org/toefl

Pearson Test of English at pearsonpte.com

FREE PRACTICE TESTS AND TEST PREPARATION

Websites

ACT Sample Test at actstudent.org/sampletest

Number2 at number2.com

SAT College Board Practice Test at sat.collegeboard.org/practice

Spark Notes SAT Practice Test at sparknotes.com/testprep/

SPECIAL INTERESTS

Learning Differences

Books

K&W Guide to Colleges for Students with Learning Disabilities or ADHD, Marybeth Kravets and Imy Wax

The College Sourcebook for Students with Learning and Developmental Differences, Midge Lipkin

Websites

Association on Higher Education and Disability at ahead.org

National Center for Learning Disabilities at ncld.org

The Arts

Books

College Guide for Performing Arts Majors 2009: The Real-World Admission Guide for Dance, Music, and Theater Majors, Carole Everett

Websites

National Portfolio Day at portfolioday.net

ATHLETICS

Books

Four Year College Admissions Data: Index of Majors and Sports, Wintergreen Orchard House

Websites

NCAA at ncaa.org

NAIA Eligibility Center at playnaia.org

GAP YEAR

Books

Before You Go: The Ultimate Guide to Planning Your Gap Year, Tom Griffiths

The Complete Guide to the Gap Year, Kristin White

Gap Year Guidebook 2010, Wendy Bosberry-Scott

The Gap Year Advantage, Karl Haigler and Rae Nelson

Websites

American Gap Association at americangap.org

AmeriCorps at americorps.gov

City Year at cityyear.org

CIEE Gap Year Programs at ciee.org/gap-year-abroad/Gapyear.com at gapyear.com

Global Volunteers at globalvolunteers.org

Global Citizen Year at globalcitizenyear.org

USA Gap Year Fairs at usagapyearfairs.org

Where There Be Dragons at wheretherebedragons.com

SELECTIVE SUMMER PROGRAMS

Websites

Telluride Association Summer Program (TASP) at tellurideassociation.org

National Hispanic Institute at nhi-net.org

College Horizons Program for Native
   Americans at collegehorizons.org
Massachusetts Institute of Technology
   MITES at web.mit.edu/mites

SEMESTER PROGRAMS
Websites
CITYterm at the Masters School in New
   York at cityterm.org
The Mountain School of Milton Academy at
   mountainschool.org
United World Colleges at uwc.org

FINANCIAL AID RESOURCES
Websites
College Board at collegeboard.org
College Goal Sunday at
   collegegoalsundayusa.org
FAFSA at fafsa.ed.gov
Fastweb at fastweb.com
FinAid at finaid.org
Federal Student Aid at studentaid.ed.gov
CSS PROFILE at profileonline
   .collegeboard.org
Paying for College at consumerfinance.gov/
   payingforcollege

FINANCIAL AID FOR
INTERNATIONAL STUDENTS
Websites
The Association of International Educators
   (NAFSA) at nafsa.org
eduPASS: The Smart Student Guide to
   Studying in the USA at edupass.org

FINANCIAL AID CALCULATORS
Websites
College Board at collegeboard.org
FinAid Calculators at finaid.org/calculators

Sallie Mae Affordability Analyzer at
   collegeanswer.com/paying
FAFSA4caster at studentaid.ed.gov

SCHOLARSHIPS
Websites
Air Force ROTC at afrotc.com
Army ROTC at goarmy.com
Coca-Cola Scholarship Foundation at
   coca-colascholars.org
College Scholarships.org at
   collegescholarships.org
College Board Scholarship Search at apps
   .collegeboard.org/cbsearch_ss/welcome.jsp
Davidson Fellows Scholarship at
   davidsongifted.org/fellows
Fastweb at fastweb.com
FinAid's Major-Specific Resource at finaid
   .org/otheraid/majors.phtml
Gates Millennium Scholarship at gmsp.org
Intel Science Talent Search at student
   .societyforscience.org/intel-sts
MeritAid at meritaid.com
Microsoft University at http://careers
   .microsoft.com/careers/en/us/collegehome
   .aspx
MoolahSPOT at moolahspot.com
Navy ROTC at nrotc.navy.mil/scholarship
   _criteria.aspx
Nordstrom Scholarship Program at shop
   .nordstrom.com/c/nordstrom-cares
   -scholarship
Peterson's Award Database at finaid.org/
   otheraid/majors.phtml
Ronald McDonald House Charities
   U.S. Scholarship at rmhc.org/rmhc-us
   -scholarships
Scholarships.com at scholarships.com

Scholarships4students.com at
scholarships4students.com

School Soup at schoolsoup.com

SMART Scholarship at smart.asee.org

Tylenol Future Care Scholarships at tylenol
.com/news/scholarship

UCF/Merck Science Initiative at umsi
.uncf.org

The Web-based Naviance system features
a scholarship search service powered by
Sallie Mae.

LOAN INFORMATION
Websites

Avoiding Deceptive Student Loan Offers at
consumer.ftc.gov/articles/0160-student
-loans

Federal PLUS Loans at studentaid.ed.gov

Federal Direct Loan website at direct.ed.gov

SCHOLARSHIPS FOR STUDENTS
OF COLOR
Websites

200 Free Scholarships for Minorities at
blackexcel.org/200-Scholarships.html

100 Black Men of America, Inc. at
100blackmen.org

American Indian College Fund at
collegefund.org

Educators for Fair Consideration at e4fc.org

Hispanic Scholarship Fund at hsf.net

Latino College Dollars at latinocollegedollars
.org

LaRaza Youth Leadership at
larazayouth.com

LGBT Scholarship Resource at finaid.org/
otheraid/gay.phtml

Ron Brown Scholar Fund at ronbrown.org

UNDERRESOURCED STUDENTS
Books

College Access & Opportunity Guide, Center
for Student Opportunity

Websites

Advancement Via Individual Determination
(AVID) at avid.org

Center for Student Opportunity (CSO)
College Center at imfirst.org

College Goal Sunday at
collegegoalsundayusa.org

Jack Kent Cooke Foundation at jkcf.org

National College Access Network at
collegeaccess.org

SPANISH-LANGUAGE RESOURCES
Websites

NSSE Pocket Guide: Questions to Ask
on Your College Visits (in English and
Spanish) at nsse.iub.edu/html/pocket
_guide_intro.cfm

Spanish Language Resource Links (Admissions
and Financial Aid) at tgslc.org/spanish

UNDOCUMENTED STUDENTS
Websites

Asian American Legal Defense and
Education Fund at aaldef.org

Chicano Organizing and Research in
Education at ca-core.org/que_llueva_cafe
_scholarship_program

Dream Activist at action.dreamactivist.org/

Educators for Fair Consideration (E4FC) at
E4fc.org

Immigration Policy Center at immigration
policy.org/issues/DREAM-Act

Mexican American Legal Defense and
Education Fund at maldef.org

National Immigration Law Center at nilc.org

The Illinois Association for College Admission Counseling at iacac.org/undocumented

LGBTQQI STUDENTS

Websites

Consortium of Higher Education LGBT Resources Center at lgbtcampus.org

Campus Climate Index at campusclimateindex.org

LGBT Scholarship Resources at finaid.org/otheraid/gay.phtml

Point Foundation Scholarship at pointfoundation.org

SAT/ACT Concordance Tables

CONCORDANCE BETWEEN ACT COMPOSITE SCORE AND SUM OF SAT CRITICAL READING AND MATHEMATICS SCORES		
SAT CR+M (Score Range)	ACT Composite Score	SAT CR+M (Single Score)
1600	36	1600
1540–1590	35	1560
1490–1530	34	1510
1440–1480	33	1460
1400–1430	32	1420
1360–1390	31	1380
1330–1350	30	1340
1290–1320	29	1300
1250–1280	28	1260
1210–1240	27	1220
1170–1200	26	1190
1130–1160	25	1150
1090–1120	24	1110
1050–1080	23	1070
1020–1040	22	1030
980–1010	21	990
940–970	20	950
900–930	19	910
860–890	18	870
820–850	17	830
770–810	16	790
720–760	15	740
670–710	14	690
620–660	13	640
560–610	12	590
510–550	11	530

CONCORDANCE BETWEEN ACT COMBINED ENGLISH/WRITING SCORE AND SAT WRITING SCORE

SAT Writing (Score Range)	ACT English/Writing Score	SAT Writing (Single Score)
800	36	800
800	35	800
770–790	34	770
730–760	33	740
710–720	32	720
690–700	31	690
660–680	30	670
640–650	29	650
620–630	28	630
610	27	610
590–600	26	590
570–580	25	570
550–560	24	550
530–540	23	530
510–520	22	510
480–500	21	490
470	20	470
450–460	19	450
430–440	18	430
410–420	17	420
390–400	16	400
380	15	380
360–370	14	360
340–350	13	340
320–330	12	330
300–310	11	310

Notes

1. John H. Pryor et al., *The American Freshman: National Norms Fall 2012* (Los Angeles: Higher Education Research Institute, University of California, 2012), 23.

2. National Association for College Admission Counseling, *State of College Admission 2013* (Arlington, VA: NACAC, 2013).

3. National Center for Education Statistics, "High School Graduates, by Sex and Control of School: Selected Years, 1969–70 Through 2020–21," Table 111, *Digest of Education Statistics*, 2011, available at http://nces.ed.gov/programs/digest/d11/tables/dt11_111.asp.

4. National Association for College Admission Counseling, *State of College Admission 2013* (Arlington, VA: NACAC, 2013).

5. Caroline M. Hoxby, "The Changing Selectivity of American Colleges," National Bureau of Economic Research Working Paper No. 15446, November 2009, available at www.nber.org/papers/w15446.

6. See the website of Solutions for Our Future, www.solutionsforourfuture.org.

7. Stacy Berg Dale and Alan B. Krueger, "Estimating the Payoff to Attending a More Selective College: An Application of Selection on Observables and Unobservables," National Bureau of Economic Research Working Paper No. 7322, August 1999, available at http://papers.nber.org/papers/w7322; Alan B. Krueger and Stacy Berg Dale, "Estimating the Return to College Selectivity over the Career Using Administrative Earning Data," Working Paper No. 563, Industrial Relations Section, Princeton University, February 16, 2011, available at http://dataspace.princeton.edu/jspui/handle/88435/dsp01gf06g265z.

8. "Look Who Harvard Blew Off," *New York Post*, May 22, 2007, available at pagesix.com/2007/05/22/look-who-harvard-blew-off.

9. Mark Schwanhausser, "Forget the Ivy League: Most Valley CEOs Went Public," *San Jose Mercury News*, November 28, 2007, available at www.mercurynews.com/business/ci_7578047.

10. Christopher Avery, Andrew Fairbanks, and Richard Zeckhauser, *The Early Admissions Game: Joining the Elite* (Cambridge, MA: Harvard University Press, 2004).

11. Caroline M. Hoxby, "The Changing Selectivity of American Colleges," National Bureau of Economic Research Working Paper No. 15446, November 2009, available at www.nber.org/papers/w15446.

12. Saul Geiser and Maria Veronica Santelices, "Validity of High-School Grades in Predicting Student Success Beyond the Freshman Year:

High-School Record vs. Standardized Tests as Indicators of Four-Year College Outcomes," Research and Occasional Paper Series CSHE.6.07, Center for Studies in Higher Education, University of California, Berkeley, June 2007, available at http://cshe.berkeley.edu/sites/default/files/shared/publications/docs/ROPS.GEISER._SAT_6.13.07.

13. *The Harvard Lampoon's Guide to College Admissions* (New York: Warner Books, 2000).

14. Denise Pope, Mollie Galloway, and Jerusha Conner, "Stanford Survey of Adolescent School Experiences," presentation at Challenge Success May Conference, Stanford, California, 2009 and 2011.

15. George Waters, "Sick of Standardized Testing?", available at georgewaters.net.

16. "Report Highlights Test Prep Paradox," press release, National Association for College Admission Counseling, May, 2009, available at nacacnet.org/media-center/PressRoom/.

17. "What Is a Galaxy? How Many Stars in a Galaxy? How Many Stars/Galaxies in the Universe?" Royal Museums Greenwich website, available at http://www.rmg.co.uk/explore/astronomy-and-time/astronomy-facts/faqs/what-is-a-galaxy-how-many-stars-in-a-galaxy-how-many-stars/galaxies-in-the-universe.

18. National Center for Education Statistics, "Number of Educational Institutions, by Level and Control of Institution: Selected Years, 1980–81 Through 2009–10," *Digest of Education Statistics,* 2011, available at http://nces.ed.gov/fastfacts/display.asp?id=84.

19. National Association for College Admission Counseling, *State of College Admission 2013* (Arlington, VA: NACAC, 2013).

20. John H. Pryor et al., *The American Freshman: National Norms Fall 2012* (Los Angeles: Higher Education Research Institute, University of California, 2012), 24.

21. Scattergram, part of the Naviance Succeed system, provided by Naviance, Inc., a Hobsons company.

22. William G. Bowen, Matthew M. Chingos, and Michael S. McPherson, *Crossing the Finish Line: Completing College at America's Public Universities* (Princeton, NJ: Princeton University Press, 2011).

23. The Common Application was used with the permission of The Common Application, Inc.

24. Reprinted with permission from the *Journal of College Admission,* number 206 (Winter 2010), copyright © 2010 National Association for College Admission Counseling.

Index

Vieira, Meredith, 7
Visits (*see* College visits)
Voice, of writer, 214

W

Waitlisted students, 306, 309–314
  advice for, 310–314
  financial aid and, 291, 310
  follow-up by, 311
  questions about, 319, 320
  responding, 309–310
  transfer applicants, 367
Wake Forest University, 102, 181, 183
Walter, Kelly A., 352, 359
Washington, James, Jr., 198
Washington & Jefferson College, 8
Washington Monthly, 127
Washington State University, 8
Waters, George, 82
Watson, Christopher, 313, 359
Wax, Imy, 340
WayToGoRI.org, 126
Websites, college, 122, 123
Weisenburger, Leigh A., 51, 62
Well-rounded versus specialist students, 71
Wenner, Jann, 7
Wesleyan University, 252, 263, 369

Westphal, Rebekah, 361
West Virginia State University, 220–221, 262
West Virginia University, 8
Wexner, Les, 8
Whitney, Jarrid, 360–361
"Why us?" essays, 215, 216
Willamette University, 222
Williams College, 221–222
Winfrey, Oprah, 8
Wiseman, Rosalind, 315–316
Women's colleges, 117
Worcester Telegram & Gazette, 5
Worksheets, 380–383
Work-study, 269, 270, 273, 275, 282–286, 289, 301
Writing section, of Common Application, 232

Y

Yale University, 4, 6, 35, 116, 133, 158, 357, 361
Yellow Ribbon Program, 293
Yelp, 125
Yeshiva University, 117
YouTube, 126, 128, 236

Z

Zinch, 124

Notes

Notes

About the Authors

CREDIT: CHI-LIN SUN

ROBIN G. MAMLET is the former dean of admission at Stanford, Swarthmore, and Sarah Lawrence, where she made over 100,000 admission decisions. Today, she helps colleges and universities find and select their deans of admission, leading the Enrollment Search Practice for Witt/Kieffer.

Journalist **CHRISTINE VANDEVELDE**'s work has appeared in the *Wall Street Journal, Washington Post, New York Times, San Francisco Chronicle, Parenting, Self,* and *USA Today.* She is the editor of collegeadmissionbook.com, the website for this book.